EMPIRE OF MANNERS

STANFORD **OTTOMAN WORLD** SERIES

EMPIRE *of* MANNERS

OTTOMAN SOCIABILITY AND WAR-MAKING
IN THE LONG EIGHTEENTH CENTURY

James Grehan

STANFORD UNIVERSITY PRESS
Stanford, California

Stanford University Press
Stanford, California

© 2025 by James Paul Grehan. All rights reserved.

No part of this book may be reproduced or transmitted in any form or by any means, electronic or mechanical, including photocopying and recording, or in any information storage or retrieval system, without the prior written permission of Stanford University Press.

Library of Congress Cataloging-in-Publication Data
Names: Grehan, James, author.
Title: Empire of manners : Ottoman sociability and war-making in the long eighteenth century / James Grehan.
Other titles: Stanford Ottoman world series.
Description: Stanford, California : Stanford University Press, 2025. | Series: Stanford Ottoman world series | Includes bibliographical references and index.
Identifiers: LCCN 2024053727 (print) | LCCN 2024053728 (ebook) | ISBN 9781503643383 (cloth) | ISBN 9781503643727 (paperback) | ISBN 9781503643734 (ebook)
Subjects: LCSH: Etiquette—Turkey—History—18th century. | War and society—Turkey—History—18th century. | Turkey—Social life and customs—18th century. | Turkey—History—1683-1829.
Classification: LCC DR432 .G74 2025 (print) | LCC DR432 (ebook) | DDC 956.1/0153—dc23/eng/20241213
LC record available at https://lccn.loc.gov/2024053727
LC ebook record available at https://lccn.loc.gov/2024053728

Cover design: George Kirkpatrick
Cover art: Jean Baptiste Vanmour, *Women Drinking Coffee*, first half of the 18th century, oil on canvas, 14.56 × 23.22 in. (370 × 590 mm). Pera Museum, Istanbul.

The authorized representative in the EU for product safety and compliance is: Mare Nostrum Group B.V. | Mauritskade 21D | 1091 GC Amsterdam | The Netherlands | Email address: gpsr@mare-nostrum.co.uk | KVK chamber of commerce number: 96249943

For my parents-in-law, Bülent and Emel Danışoğlu

CONTENTS

	List of Illustrations	ix
	Acknowledgments	xi
	Map of the Ottoman Empire, c. 1750	xiii
	Introduction	1
One	**Presenting the Body**	20
Two	**Pleasure Wins Again**	59
Three	**Polite Manners**	91
Four	**The Expansion of Polite Society**	122
Five	**Honorable Manners**	154
Six	**Rough Manners**	184
	Conclusion	217
	Notes	233
	Bibliography	301
	Index	333

ILLUSTRATIONS

FIGURE 1.1	"An Albanian woman"	23
FIGURE 1.2	Depictions of "popular" dress in Egypt	25
FIGURE 1.3	"Greek man from Yanina"	27
FIGURE 1.4	Portrait of a lady from the Ottoman palace	32
FIGURE 1.5	An Armenian gentleman wearing a *kalpak*	37
FIGURE 1.6	Portrait of a prince (*hospodar*) of Moldavia	39
FIGURE 1.7	"Albanian soldiers"	42
FIGURE 1.8	Portrait of an Ottoman lady and servant	44
FIGURE 1.9	"Women of Scio"	46
FIGURE 1.10	"An itinerant barber"	50
FIGURE 2.1	"A Turkish girl taking coffee on a divan"	64
FIGURE 2.2	Ottoman tobacco pipes from the fortress of Smederevo in Serbia	68
FIGURE 2.3	Ottoman official holding a long-stemmed pipe	69
FIGURE 2.4	An Egyptian coffeehouse	75
FIGURE 2.5	"Marines of the Ottoman Navy"	85
FIGURE 3.1	"Ottoman ladies at a banquet"	117
FIGURE 3.2	"Dinner at Chrisso"	118
FIGURE 4.1	Portrait of Selim III	138
FIGURE 4.2	Depiction of a military band (*mehter*)	149
FIGURE 5.1	The grand vizier crossing Atmeydanı	174

ACKNOWLEDGMENTS

This is my Covid book, launched during a period of uninterrupted reading and reflection that only the seclusion and tedium of a pandemic can seemingly guarantee. Yet even in an era of social distancing, researchers accumulate debts. ChiaYin Hsu, my colleague in the history department at Portland State University, provided invaluable tips about scholarship on the Russian Empire. Maureen Healy of Lewis and Clark College similarly helped to ease some of my perplexities about the historiography of the Habsburg Empire. In the groggy aftermath of the pandemic, Cihan Yüksel at the University of Houston was kind enough to invite me for a lecture on an early version of what became chapter 4. Her colleagues in the history department, together with faculty from Rice University, were a gracious and stimulating audience. At Stanford University Press, it has been a pleasure to work with my editor Kate Wahl, who has been a patient and reassuring shepherd for this project. Two anonymous readers of the original manuscript have my thanks for their attentive criticisms and suggestions. My copy editor, Paul Tyler, was helpful in sharpening the final draft and sweeping away the last bits of verbal detritus. At Portland State University, Travis Anglin-Dodd created the map of the Ottoman Empire with impressive efficiency and flexibility. To my family belongs the biggest debt of gratitude. My son, Sinan, went off to college and earned his degree while this book was being written. During visits home, he indulged my moments of distraction with good humor and kept me on my toes through many a spirited debate. My wife, Pelin, above all, deserves special thanks for all her support and encouragement. She showed boundless patience and understanding as yet another book project took up prolonged and intrusive residence in our home.

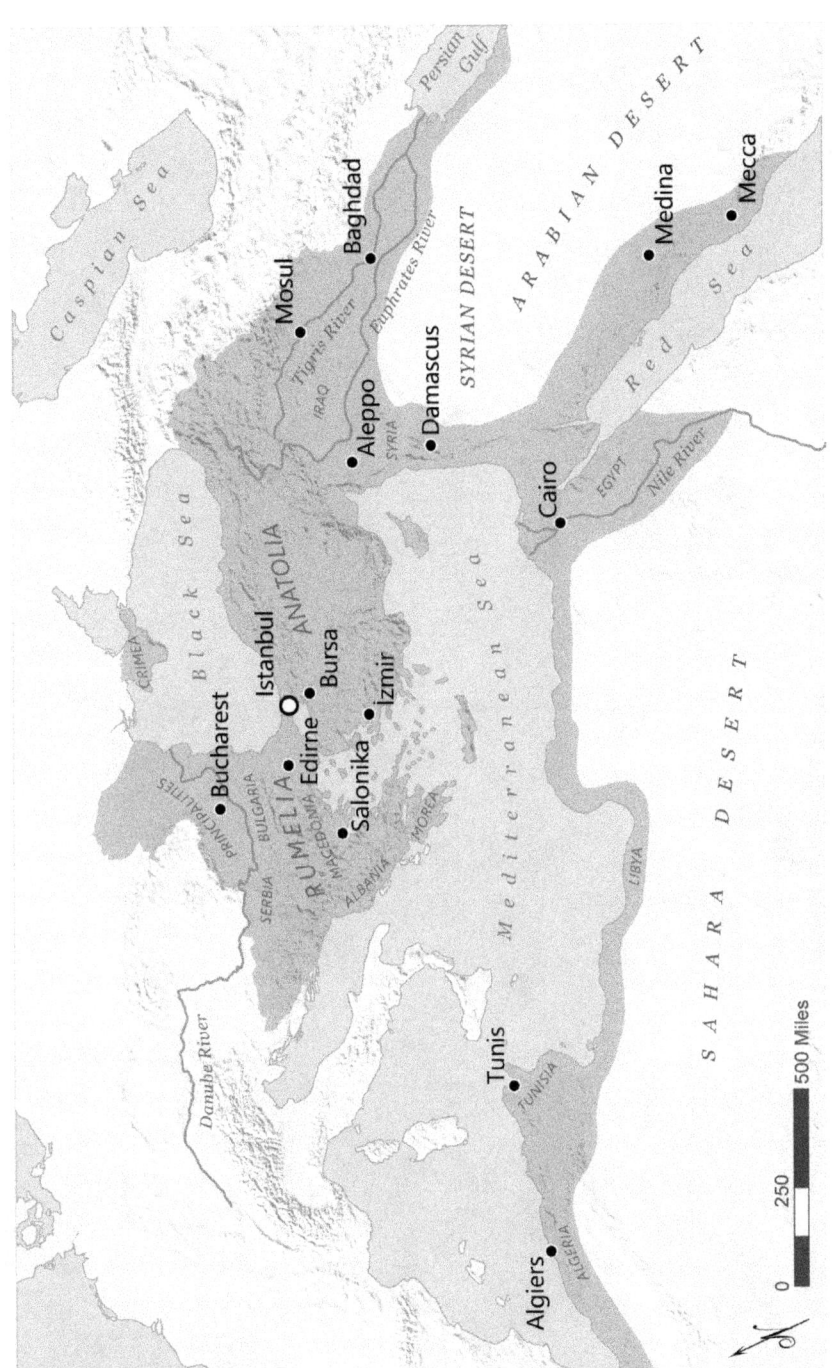

The Ottoman Empire, c. 1750

INTRODUCTION

One afternoon in the spring of 1770, a small group of Janissaries was passing the grand country house of the French ambassador at Büyükdere, a quiet retreat along the northern reaches of the Bosphorus, up a short way from Istanbul. Occupying one of the rooms was Baron de Tott, a French military officer who would enter the Ottoman service during the Ottoman-Russian war of 1768-74. As recollected in his memoirs, he happened to notice an ugly scene that was developing below his window. A couple of Janissaries had been passing in front of the house, engaged in spirited conversation, when they heard a voice from a high window repeating exactly what they were saying. They thought that someone was mocking them and became enraged. They began to swear in the most florid Turkish. The voice repeated their insults, word for word. It was too much to bear. In broad daylight, an infidel inside the French ambassador's house had the temerity to shout abuse at them, just as the empire was marching to war against Russia. They pulled their guns and prepared to storm the residence.

At that moment, a fellow Janissary stepped out the front door. He was one of the guards posted to the French embassy, for the sultan's government took care to ensure the safety of all foreign diplomats residing in Istanbul. Clustered high in the neighborhood of Pera (modern Beyoğlu) overlooking the Golden Horn from the north, the European embassies were valuable conduits of intelligence from states that, by the eighteenth century, had come to play a large role in the empire's external affairs. The Janissary at the gate tried to calm the soldiers. He could explain everything if only they would wait a moment. As they continued with their threats, he went back inside and brought out something entirely unexpected: a talking parrot. The Janissaries could hardly believe their eyes. The guard tried to reassure them. He had them seated and made the bird demonstrate its foul-mouthed talents again. (The parrot obviously had excellent preceptors in the Janissary guards at the embassy.) Realizing that more needed to be done, he immediately called for cups of coffee, fell into jocular conversation, and served several more rounds before the soldiers were fully placated and the incident drew to a peaceful close.[1]

This curious encounter contains several points of interest for anyone who is trying to "decode" the soldiers' interaction. The first detail to attract our attention is the setting: the residence of the French ambassador. In 1770, as the Romanov Empire was gaining the upper hand against the sultan's forces, European states were just beginning to exercise the indisputable military superiority that would later, in the streets of the empire, compel deference, or at least a certain precautionary self-restraint, in dealing with their diplomats and subjects. At that moment, Ottomans still retained an older image of "Franks" as outsiders from a marginal, uninteresting part of the world who were expected to know their place. Another central detail, impossible for the guard to ignore, was the soldiers' extreme sensitivity to insults, which they would not allow to pass on any account. Any person who uttered slights would have to suffer the consequences. The guard instantly understood how explosive the encounter was, and how it might end very badly if he could not soothe his offended guests. As a Janissary himself, he would have realized how easily they could be provoked. Only after seeing with their own eyes that a mere bird had been mocking them would they judge their honor safe and intact. Helping along this reconciliation were the obligatory social graces. Almost as a matter of instinct, the guard welcomed his comrades and treated them to coffee. He knew that the arts of hospitality would be essential to any efforts at peacemaking. On this point of conduct, too, we would want to know more. Something about the symbolism of sipping cups of coffee together was likely, as their host knew, to put them at ease and defuse their outrage.

Puzzled readers might well ask why we should pay any attention to such a scene in which soldiers confronted a cursing parrot. This incident, on its surface strange and even comical, is more revealing than it might at first seem. It helps to lead us inside a social world whose manners are not so straightforward and comprehensible for observers looking far back in time. Such details about social interaction are not bits of historical trivia. They reflect larger modes of social and political organization. From the humble norms and niceties of everyday speech and gesture, grand historical structures can come suddenly and uncannily into view.

Most studies of manners take polite and formal modes of behavior as their main themes. Thus in the scene above, we might well imagine that the soldiers had come very close to losing self-control. It was a case of intemperate passions being tamped down thanks to quick-thinking diplomacy, which allowed everyone, in the end, to regain their composure and return to their proper "manners." Though the emotions and gestures were no doubt real and sincere, not everything about this altercation was as rash and impulsive as it might seem. The soldiers quickly swept over a gamut of poses that seemed almost expected of them, as if they knew what to do, how to hold themselves, how far they could go, and how they might, if they wanted, navigate back to safer ground. They were, at least in part, activating a set of manners that were as elaborate as any conventional etiquette. In fact, all social situations draw on elements of social artifice, formula, and cliché that people absorb in the course of their upbringing and socialization. Viewed in this light, no social interaction can be entirely free or spontaneous. To better make sense of manners, then, it is necessary to lay them out along a much broader spectrum of sociability, running from the polite and restrained, to the staid and dignified, to the offensive and downright violent. The real task for historians is to determine what contemporaries understood as correct or expected in any given social situation and to "read" the informal, unspoken rules that guided them.

It is not enough, of course, to study patterns of sociability. Manners need to be placed within the larger social forces that ultimately shape them. To return once again to the soldiers' altercation: the outbreak of war with Russia in 1768 was not an extraneous detail. Seeming to hover in the background, the conflict was actually a turning point for Ottoman political and military might, which had been slowly ebbing since the late seventeenth century and would now begin to falter more precipitously. What does all this have to do with the study of manners? The answer, this book argues, is that patterns of sociability and violence are always intertwined. Sometimes this entanglement shows itself in everyday social interaction through low-level intimidation or aggression, as the Janissaries above came close to demonstrating. Far more decisive, however, is organized violence, most notably in the form of war-making, whose repercussions were as much cultural as political and economic. Thus in investigating manners, this study inevitably considers the broader question of what war-making does to culture.

It was during the eighteenth century that the relationship between warfare and manners became more obvious and pressing. War-making was beginning to assume a greater scope and complexity whose consequences would stretch far beyond the raising of armies, requisitioning of resources, levying of taxes, and arming of ever more soldiers. Increasingly, on account of mounting social costs and disruptions, it generated far-reaching cultural anxieties and uncertainties, which often expressed themselves through manners. Over the long eighteenth century, the cultural consequences of warfare would thus presage, however faintly and distantly, the broader and more traumatic shocks to manners and mores that war-making would inflict on modern societies.

Manners as a Historical Problem

The main model for anyone exploring the history of manners remains the thought of Norbert Elias, one of the most influential sociologists of the twentieth century, who first put forth his ideas in *The Court Society* (1933) and *The Civilizing Process* (1939).[2] Looking back at European history, he argued that a crucial turning point had arrived in the sixteenth century, as the "courtesy" of medieval courts gave way to a more comprehensive code of "civility." This latter concept corresponded to a more rigorous form of self-restraint and muting of bodily urges. The social process most responsible for promoting these new manners was the rise of the "centralized" state. From the sixteenth century onward, monarchs were able to bring aristocrats to heel and turn them into courtiers, who, in keeping with their newly subordinated social position, renounced the use of personal violence and cultivated self-restraint. They adopted a more formalized set of manners for eating, sleeping, and the management of bodily functions like spitting, yawning, blowing the nose, and urination. These habits slowly lowered the "threshold of embarrassment and shame" and introduced a more reserved "personality structure" that kept a tighter rein on emotional expression.

Popularizing this new model of comportment were authors like Desiderius Erasmus (1466–1536), whose *Manners for Children* (1530) created a new genre of etiquette manuals, addressed to all readers regardless of social status, and spawned a trail of numerous imitators and commentators.[3] Carried by the tide of this expanding literature, civility began its subsequent diffusion from the aristocracy to affluent townsmen during the seventeenth and eighteenth centuries. It gained further impetus from a burgeoning market economy, another legacy of the centralized state, which enmeshed individuals in ever greater "chains of interdependence." To cope with this greater social complexity, Elias argued, people had to adjust their conduct ever more precisely to the actions of others and cultivate heightened self-control and foresight. Hence the appeal of civility: it helped to facilitate interaction within a denser social environment in which individuals had to confront and deal with many more people than before, most of whom they did not know very well, if at all. In modern times, civility would make yet wider conquests as self-restraint became a central pillar of the sober, thrifty, time-keeping culture of the bourgeoisie and urban professional classes.

In the decades since Elias's publications first gained a wide audience (from the 1960s onward), his ideas have continued to shape the main debates about the history of manners. Historians of Europe have been particularly receptive. One may speak of a loose consensus, a kind of courtly model, linking the rise of absolutist courts to a shift from medieval courtesy to early modern civility.[4] As Roger Chartier has put it, "A new type of state instituted a new way of being in society."[5] Outside Europe, too, Elias's ideas have proved alluring.[6] Historians, we might say, have fallen into the habit of tracking the diffusion of manners from absolutist courts and looking for evidence in etiquette manuals.

Yet there are reasons to question this courtly model. Some of the most sustained objections have to do with Elias's depiction of medieval society as impulsive, violent, even dangerous. Manners and civility, his critics contend, have a much older history that predated the early modern period and did not originate in royal courts. As Hans Peter Duerr argues in considerable detail, medieval Europe evolved social codes of self-restraint that were no less demanding than modern ones.[7] There is no reason, for that matter, why such codes should not be present in earlier periods, extending far back to remote antiquity. Civility would have appeared as a social adaptation wherever towns or complex societies sprang up.[8]

A bigger problem in the history of manners is precisely this general preoccupation with civility. It restricts our field of investigation to a single behavioral ideal. Yet every society recognizes, and often encourages, other modes of conduct that touch on questions of honor, rank, and status. Social encounters could, depending on circumstances, require manners that veered far from the norms of polite speech and gesture and call forth anger, vituperation, physical confrontation, even full-blown violence. This alternative register of emotion and self-expression was not necessarily the same as breakdown or loss of self-control. It had to be learned and internalized as much as the intricacies of any gentlemanly etiquette. No aberration, it was as central to manners as civility. So the "social constraint towards self-restraint"—to use Elias's phrase—was never the only process at work. Social complexity did not, as Elias would have it, exclusively drive social relations toward civility; on the contrary, it simply bred a complementary complexity in manners.

The courtly model talks so much about civility and self-restraint because it conceives of political and social relations as sharing a common trajectory toward greater order and harmony. The early modern state's pacification of its territory, in this view, led to the pacification of manners. The argument decorously pushes violence to the frontiers of the state. But this pacification is overstated. Violence continued to stalk early modern society: in brigandage, crime, rough justice and social control, codes of honor, various forms of popular protest, and all the little scuffles and fisticuffs that could erupt in the course of interpersonal disputes.[9] It was precisely during this period, moreover, that the state presided over the intensification of warfare. The courtly model underplays, or altogether fails to consider, the growing role of this violence in the shaping of culture. It refuses to acknowledge that violence has acted (at least so far) as a key constitutive process of "civilization."

Perhaps the most explosive charge laid against the courtly model is that it harbors a Eurocentric bias. Indeed, the entire narrative about the evolution from courtesy to civility comes out of the study of European history. To say the least, it would be reckless to assume that other parts of the world shared the same cultural trajectory. For his own part, Elias always protested that he was writing about Europe, not other parts of the world. Nevertheless, he could not resist venturing occasionally into a comparative mode of study that, in his telling, pitted the West against "simpler" societies in Africa and Asia, where self-restraint was less developed.[10] Most revealing was his treatment of colonialism, which, as he blandly argued, would inevitably bring colonized peoples in line with prevailing "Western" manners. Although he insisted that it was not a cultural judgment, and that it was only a scientific assessment about a stronger "sociogenic" process integrating others, he slipped too easily into stereotypes about "primitive" peoples who were closer to nature and freer and more honest about their impulses. He seemed oblivious to studies that demonstrated how even the poorest, most isolated communities would necessarily inculcate intensive self-restraint.[11] More curious still was the lack of effort in investigating the manners of non-European cultures, which would surely be essential for any truly scientific model. A strange asymmetry haunts his work. Later in life, as he struggled to reconcile the "civilizing process" with the devastation of two world wars and death camps in the midst of Europe, he turned a blind eye to the violence committed in Europe's overseas colonies.[12]

In view of this problem with Eurocentrism, this book invites readers to venture to the Ottoman Empire. Like most parts of the world outside the North Atlantic zone, it has generated few studies on manners. Even without this research, a quick glance at Ottoman culture is enough to confirm that the "North Atlantic" historical experience will not be a useful guide. The Ottoman dynasty ruled over societies in the Balkans and Middle East that had practiced sophisticated forms of civility (or "urbanitas") stretching back to antiquity. Ottoman culture reflected this continuity. There was no sixteenth-century figure like Erasmus. To the extent that Ottoman authors dealt with manners, they introduced no innovations in etiquette, bearing, gesture, or forms of address.[13] Nor did the formation of a powerful royal court in the sixteenth century, attaining full ceremonial splendor under Suleyman the Magnificent (r. 1520–66), lead to anything like the social remolding of either courtiers or provincial elites, let alone ordinary Ottoman subjects.[14] The palace is the wrong place to search for the origins of long-term social and cultural change. Despite its self-inflating propaganda, it was never the main cultural trend-setter or bellwether of modernity.[15]

Indeed, the entire model of top-down diffusion is misleading. Instead of looking to the royal court, we should go out and explore society, which, for the most part, followed its own customs without waiting for promptings from "above." Very much in this fashion, Ottoman society took its bearings from long-established manners that no one had to contrive or ever thought about reforming. But this weighty inheritance did not preclude social change. Over the long eighteenth century, Ottoman manners would begin to express questions about social identity and lifestyle, hierarchy and mobility, and order and disorder that were becoming ever more urgent, conspicuous, and combustible.

The long eighteenth century, as it happened, spanned the heyday of the Ottoman *ancien régime*. It looked both backward and forward, acting as the culmination of the "early modern" period (c. 1500–1800) and the gateway to the dawning modern age. The next section will explain why this critical hinge in Ottoman history has not received more attention.

Visions of the Ottoman Old Regime (c. 1680–1830)

The eighteenth century has suffered from curious neglect in Ottoman studies. To an older, disapproving view, which has yet to be fully supplanted, it represents the nadir of a long "decline," signified by mounting military losses and territorial contraction.[16] The sinews of the Ottoman state were fraying. The empire had lost the rude, battle-ready health of its military prime, which reached its summit, according to this view, back in the sixteenth century with the last phases of grand conquest in the Balkan and Arab lands.

This gloom is rather curious. The greater part of the eighteenth century, as it turns out, was relatively sunny for the empire's economy and population. After the demographic stagnation and political upheaval that had characterized much of the seventeenth century, both in the Ottoman Empire and across much of the world, a recovery gathered pace during the early and middle decades of the eighteenth century (c. 1720–70).[17] This general expansion was a broadly Eurasian phenomenon. Though not as vigorous or prolonged as the surge of the sixteenth century, it helped to propel trade and commercialization in the Ottoman economy and elsewhere. While precise population estimates are difficult, the empire held perhaps thirty million people by the end of the eighteenth century—a total roughly comparable to the late sixteenth century.[18]

Floating atop these demographic and economic tides was the Ottoman Old Regime. With its deep origins in the late sixteenth century, and fully mature by the eighteenth, it had come into being not as the long-term fruition of deliberate plans and policies but as the unintended sum of countless expedients and pragmatic compromises.[19] The Ottoman state had evolved very much like other Eurasian empires, all of which had passed through a heyday of territorial expansion (mostly in the sixteenth century) and afterward struggled to maintain the vast military juggernauts that they had assembled. By the eighteenth century, warfare required the mobilization of men and materiel on an unprecedented scale. The unrelenting pressure of these expenses, which never ceased climbing, drove imperial authorities to frantic short-term policies whose main purpose was to bring in revenue as quickly as possible. Like most other eighteenth-century empires, the Ottoman state resorted routinely to the sale of tax-farms (the right to collect, at profit, particular taxes on behalf of the treasury) and state offices. So embedded had this official venality become that most state revenue was raised from tax-farming, usually on short-term leases (of one to three years), and after 1694, supplemented through the auctioning of lifetime tax-farms.[20] Nearly all provincial governors and chief judges had to buy their appointments, typically for a term of one year. As officials everywhere knew, these policies were open to abuse and corruption. But the imperative to fill the treasury took precedence.

By 1700, political power had become more widely dispersed. Once active both on the battlefield and in councils of state, the sultan had settled into the role of a symbolic leader who delegated real authority to high officials in his administration. Since 1656, with the appointment of Mehmet Köprülü to the office of grand vizier, this disposition of power had in effect gained formal sanction, after Köprülü had won a promise that the court would not interfere in political decisions. Thereafter grand viziers, serving at the sultan's pleasure, wrested away day-to-day supervision of the state as the Porte, their official residence in Istanbul, became the true center of government rather than the palace. Surrounding the grand vizier were other grandees: top-ranking bureaucrats, military officers, and leaders of the religious establishment.[21] Pashas of different ranks served both as military commanders and as governors of various provinces around the empire. They now formed their own political households, with scores or even hundreds of dependents and armed retainers who would follow them from one appointment to another.[22] To win office, they had to raise large sums of money, which became as pressing a concern for them as for the imperial treasury.

The pursuit of power was impossible without familiarity with the intricacies of high finance and access to the right political and financial networks in the capital. These essentially fiscal rules of politics soon extended throughout the whole empire. To use a term that has been fashionable for too long: it bred "decentralization."[23] The state drew more and more subjects into its fiscal operations as it came to depend ever more heavily on the "privatization" of tax collection through tax-farming schemes. The chief beneficiaries were undoubtedly the provincial notables, who comprised a diverse cast of social figures found mainly in the towns: military officers (or tribal leaders in remote areas), wealthy merchants, leading members of the religious establishment, and heads of prestigious lineages.[24] They attached themselves to powerful patrons in the capital, sought out tax-farms, and maneuvered amid constant factional intrigue for control over local offices and resources.[25] They grew rich, and identified their interests closely with the Ottoman order.

To many historians, who used to imagine the sixteenth-century state as strong and "centralized," these social and political trends seemed like a sure sign of internal weakness and gathering centrifugal dysfunction. But among early modern states, the Ottomans were hardly alone in resorting to strategies of political and fiscal devolution—or to put it another way, the widening and deepening of the political class.[26] Nor did such choices necessarily lead to administrative decay or breakdown. On the contrary, the greater visibility of provincial notables testifies to their absorption into imperial networks that had become far more extensive and cohesive by the eighteenth century.[27] More curious is the invidious contrast that many historical accounts continue to draw with the sixteenth century, the apogee of the empire's so-called "classical age."[28] Did the later Ottoman state really become less effective? To take one fiscal measure: around 1750, the Ottoman treasury was still extracting approximately the same percentage of revenue from the overall economy (on an estimated per capita basis) as it had around 1550.[29] And by the eighteenth century, monetary and fiscal links between Istanbul and its provinces had, if anything, become far better integrated, not decentralized.[30] The real problem was that, since the sixteenth century, the costs of warfare—the main expense of any early modern state—had risen dramatically.[31] Meanwhile the Ottomans had to confront the armies of the more muscular "fiscal-military" states that their European foes had been building.[32]

One suspects that bleak assessments of the eighteenth century really have to do with the empire's sinking fortunes on the battlefield. The final decades of the seventeenth century were a watershed for Ottoman arms. In the War of the Holy League (1683-99), a long conflict of attrition, the sultan's armies suffered an exhausting defeat against a tripartite alliance of Austria, Russia, and Venice. For the first time, the Ottomans had to cede territory, forever parting with Croatia, Hungary, and Transylvania and temporarily relinquishing the Morea (1687-1715). The next few decades brought mixed success on the battlefield over several campaigns, on both western and eastern frontiers. More unmistakable was the shift in perceptions. By the middle of the eighteenth century, Ottoman rivals to the west and north retained a certain wariness of the sultan's forces but no longer feared them.

The lasting image of the long eighteenth century, which has left its imprint on so much historical writing, unquestionably belongs to the decades of what we can call the Great Crisis (c. 1770s-1830s). The strains of prolonged warfare during this period led to economic hardship, inflation, repeated currency debasements, and rampant political instability and insecurity.[33] A disastrous defeat against Russia (1768-74) inaugurated a series of wars that plainly exposed the Ottoman Empire as a second-rate power and resulted in further loss of territory along the northern frontier (starting with the Crimea in 1774). A second crushing defeat against Russia (1787-92) persuaded the Ottoman leadership to undertake its first attempt at large-scale military and administrative reform, the so-called New Order (1792-1807), which was designed on the very European models that had been arrayed so formidably against them.[34] Unfortunately for Selim III (r. 1789-1807), the sultan who presided over these efforts, reform provoked intense opposition from the Janissaries and other established interests, who ultimately brought about his murder and ended his initiatives. In any event, military reform yielded no immediate returns. Under the command of Napoleon, a French expeditionary force easily occupied Egypt (1798-1801), and was dislodged only with help from the British navy. Two further wars with Russia (1806-12 and 1828-29) merely confirmed Ottoman military weakness.

The military defeats of the late eighteenth and early nineteenth centuries reverberated throughout the empire. Owing to the distraction of the central state, provincial warlords soon entrenched themselves within regional strongholds, sometimes for decades at a stretch.[35] Overmighty governors or provincial notables who had climbed to high office, they nonetheless continued to think of themselves as Ottomans. Never questioning the legitimacy or authority of the sultan, they regularly forwarded taxes and gained reappointment by cultivating powerful patrons in the capital and smoothing away the doubts and frustrations of central bureaucrats with well-placed gifts, favors, and bribes. The most cunning and successful raised private armies that they had no hesitation about deploying in regional political struggles, sometimes against each other.

The crowning humiliations of these decades arrived with two internal rebellions in Serbia (1804–16) and the Morea (1821–30), which respectively ended with Serbian autonomy and the creation of the independent kingdom of Greece. It was only during this latter conflict that reformers inside the Ottoman state, led by Mahmud II (r. 1808–39), finally gained the upper hand. The sultan and his advisors abolished the Janissary corps (1826), which had been permanently discredited in combat against Greek rebels. Freed of this reactionary opposition, they were then able to launch the Tanzimat, the second and more successful program of military and administrative reform that would carry the empire forward into the early twentieth century.

So the Ottoman Old Regime of the "long eighteenth century" ultimately crumbled amid the challenges of the Great Crisis. To search for a cause and point an accusing finger, one might ask: What went wrong? Here a moment of wider reflection is both necessary and salutary. Across large parts of Eurasia, the Old Regime of fiscal states was gradually buckling under the same stresses generated by the mounting demands of warfare, corrosive effects of inflation, difficulties with debt and taxation, and contestation over the terms of imperial government.[36] In Europe, it was the age of Atlantic revolutions, Napoleonic wars, and intermittent turbulence as conservative regimes tried, before and after Napoleon, to keep the old dispensation intact. The political fallout reached far beyond Europe. By 1783, colonists in North America had broken away from the British Empire. Later Napoleonic turmoil in Spain led to the collapse of the old colonial order across most of Latin America (1810–25). In British India and Dutch Southeast Asia, the rudimentary fiscal-military states cobbled together by the East India Company and VOC, each of which was deeply dependent on partnerships with local notables, were yielding by the early nineteenth century to reorganized polities of a more centralized and nakedly colonial character. All these parallel transitions are reminders that the Ottomans cannot be treated as anything like an aberration as their own version of the Old Regime progressively cracked and fell apart.

War-Making as Manners-Making

The Ottoman Old Regime was very much like other eighteenth-century states insofar as no single task consumed more of its resources than war-making. To generate revenue for all its campaigning, it issued a regular flow of edicts related to taxation, trade, consumption, and military recruitment. Without any intention on the part of officials, all these military and administrative decisions played out far beyond the battlefields, barracks, and chanceries of the empire. In entirely unforeseen ways, they both stimulated and disturbed Ottoman society and culture.

The first step in tracing out all these indirect and unplanned consequences of war-making is to recognize how the state was interacting with a society that, like elsewhere in the early modern world, had become more thoroughly networked and commercialized. Most critically, it was more urban. Indeed, eighteenth-century Ottoman society was heir to long-term urbanization that had been steadily taking place since the sixteenth century. The Ottoman Empire now held towns that had not only grown more numerous but noticeably larger and richer. The career of Istanbul alone testifies to the extent of this transformation. From a population of about thirty-five thousand at the time of the Ottoman conquest in 1453, it would surpass one hundred thousand during the sixteenth century and climb to approximately four hundred thousand by the late eighteenth century, making it the third-largest town in Europe (after London and Paris).[37] Izmir, once a tiny port on the Aegean Sea, boomed during the seventeenth century as a hub for long-distance trade; by the eighteenth century, it easily ranked (at about a hundred twenty thousand inhabitants) among the five largest Ottoman towns.[38] Wherever we look, Ottoman urbanism was thriving. All the great Arab towns experienced the same long-term growth (in the range of 50–100 percent, c. 1500–1800).[39] By the late eighteenth century, Cairo, the second city of the empire, had swollen from one hundred fifty thousand in 1517 to about two hundred fifty thousand, making it, along with Istanbul, one of seven cities in the Mediterranean basin to exceed two hundred thousand (together with Madrid, Naples, Milan, Rome, and

Venice). Comparable rates of growth lifted Aleppo, Baghdad, Damascus, Tunis, and Mosul. To the north and west, the Ottoman centuries likewise nurtured urban expansion. Though the Balkans had few towns that could match the biggest in the Arab provinces—with the notable exceptions of Edirne, Salonika, and Bucharest—the region had acquired a dense urban network by the eighteenth century.[40] As a consequence of all this urban dynamism, the Ottoman Empire was home to more townspeople. And it was precisely this urban population, then as now, which proved the most fertile ground for the self-conscious cultivation of manners.

Against this backdrop of long-term urbanization, the crucial source of disruption was Ottoman war-making. Or to put it more paradoxically, questions about manners became more salient as the organized violence of the state escalated. The cultural repercussions of all this war-making were never a direct result of state action or policy. The administrative mechanisms at the disposal of the Old Regime, whether in the Ottoman Empire or any other eighteenth-century state, were still too feeble and rickety. Nor did the state have anything like a cultural policy. It gave little thought to manners, and in any case, had little power to reshape them. No new modes of bodily comportment were invented or foisted on Ottoman subjects during the long eighteenth century, as would happen, for example, in Russian society under Peter the Great (r. 1689-1725). Among the latter's cultural reforms were edicts requiring nobles and townsmen to shave their beards and wear European-style clothing. At court, men and women were compelled to dance together and mingle.[41] The Ottoman state never contemplated any comparable social legislation.

Far more consequential for Ottoman subjects were the social opportunities and incentives—for lifestyle, status, and social mobility—which emerged from a corrosive mix of commercialization, consumerism, and venality. Making the biggest difference by the eighteenth century was the state's relative capacity for mobilization—which is to say that the state was slowly drawing more subjects into its efforts to wage war. Though still a long way off from the "total wars" of the twentieth century, the mature fiscal state began, bit by bit, to tap the wealth and labor of society ever more creatively and extensively. As it scaled up its military networks and operations, it put more men under arms. To pay for this larger army, it taxed more heavily. Sensitive to its self-image as a just state, it was willing to bargain and compromise to get its way—and essentially had no choice about it.

In dealing with the general population, it could offer tacit "concessions," like more lenient social policies to accommodate a vibrant (and lucrative) consumer culture.[42] To co-opt and entice a wider Ottoman political class, it wielded fiscal blandishments, mainly the sale of state offices and tax-farms, which encouraged social mobility (or at least rising social expectations), both in Istanbul and the provinces. Mostly indirect in application, and entirely piecemeal in formulation, these policies nonetheless stirred resentments. What were opportunities and incentives for some Ottoman subjects proved, with varying degrees of alarm and outrage, threatening and subversive to others who feared social instability or their own seeming loss of status.

The pall of military defeat and internal disorder magnified social anxieties. It tarnished the legitimacy of the state. It raised unwelcome questions about the sultan and his officials. More troubling still were the cultural consequences of fighting losing wars. The Great Crisis of the late eighteenth and early nineteenth centuries, in which these setbacks culminated, was a cultural as much as a political episode. Demoralizing losses, with little respite in sight, made it easier to imagine the entire edifice of society as standing on shaky ground. Seemingly small issues could assume outsized significance: what people wore; what they ate and drank; the gestures they used; the way they moved through the streets. All these quotidian details, far from the battlefields, require an extensive consideration of the manners that seemed to constitute the very guarantee of social order and public morality.

The Ottoman sources for such a history are richer than might be expected. Most obviously useful, though not to the degree that one might hope, are etiquette (*adab/edep*) manuals. The authors within this literary tradition were members of the religious establishment (or at least had a religious education) and therefore devoted far more attention to religious and moral questions than practical advice for everyday social exchange. They taught piety, self-possession, and deliberation in thought and deed. The audience was presumed to belong to the same religious and literary circles as the authors themselves. Sünbülzade Vehbi (d. 1809), an Anatolian scholar and author of one admired etiquette manual, wrote it explicitly for his son, who would, of course, follow his father's career in the religious establishment.[43] Vehbi's tone veers from religious idealism to acerbic world-weariness. Early chapters on various branches of learning give way to a high-minded celebration of modesty and piety, along with warnings about the dangers of arrogance, envy, gossiping, and other moral defects. The good person, we learn, will honor his parents and respect scholars. The few practical-minded chapters urge his son not to get mixed up with state officials or incur too many debts. A section on fashion ventures no further than a few lines of sage counsel on the necessity of wearing clean clothes, eschewing excessive ornamentation, and dressing with the dignity incumbent on all scholars.

The idiosyncrasies of such authors, however arresting or diverting, should not blind us to their broader limitations. They thought in prescriptive terms and mused about the world as it ought to be. Their pages are undoubtedly useful for reconstructing general models of conduct. But the very real danger is that they can trap us in an imaginary world of social and religious norms that are presented, with few references to contemporary social conditions, as obvious, widely acknowledged, and uniformly applied. They reveal more about ideals than everyday social practice. And since such Ottoman guides drew their authority from religious teachings, they extolled values that were imagined as valid for all times and places, making it still harder to see how, or whether, authors were responding to contemporary social trends.[44] They show us, at best, what the cultural elite thought was proper.

If we want to catch various members of society "in action," other sources will tell us far more. Particularly valuable are chronicles, among the most abundant literary materials available to historians for nearly all parts of the Ottoman Empire. Once consigned to political history, they appear at first reading as straightforward accounts of urban or provincial politics, whose dramas almost always loomed as their main preoccupation. They recount the comings and goings of Ottoman officials, local political quarrels and intrigues, outbursts of factional or popular unrest, bits of gossip and rumor, and memorable events and personalities that, for one reason or another, had become the subject of local conversation or speculation. In short, they try to describe their world. The sketches are often patchy or partial, if not downright garbled or misinformed, but furnish precious details about social life that other sources were simply not interested in preserving. Chronicles will show us social encounters in which individuals, or sometimes groups, are speaking and physically moving. At these moments, nothing is abstract or idealized. Authors record, or realistically imagine, entire social scenes, sometimes adding extra touches like gesture, tone of voice, or even bits of direct speech.

The same opportunities abound in biographical dictionaries, another common genre in Arabic and Turkish letters. Essentially collections of obituaries, they memorialized members of the Muslim religious establishment, state officials, and literary lions. Though highly uneven in quantity and quality of detail, they sought, at a bare minimum, to record their subjects' main accomplishments. The best entries contain anecdotes or flashing recollections in which we can watch individuals acting in the heat of the moment. Memoirs, too, potentially furnish the same kinds of observations. Looking back on their life, authors might reconstruct a pivotal conversation, sketch a dialogue, or rarest of all, confess to some inner emotion.

Of more variable quality are the accounts written by European travelers to the Ottoman Empire. By the eighteenth century, they were coming in greater numbers, usually as merchants or diplomats, but were also joined by a new figure, the educated gentleman committed to the scientific study of other cultures. Not all these authors assumed European superiority. They might write about distant places with an attitude of curiosity and detachment, and sometimes with open admiration.[45] A few of them actually spoke local languages and through long residence had acquired deep familiarity with the society that they sought to describe and explain. Even when authors were less knowledgeable, or were merely passing through, their accounts still contribute invaluable information. Precisely because they knew so little, they were determined to set down whatever they saw in detailed fashion. They present the useful perspective of the outsider, for whom manners and customs are never self-evident and always need to be laid out and decoded. Only in the early nineteenth century does the tone of European travelers begin to shift overwhelmingly into hostile chauvinism. Even then, an author like Edward Lane, who learned Arabic and lived among Cairenes for many years (during several stays, 1820s–1840s), might still produce a valuable ethnography.[46]

From all these different sources, the manners of the Ottoman Empire come alive. To see them better, we first need to clear away accumulated myths that would obscure our view. Perhaps the most pervasive misconception is that the Ottoman Empire presided over an essentially "Islamic" (or "Islamicate") culture, whose mores and customs somehow bore the deep imprint of religion at every turn. But the manners that governed the body, whether through patterns of dress or taboos about self-presentation (chapter 1), had little to do with state policy or religious identity and far more likely reflected long-standing regional preferences. Sporadic attempts by the state to enforce religious codes went nowhere. The slippery hold of religious ideals over everyday sociability becomes still more obvious when we turn to the expansion and consolidation of Ottoman leisure culture during the long eighteenth century (chapter 2). Leisure culture reveals people in "free play," pursuing fun and recreation. These "unscripted" moments liberated them from official cultural norms and expectations and opened up opportunities for escapism. Ottoman society began to press ever more persistently on these exits from everyday routine. For its own reasons, the Ottoman state went along. Except in a few sporadic and short-lived moments of ideological distress, it gave up on earlier campaigns against coffeehouses and public smoking. Alcohol, opium, and other illicit substances, though proscribed by Islamic law, circulated actively in hedonistic subcultures, both inside the elite and among common subjects. In its unceasing and ever more urgent quest for revenue, the Old Regime was deeply complicit in this unabashed progress of pleasure.

No less decisive in shaping manners were ideals of self-presentation in speech, gesture, and bodily deportment. Particularly within urban society, one can actually speak of an empire of manners that corresponded to the empire of arms and officials that we are used to imagining as the face of imperial rule. From one end of the sultan's domains to the other, anyone who participated in official circles or nurtured aspirations to social respectability would have internalized a common set of polite manners (chapter 3). The study of this refined code of speech and gesture thus helps us to recognize the durability of Ottoman cultural models. Even during an era of supposed "decentralization," the "soft power" of Ottoman rule remained more potent than ever. This shared imperial culture was obvious to contemporaries, though not always to later historians.

The second half of the book considers more directly how manners became a cultural flashpoint across the long eighteenth century. The implacable demands of war-making brought into existence a vast paramilitary complex, which put rising numbers of men under arms and looked the other way as military units steadily integrated themselves into local society. More military officers were earning fortunes and turning gradually into urban notables. Affluence recast them increasingly as devotees of civility, and sometimes even ignited ambitions to become lettered and self-consciously cultivated gentlemen (chapter 4). But civility was never the entire story of manners. Coexisting with it, in constant tension and potential contradiction, was a parallel code of honor, which might authorize or even require displays of extreme emotion, including physical violence (chapter 5).[47] As more Ottoman subjects entered political networks and gained a claim to such prerogatives, old social hierarchies became blurrier, harder to define, and more subject to strain and dispute. Perhaps the most destabilizing legacy of the paramilitary complex was the unprecedented influx of new recruits, largely of rural background, who began to fill Ottoman towns. They quickly created their own unruly subculture (chapter 6). "Respectable" townspeople reacted to them with horror and outrage. In retrospect, we can recognize how these paramilitary elements were struggling, albeit unsuccessfully, to adapt rural norms and behavioral codes to an urban environment in which they proved incongruous and disruptive.

Taking different cross-sections of Ottoman society allows us to see how the evolution of manners was never unidirectional. It never consisted of the "downward" diffusion of civility throughout society, which has served as the main paradigm for the study of manners. The emphasis should fall instead on the role of war-making, which needs to be acknowledged, no matter how ironic or contradictory it may seem in relation to behavioral ideals that extend all the way to civility and politesse. But should it really be so surprising? Manners are, after all, fundamentally political. They expose the fault lines where stresses and tensions are silently accumulating. Viewed over the long eighteenth century, manners offer a new way of tracking the development of Ottoman society, and more fatefully, of understanding how the Ottoman Old Regime ultimately unraveled and gave way to the era of state-led modernization in the nineteenth century. The "dialogue" between manners and violence, an inextricable pair, unexpectedly narrates this path to modernity.

ONE

PRESENTING *the* BODY

Surveying the sheer breadth of the Ottoman Empire, the Swedish diplomat Mouradgea d'Ohsson (1740–1807) could hardly contain his amazement at its diversity, even though he was by birth an Ottoman Catholic Armenian (originally known to his peers as Ignatius Muradcan Tosunyan) who came from this social world. There was no better proof of it, he thought, than the dazzling profusion of fashions that even the most casual observer could not possibly overlook:

> Independently of the costumes reserved in general for the various peoples of the country, as well as the state, rank, and condition of each individual in the political order, we still notice an infinity of others, particularly those affected by the inhabitants of each province, each town, and each island of the Mediterranean Sea: this diversity, so striking in the Ottoman lands, but especially in the maritime towns, and even more particularly in the capital, offers everywhere and at every moment the most amusing and picturesque portrait.[1]

So the question of fashion was challenging even for contemporaries. From one part of the empire to another, innumerable local styles and usages predominated. We should therefore open our eyes to a sartorial landscape in which riotous variation was taken for granted by the subjects of the Old Regime themselves.

Fashion, however, is not the mere sum of costume and ornamentation.

It expresses basic standards of decency and propriety and therefore leads to the larger question of manners. At the center of these concerns was the body. As a general ideal, the cultures of the Ottoman Old Regime preferred to shield as much of the human form as possible from public view. But by no means did this ideal of deportment work itself out in the same way across the full breadth of the empire. Every region followed its own whims. In this regard, fashion takes us far beyond myths about "Islamic" culture or "national" tradition that still infect so much historical writing. It asks us instead to look beneath ideological surfaces. It reveals an empire that accommodated manifold customs, and that, to put the matter more bluntly, was quite powerless to impose any kind of cultural uniformity. In making sense of fashion, geography will thus be a far better guide than religion or "ethnicity."

Manners took many of their bearings from the interplay between fashion and body. People looked first to the head. As one British traveler observed, it was "commonly esteemed the noblest part, which is always chosen to bear the mark of an enjoined distinction."[2] As a result, headgear was the most expressive element of an individual's outfit. It instantly announced social status, and in this role was subject to the greatest variation in design and decoration. Clothing, too, was as much a social as a practical matter. It undoubtedly responded to the twin imperatives of climate and custom, but from one region to the next also gave rise to many different styles that sorted men from women and rich from poor and marked the sartorial frontiers between townspeople and villagers.

These fashions, at best, only partially and inconsistently conformed to the dictates of state law and Islamic tradition. Across the eighteenth century as the Great Crisis intensified, official decrees would call, ever more shrilly and fitfully, for legal and religious hierarchies to be upheld. Amid a deepening sense of insecurity, as Ottoman war-making faltered on the frontiers, this legislation sought to project strength, competence, and order. Despite the ideological bravura, all these initiatives came to naught. The state's failure to dress subjects according to official and Islamic regulations was not a consequence of the Great Crisis itself, but stemmed rather from the larger political and cultural limitations of the Old Regime, which never constituted anything resembling an "Islamic society."

Face and Hair

Across the societies of the Ottoman Empire, nearly everyone could agree on one basic rule: the head was not to be improperly exposed to public view. But this rule did not apply equally across the social order. Nearly everywhere, it weighed more heavily on women than men.

At the root of this injunction was a pervasive anxiety about women's hair, which, as folk judgment firmly maintained, carried an erotic charge that made it a disruptive incitement to men. It was an endless source of sexual provocation, and therefore of danger and disorder. Across the Mediterranean and Middle Eastern portions of the Ottoman Empire, women were expected to obey the same commandment to keep it primly out of sight. If taken unawares, while bathing or in any state of undress, they would instinctively cover their hair before thinking of doing anything else. These reflexes amused European travelers, whose own cultures taught women, above all, to shield their breasts from exposure. Wandering through Egypt in the 1760s, Carsten Niebuhr could not hide his astonishment: "There have been many instances of women, who, upon being surprised naked, eagerly covered their faces, without showing any concern about the other charms."[3] Working as a physician in eighteenth-century Aleppo, Alexander Russell later recalled this unwillingness to reveal the hair. His female patients did "not hesitate to expose the neck, the bosom, or the stomach" to his examination. But they would "never without extreme reluctance consent to uncover the head." Even women whom he had known since youth had this aversion to showing their hair.[4] The English traveler Richard Pococke had earlier discovered (1745) a more fashionable version of these attitudes on the Aegean island of Ipsos. He could not conceal his amazement at the local outfits. "The women have a veil or towel that comes over their heads and is brought around the neck, and sometimes they put it over the chin and mouth; but they expose the breasts in a very indecent manner, which seemed rather owing to an ignorance of decorum than out of lewdness."[5] From the local point of view, the traveler was the one who was guilty of ignorance. As long as women took care to conceal their hair, they were still dressing within the bounds of propriety.

Only in the interior of the Balkans, as the hold of Mediterranean values receded, did laxer views prevail about showing the head. When Charles Colville Frankland later passed through Ottoman Bulgaria (1827), he divided women's habits into two. Mature Bulgarian women wore "a kind of half-turban," whereas maidens were free to show off their hair, wound in long braids and "ornamented with gold coins."⁶ It was not, to be sure, a strictly "Bulgarian" custom. In the many Albanian villages around Athens (1806), young women also liked to decorate their hair "with medals and small pieces of money."⁷ Most parts of the Balkans, then, were not overly restrictive about women's hair (fig. 1.1). Though a relatively small detail, this freer exposure of the head signals the outlines of a broad cultural zone that predated Ottoman rule and continued to preserve its ways throughout the Old Regime.

FIGURE 1.1. "An Albanian woman" (c. 1700–1714). Portrait by Jean-Baptiste Vanmour (1671–1737), who arrived in Istanbul in 1699 as the painter for the French embassy and stayed the rest of his life, making a living with his brushes in the European diplomatic circles of the Ottoman capital. Among his works were portraits of different Ottoman social types. Here he represents an Albanian woman in clothing that one could have found in many parts of the Balkans: a kerchief, only partly covering her hair; a petticoat over most of the body; and boots adorning the feet. SOURCE: Rijksmuseum, Amsterdam.

Yet it would be a mistake to dwell entirely on geography as the single factor that determined how women would present themselves. Social context mattered at least as much and might vary throughout the course of daily routines. Even in the towns, which upheld a tighter surveillance over female dress, most women did not have to obsess over such questions. They spent their time within the confines of their own neighborhoods, where social interaction was frequent and casual. Neighbors knew each other and dispensed with formalities. They observed a minimum standard of decency: hiding their hair with a kerchief or some other cloth wrapped around the head. Further precautions were unnecessary. Networks of kinship and religion magnified this social latitude. In eighteenth-century Aleppo, for example, Jewish women were laxer about veiling within their own religious community "from the common occurrence of several families living in the same house and of intermarriages among near kindred."[8] Poverty further loosened communal restrictions. It reduced women to threadbare wardrobes and put refined accessories like face-veils out of reach. As Edward Lane observed for early nineteenth-century Egypt, "Many of the women of the lower orders, even in [Cairo], never conceal their faces."[9]

In the countryside, where most households lived close to subsistence, standards of modesty were proportionally eased. Basic questions of deportment, then, always adjusted to class and status (fig. 1.2). Lane continued, "I have often seen in this country women but half covered with miserable rags; and several times, females in the prime of womanhood, and others in most advanced age, with nothing on the body but a narrow strip of rag bound around the hips."[10] Rural attitudes were hardly different elsewhere. Kurdish women in the hinterland of eighteenth-century Aleppo were used to going about "bare-headed, without any veil, and converse freely with the men."[11] Hiding the face was an obviously urban affectation across most of Ottoman society. As John Lewis Burckhardt remarked (1812) of the Hawran, in southern Syria, the women "dress in the Bedouin manner; they have a veil over their head, but seldom veil their faces."[12] In the more familiar social environment of the village, they had no need to make a bigger show of respectability. Applying a further brake on ostentatious modesty was the necessity of working outside the home. Attaching a veil or full-body cloak as they went about their business was an unwelcome nuisance. Only in encounters with strangers or while traveling away from their village, perhaps on the road, would peasant women resort to fuller forms of veiling.

FIGURE 1.2. Depictions of "popular" dress in Egypt. The man is a groom, clad in an ample robe, with a turban and skullcap. He wears simple slippers. The peasant woman has a long, loose shirt, and has thrown a cloak over her head and body for a modicum of decency. Both individuals reveal the basic wardrobes available to most of the population, especially in the countryside.
SOURCE: *Description de l'Égypte* (Paris: Imprimerie de C.L.F. Panckoucke, 1821–30).

Though men might seem less encumbered from a distance, they too observed the same general restriction as women not to bare the head. The main male privilege was to be spared the face-veil, which automatically signaled "female" status. The vanishingly rare exceptions only prove the rule. Hence some Janissaries were known to keep young male lovers whose faces they might veil in public.[13] But the head was a different question. Unlike Europeans, Ottoman townsmen would never think of removing their headpiece or cap; it would be tantamount to an "affront."[14] They mocked the European gesture of doffing the hat and stepping backward, which made it seem, as one French visitor learned, "as if we were driving away flies."[15] Keeping the head from view was, for men as much as women, a matter of decency and good taste.

In contrast to women, men did not have to worry too much about showing their hair, mainly because they kept so little of it. Throughout the Mediterranean and Middle Eastern portions of the empire, as well as parts of the northern Balkans, the general fashion was to shave all the hair except for a "tuft" at the top. It was mainly a practical hygienic measure taken for the sake of cleanliness and as a precaution against lice and other vermin. As European travelers could not help noticing, Ottoman and "Frankish" fashions pursued opposite paths: whereas European men had long hair and often shaved the beard and mustache, Ottoman taste prescribed a shaved head and lavish facial hair.[16] Barbers necessarily did a brisk business. The Frenchman Volney thought (1783) that Egyptians used their services about once a week.[17] Haircuts were a fairly straightforward job, with little styling, and so customers allowed barbers to pretty much cut as they pleased.[18] In the name of simplicity, one Istanbul Sufi, Muhammed Nuri Efendi (d. 1823), dispensed with their services altogether and cut his own hair, which would not have required much coiffing anyway.[19] The main art to barbering consisted of twisting and perhaps scenting the knot of hair that would remain under the headpiece.[20]

The lone divergence from these customs—again—appeared in the Balkans. Two separate fashions prevailed. In the southern Balkans, most notably among the Greek population, the main hairstyle was a kind of tonsure. Men usually shaved away the front part of the head and let the hair grow down from the back (fig. 1.3). On the face, moustaches were sufficient.[21] In the western Balkans, as one English traveler reported (1673), men sprouted the main alternative, which he called the "Croatian" fashion: "One side of the head [is] to be shorn, and the other side is neither shorn nor cut, but the hair is let to grow as long as it will."[22] Thus this Balkan exceptionalism mirrors the different treatment of women's hair that we observed earlier. With men, too, the Balkans took a more relaxed view on the display of hair and preserved its own distinctive regional fashions.

There were few dissenters to these prescribed hairstyles. Almost without exception, nonconformists occupied narrow social niches, where deviations from the norm were tolerated. Some members of the religious establishment wore their hair differently as a means of expressing symbolic renunciation of the world. The great scholar and Sufi of Damascus, ʿAbd al-Ghani al-Nabulsi (d. 1731), once suffered a midlife bout of depression in which he kept mostly to himself at home. Friends later remembered this period for his unusual antics, such as refusing to cut his hair or trim his fingernails.[23] In Cairo, ʿAbd al-Latif al-Maktabi (d. 1748) made the same decision from strictly pious motivations. He was a scholar and popular

FIGURE 1.3. "Greek man from Yanina." His head is shaved in the Greek style, leaving the front part bare and the hair long in the back from under a small cap. He wears the *fustanella*, the kilt-like garment favored throughout the southern Balkans by many Greeks and Albanians.
SOURCE: Louis Dupré, *Voyage à Athènes et à Constantinople* (Paris: Imprimerie de Dondey-Dupré, 1825).

teacher who went on the pilgrimage late in life. When he returned, his religious devotion now redoubled, he turned his back on society, stayed at home, and "let down his hair."[24] Association with mystical rites also raised the likelihood of violating customary hairstyles. Whether in the Balkan or Middle Eastern parts of the empire, long hair was one of the hallmarks of such figures as Christian monks and wandering Sufi dervishes.[25] Socially marginal groups were other candidates for wearing their hair differently. The Dutch traveler Aegidius van Egmont recalled his meeting at Tiberius with a local commander, a son of Zahir al-`Umar, the most powerful figure in northern Palestine in the mid-eighteenth century. The commander and his small detachment of men "wore their own hair braided in two locks, hanging behind the ears, the fore part of the head being closely shaved."[26] It was a signal, instantly conveyed, of their rustic origins in remote districts. Bedouin-style warriors were certainly not the only ones to create such a peculiar impression. Landing on the coast of the Morea with his shipmates, Antonio Katsaites, a gentleman from Corfu, was startled by a party of local peasants. They could hardly believe their eyes. With their overgrown hair, beards, and fingernails, the villagers "resembled bears."[27] In these deep rural enclaves, urban standards of refinement were both irrelevant and ignored.

Outside the Balkan zones, then, men's hair was to be kept trimmed and concealed. Yet Ottoman gentlemen certainly did not feel this way about their facial hair. Luxuriant mustaches and beards were to be cultivated and conferred the very proof of manhood. Across all social groups, the symbolic passage to male adulthood was to grow a beard. In the principalities of Wallachia and Moldavia, the Romanian landowners (*boyars*) attached so much importance to their beards that they used them as an emblem of social rank: the higher a man's status, the longer his beard would grow. They would not part with their magnificent beards until the mid-nineteenth century, when Ottoman suzerainty had dwindled to a quaint political fiction, and with it, the old hirsute tastes.[28]

Endowed with this symbolic potency, the beard commanded respect. It was one of the chief emblems of masculine self-regard, which every man sought to protect. Under no circumstances was anyone to touch it. Those who ignored this precept were committing an unmistakable act of aggression or impertinence. In 1805, the sharif of Mecca, chief notable of the city, met with the governor of Damascus and warned that the pilgrimage caravan could not proceed safely and should turn back. The sultan's mother happened to be traveling with the pilgrims that year, and her steward (*kahya*) objected to such an ignominious retreat. His honor wounded, the sharif jumped up and grabbed the steward by the beard. He swore that he would have killed him at that instant if only the murder were not more trouble than it was worth. He reminded the imperial party that he had visited Istanbul five years earlier and pleaded for help from the Ottoman state in dealing with Wahhabi raiders who now blocked the way.[29] In the midst of his outburst, he could think of no more demeaning gesture, short of murder itself, than taking hold of the steward's beard.

Once a man was bewhiskered, he was expected to remain so. Refusing to keep a beard would be like renouncing manhood itself.[30] With this cultural shame in mind, many youths fled Damascus (1808) after a decree from the puritanical governor, Genç Yusuf Paşa, forbade them from shaving and threatened barbers with the amputation of any hand that would put a razor to a beard.[31] The fugitive youths were aware of social expectations, and knew that, once they started growing a beard, they would have to keep it. Rare was the man who defied these pressures. When Rufa'il Bijut, a Jewish merchant, became the Austrian consul in Aleppo (1784), he had to submit both to wearing Austrian clothes and shaving his beard, as if he were a European himself.[32] He consented only because it was the ritual price of the appointment, which conferred too many rewards to be declined for the sake of facial hair. Only a few eccentrics—from religious motives or otherwise—would have ever considered keeping a clean-shaven face.[33]

Male slaves were automatically subject to this symbolic social demotion. Found mostly in elite households, they were regarded as dependents, who, under both law and custom, should not look the part of free men. For this reason, the mamluks, or slave-soldiers, of Egyptian commanders kept a bare face until their formal manumission. Sprouting facial hair could become a virtual rite of passage. When the governor of Egypt formally elevated one of his mamluks to a state office (1697), he gave permission for his protégé to wear a beard.[34] It announced his transition to a new social status and allowed him to command the corresponding social respect. By the same logic, Janissaries kept only their moustaches.[35] Technically, they were "slaves" (*kul*) of the sultan; in reality, nearly all Janissaries had become free-born Muslims by the seventeenth century. The shaven portion of their face remained only as a token of loyalty and submission to the throne.

Ottoman men took pride in their facial hair and lavished attention on it. Long full beards, in particular, evoked admiration. Gray conferred dignity, but some Ottoman dandies waged their own war against time by using black dye. An alternative was to daub the beard with henna, which imparted a reddish hue. Some objected that the practice of dying beards was improper, even though proponents could cite the example of the prophet Muhammad, who was reported to have colored his own beard.[36] Hence Genç Yusuf Paşa, the puritanical governor of Damascus whom we met earlier, tried (1808) to make the men of Damascus apply antimony (*kohl*), a black tincture, to their beards and eyes. Townsmen viewed this measure, like the other initiatives that he pushed, as a strange imposition; and like those earlier measures, it was soon defeated through passive resistance.[37]

Much of this opposition had to do with prevailing aesthetic norms, which in most parts of Ottoman society assigned the use of antimony to women.[38] It was applied around the eyes or along the eyebrows. Like all such customs, it adapted to local differences in taste. In Athens, for example, women highlighted their eyes with blue, not black.[39] Henna, on the other hand, served as a decoration for women's fingernails, staining them with a reddish hue.[40] Apart from these embellishments, Ottoman women used hardly any makeup. By the eighteenth century, only wealthy Greek women had acquired this habit. They painted their faces with a kind of rouge, "which imparts a beautiful redness to the cheeks and gives the skin a remarkable gloss." Since this mixture contained mercury, it had the regrettable side effect of causing teeth to fall out.[41]

Bodily decoration consisted mainly of jewelry. Respectable opinion allowed both men and women to wear rings. But religious commentators were uneasy about men who took these habits too far. Gold was ruled out for men, who mostly conformed to this prohibition (if we can extrapolate from tastes in Damascus); they were counseled to wear silver instead. One ring on the left hand, the stone discreetly turned downward, would suffice.[42] Many men had practical reasons for owning a ring too. In early nineteenth-century Cairo, "almost every person who can afford it has a seal-ring, even though he be a servant."[43] Women had more latitude. They could wear gold or silver and could more freely indulge their fancy for decoration. Besides rings for the fingers, they availed themselves of different styles of necklaces and earrings, as well as bracelets for the arms and ankles.[44] In Egypt, the most adventurous used "pieces of coral hung about their faces" or tied "small bells to the tresses of their hair" or even to their feet.[45] The custom was not much different from the "great variety of colored glass beads" that Bulgarian women liked to hang on themselves.[46] Nose rings were a fashion that appeared in many places, though they were most popular in small towns or villages. Near Malatya, in southeastern Anatolia, a French traveler noticed how women's noses became "deformed" from the big rings that they inserted.[47] Less distasteful, at least for urban women, was the wearing of rings on toes.[48] The stitching of gold or silver coins into women's headdresses or necklaces was an overwhelmingly rural affectation.[49] Townswomen partook of the caution and reserve that reigned throughout urban culture and counseled against flashy ostentation. Feeling these inhibitions most keenly were the middling ranks of urban society. Having achieved a modest prosperity, they were haunted by a lingering insecurity, which made them wary of the state and its grasping officials. The gaudy display of good fortune was judged unwise, whether for men or women.[50] On the streets, well-to-do families learned to express their status more subtly in the high quality of the fabric and workmanship of their clothing or perhaps the fur that lined cloaks and vests.

Dressing the Body

As a general rule, affluent townswomen took the greatest pains with veiling and adorned themselves with the most elaborate outfits. Here we can begin to consider fashion in its fullest sense and view the headdress along with the rest of the female wardrobe. This bodily survey of Ottoman attire will once again confirm the predominance of regional fashions over religious or "ethnic" ones. Neither the state nor the religious establishment could set these tastes, which answered to local custom and geography, not the grand pronouncements of officials or scholars.

Our tour will start in the imperial capital, not because it defined an official "Ottoman" fashion but because, more than any other place, it served as the implicit model of dress for leading townspeople. Emulation always looked first to Istanbul. We can get a quick sketch of an upper-class outfit from Lady Mary Wortley Montagu, wife of a British ambassador who arrived in Istanbul (1717) with her husband's diplomatic mission. She quickly set about learning Turkish and gained entry into the homes of Ottoman grandees, conversing with their wives, and unlike other European travelers, getting a far more intimate perspective on Ottoman society. She liked what she saw. One of her early delights was the Ottoman wardrobe prepared for her. It contained all the items that any Istanbul lady would have insisted on having. In a letter to a friend back home, she worked up a concise self-portrait.[51] First came her headpiece, built around a cap, "in winter of fine velvet, embroidered with pearls or diamonds, and in summer of a light shining silver stuff." Tasteful ladies surrounded it with kerchiefs, ribbons, or even feathers, and perhaps overlaid jewelry like diamonds, gems, or pearls if they aimed at extravagance.[52] On her body, she wore a wide-sleeved shirt, and loose trousers hung down to her feet. Over the shirt came a tight-fitting "waistcoat" (*entari*) with long sleeves, over which she placed a long-sleeved robe (*kaftan*) that reached to her feet, secured around the waist with a belt. Outdoors she sported a greatcoat (*ferace*), "which no woman of any sort appears without; this has straight sleeves that reach to their finger-ends."[53] As a face-veil, two cloths were attached to the headdress, one thrown to the back and the other, called a *yaşmak*, brought around front to conceal all of the face except the eyes.[54] In Istanbul, as well as many other towns in the central Ottoman lands, the latter piece was commonly made of a gauzy white material (fig. 1.4) that, at the edge of acceptable fash-

FIGURE 1.4. Portrait of a lady from the Ottoman palace. Painting by Abdülcelil Levni (d. 1732), an artist at the Ottoman court. The subject of this portrait is dressed for outdoors, clad in a long overcoat and shrouded in the light, gauzy face-veil (*yaşmak*) favored by the respectable women of Istanbul. SOURCE: Topkapı Palace Museum.

ions, might almost attain a kind of translucence and seemingly defeat the purpose for which it was designed.[55]

Lady Mary's outfit by no means exhausted all the possibilities for upper-class wardrobes. There were many versions of this ensemble, including some garments that she did not name or perhaps never saw. Religious identity made hardly any difference in what women wore. The same tastes in clothing crossed all communal boundaries.[56] Within this spectrum of choices, established fashions tended to endure. To Mouradgea d'Ohsson, it seemed as though they hardly ever changed at all.[57] This judgment, of course, is not quite true. As Lady Mary herself observed at close quarters, Ottoman ladies were adept at introducing little variations, particularly in the headdress. But all this tinkering was not enough to disrupt the main outline of upper-class attire. When Elizabeth Craven visited Istanbul in 1786, she gazed on fashions that Lady Mary would have instantly recognized.[58]

Away from the capital, regional fashions quickly asserted themselves. Some were relatively subtle or understated. In Izmir, one traveler observed (1700) that Greek ladies "differ from other chief Greek women through all the cities and towns in Turkey only in respect of their headcloths, which are pretty like that of the Turkish ones, viz., of smaller bulk than that of the others."[59] At the small town of Manisa, in western Anatolia, few women had any thought of a fancy headdress. They sufficed instead with a simple white kerchief, "which is fastened around the neck under the vest and in the same measure resembles the mob worn by the women of Europe."[60] Set against these sedate preferences, the fashions of the Aegean islands were positively whimsical. Perhaps nowhere else in the Ottoman lands did diversity in costume reach such extravagant proportions. On eighteenth-century Lesbos, these differences were so extreme that the women on one part of the island wore "high turbans" on their head, while those of the main town followed another fashion.[61] Stopping at Naxos (1786), Elizabeth Craven confessed to a mixture of wonder and contempt. She recalled one "Naxiote maiden" whose "short shirt reaching to her knees served as a petticoat," over which she wore a vest "fantastic beyond conception, pearls, feathers, beads, sewed on, in various forms—and two wings like those of a butterfly, stuck between the shoulders."[62] It seemed to another British traveler that, on Rhodes, the women merely set "a large bundle of handkerchiefs and wrappers on the head."[63] These picturesque variations drew the attention of all travelers.[64] As Edward Dodwell concluded (1819), "Every island has its fashion."[65]

Amid this welter of styles, we might search for some "ethnic" Greek unity, as if there must have been some elements that tied them all to the Greek-speaking "mainland." But this imaginary bond is not something that was obvious to contemporaries, who took their bearings from a more restricted worldview, bound to their town, local district, or island. In the towns, affluent women tended toward cosmopolitan tastes and wore the usual Ottoman articles of clothing. To the eye of one early nineteenth-century traveler, the dress of Greek women "varies not materially from the Turk." Muslim or Christian, they veiled.[66] Leaving behind the islands, one soon encountered fashions from the Balkan interior, none of which were uniquely "Greek." Around the Gulf of Corinth, Dodwell found what he called the "Albanian styles." Atop the head was a "white handkerchief, hanging carelessly down the shoulder and turned around the neck." Maidens had a "red skull-cap, which is covered, more or less with money according to the wealth of the person."[67] His portrait is not very helpful, mainly because it glossed over so many variations in Albanian dress. As another British traveler had to admit (1809), Albanian attire was "very fantastical and different in different villages."[68] From one valley to another, generalizations tended to disintegrate. The rugged landscape imposed isolation and therefore favored eccentricity.

The same warning awaits us in the Arab provinces. No single "Arab" attire presents itself. Every region left its own stamp on sartorial styles. As always, headpieces were the most distinctive articles of dress. In Cairo, proper ladies wore a kind of turban, made from a cap wrapped tightly in one or more kerchiefs. From the top of the head, they suspended a two-piece face-veil (*burqu'*). The top part, attached to the headdress, fell down to the eyes, from which a second piece hung loose, over the nose and down to the chin. Further marking them off from the fashions of the capital was the different way in which they assembled and held their outer cloak.[69] In Aleppo, the fashions of Istanbul cast a bigger shadow. Some of the "Turkish" ladies dressed like their counterparts in the capital, although most women preferred the local style of headdress: "a linen sheet, large enough to cover the whole habit, from head to foot, and ... brought over the face in a manner to conceal all but one eye." It was lighter than the Istanbul outfit and less tiring to wear.[70] Away from the big towns, the design of headdresses grew ever more exuberant and parochial. It sought release in forms as varied as cones or discs. Across much of the Syrian countryside, women's fashions adhered to "a sort of lackered hat, shaped like a cone, a platter, or some other fantastic form."[71] The Maronite women of Beirut and Mt. Lebanon favored a cap made with a "long horn of silver in the richer, and wood in the poorer classes, which stands out from the forehead, inclining upwards, and about fourteen inches in length."[72] The same fashion, in silver or copper, predominated as far off as Adana.[73]

There was nothing about these shapes that tied them specifically to the Arab lands or any other region. In the countryside of southwestern Macedonia, women likewise wore a tall hat, "a species of mitre," and swathed the bottom with a long piece of muslin.[74] But this, too, was a local peculiarity. In many parts of Serbia, the female headpiece was a circular hat worn at the back of the head. The most extravagant versions were enormous and proved so cumbersome that, whenever the wind blew, women either had to bend down or hold onto them tightly with their hands.[75] This fondness for circular hats also surfaced, quite independently, as far away as Malatya, a town in southeastern Anatolia. Fashionable women wore "broad flat pieces of metal" that "resemble common eating plates and are fastened with strings under the chin." The well-to-do had them in silver; the poor, in copper.[76] In short, every district had its own peculiar costume, which reflected the immense variety of customary laws and usages that guided social and economic life. All travelers were used to these local idiosyncrasies of dress and took them in stride. Clothes would, of course, change like the landscape.

Very much like women, men sported highly distinctive regional styles of headgear that neither state officials nor anyone else ever thought of trying to unify into a grand imperial fashion. At the same time, these styles spoke a social language that was impossible to ignore. Size, ornamentation, and quality of material helped to signal social status, confirmed affiliation with the state, and distinguished townsmen from villagers. As a first step, we can divide this male headgear into two categories: turbans and caps. Preferences had little to do with religion or "ethnicity," and in most places, predated Ottoman rule.

Turban is a term that actually encompasses a wide range of head coverings. To start at the top of society: the powerful and well-to-do would have demanded visual magnificence as their due. Their turbans were therefore tall, and typically consisted of three main components: a stiff cap (*tarbush*) that acted as a kind of inner scaffolding; the cloth that they wrapped around it, whether of muslin, satin, or linen; and a sash, of one color or another, which girded the base. From this basic architecture numerous designs took shape. "The oriental headdress admits of great variety in its fashion," as Alexander Russell observed of eighteenth-century Aleppo.[77] Many of these wrappings corresponded to specific offices or ranks. Still others were the product of regional styles, identifiable at a glance. In Cairo, the great scholar Murtada al-Zabidi (d. 1791), who had migrated from India by way of Yemen, wore a turban in the style of Mecca, "wound around with a white sash. It had ends which fell down to the back of his head, and they had fabric and tassels of silk about a span long, the other end of which entered the fold of the turban while some ends showed."[78] Other new arrivals in Cairo signaled that they were putting down roots by abandoning the fashions of their homeland and dressing "local."[79] High officials felt no such desire to blend in. At the palace, the viziers, Janissary officers, courtiers, and high-ranking religious officials all had their own distinctive headgear, bedecked with jewels, pendants, or exotic feathers, which they automatically donned for state ceremonies and parades.[80] Across the towns of the empire, members of the social elite produced their own versions of these displays according to local fashions.[81] Turbans of such lofty proportions, which depended on intricate wrapping, required specialists who knew how to wind or repair them.

Few townsmen could indulge in such outsized tastes. By necessity—which is to say, by virtue of their more restricted purchasing power—most Ottoman subjects favored simplicity. Tradesmen and shopkeepers might make their turbans with a small tarbush swathed in a piece of cloth.[82] Among the poor, a cheap felt cap, with only a sash around it, could serve as a substitute. Humbler still was a piece of cloth directly wound around the head, as many villagers were accustomed to dressing it.[83] Whichever style they chose, men would honor two basic rules. Under no circumstances would they uncover their heads; and they would not exceed their social status by wearing a turban that was too grand and ostentatious.

The main rival of the turban was the cap. And much like the turban, this term conceals a surprising complexity. Found across most of the empire, every region had its popular designs. In the highlands of eastern Anatolia, it was a tall cylindrically shaped hat, known as a *kalpak*. One of the telltale fashions of the Kurds and Armenians, it was made from animal skins, which made it ideal for the rigors of the cool mountainous climate. The best ones were lined with fur; inferior versions used felt.[84] Comparable hats appeared across the northern tier of the empire (fig. 1.5), circulating from the highlands of Anatolia to the Crimean peninsula, and then across the northern Balkans. Local styles tended to vary by color and height, like the towering Bosnian headpiece known as the *kovrdjak*.[85] Among the privileged, the kalpak actually had a wider range, serving as the favorite headgear for affluent Christians even where it was uncommon. In Cairo, one Christian physician was remembered (1766) for donning a "kalpak of sable fur," which would have instantly stood out in the turban-wearing lands along the Nile.[86] Throughout the Arab provinces, Christians and Jews who had joined European consular staffs would have also identified themselves with a tall kalpak.[87]

FIGURE 1.5. An Armenian gentleman wearing a *kalpak*, the tall skin hat whose main fashion zone stretched across the northern tier of the empire. It was also common headgear for well-to-do Christians and Jews in towns across the Ottoman Empire.

SOURCE: Louis Dupré, *Voyage à Athènes et à Constantinople* (Paris: Imprimerie de Dondey-Dupré, 1825).

As one passed into the southern Balkans, the supremacy of the kalpak faltered, and a third sartorial zone came into view. It encompassed Greece, the Aegean islands, and Cyprus, and then dipped south to North Africa, where it hugged the coastline as far west as Algeria. Here was a separate world of fezzes and cloth caps, which came in different styles. Most were short and somewhat conical, sometimes with a tassel attached at the top. With use, they tended to lose their shape and sag. Not to be deterred, Greek peasants used the drooping ends "as a handkerchief and sometimes for the purse." The chief alternative, recommending itself mainly to the poor, was a small red skull-cap.[88]

The competition between turbans and caps did not play out on an equal footing. Turbans more readily entered the lands of the caps and were to be seen throughout the empire. Towns were particularly receptive settings, mainly because turbans were more closely associated with urban lifestyles. Equally decisive was the endorsement of the state, for which turbans functioned as part of the ceremonial language of power and status. The Balkans best illustrate this dual attraction. Turbans were a commonplace in the streets of the towns. Strolling through early nineteenth-century Athens, one British traveler marveled at a "crowd of Greeks and Turks, seen at a distance with their colored turbans, with the predominant tints of red, blue, yellow, and white."[89] These fashions remained uncontroversial, and unchallenged, even on the eve of the Greek war of independence. The attachment to turbans was doubly true of Christians who held high office. In Wallachia and Moldavia, the two tributary provinces north of the Danube, the Ottoman state implemented a long policy (1711–1829) of selecting governors (*hospodar*) from wealthy Greek notables in Istanbul, the so-called Phanariot families. Just like their Muslim counterparts, they lived and dressed like Ottoman grandees (fig. 1.6), sat on Ottoman-style furnishings, and self-consciously placed a turban on their head.[90]

Looking "below" to the dress of the majority, we can apply a slightly different rule. If officials and soldiers showed a sartorial fealty to Ottoman styles, recognizable across large parts of the empire, Ottoman subjects clung to their regional fashions. In these choices, religion once again made little difference. A British traveler touring Ottoman Greece had to concede that Muslims and Christians dressed alike. The only significant variation, as far as he could tell, was that wealthy Christians wore an "immense calpac" instead of a turban.[91] Ottoman observers already knew the

FIGURE 1.6. A portrait of a prince (*hospodar*) of Moldavia. The Ottoman government appointed (1711–1829) the princes of Wallachia and Moldavia (modern Romania) from the wealthy Greek Phanariot families of Istanbul, trusted agents of the sultan. The prince here, Michail Soutzos (r. 1819–21), appears in the fine apparel that high Ottoman officials would have routinely donned. SOURCE: Louis Dupré, *Voyage à Athènes et à Constantinople* (Paris: Imprimerie de Dondey-Dupré, 1825).

rule: region mattered more than religion. Villagers at Dayr al-Qamr, on Mt. Lebanon, quailed at the approach (1792) of what they initially assumed were a contingent of Anatolian mercenaries (*dalatiyya*). At the last moment, their apprehension turned to relief when they realized that the troops were actually local Druze who had routed the mercenaries and plundered their tents.[92] The villagers were almost certainly looking at tall kalpaks, taken as booty from the defeated troops, the latter of whom continued to wear them even during service in the Arab provinces.[93]

Regional "traditions" were an outgrowth of historical experience. New fashions might require generations to take hold; likewise, older ones might stubbornly persist in the face of new conditions. Several Aegean islands preserved Italianate dress long after the departure of Venetian or Genoese rule. At the end of the seventeenth century, one French traveler was amused by the scene at Scio (Chios), which the Ottomans had conquered much earlier from Genoa in 1566:

> This is the only island in the Levant where the custom of wearing long garments does not prevail: for the Scios retain'd the fashion us'd by the Franks after their subjection to the Turks. They still use doublets or waist-coats, breeches, and shooes; and besides they wear their hair long: but we have changed so many fashions since that time that they who have kept that which was then in use appear very ridiculous at present. Their hats have broad brims, not cock'd up, and tapering crowns, somewhat resembling a sugar-loaf: the sleeves of the doublets are wide and open, but close at the waist: their breeches are open below, edg'd with ribbons, and their drawers appear under them: their shooes have large open ears and are sharp-pointed at the toe, as they were usually made in our country about twenty years ago.[94]

These peculiarities in dress were, as we have already observed, characteristic of the Aegean basin as a cultural region. The sea acted much like rugged mountain terrain in isolating communities and encouraging them to foster and maintain their own idiosyncrasies. On Cyprus, too, the Ottoman conquest (1570) did not lead to the abandonment of the older Italianate fashions until the eighteenth century.[95]

Further uniting neighbors were shared notions of propriety and decency. For men, no less than women, clothing functioned as a polite screen designed to shield the body from view. We can return to Istanbul for a snapshot of a common urban ensemble for men: a loose shirt with wide sleeves (*gömlek*); baggy trousers (*çakşır*); a belt or sash wound around the waist; a short vest or robe (*dolaman* or *cübbe*); and over the whole outfit, one or perhaps two long-sleeved robes that hung nearly to the ground.[96] In general outline, the same items will appear familiar from women's wardrobes. Nevertheless, men's garments did have distinctive features. Their shirts covered the neck and upper chest more closely, and had none of the plunging necklines that would become so fashionable among Istanbul women by the eighteenth century.[97] Men's vests were also somewhat longer, reaching down to the knees, and were not as close-fitting as those designed for women.

At the summit of male fashion, no article of clothing better defined the stylish urban gentleman than the outer cloak. For at least half the year, it was an indispensable garment, not only for outdoors in cold weather but inside as well, primarily due to the difficulty of heating and insulating interiors, even in the best houses.[98] The fanciest cloaks were trimmed with fur and immediately marked out the urban gentleman from the more commonly dressed. So prestigious were these garments that Ottoman ceremony had long used the robing of officials, mainly in sable, as the ultimate mark of imperial favor. As if confirming a hierarchy of furs, the palace went so far, in 1756, as to order all members of the imperial council to prefer sable alone.[99] Among others donned by the affluent were ermine, marten, and fox, all of which reached Ottoman markets from either the Balkan provinces or the Russian Empire.[100] The poor had to seek warmth and consolation in inferior furs, such as squirrel and cat, or in imitations made from felt.[101] In desperation, many Wallachians wrapped themselves in ragged motley cloaks, stitching together "one patch of fur from every creature."[102] Warmer weather brought out cloaks and robes made from cotton, silk, or broadcloth, all of which covered a vast range of prices. Gentlemen displayed their social credentials through high grades of fabric, fine workmanship, and the lavish use of gold and silver brocade. Ample garments with large sleeves, outer cloaks descended nearly to the feet and concealed the entire figure. Thus in the same manner as women, men would show as little of the body as possible. The dictates of modesty granted little leeway to the respectable.

Only in the Aegean basin, and along the Mediterranean coastlines stretching across North Africa, did men's fashions deviate from this preference for enveloping cloaks. These were the same regions where, as we noted earlier, men wore caps instead of turbans. They went their own way in clothing too. Along the Mediterranean littoral the prevailing fashion called for relatively short and close-fitting dress: a tunic and sleeveless vest for the upper body; together with baggy pants, no lower than the knees, held by a loose belt.[103] This ensemble was most closely associated with Greeks, Albanians, and North Africans, who often kept these clothes as they moved about the empire as soldiers, sailors, and laborers (fig. 1.7). The French writer François-René Chateaubriand encountered a contingent of Albanians stationed in Alexandria (1806) and was smitten by their costume.

FIGURE 1.7. "Albanian soldiers." They wear the characteristic attire of the Mediterranean zone: tunics, vests, short pants; and for the head, a small red cap. For Greek and Albanian highlanders, the weapons, always tucked into the belt, were as much a social statement as a means of self-defense. SOURCE: Marie-Gabriel-August-Florent Choiseul-Gouffier, *Voyage pittoresque de la Grèce* (Paris, 1782).

> Their dress consists of very wide trousers, a short petticoat; a waistcoat covered with plates, chains, and several rows of large bells of silver. They wear buskins, fastened with thongs of leather, which sometimes come up to the knees to keep on the calves of the legs plates which assume their form and preserve them from rubbing against the horse. The cloaks, bordered and laced with different colors, render their dress still more picturesque. They have no other covering for the head than a red cap, and this they throw off when they are going into battle.[104]

Like other outfits, the details were subject to local variations and accents. Greeks and Albanians often wore a loose kilt (*fustanella*) over their pants. Some tastes were entirely regional. To take the Albanians again: the red cap was often displaced by "a colored or white handkerchief, folded two or three times around the head" in the villages of Thessaly, where many had long settled.[105] The same lessons can be applied, independent of "ethnicity," across the entire Mediterranean cap-wearing zone where these fashions held sway.

The last stop on our tour of Ottoman bodies brings us to the feet, which received perhaps the most subdued attention. Shoes were literally the most pedestrian article of clothing and served a mostly utilitarian function. Few pairs lasted very long, allowing urban shoemakers to keep ample inventories in their shops, as customers had to regularly seek out replacements.[106] Across most of the empire, the biggest differences in footwear fashion ran between towns and villages. Most Ottoman townspeople, men and women, walked outside the home with soleless slippers (*mest*), placed inside shoes (*pabuç*) of red or yellow leather. Calf-high boots (*çizme*) were the first choice of many soldiers (or those who wanted to strike a more dashing and equestrian pose).[107] In rainy conditions, or merely at the bathhouse, elevated wooden clogs came into service, albeit mainly among women (fig. 1.8).[108] Peasants, on the other hand, often shod themselves with simpler footwear. In the Aegean region, leather sandals were the norm; throughout the Balkans and Anatolia, black boots or skin buskins.[109] Some Serbian peasants dispensed with shoes altogether and swathed their feet in thick socks.[110] Easier still was the option of going about barefoot. In balmy regions like Egypt, it was utterly commonplace;[111] but even in Bulgaria, as one traveler attested, women might in fair weather do without shoes, as "their feet are always bare, and beautiful."[112] From this overview of footwear, then, we can conclude that the feet submitted to the same general principle as other parts of the body: respectability demanded concealment. This expectation applied most strictly in the towns, where the affluent would never allow themselves to be seen barefoot. Although few shoes could be considered stylish, they still conveyed status in a plainer, more functional language. A glance at the boots and sandals of many peasants would confirm their lower social standing, betrayed by the basic design and manufacture that was evident in nearly all the clothing of the countryside.

FIGURE 1.8. Portrait of an Ottoman lady and servant. The painter, Jean-Etienne Liotard (1702-1789), spent part of his career (1738-42) in Istanbul. The two figures here stand in a bathhouse, where women often wore high wooden clogs.

SOURCE: Nelson-Atkins Museum of Art.

Fashion and Official Hierarchies

In a series of decrees that gained intensity and urgency across the eighteenth century, Ottoman authorities took a new interest in the clothing that the sultan's subjects were wearing. Two separate trends form the backdrop for all this legislation. The first was the sustained economic expansion of the mid-eighteenth century (c. 1720–70), which fanned commercialization and consumerist impulses. The affluent and ambitious could more freely indulge in sumptuous expenditure. The second, and far more portentous, trend was undoubtedly the downturn in the empire's military performance. As defeats on the frontiers mounted, especially in the late eighteenth and early nineteenth centuries, the state rushed to defend hierarchies of status and power that these military troubles now seemed to tarnish. The sultan and his officials sought to reassure the public. They would deal with both threats, military and social, which were increasingly viewed as intertwined. The legislation had two main targets: women and non-Muslims. At the core of these initiatives, which were entirely symbolic and had little practical effect on sartorial custom, was the state's concern with upholding an idealized social order sanctioned in Islamic law. That such a social order had never existed was hardly a deterrent, whether to officials who were clamoring for its alleged restoration or to moralists who imagined themselves as rallying to its defense.

The decrees directed against women, which we will take up first, always had to strike a delicate balance. Though firmly committed to ideals of female modesty, law and custom readily conceded that women had a right to be present in public places. At a bare minimum, the everyday routines of the household—not to mention their participation in the local economy through activities as varied as spinning and peddling—positively required their circulation in streets and markets for the sale and purchase of essential supplies. Wandering through the crowds at the Egyptian Market in Istanbul, one British observer (1834) judged that "the fair sex form by far the majority."[113] Women made their way with equal freedom to the outskirts of towns, where they might pass the time in the gardens, orchards, and cemeteries that constituted the principal leisure spaces of towns under the Old Regime. Here they amused themselves with conversation, graced ideally with coffee and pipes (and sometimes alcohol).[114] In Aleppo, one British traveler (1805) ventured out to the gardens and met with a party of women who playfully encircled him and briefly made him their "plaything" before moving on to other entertainments.[115] Guiding their movement through urban spaces were informal expectations about modesty and social distance that weighed on all women who had any claim to respectability. They were not to go out alone. A proper lady would have an escort (preferably a train of attendants). Even a woman of humbler station would still know to walk with a companion, male or female, or join a group outing.[116] Few were the women, like those on the island of Chios (fig. 1.9) where more Latinate ways prevailed, who could dispense with head coverings, sit boldly in their doorways, and strike up conversations with strangers.[117] Modest women would maintain a demure distance and avert their gaze. More primly still, they would swathe themselves in ample, unassuming dress. It was per-

FEMMES DE L'ILE DE SCIO.

FIGURE 1.9. "Women of Scio." This portrait features women's fashions from the island of Chios. The headdresses were particularly idiosyncratic. As late as the eighteenth century, European travelers regarded Chios as the most "Latinate" of the Aegean islands.

SOURCE: Marie-Gabriel-August-Florent Choiseul-Gouffier, *Voyage pittoresque de la Grèce* (Paris, 1782).

ceived violations of this last stricture that were most likely to touch off active surveillance of female mobility by the state.

The first wave of eighteenth-century legislation about women's clothing can be traced back to the reign of Ahmed III (r. 1703–30). An edict from 1726 chastised women—presumably those who belonged to elite families in Istanbul—for wearing headdresses that resembled European designs.[118] The document provides no background about official motivations, but the most probable chain of transmission for these provocations ran through the powerful Phanariot families, who supplied the Porte with its main diplomatic staff. Contact with European embassies would have exposed them to European fashions, which for a moment settled into an exotic niche among the upper reaches of Istanbul society. In the early eighteenth century, a strong sense of imperial identity was still comfortable with such cosmopolitan eclecticism, which happily absorbed tastes and styles of different provenance.[119] But even during this last phase of imperial self-confidence, which only began to evaporate toward the end of the eighteenth century, political instability could foster cultural reaction. After the Patrona Halil uprising (1730), which overthrew Ahmed III, anxieties about public order persisted. In one famous incident (1732), authorities executed a prostitute (*kahpe*), dubbed "Satan's Deputy" (*Şeytan Eminesi*), whom they arrested and threw into the sea. She was made an example for other women who were dressing provocatively with fancy, pleated turbans, veils that hid little of the face, tight-fitting cloaks, and long collars that fell down to their waist. Critics lamented that these fashions were fomenting a breakdown in social hierarchy and encouraging women of modest means to dress like their superiors.[120]

The next burst of sartorial legislation corresponded largely with the short reign of Osman III (r. 1754–57). Women again bore the brunt of official surveillance and regulation. The champions of law and order took umbrage at the many women who felt free to promenade in streets and gardens around the capital. Many of the earlier complaints were repeated as well. Some women, we hear, wore fancy clothing and tight-fitting cloaks and loitered around shops in the market. They staged excursions outside the capital, where the wealthiest among them drew attention by touring in carriages. So many filled the streets that the sultan sent out an order to neighborhood headmen forbidding women from leaving their homes without good reason.[121] Over the next several years more decrees would follow with monotonous scolding. Women were sporting (1755) multicolored overcoats (*ferace*) and continued to indulge in a shameless fancy for long collars that they showed off in the markets.[122] A decree of 1757 harped again about overcoats and collars that violated "the attitude of propriety"; it added that headscarves were now becoming overly long and immodest.[123] A warning issued in 1759 trained its ire on outlandish headdresses and skimpy veils that left half the face exposed.[124] The repetition of these prohibitions only confirms the helplessness of officials. Women were still promenading as Osman III had observed them. And these scenes played out in the capital. If official monitoring proved so futile in the very seat of the imperial government, it had no chance of reshaping fashion elsewhere.

The sartorial legislation of the eighteenth century had a second target in the Christians and Jews of the capital. In the aftermath of Ottoman defeat in the War of the Holy League, imperial authorities were already reproving them (1702) for dressing with articles like yellow shoes and red and "Tatar" kalpaks, which state law had previously assigned to Muslims.[125] In 1757, the newly enthroned Mustafa III took up the same refrain. Christians and Jews had overstepped their place by wearing elegant furs, yellow leather shoes, red fur caps (kalpaks), and red broadcloth. The same decree wagged its finger at Europeans in Istanbul, who carelessly wandered the streets in their native garb, which Ottoman opinion regarded as overly snug and therefore indecent.[126] The sultan underscored this initiative by summoning to the palace the heads of the Christian and Jewish communities of Istanbul and personally commanding them to enforce the sartorial regulations.[127] A second order, proclaimed in 1759, dealt more specifically with the colors assigned to different religious communities. Muslims had the right to wear green and red. Christians and Jews were to identify themselves on the streets with blue or black, usually signaled by a sash in their headgear. Their women, who had not escaped official notice, were to content themselves with red leather shoes, not the yellow ones formally reserved for Muslims of high status.[128]

All these measures, as if repeated in an irate staccato, once again reveal how little the Ottoman administration could do in the streets of the capital itself. Boundaries meant to separate Muslims visually from their Christian and Jewish neighbors were being routinely trampled or blurred. The hand of the state might find a few random victims to punish for breaches of the formal sartorial order. But fashion would have its way. The very styles and articles of clothing that were the prerogative of Muslims corresponded to the furs, fabrics, headpieces, and accessories that conveyed high status. Christians and Jews showed a wily determination to chip away at the edges of these regulations as much as they could.[129]

On the official side of these campaigns, the authorities were not used to being so severe in enforcing sartorial distinctions. In Istanbul and Izmir, well-to-do Christians had once gotten away with donning white turbans, which, minus the telltale colored sash, should have been available only to Muslims.[130] This leniency could fluctuate according to local conditions or might even depend on the vagaries of particular social encounters. One French traveler (1682) spied several Christians wearing green on the streets of Istanbul; while visiting Aleppo during the same journey, he claimed to have watched as a group of Muslim women attacked a Christian woman for having it in her clothing.¹³¹ So the Christians and Jews of the towns were aware that they could not altogether ignore the color scheme. Nevertheless, there were no police to monitor them or enjoin compliance; and in the tight-knit residential quarters, townspeople knew the religious identity of their neighbors anyway and did not need the external symbols to remind each other. In the countryside, the color scheme was practically a dead letter. Regional styles prevailed across the peasantry regardless of religious identity. As European travelers discovered on Mt. Lebanon, Maronite Christians freely wore green turbans.¹³² On the island of Chios, Christian peasants actually had formal permission to wear the white turbans that, as we have seen, were the prerogative of Muslims. Only if they entered town—by definition, prone to more ideological surveillance—did they have to wind the requisite blue sash around their head.¹³³

Complicating these formal restrictions on colors were variations from one region or period to another. The empire had never had a single Ottoman color code. Contemporaries were aware, moreover, that the scheme was far from immutable. The Ottoman historian Hüseyin Ayvansarayi (d. 1786) could recall how Abdülkerim Efendi, spiritual advisor to Murad III (r. 1574–93), had brought about a switch of colors in which the Christians and Jews of Istanbul replaced their blue and yellow sashes, respectively, with black and red; and shortly afterward, as if to further demonstrate how there was nothing sacrosanct about these choices, Jews were told to wear purple.¹³⁴ This order appears to have rippled out to at least some provinces. In Egypt, one governor (1582) had Christians use black and assigned red to Jews, the latter of whom were commanded to wear black only a little later (1595).¹³⁵ By the eighteenth century, Christians in Egypt and Syria were putting black or blue (or blue-and-white striped) sashes in their turbans, whereas Jews resorted to red—except in Aleppo, where the latter had, since 1600, worn violet for their turbans and shoes as the result of a single governor's whim.¹³⁶ More stable were the regulations on footwear. Yellow was the privilege of Ottoman officials and the upper social stratum, which included Christian officials and notables.¹³⁷ By law, European officials and their local diplomatic staff qualified for this exemption as well. Other townspeople would have to wear red shoes.¹³⁸ Sartorial legislation jealously guarded this distinction, but if the footwear of eighteenth-century Aleppo is any indication, it seems to have been implemented unevenly.¹³⁹

As the palace surveyed the fashions of the capital during the reign of

Mustafa III (r. 1757–74), a broader set of concerns entered its field of vision. A decree of 1760 repeated the earlier commands to non-Muslims about observing the proper sartorial restrictions.[140] At the same time, officials leveled new objections at artisans, servants, and other townspeople of middling status who were now trying to "imitate" men of state (fig. 1.10). They were dressing up with expensive furs and betraying a sartorial exuberance unbecoming of their social station.[141] In 1764, the state reissued the same warnings and extended the prohibition to robes and belts decorated with

FIGURE 1.10. "An itinerant barber." Portrait by Jean-Baptiste Vanmour (c. 1700–1714). The barber wears the simple turban and robe of an ordinary artisan. More defiant are the yellow leather shoes, formally reserved for the social elite. Whether in Istanbul or other Ottoman towns, this flouting of sartorial boundaries was rampant, and to the chagrin of imperial authorities, proved impossible to monitor and control.

SOURCE: National Trust Collections, UK.

floral themes (probably of Indian manufacture).[142] We hear the same refrain about those who would "exceed their rank." Runaway fashion now seemed to endanger the social order. If new styles were allowed to establish themselves, they would confuse social hierarchies that were imagined as proper and permanent, and positively invite social competition. Bemoaning the "profligacy" of artisans and servants who were trying to emulate their superiors, these official lamentations testify to the long economic expansion of the eighteenth century. Steady growth had unleashed a spate of luxury spending that was disproportionately concentrated in Istanbul: hence the state's fixation on sartorial trends there.[143]

Over the next several decades, the state would continue to confess its anxieties about status and order. Some dandies, decrees grumbled, had acquired a taste for fashions "resembling those of women's clothing." Worse than this effeminacy was the reckless spending that it encouraged among these "fools" (*sufaha*). Notices had to be posted (1776) outside tailor shops in Istanbul to discourage extravagance.[144] The same ordinance had to be repeated in 1783, again with threats to tradesmen and wailing about excessive spending. So concerned had officials become that on this second occasion they forbade the general population from buying Indian textiles, whose popularity, they insisted, was now harming Ottoman industry.[145] Selim III (r. 1789–1807) personally complained that he wore clothing of Ottoman manufacture, whereas his ministers and other grandees preferred Indian and Iranian garments.[146] Official scrutiny soon turned to women's towering headdresses and brightly colored overcoats. Collars had once again grown so long that neighborhood headmen were empowered to snip them off with scissors. Provoking a separate prohibition (1792) was the craze for English broadcloth so fine that passersby could see whatever garments were worn underneath.[147] This official hostility to flamboyant fashions would continue into the early nineteenth century, reaching a new pitch of indignation with the toppling of Selim III (1807), which intensified hand-wringing about hierarchy and order. During one of Mahmud II's incognito patrols on the streets of Istanbul, his bodyguards apprehended a youth who was wearing expensive fabric in his turban that a recent edict (1811) had forbidden. They pulled it off his head and tore it to pieces. If a crowd of women had not gathered around the youth and pleaded for mercy, he might have suffered far worse.[148]

The sartorial legislation dating from the early and middle decades of the eighteenth century had taken aim at the streets of the capital. By the 1770s, the same directives were now being proclaimed in the provinces as well. Military defeat against Russia (1768–74) was the trigger for a general ideological crisis of confidence that now seeped into all corners of the empire. Fresh from the catastrophe on the northern frontier, the governor of Aleppo announced (1772) new sartorial regulations for local Christians modeled on the customs of Istanbul. They were to wear a fur cap (kalpak), black garments, red shoes, and violet trousers (*jaqshir*). The poorest Christians, it was said, had to scour the markets for small caps and old garments of fur and broadcloth so that they could comply. Only after numerous warnings and fines did the governor, having filled his pockets, allow Christians to revert to their original clothing.[149] In 1775 and 1780, governors tried to switch the color scheme again. On both occasions, Christian and Jewish leaders had to negotiate payments before the order was rescinded.[150] Then in 1784, a new governor arrived and once again accused Christians of not following the color code scrupulously. He admonished them to take greater care with their dress and keep their women from wearing green to church.[151] The unspoken subtext, understood by everyone, was that many Christians were not so readily identifiable on the street, and that green was by no means a strictly "Muslim" color. In Damascus, Mikha'il Burayk, a Christian priest, remembered the governorship of As`ad Paşa al-`Azm (r. 1743–57) as a time of relaxed supervision of the dress code. Christians could wear whatever they wanted, including the color green, and drink alcohol in the gardens without the slightest harassment.[152] These easygoing attitudes were now beginning to fade. Meanwhile on the Levantine coast, the same ideological pressures were building during the last decades of the eighteenth century. The governor of Acre, Ahmed Paşa al-Jazzar, ordered the Christians of Beirut (1782) to place a blue or black sash in their turbans. He repeated the proclamation in 1785.[153] Memories of two Russian raids on the port, in 1772 and again in 1773, were still fresh. The provincial administration would now take measures, even if only symbolic, to shore up its authority.

Wherever the Ottoman order seemed threatened or showed obvious strains, legislation about non-Muslims was likely to follow. In Egypt, mamluk factions exploited the distraction of the central state, still trying to cope with defeat against Russia, and turned themselves into unaccountable strongmen. Their grab for power provoked an Ottoman expedition

(1786) to bring the province back into line. Under the leadership of Kapudan Hasan Paşa, it landed at Alexandria and quickly made its way to Cairo. The grand admiral chased the leading mamluks to Upper Egypt, where they adopted a strategy of waiting out the Ottoman forces. In the meantime, Hasan Paşa turned his attention to implementing various administrative reforms, which also carried an ideological component. He introduced new laws aimed specifically at Christians. They were not to ride horses, hire Muslim servants, or buy and own slaves and concubines. He followed up with a second decree insisting that Christians would continue to enjoy their customary guarantees to property and security. He had become aware of popular "agitation" against them and hastened to calm the populace. This precaution did not prevent him from repeating his earlier demand that all Christians and Jews sell their slaves and concubines. He threatened them with house-to-house searches if they did not comply. Christians and Jews, we learn, either sold their slaves or entrusted their favorites, with whom they would not part, to Muslim friends.[154] The admiral's concern with upholding an imaginary social order extended to the clothing of Cairenes, who were warned not to wear rings or dress in cashmere shawls.[155] Women were later forbidden from wearing cloaks made of taffeta or "Frankish material," as well as a new kind of turban that was made of colored sashes twisted into the shape of a "cake" and bent slightly over the forehead.[156] Like other such legislation, these decrees were soon forgotten.

The heightened concern with the dress of non-Muslims became something of an ideological reflex as the military predicament of the empire worsened after a second defeat to Russia (1787–92). The French invasion of Egypt in 1798, totally unexpected, further underscored Ottoman vulnerability. Napoleon's army easily defeated mamluk forces outside Cairo and cast the remnant to Upper Egypt, where the surviving emirs waged a guerrilla campaign for the next three years. The French brazenly, though ineffectually, presented themselves as "Muslims" who had made war on the papacy itself and were now delivering Egypt from the "oppression" of the mamluks.[157] Once installed in Cairo, French rhetoric about "liberty" induced them, in the early days of their occupation, to pass a decree requiring all townspeople to wear a tricolored rosette, symbol of the French Revolution, as a badge of their submission.[158] In the Ottoman political context, the act held no meaning. So the French quickly switched back to "Muslim" tactics. They actually paid the head of the Bakriyya Sufi order to hold celebrations for the birthday of the prophet Muhammad, as if normal times had returned.¹⁵⁹ Before leaving for an unsuccessful campaign in Syria (1799)—where, at Acre, Napoleon would suffer his first major defeat as general—he sought to shore up the fiction that the French were promoting a Muslim social order. He called on local Christians to revert to the old dress code. They were to wear black or blue turbans and forswear cashmere shawls. As a further warning, he instructed them not to eat or smoke in the streets during Ramadan.¹⁶⁰ These ideological tactics were one of the great ironies of Napoleon's time in Egypt. The scion of the French revolution now assumed the same pose as the Ottoman officials whom he was fighting.

Despite all these punctilious decrees, meant to mollify Muslim opinion, the French were never viewed as anything but invaders and usurpers. Their government had no hope of earning legitimacy and had to put down two separate revolts in Cairo: the first in October 1798, the second in March 1800.¹⁶¹ Only within the various Christian communities did they find any recruits to their cause. French merchants had long sought out Christians as intermediaries and protégés; now the military authorities were doing the same. Small numbers of local Christians, mostly Copts, entered the French army, though most kept their distance. By 1801, the last year of the occupation, these regiments had their own French-style uniforms, shaved their beards like the French, and wore a distinctive fur hat of black sheepskin.¹⁶² This cooperation, however uneven, badly strained Muslim-Christian relations. During the two revolts in Cairo, Christian homes became a target for insurgents. And even in peacetime, violent quarrels periodically erupted in the markets.¹⁶³ Muslims accused Christians of acting insolently. They bitterly resented Christians who openly adopted privileges such as riding horses and carrying weapons which, under the letter of Islamic law, belonged exclusively to Muslims.¹⁶⁴ That wealthy Christians had long evaded these restrictions no longer seemed to matter. The French presence cast everything in a new light.

When the French finally withdrew during the summer of 1801, Ottoman troops reentered Cairo and immediately set about restoring symbolic order. They invoked the Islamic sartorial code. Christians were again relegated to black or blue turbans and forbidden to wear multicolored garments. Some Ottoman soldiers took revenge on passing Christians and harassed them, with no regard to who they were or what they might have done. They stripped them of forbidden articles, and sometimes took turbans and shoes as plunder, forcing Ottoman commanders to issue proclamations that warned their troops against theft and harassment.[165]

The damage from the French occupation was lasting. One of its main legacies was to harden the dawning perception—first within officialdom and then more slowly among the populace—that Christians were somehow complicit in the military designs of European states. At the same time, the provincial administration continued to protest that it was a Muslim political order—precisely because it now seemed more fragile and unstable, and therefore in greater need of assertions of legitimacy. Symbolic hierarchies now mattered more than ever. Even after Mehmed Ali had consolidated his grip as the new governor of Egypt (1805), he felt it necessary (1818) to insist on the usual dress regulations. The complaints were the same. Christians ought to confine themselves to blue and black turbans. They should not ride horses, parade through the streets with retinues, or cavort in the countryside with guns as they went out for target practice and amusement.[166]

The sectarian antagonism provoked by the French occupation soon found scapegoats. As Christian bureaucrats and merchants prospered under Mehmed Ali (r. 1805-48), who deliberately promoted them, much of the older elite lost their former sources of wealth through state confiscation of tax-farms and religious foundations. They now turned a baleful eye on their social competitors, who had passed over them, it seemed, in flagrant violation of the proper hierarchies. They noticed the fine houses of leading Christians, which were in some cases bought or taken from the hands of the very notables whose fortunes had begun to decline. They fumed at the Christian notables' sumptuous clothing, long trains of servants, and proud passage through the streets on horseback.[167] Heightening the identification of Christians with external enemies was the presence of Europeans, who worked in the Egyptian army and administration and likewise conducted themselves like grandees.[168] These tensions occasionally burst into the open. In Cairo (1820), a jurist declared that it was forbidden for Muslims to eat meat slaughtered by Christians and Jews. The opinion stirred up outrage among his fellow scholars, who objected, quite accurately, that Islamic law had never held such a view. They challenged him to a formal debate; he responded with insults. The controversy soon died away, mostly because the scholar spoke only for himself and the small community of North Africans in Cairo who had begun to favor more militant interpretations of Islamic law.[169] That unpleasant disputes about Christians and Jews could ruffle the normally placid round of lectures and lessons indicates how external political pressures could create new and unwelcome social strains.

The French occupation of Egypt coincided with pressures that were beginning to sweep across Ottoman Syria. The French campaign against Acre in 1799 fed more of the same ideological posturing, here as in neighboring regions. The arrival of Ottoman reinforcements led to the revision of the color codes for the Christians and Jews of Aleppo and Damascus. Once these forces left, the old scheme returned, eased back into place with payments arranged by communal leaders.[170] In Damascus, the surveillance of Christian attire intensified under the puritanical governorship of Genç Yusuf Paşa (r. 1807–10), whose curious views about fashion, such as forbidding barbers from shaving beards, we have already encountered. His draconian notions of morality and deportment almost certainly had their origins in the impotence of his administration, which was unable to conduct the annual pilgrimage to the Holy Cities after Wahhabi forces had seized Medina (1803) and Mecca (1806). The Wahhabis denied the legitimacy of the Ottoman state and proclaimed their own purified Islamic creed. Genç Yusuf could do nothing. As Wahhabi troops harassed outlying districts, he was unable to mount anything like an effective campaign that might restore Ottoman authority. So he turned to what he could control and began to police morality in the streets of Damascus. Mirroring the rhetoric of his Wahhabi adversaries, he committed himself to making Damascus more properly Muslim. One of his leading initiatives was to introduce a stricter dress code for Christians and Jews. Christians now had to dress in black; more emphatically, their women were ordered to cover themselves down to the feet with this color. Green was absolutely forbidden to them. He also ordered Christians and Jews not to raise their voices in the streets. He relented with his initiatives only when local Muslim scholars (`ulama') protested that he had gone much too far and that there was no precedent for his actions.[171]

Christians did not have a long reprieve. The outbreak of the Greek war of independence set off official panic throughout the eastern Mediterranean. In Syrian towns, it led again to a more stringent application of the color scheme for Christians.[172] In Istanbul, above all, sartorial legislation reached a staggering crescendo as wild rumors about Greek spies and saboteurs filled the streets (1822). Officials railed against the same infractions that they had been protesting for decades: subjects dressing beyond their social station; popular devotion to Indian fabrics; outrageous collars and long sleeves on women's overcoats; and excessively ornamental designs on clothing.[173] The equation of sartorial order with political stability had become unmistakable. By the 1820s, both seemed to be crumbling. More ominously, the obsession with religious hierarchies foreshadowed the deep sectarian tensions that would rack Ottoman society across the nineteenth and early twentieth centuries. This later turmoil originated neither with state-led modernization nor the disruptive integration of Ottoman markets into the European-dominated world economy. Rather, its roots lay in the final decades of the Old Regime, as anxieties about order and status were already beginning to undermine older notions of community and identity and place the loyalties of Christians, in particular, under growing suspicion.[174]

Conclusion: Beyond Islamic Illusions

We can make two observations about all these clothing regulations. The first is that officials confined their attention almost entirely to the towns. The early modern state had few personnel at its disposal and could never hope to monitor the vast rural world in which most Ottoman subjects lived. More than a logistical question of ways and means, this urban bias also had to do with the ideological nature of sartorial regulations. Towns were the main spaces in which the state transmitted the rhetoric affirming its justice and legitimacy. Decrees about clothing helped to reinforce symbolic hierarchies that all subjects would, in theory, acknowledge and respect. Across the eighteenth century, the state felt compelled to assert these hierarchies because of a rise in luxury expenditure, which was most conspicuous in the large towns, and because of repeated military setbacks, aggravated by inflation and monetary instability, all of which seemed to cast doubt on its fitness to rule. Towns inevitably served as the main centers for purveying ideological messages.

The fundamentally ideological nature of sartorial regulations leads to a second observation about the ultimate ability of the Ottoman state—or for that matter, any early modern state—to shape sartorial habits and preferences. Despite the rising frequency of decrees, the state's efforts had almost no effect whatsoever on what Ottoman subjects wore. Habits and tastes hardly budged at all.[175] Broad continuities in fashion corresponded, in turn, to notions of decency and self-presentation that endured without challenge or dissent under the Old Regime.[176] Each region of the empire preserved its inherited sensibilities related to modesty and the display of the body.

In any case, the state's decrees worked at repairing a sartorial order that was far more prescriptive than real. Members of subordinate social groups were always testing the boundaries of the permissible; they were always trying, however stealthily, to "dress up" and appropriate styles and colors formally reserved for the powerful and prestigious. Christians and Jews did not necessarily—or at least, consistently—observe the color scheme laid down for them. Affluent women, in particular, were willing to probe the limits of modesty and fashion by altering the shape or cut of outer garments and decorations.[177] In practice, sartorial distinctions were always blurrier than the pronouncements of officials or jurists might make them seem.

Beneath this ideological posturing, regional fashions hardly took notice and continued to set the real standard for everyday attire. This was especially obvious in the countryside, where nearly everyone dressed in the same local styles. On Mt. Lebanon, the French traveler Volney was struck (1785) by this rude egalitarianism in lifestyle. The ruling shaykhs, he observed, "are only distinguished from the people by a bad pelisse, a horse, and a few slight advantages in food and lodging."[178] This simplicity generally seems to have been most extreme in mountainous regions, where life was perhaps hardest. To one Ottoman traveler, it seemed that the clothing and headgear in Erzincan (in eastern Anatolia) were "like Albania" insofar as male and female dress were virtually identical (*yek-resm*) and even interchangeable.[179] This judgment expressed more than urban condescension. It testified to the constraints of poverty, which always put cultural ideals out of reach. Nor did one have to visit the mountains or any other part of the countryside to view deprivation. As the British traveler Aaron Hill noticed (1709) on the streets of Istanbul, "The meaner sort of people go bare-legged, with girdles twisted around their middles and a dirty towel wrapt about their heads or sometimes a small scarlot skull-cap."[180] The capital was no special case, and should remind us how the poor of both town and countryside were subject to continual compromises and sacrifices in lifestyle. For the majority of the population, the norms prescribed by law and custom were often as unobtainable as the fine garments that they might dream of owning without ever having any prospect of actually putting them on.

TWO
PLEASURE WINS AGAIN

Fashion, as we learned, never submitted to religion. It could never be reduced to anything as simple as an "Islamic" set of symbols and tastes. The manners surrounding the clothing and ornamentation of the body were far more likely to follow variations that expressed regional identity and social status. But what about the social life of manners? Might the mores that governed sociability reveal a different side of Ottoman culture which was more faithful to the dictates of Islamic law and piety? For one of the most revealing tests of "Islamic" sociability, let us turn to Ottoman leisure culture. In the midst of their pastimes and recreations, people entered relatively unstructured social settings in which they could act more "naturally"; or at any rate, the quest for fun and diversion required, across most of the social spectrum, less artifice and acculturation than most other social situations. It is precisely at these moments that Ottoman society betrayed its true desires and predilections.

The temptations were perfectly apparent to the scholar Sünbülzade Vehbi (d. 1809), whom we briefly met earlier as the author of an etiquette manual addressed to his son. The manual became well known and was full of learned recommendations that received the endorsement of his peers. Doting yet firm, and no doubt thinking of popular habits, Vehbi went out of his way to warn, in one particularly irate passage, against coffeehouses:

> Don't stink in the corners of a coffeehouse
> Don't stick your head in those sorts of shabby places.[1]

His verses invoked an old suspicion, continually reaffirmed by Muslim jurists since medieval times, about worldly distractions that would divert worshippers from the essential task of living uprightly and preparing for the afterlife. They adopted a stern tone about "fun and games" (*lahw wa lu'b*) and viewed anything that drew the faithful toward idle pursuits as a spiritual peril. As late as the eighteenth century, they were still repeating the same refrain.[2] The pleasures of this world were not to be denied or despised. But people should partake of them only in a measured and lawful manner. Time was finite; no one should casually fritter it away.

But if we are honest about Ottoman social routines and look at the living culture, as opposed to religious ideals, all these exhortations hardly mattered. Few people listened, as the grave counsel of scholars and preachers never traveled very far beyond the pages of their books or earshot of their sermons. On the contrary, an expansive leisure culture had already come into being by the sixteenth and seventeenth centuries with the advent of coffee-drinking, smoking, and most potent of all (as Sünbülzade Vehbi conceded), the flagrant escapism of coffeehouse culture. A moralizing opposition, which became known as the Kadızadeli movement, peaked in the mid-seventeenth century. It sought to check, or if possible suppress, these fun-loving innovations by outlawing smoking and closing coffeehouses. But the efforts of these hardliners had come to naught by the eighteenth century, which brought the equivalent of a breakthrough in both state policies and social attitudes. Puritanical impulses, never broadly representative or popular, would thereafter retreat to the margins of Ottoman society as everyday forms of hedonism fully and irrevocably triumphed, most enthusiastically in the towns.

Let us acknowledge, too, that leisure culture could not secure this victory unaided. It had a powerful ally. For entirely self-serving reasons, the state came to its side and learned to nurture and encourage it—the better to tax it and fill coffers that constantly needed to be replenished. War-making put pleasure in its service. It thereby helped to remold sociability, without any official intention of doing so.

In following this progress of leisure culture, we will first take stock of coffee and tobacco, which became ubiquitous in the Ottoman lands and infiltrated so many social routines that people could hardly imagine life without them. The true measure of this invigorated leisure culture, which could no longer be penned into private spaces, was the multifaceted hedonism of the Ottoman coffeehouse, home of public fun and entertainment. We must not assume, however, that pleasure submissively bent the knee to state and religion and advanced only as far as it was allowed. Though technically illegal under Islamic law and condemned as immoral, alcohol and opium sustained subcultures of intoxication that remained indifferent to the voice of authority, whether in official or moral guises.

The advance of leisure culture did not thereby defeat some preexisting "Islamic culture" that was fundamentally rooted in religion. To take the impressions of Haşim Efendi, a late eighteenth-century visitor to Erzurum, a small town in eastern Anatolia and early haunt of the Kadızadeli preacher Vani Mehmed Efendi (d. 1685): "Its people's natures are inclined toward amusement and delight. Day and night, they pass the time with games of song, music, and dancers."[3] Kadızadeli activism—by that time only a distant memory, if that—never had a chance. The allure of fun and diversion easily won over societies that were eager for new outlets to sociability and in which official barriers were rapidly falling. By the eighteenth century, these opportunities were arising with greater frequency, not only in the Ottoman Empire but across the world, and were helping to bring forth a distinctively modern outlook that reveled in pleasure and recreation for their own sake.

Everyday Pleasures: Coffee and Tobacco

No two commodities were more responsible for remaking early modern Ottoman social life than coffee and tobacco. Both touched off lively legal controversies as they quickly—one is tempted to say, inexorably—established themselves as popular pastimes.

First introduced from Yemen and Ethiopia at the turn of the sixteenth century, coffee enjoyed a rapid ascent onto Ottoman palates. Celebrated by Sufi mystics as a boon to all-night spiritual vigils, it earned the enmity of the most stringent religious scholars, who objected that it was a mind-altering drug not essentially different from wine in its intoxicating properties.[4] And if the Qur'an itself had banned wine, who could defend wine-like substances? Popular opinion paid no heed. By the late sixteenth century, these early quarrels over Islamic law had long faded into irrelevance as coffee-drinking entrenched itself in Ottoman culture.

The last reverberations of these debates had not quite subsided when tobacco made its first intrusion into Ottoman markets at the beginning of the seventeenth century. An American plant, resilient and adaptable to many different climates and soils, it soon made itself at home with an astonishing rapidity, as it would across large parts of the world over the next several decades. Much like coffee, tobacco wasted no time in winning adherents. In the same measure, it ignited acrid legal debates in which critics mounted the same attack against another mind-altering innovation that seemed to them every bit as intoxicating as wine. Equally shocking was the act of smoking itself, which represented a veritable revolution in bodily habits. Ancient and medieval populations in the Balkans and Middle East had never previously taken any substance in this manner. So it seemed utterly outrageous that smokers would "drink" tobacco smoke, whose offensive odor, contended hostile jurists, was yet another reason for outlawing the new pastime. Like coffee, tobacco was able to shrug off these objections.[5] Smoking spread everywhere throughout the empire—probably faster and farther than even coffee on account of its cheap cost and expanding domestic supply. But in the capital and central provinces, the resistance to tobacco was initially more sustained and better organized. By 1635, the palace had formally banned public smoking, siding with the puritanical Kadızadeli movement (named after the famous preacher Mehmed Kadızade), which demanded the application of strict moral and legal reforms.[6] Prohibition nonetheless proved a total failure. Despite official opposition, concentrated mostly in and around Istanbul, tobacco would continue its triumphal progress throughout Ottoman society. By the reign of Süleyman II (r. 1687-91), official policy had fully changed course. Exhausted from protracted warfare on its western frontiers, and desperate for revenue, the Ottoman state promulgated its first set of tobacco taxes.[7] The fiction of moral policing had effectively ended. The fiscal demands of war-making, steadily climbing, became the most persuasive argument for toleration. Leisure culture thus owed secret debts to organized violence.

By the eighteenth century, then, both coffee and tobacco had become an ineradicable part of everyday sociability. The lasting consensus about their permissibility is one of the long-term achievements of the Old Regime. But acceptance was more than a legal or moral question, to be decided by officials, jurists, and moralists. It came about from the overwhelming popular enthusiasm for these new pastimes, from which there was no turning back.

The thirst for coffee was irrepressible. Urban society led the way in pushing up demand, and townspeople were happy to enjoy as many cups as they could afford. As Mouradgea d'Ohsson reported (thinking mainly of Istanbul), coffee-drinking took place throughout the day. The craze extended across the entire population—men, women, and even children.[8] For Aleppo, Alexander Russell estimated, "Few of the lower people drink less than three or four cups in the twenty-four hours; their superiors drink more: and persons who frequent the great, drink perhaps twenty cups daily."[9] Drinking habits were simple. The Ottoman custom was to take coffee black and strong, without sugar or milk. Porcelain cups were small, "generally not holding quite an ounce and a half of liquid."[10] By the eighteenth century, large numbers of urban households owned their own cups and coffee-pots, further confirming a vigorous level of demand (fig. 2.1). Even common soldiers carried coffee to the front. Amid the most arduous campaigning, they still expected a regular daily supply.[11]

Most coffee came up from Yemen by way of Egypt, which had long acted as the center of the Ottoman trade. Cargos were plentiful enough to make it available to most urban consumers. Draining away a disproportionate share of supplies were the biggest towns. At the front of the line was, of course, Istanbul, which generated about half of Ottoman demand and therefore effectively set the price of coffee for the entire Ottoman economy.[12] Fortunately for coffee drinkers around the empire, prices were falling by the middle decades of the eighteenth century as the first imports of Atlantic colonial coffee began to seep into Ottoman markets and gradually overtake the older Yemeni trade.[13] The resulting economic and pyscho-social stimulus, however, remained an essentially urban blessing. Throughout most of the countryside, coffee remained unaffordable, insofar as few could enjoy it as an everyday drink. Rural notables would have their own stocks, whereas most peasants would taste it only on ceremonial occasions or perhaps as a token of hospitality. As the Old Regime was drawing to a close in the early nineteenth century, consumption had still not risen very much. Making sure to pack ample supplies, the traveler John Lewis Burckhardt used this rural scarcity as a kind of social passport, making coffee wherever he traveled throughout southern Syria. He could always repay the hospitality that he unfailingly received by boiling a few cups of coffee.[14] European merchants and travelers quickly learned that making a present of coffee, as well as other goods like sugar, was an excellent way of ingratiating themselves with officials or entire villages.[15]

FIGURE 2.1. "A Turkish girl taking coffee on a divan" (c. 1707). Painting by Jean-Baptiste Vanmour. A servant brings the coffee in a small cup. Her lady will sip it black, without adding sugar or milk. At eighteenth-century rates of consumption, a person of her status probably enjoyed coffee throughout the day.

SOURCE: Houghton Library, Harvard University.

Any stigma about coffee-drinking had vanished by the eighteenth century. The religious establishment had long made its peace with it.[16] Only a few scattered hardliners, regarded as eccentrics, could muster any outrage. In Cairo, `Ali al-Hanafi (d. 1733/74) waged a lonely campaign for this long lost cause. He railed against coffee-drinking, and once took a present of coffee beans that someone had made to him and threw it into the latrine.[17] His biographer does not record any converts to his decaffeinated morality. No doubt Egypt's central role in the Ottoman coffee trade, which made many a fortune, did little to help such rearguard harassment.

Despite having overcome the enmity of the state, tobacco found it harder to shake off connotations of immorality and licentiousness.[18] Although its foes were likewise few in number and had no hope of suppressing it by the eighteenth century, they carried on a stubborn opposition from the margins of the religious establishment. Impotent in their fury, they were all the more prone to histrionics to make their point. `Ali al-Sa`idi (d. 1775), another Cairene scholar, forbade all companions, even powerful officials, to smoke in his presence. If he entered an official's house and found people smoking, he would berate them and break their pipes. He was utterly fearless, and on one occasion, did not hesitate to snatch a pipe from the hand of a military officer. So notorious did his meddling become that smokers, on seeing him approach, would signal to each other and put out their pipes.[19] Onlookers indulged his antics. Protecting him from harm was his reputation as a first-rate scholar and model of upright conduct, which granted him a certain leeway in thundering about morality.

By the eighteenth century, there were so many smokers that the religious establishment had learned to tolerate and even abet the habit. Scholars argued that smokers should not have to endure the agonies of withdrawal. Showing compassion was far better. A renowned Sufi in Istanbul, Muhammad Nasuhi (d. 1718) did not smoke, but unlike the previous head of his order, he would not hinder those who did and actually went out of his way to welcome them to his Halveti-Şabani lodge in Istanbul.[20] In Damascus, the great scholar and Sufi `Abd al-Ghani al-Nabulsi (d. 1731) also counseled forbearance; late in life, he made use of his own arguments and became an avid smoker himself.[21] Perhaps the most disconcerting turncoat was Kadı Süleyman Efendi (d. 1714), a former judge who later in life experienced something like a breakdown and turned into an enraptured folk saint. He would sometimes wander naked through the streets of Istanbul, shouting, "Scatter infidels! Hypocrites!" Even in his most extreme state of undress, he would still have a tobacco pipe in hand.[22] One might smile and assume that such folk saints, bereft of any conventional sense of propriety, were not the best measure of social attitudes. But many scholars and Sufis took up smoking without the slightest compunction. While enjoying a pipe at his lodge, another Sufi, Neş'et Efendi (d. 1807), had to parry an impertinent question from a disciple who asked how he would light his pipe in heaven. "From the oven that cooks your kebab," came the instant retort. The implication was that smoking was a minor vice of this world, and that no one would smoke—or, for that matter, eat kebab—in the afterlife.[23] Confronted with objections to his own smoking, Kuşadalı İbrahim Efendi (d. 1846) retorted that those who did not smoke should not start, and that those who had started need not give it up. His reasoning was that smokers should not have to undergo the agony of a withdrawal that nonsmokers themselves would find unbearable.[24]

Memories of the original seventeenth-century campaigns against tobacco did not fade away entirely. Whenever the state wished to make a show of restoring moral order, it might revive the old rhetoric and try to ban public smoking. The common fate of all such efforts, turning up here and there at odd intervals, was to sputter out immediately. In 1758, and still later in 1812, imperial authorities got nowhere when they tried to outlaw smoking in the streets of Istanbul. From the moment of their reading, both edicts were stillborn.[25] In 1744, the governor of Egypt took up the same lost cause, mounting patrols in the markets of Cairo and making offenders eat their own pipes.[26] But this furor, too, quickly passed. In Damascus, smokers heedlessly puffed their way through at least four separate campaigns: in 1699, 1711, 1713, and then again through one final bout of harassment in 1749.[27] Nor was this smoldering hostility to tobacco, however fitful and doomed, a strictly "Muslim" obsession. As late as 1774, the Maronite Church tried its own hand at stamping out smoking among congregations on Mt. Lebanon. The crackdown was notable only for its complete failure.[28]

In short, smoking was rampant in eighteenth-century society. "If fifteen men were in a room, only two or three would not smoke." So ubiquitous was tobacco in social gatherings that pipes had become ostentatious fashion accessories that smokers would adorn according to their means. A fad for gilding pipes or encrusting them with jewels provoked (1781) the indignation of the palace, which subsequently forbade these embellishments.[29] Mouradgea d'Ohsson, reflecting on the diligence of contemporary smokers (1788), recalled how no townsman would think of leaving home without his pipe and pouch of tobacco. He gives an idea of their industry: "Should only two men smoke in a room, especially in winter, one will find an atmosphere that resembles a dense fog. Cloaks, furs, clothes, furniture: in a word, everything in the houses is impregnated with the odor of tobacco."[30] In Aleppo, Alexander Russell marveled that "the men begin to smoke as soon as they awake in the morning, and, the time of meals excepted, hardly cease the whole day." He noticed that children partook as well; the latter would "acquire early a taste for tobacco, by being occasionally employed to light the pipe of their parents."[31] Accompanying the male smokers were many women, who partook with a gusto that tormented moralists to no end.[32] Pipes might come out at nearly any time. One British visitor to Istanbul was mildly shocked by the smokers who calmly puffed away during funerals.[33] An anonymous Istanbulite railed (c. 1740) against smokers who broke the Ramadan fast by lighting up their pipes.[34] Many were in the grip of an addiction that they were powerless to overcome. As one governor of Egypt meekly confessed, "If I were able to quit, I would do so."[35]

Soldiers were perhaps the most enthusiastic smokers. At any rate, they were closely identified with the pastime and did not object to the association. Smoking had become almost inseparable from their self-image. During factional street battles in Cairo (1711), one soldier had to scold a comrade for casually smoking around a cannon that was being loaded.[36] This unthinking addiction was by no means confined to the rank and file. We get a quick sketch (1807) of Janissary officers aboard an Ottoman warship anchored in the Bosphorus as an English flotilla approached Istanbul at the onset of the brief Anglo-Ottoman War. They insisted on freely roving about the deck with pipes and hookahs until the frantic captain, seeing the futility of his warnings, broke down and swore, "We are all one ship. If we burn—the matter is God's—we burn together!"[37] Heedless habits did not always end well. Soldiers puffing on their pipes occasionally set off stocks of ammunition with a chance cinder.[38] These cautionary tales did nothing to suppress demand. Smoking became a virtual entitlement for the sultan's soldiers. One of the winter hardships endured on the Balkan frontier at Şumnu (1809) was a shortage of salt; equally disquieting were the dwindling supplies of tobacco.[39] The state, after all, could not ask soldiers to go without smoking.

Whether for soldiers or other smokers, two advantages recommended tobacco. The first was its convenience. It conferred instant access to pleasure, almost at any time. One could smoke anywhere: at home, on the road, at work, with or without company. The second advantage was low cost. Tobacco was easy to grow and transport. By the eighteenth century, Ottoman production in Macedonia, Anatolia, and Syria easily met domestic demand and had long displaced more expensive imports, mainly of North American origin. The only other requirement was a cheap clay or wooden pipe, which among the poor, might be nothing more than a bowl (fig. 2.2).[40] With such negligible "start-up" costs, anyone could become a smoker.

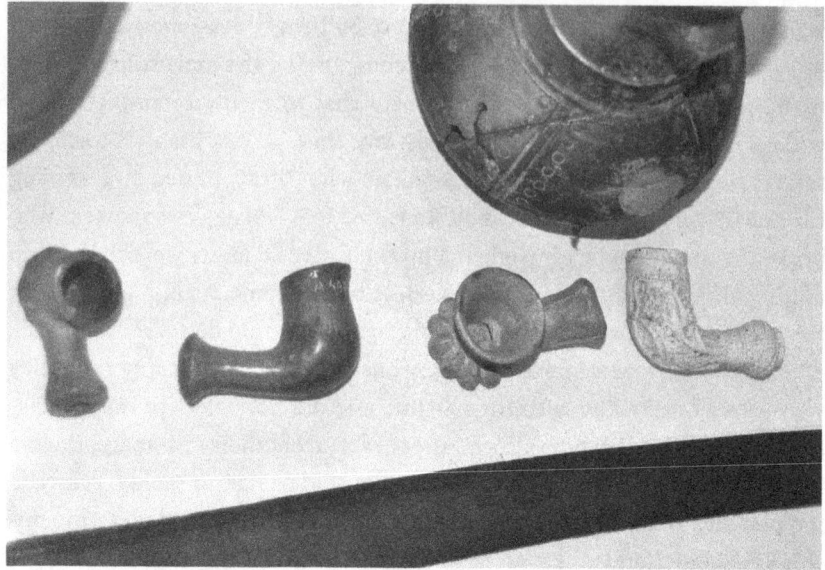

FIGURE 2.2. Ottoman tobacco pipes from the fortress of Smederevo in Serbia. These are simple models made from clay that most smokers would have used. The owners of these pipes were almost certainly soldiers stationed there.　　SOURCE: Smederevo Fortress Museum, CC BY-SA 4.0.

Beyond the utilitarian majority, smoking lent itself to the same distinctions in taste that defined other pastimes. Stylish smokers would prefer a hookah, which cooled the smoke with water, usually in a glass bottle. Expensive and cumbersome to carry, this device was largely restricted to the homes of the well-to-do or to coffeehouses. Making its own fashionable statement was the long-stemmed pipe, whose tube had the same function of cooling the smoke.[41] It was in Ottoman officialdom that these longer pieces gained the biggest following (fig. 2.3); and as an extra feature, they could double as compartments for secret messages.[42] From this basic design, fancy variations came into vogue. Lady Craven admired one setup during her stay in Istanbul (1786): "Among the higher order of Turks, there is an invention which saves them the trouble of holding the pipe: two small wheels are fixed on each side the bowl of the pipe, and thus the smoaker [sic] has only to puff away or let the pipe rest upon underlip, while he moves his head as he pleases."[43] Minimizing contact with the pipe would have appealed to upper-class smokers, who tried to keep themselves as neat as pos-

FIGURE 2.3. Ottoman official holding a long-stemmed pipe. These stylish pipes came in different lengths and designs and were prized for cooling the smoke. Most owners were affluent; all wished to make a visual statement about their status.
SOURCE: William Alexander and Octavian Dalvimart, *Picturesque Representations of the Dress and Manners of the Turks* (London: T. M'Lean, 1816).

sible, and never spit (unlike most European smokers who burned the harsh North American varieties of tobacco).[44] Snuff did not begin to carve out its own niche in the Ottoman market until the mid-eighteenth century.[45]

Were there no limits to smoking? We cannot translate the obvious enthusiasm for tobacco into an absolute license to light up anywhere at any time. The only effective restrictions were imposed not by the state, but society itself. Smokers had to bow to pervasive social hierarchies that demanded gestures of recognition and deference. Age and status required those of lower rank to put out pipes or refrain from smoking unless they had received permission from fathers, elders, or superiors.[46] It was indifference to these sensitivities that pushed the governor of Egypt into outlawing public smoking in 1744. He complained that the people of Cairo were "impolite." They showed "no respect" to military officers and kept blithely "smoking their hookahs and pipes in front of them." He would have none of their impertinence and decreed that no one should smoke "while sitting on stone benches and at the doors in front of shops, coffeehouses, or in the streets"—in short, anywhere in public where social hierarchies might be singed and offended.[47] Even if the idea of a total ban receded into absurdity, public smoking continued to irritate the most unyielding champions of propriety and formality. In Cairo (1787), one decree sought to bar mamluks from venturing out, unaccompanied, from the houses of their commanders. In the old days, they would never have dreamed of taking such liberties and would have always joined their patron in procession. The most glaring symbol of this ceremonial disorder was the ease with which they lit their pipes and openly smoked as they rode in public.[48] Not all taboos fell so easily. At the court of the bey in Tunis, Muhammad Bey (r. 1756-59) refused to smoke his hookah in front of scholars whom he invited to social gatherings in the palace gardens. This self-denial, he explained, was a tribute to religion and learning. He kept up this personal prohibition even after local scholars insisted that he could relax and enjoy his tobacco and that there was nothing in Islamic law which required him to refrain. It thereafter became a court custom that his nineteenth-century successors would continue to uphold whenever scholars were present.[49]

Coffeehouse Culture

By the eighteenth century, coffee and tobacco had emphatically secured their place in Ottoman society, becoming fixtures in everyday life. They wound their way into private social settings, making themselves at home throughout the day, lending their services to official interviews and meetings, and helping friends simply pass the time. In public spaces, too, the tandem could be seen nearly everywhere. People sipped coffee and smoked tobacco in the orchards, fields, and cemeteries on the outskirts of towns as they picnicked or held bucolic excursions. Nor did they see any reason not to enjoy these pleasures in plain sight. As we have already observed, tobacco was especially convenient. Smokers could savor it whether they were walking at leisure or sitting in a shop. But coffee was not to be entirely outdone. Ottoman markets were full of itinerant vendors who constantly made their rounds and were happy to supply anyone who wanted a quick cup. In Istanbul, they were so numerous that one decree (1759) forbade the sale of coffee in front of shops.[50] In pouring for customers, went the complaint, they attracted swarms of the unemployed and shiftless and thereby created a public nuisance.

For those who sought more than convenience, there was the coffeehouse, the single greatest social innovation of Ottoman times. Nowhere else did coffee and tobacco find such a congenial welcome; and nowhere else did leisure culture so openly and wantonly thrive. Like coffee itself, the coffeehouse had experienced a difficult entry into Ottoman culture. First appearing in the sixteenth century in one town after another, as if spontaneously generated by the introduction of coffee-drinking, it had quickly acquired a dubious reputation as a haven for the immoral, dissolute, or merely idle. Nor could disapproving commentators overlook the tendency of patrons to mingle in close proximity without regard to social rank or to freely wag their tongues about affairs of state. Hence moral activism found a new target for its ire.[51] Throwing in his lot with the Kadızadeli movement, Murad IV (r. 1623-40) closed the coffeehouses of Istanbul (1635) amid his campaign to crack down on smoking. In the capital and nearby towns—though not elsewhere in the empire—this ban on coffeehouses would remain nominally in effect for several decades, lifted only by the same fiscal exigencies that would liberate tobacco during the War of the Holy League (1683-99).

Ottoman authorities would afterward renounce such extreme policies. During the eighteenth century, they preferred to exercise a worldly toleration, imposed by the knowledge that coffeehouses had become too ingrained in urban culture to be shut down and driven out. To one Ottoman traveler alighting in Ankara, it seemed that "nearly a third [of the townspeople] talked and gossiped in the coffeehouses."[52] Sheer numbers had made them impossible to suppress. And so at the turn of the nineteenth century, roughly one out of every seven or eight shops in Istanbul was a coffeehouse.[53] In Cairo, a city of about a quarter-million inhabitants, there were approximately twelve hundred of them in operation in the same period.[54] Only on rare occasions might moral clucking rouse some official to take disciplinary action. In Damascus, the governor ordered sweeps of the coffeehouses (1699) because so many people seemed to prefer sitting in them to attending Friday prayers. Damascenes were so resistant to this initiative that he had to oversee several raids and make ever sterner threats.[55] But the campaign soon passed, and patrons returned to their accustomed ways. In general, it would take moments of extreme ideological vulnerability, like the decades of the Great Crisis, before officials would again contemplate such moralizing poses. We can take these crackdowns as signals of a wounded sense of legitimacy following some setback or challenge to the established order. Putative remedies therefore acquired a moral and religious tone, as the authorities publicly committed themselves to setting things right. Acting on precisely such motives, the grand vizier ordered the closure, in 1808, of a coffeehouse outside Sultan Mehmed Mosque in Istanbul. He had passed by it one Friday afternoon and noticed that it was completely full; no one had gone to communal prayers. In a fury, he dispatched troops and shut down the establishment for an entire month.[56] Not long afterward (1809) the authorities issued a proclamation threatening to jail anyone who sat in coffeehouses during nighttime prayers (*teravih*) in Ramadan. In one raid, more than three hundred patrons were taken away.[57] Unfolding against the background of political instability in the capital that followed the overthrow of Selim III, as well as a war on the northern frontier which was not going well, this religious policy served as a kind of ideological balm. But it was nothing more than a temporary feint. In the limited nature of the closings, the state recognized that the coffeehouse, as an urban institution, had become untouchable. There were too many patrons, and they were happy to visit at nearly all hours.

Indeed, the coffeehouse would extend its cultural conquests into the night. Especially in the biggest towns, some establishments were keeping longer hours, well past dark, by the eighteenth century. The urban clientele was now so sizable, and so accustomed to having regular access, above all for entertainment, that this demand began to break down taboos about nightlife.[58] As a matter of habit, most townspeople did not stay up late, and retired to sleep not long after sunset.[59] Coffeehouses now began to challenge these rhythms with nocturnal amusements as well as the usual refreshments. To the guardians of morality, this hedonistic advance into the night was a shocking affront to public decency. In 1764, the governor of Aleppo received reports that some of the local coffeehouses had been keeping nighttime hours for the previous six years. Under cover of darkness, complained petitioners, "rabble and prostitutes" were now gathering with impunity. They drank wine and committed the most reprehensible acts. Conducting an inspection from nearby rooftops, the governor had himself observed these nocturnal scenes in which men and women mingled openly. The presence of women was particularly provocative. Coffeehouses functioned as overwhelmingly male spaces that were barred to women—or at least to those women who cared about appearing "respectable." To the praise of moralists, the governor went into action at once: without banning coffeehouses altogether, he nonetheless ordered them to close at sunset.[60] But such initiatives could secure only a temporary victory. Coffeehouses were answering to social pressures—and opportunities—that the authorities could not suppress. By the eighteenth century, the invasion of the night was gaining momentum—most conspicuously in Istanbul, where nightlife was most active and had the most outlets at its beck and call.[61]

Despite their popularity, coffeehouses could not entirely escape the unsavory images that moralists had long attached to them. Respectable opinion continued to cast a wary eye. The prim and pious imagined scenes that ranged from outright depravity to mere sloth and vagrancy.[62] They still conceived of many coffeehouses as portals to a nefarious underworld, a slough of vice and corruption that subverted religion and morality. The truly God-fearing would shun them. In Aleppo, Armenian monks founded a new religious order in 1752 and committed themselves to a chaste regimen of prayer and self-denial. One of the restrictions that they placed on themselves was to avoid all contact with coffeehouses.[63]

The moralists did protest too much. So irresistible was the lure of coffeehouses that even a few members of the religious establishment were known to patronize them. These visits, however, carried a damaging social opprobrium. In Aleppo, the chief judge lost his office (1764) after it was discovered that he had dressed as a Janissary and frequented local coffeehouses.[64] Perhaps the embarrassing disguise, more than the unseemly venue, had made the scandal intolerable. Somehow eluding this fate was Ahmad al-Hamaqi (d. 1774), a respected scholar who taught at al-Azhar Mosque in Cairo. Colleagues praised his mild and upright character. Yet he horrified them with his habit of casually sitting in shops or, worse still, in coffeehouses. Prompting further dismay was his elevation to the position of mufti of Cairo, the highest office to which local jurists might be appointed. Al-Hamaqi was unfazed by their objections and kept making his customary rounds until his death.[65] In his indifference to colleagues' anxieties, and polite dismissal of concerns about their collective self-image, we can begin to measure the pull of the coffeehouse on townsmen across the social spectrum.

Beyond this perceived assault on the dignity of scholars, al-Hamaqi was guilty of a second gaffe that had much less to do with moral probity than it did with expectations about members of the social elite. As Alexander Russell observed for Aleppo, "The coffeehouses are not frequented by persons of the first rank, but by all others indiscriminately."[66] This had not always been the case. Visiting Aleppo in the middle of the seventeenth century, Evliya Çelebi fondly recounted his time at the "Arslan Dede Coffeehouse," which could accommodate up to "two thousand" patrons. Making a strong showing among its enlightened and sophisticated clientele, he tells us, were members of the religious establishment.[67] In Istanbul, too, the French traveler Jean Thévenot (1655) discovered that coffeehouses still fostered mingling across the social spectrum, exactly as the first generation of critics had charged. They were essentially open to anyone who could pay.[68] But by the eighteenth century, a new degree of social segregation seems to have set in. Members of the elite had learned to stay away and sip their coffee in private spaces, joined only by those who partook of their exclusive social circles.

The retreat of the urban elite from coffeehouse culture did not necessarily condemn all coffeehouses to a squalid decline. They continued to take their place along a hierarchy of size and prestige, which was most obvious in the largest towns. The most popular venues bore proud names. Along the waterfront of Galata in Istanbul (1792), visitors could call at such renowned retreats as Freckled Sergeant's Coffeehouse (Çil Çavuşun Kahvesi), Cretan Ahmed Ağa's Coffeehouse (Giritli Ahmed Ağa'nın Kahvesi), and Widow Lady's Coffeehouse (Dul Hatunun Kahvesi).[69] The grandest coffeehouses were spacious, ringed their interior with comfortable divans, and could hold more than a hundred customers at a time. Others, equally select and elegant, offered relaxation by rivers or streams, ideally on the outskirts of town amid gardens.[70] Below these trend-setters was a multitude of smaller shops. Interiors were spare and utterly functional: perhaps a few divans or benches covered with pillows (in the better places) or plain straw mats.[71] As Aaron Hill described the scene in Istanbul (1709), this humble set consisted of "only a sort of Stalls, like Tailors Shopboards, open to the Street, and capable of holding twelve or fourteen Men."[72] In Egypt (fig. 2.4), which was no different from other Ottoman provinces, the average coffee-

FIGURE 2.4. An Egyptian coffeehouse, depicted by the British painter David Roberts (1796–1864). Like most Ottoman coffeehouses, this one was little more than a small room or compartment that could seat only a small number of patrons at a time. The clientele would have needed no prodding to light their pipes. During his visit to Egypt and Syria (1838–39), Roberts would have encountered many such shops.

SOURCE: William Brockedon, *The Holy Land, Syria, Idumea, Arabia, Egypt & Nubia*, illustrated by David Roberts (London: Day and Son, 1855–56).

house comprised "only one apartment, not very large. Only coffee and fire for the pipe are furnished."[73] This was the basic standard of service among most of the trade.

From these relatively plain accommodations rose far-reaching social consequences. Devoid of social barriers and restrictions (at least below the social elite), coffeehouses helped to accelerate public sociability. Like coffee itself, they stimulated social exchange. Even the smallest shops could count on a regular clientele from their local neighborhood or market. They brought people together and encouraged them to linger.[74] Patrons gossiped, shared the latest news, or simply sat and took comfort in each other's company. Proximity and familiarity tended to dissolve or at least suspend hierarchies that immediately imposed themselves in other social spaces.

To take one random scene from the Ali Paşa coffeehouse on the wharf at Hasköy in late seventeenth-century Istanbul: Kalyoncu Süleyman, a young sailor, was lounging "free and easy, barefoot, dressed like a vagabond, his chest open." An admiring bathhouse owner, Hasan Ağa, had no hesitation about approaching, striking up a conversation, and ultimately offering him employment as a masseur (among other more intimate services for his male clientele).[75] The open atmosphere of the coffeehouse helped to foster such chance encounters, minimize social distance, and override boundaries decreed by propriety and convention.

More tempting than conversation alone were the prospects for entertainment, which at the best coffeehouses became one of the main draws. The simplest diversions were games like chess and backgammon that patrons could play among themselves. But the most distinctive achievement of the coffeehouse was to create a public venue for spectacles of fun and recreation. Among the most common fare were the one-man dramas staged by storytellers and shadow puppeteers.[76] The largest and finest establishments could host much grander shows. In Aleppo, as the Ottoman bureaucrat and traveler Mehmed Haşim Efendi recounted (1798), patrons might watch dancers or tightrope walkers or sit for musical performances.[77] The latter were easily accommodated as Ottoman musicians played a kind of "chamber music" consisting of voice and small ensembles of instrumentalists, no more than four or five in most settings.[78] Though all of these various pastimes predated the coffeehouse, they were now brought increasingly into the sphere of public entertainment, which as a result became more widely accessible to Ottoman townspeople. The new opportunities were a boon to entertainers, who could now earn at least part of their income by performing to paying audiences. For all but a very fortunate few, who were employed at the court or perhaps a Sufi lodge, full-blown professionalization was still far off.[79] Nevertheless, the coffeehouse looked ahead to larger possibilities, mainly by ending their complete dependence on wealthy patrons.[80]

So popular was the coffeehouse, and so inextricable had it become to urban routines, that it would spring up wherever people gathered in large numbers. The demand was seemingly spontaneous. In 1758, the death of the great Sufi ʿAbd al-Wahhab al-ʿAfifi led to the founding of a new shrine outside Cairo near the mausoleum of Sultan Qaytbay. It soon had its own annual festival that attracted not only throngs of pilgrims but the services of myriad tradesmen and peddlers. Attendees, male and female, represented nearly every part of the social spectrum, from the social elite (including emirs and scholars) to ordinary townspeople and peasants. For ten days or so, they gave themselves up to music, dancing, games, and carefree cavorting. Amid the sprawling scene of tents and makeshift stalls were coffeehouses, erected on the spot to accompany the celebrations.[81] The religious side of this commemoration never got in the way of the revelry, which eagerly sought routes to pleasure and escapism. The impromptu coffeehouses simultaneously fanned and served these desires.

Outside the largest towns, coffeehouses had a more functional character but continued to act in their own way as social hubs. Many doubled as inns. This contribution was welcome since the main Ottoman equivalent for housing travelers, the caravansary, was unevenly distributed across the empire and provided no services beyond basic shelter and protection. Travelers who availed themselves of these accommodations found only unfurnished rooms and had to bring their own provisions. Where no caravansary stood, coffeehouses had little difficulty meeting the same minimal expectations. At night, visitors to the Thracian town of Rodosto (Tekirdağ)—to take one example—could make inquiries and put themselves up in the nearest coffeehouse, which would act, in effect, as an unofficial guesthouse.[82]

Rural infrastructure was spottier still. Across large parts of the countryside, travelers could by no means always count on staying at a caravansary, which, in any case, would have consisted of nothing more than a fort with high walls enclosing a courtyard and small rooms. Village coffeehouses were becoming more numerous during the eighteenth century and helped to increase this supply of rudimentary lodging. The British traveler Richard Pococke relates how he stayed at a coffeehouse in a small village near Denizli (in southwestern Anatolia). Even from this lonely social outpost, word quickly spread of his archeological interests, and "half the village" accompanied him to the nearby ruins, "laughing and jesting and with much good humor."[83] These rural coffeehouses were not to be scoffed at. In the early nineteenth century, there were still small towns that had none. Reflecting on his youth in Epirus, the Greek general Yannis Makriyannis (1797–1864) could remember the evening gatherings in the small town of Arta. Having no better option, the chief townsmen and merchants used to sit until midnight in the town square during summer.[84] They were essentially following the custom that still prevailed in most Greek villages. Since so few of the latter had coffeehouses, peasants would simply congregate around a "kiosk" (i.e., wooden platform) or large tree, where they would talk and smoke at leisure.[85]

Disreputable Pastimes: Alcohol and Opium

If tobacco was controversial in some quarters, Islamic law would seem to leave no doubt about the question of alcohol. Verses from the Qur'an explicitly forbade Muslims from drinking wine, and jurists extended the prohibition to all alcoholic beverages, which were ruled intoxicants. These legal strictures against alcohol helped to discourage Muslims from drinking it.

More effective still, especially among Muslim townspeople, was the aspiration to social respectability. To drink openly was to damage one's social status. This taboo weighed most heavily, of course, on members of the religious establishment, who were expected to model their conduct on religious ideals. Lapses were not easy to forgive. In 1811, the judge of Galata, in Istanbul, could not escape the consequences of his "drinking and fornication" (or at least of being accused of such pastimes). He was immediately dismissed and sent away to Edirne.[86] Ordinary Muslims, too, plainly felt varying degrees of guilt or shame. One eighteenth-century traveler came across a group of Anatolian villagers, one of whom asked for wine. "He took his turban from his head, kissed and laid it aside; and after drinking, replaced it with the same ceremony."[87] So this Muslim villager was happy to drink wine, but signaled, in a symbolic gesture, that it was reprehensible.

As a result of this religious disapproval, alcohol tended to flow along less conspicuous pathways. Drinking retreated from public spaces and took place mainly behind closed doors. Yet it did continue. Muslims had their excuses at the ready. The real shame, drinkers insisted, was public drunkenness. A French traveler summed up these complex attitudes (1700):

> Tho' I've said that the Turks ought to abstain from wine according to the law, 'tis generally the least observed of any article in the religion; for I believe I should not exaggerate, if I should say, that they drink more in proportion than the Christians; and the Greeks, Armenians, and Jews receive the greatest profit by them, tho' at the same time they run the risk of the falake [bastinado] for selling it to the Turks, as well as the Turks for drinking it. Even the discreetist of them, who will give the

falake to anyone who has violated the law in this respect, and is seen to be overtaken with liquor in publick, will themselves drink it during the great part of the night, as I have seen several of them, and then go to bed and sleep; and in the morning, before going to mosque, they wash themselves, and breakfast upon baked apples and coffee to dissipate the fumes and smell of the wine; after a second lotion, they pray and then do business: they explain the law in their favour by saying that the sin lies only in the publick scandal or the disorders which it causes, which they avoid by drinking it only at night, and secretly, without doing wrong to anyone.[88]

A Muslim might enjoy wine, or even get drunk from it. As long as he did not make a spectacle of himself or harm others, his conscience had no reason to feel any twinge.

To the astonishment of European observers, Ottoman patrons could imbibe "prodigious quantities" if they set their mind to it.[89] For some Muslim drinkers, intoxication was the point, and so they drank heavily.[90] Having witnessed many scenes of excessive drinking, Aaron Hill sketched an imaginary plan (1709) to lure poor English brewers to Istanbul, where, as he assured his readers, they might secure a steady trade.[91] On the road, Europeans discovered that they were assumed to be carrying wine, and that local acquaintances might hope to partake of it. Staying at the Anatolian town of Manisa, one Englishman called (1699) at the home of "a certain Suleyman Efendi," who immediately returned the favor. He came with the expectation that the traveler should share his wine and kept drinking "till 2AM."[92] Muslims were not alone in slaking an outsized thirst. Free to manufacture and sell wine and other alcoholic beverages, Christians and Jews did not deny themselves in tippling either. After a visit to Homs (1831), Mikha'il Mishaqa (a Christian) sniffed, "I did not see a single Christian there not lit up with intoxicants." Not to be taken literally, this judgment ought to be treated rather as a testament to the freedom with which local Christians drank.[93]

Ottoman drinkers generally preferred wine, which was the default beverage in most drinking sessions. Europeans noticed that much of it, in regions like Greece, was still made with resin in the manner of wine-making in antiquity.[94] Impecunious tipplers found solace in boza, which (in its alcoholic version) was fermented from millet, barley, or rice, and served as the

Ottoman version of beer.⁹⁵ A distilled spirit flavored with anise, rakı (also 'araq or ouzo) was manufactured, usually from grapes or raisins. Its higher cost undoubtedly gave pause to many a drinker under the Old Regime.⁹⁶ In Istanbul, it did not become truly fashionable until the late nineteenth century, when the self-consciously modern made it their drink of choice.⁹⁷

Much drinking took place discreetly inside homes or in relatively secluded spaces like gardens, where the uninvited could neither see nor judge. To lubricate these entertainments, Ottoman townsmen turned to shops that dispensed alcoholic beverages. Most were hardly more than stalls in the market. Their proprietors were Christians or Jews, who acted simply as producers and retailers, not publicans. But consumption was by no means banished entirely from public view. A few coffeehouses were known to serve alcohol, albeit at some cost to their reputation, as did some of the caravansaries catering to travelers.⁹⁸ Functioning explicitly for this purpose, at least in the towns of the Balkan and central provinces, were taverns of various sizes and social pretensions. They spanned roughly the same spectrum of possibilities as coffeehouses. A select few could assume comfortable, even stately proportions. One British traveler entered a high-end tavern in Istanbul and found "large halls floored with Dutch tiles, having a fountain in the middle of a wooden gallery for the guests running around the sides of the room about halfway between the ground and ceiling."⁹⁹ Most, however, were unassuming and plebian, a small room with a few tables and stools and simple furnishings.¹⁰⁰

Distinct social spaces, the taverns were even freer and less inhibited than the coffeehouses. In Istanbul, the urban imagination filled them with the denizens of the underworld: pimps, prostitutes, local toughs and ne'er-do-wells, a few assorted criminals.¹⁰¹ As one traveler primly reported, "We entered a Turkish tavern, but found such entertainment that we did not chuse to make a second visit."¹⁰² Some suspicions were quite justified. A number of taverns busied themselves in the local sex trade, procuring both women and young men for their (male) customers.¹⁰³ On late eighteenth-century Chios, it was common knowledge that many of its fifty-eight taverns doubled as brothels.¹⁰⁴ In Wallachian towns, patrons looked for visual clues. Telltale insignia placed over the doorway—crosses mounted inside rings of straw—identified the brothels from the regular taverns. This clarification was no doubt welcome since Wallachian taverns operated from inside homes and women routinely worked alongside their proprietor husbands, helping to serve drinks as they titillated the "lady lovers" and "Crimean gentlemen."[105]

Like the coffeehouse, only more heedless of moralizing opinion, the tavern had become a "countercultural" bastion of sensual escapism and masculine sociability. It likewise did its part, wherever there was an established tavern culture, in pushing social life deeper into the night—as it did most provocatively in Istanbul.[106] But unlike the coffeehouse, the tavern never gained full social acceptance. Nearby residents tended to view it as little better than a moral blight to be heavily monitored or perhaps extirpated altogether. In one Istanbul neighborhood (1815), a group of some two hundred women descended on a newly opened tavern; so badly did they wreck the place that the proprietor sought permission afterward to set up in another part of the capital.[107] Religious scruples could achieve the same end, with Muslim neighbors occasionally filing into the courthouse and asking a judge to shut down a tavern on the pretext that it stood too close to a mosque.[108]

Yet the Ottoman state had no interest in suppressing this trade. Only during a few fitful interludes had it briefly yielded to the demands of religious hardliners. First in 1596, and again in 1613, the taverns of Istanbul were subject to short-term closures (even though Islamic law allowed Christians and Jews to make, sell, and drink alcohol).[109] During the height of the Kadızadeli agitation, in 1670, the authorities announced yet another ban on alcohol, which took effect in Istanbul and nearby towns. In spite of the pious din, the measures did little to dent demand. The English traveler John Covell had no trouble (1675) quenching his thirst in Edirne. "Yet I believe there is as much wine drunk (or more) as many taverns by connivance and bribery as ever there was." Wandering out to the nearby village of Karaağaç, he discovered that the whole community "lived by the selling of wine," and "every day come hundreds of people from Edirne to be drunk."[110] Whatever inconvenience the shutting of Istanbul taverns had caused, wine continued to find its market. By the 1690s, the same fiscal pressures that had led to the full legalization of tobacco conspired to bring back the open sale and regulation of alcohol. Here and there, a few local initiatives to close the taverns might sputter briefly into action.[111] But the Old Regime had now committed itself to greater toleration—and regular taxation.[112] Another path to pleasure and sociability had opened wider.

Very much like the policy toward coffeehouses, this toleration wavered only for brief moments of ideological crisis in which the state (or local authorities) self-consciously protested their Islamic legitimacy. In Cairo (1703), monetary disorders prompted the head of the local Janissary corps to close boza and wine shops, as well as brothels.[113] More serious were the tribulations of the late eighteenth and early nineteenth centuries, which magnified these ideological reflexes. Having inherited a foundering war effort against Russia and Austria (1787–92), Selim III hoped to allay doubts about his leadership and prove that he was a just ruler who would see the fighting to a triumphant conclusion. He therefore forbade Muslims from drinking alcohol and decreed the closing of all taverns in the capital.[114] Evasion was immediate, as smugglers and private sellers sprang into action. Within a short time, the taverns began to reopen despite official attempts at monitoring. Popular demand was irresistible—as was official hunger for revenue. And since the alcohol tax was one of the treasury's most remunerative dues, the state soon relented.[115] This exercise in futility was briefly repeated a second time in 1826, when the abolition of the Janissary corps initiated several months of ideological posturing.[116] In provinces with large Muslim populations, local authorities also carried out their own campaigns against alcohol. Once again, the triggers were moments of political and ideological stress amid the Great Crisis. In 1802, the governor of Aleppo, recently returned from the victorious Ottoman campaign in Egypt, executed several Janissary officers for committing abuses in his absence; symbolically signaling a restoration of order, he announced a ban on alcohol.[117] In 1804, and again in 1807, it was the turn of Damascus, where the provincial administration was unable to subdue the Wahhabi threat from the desert.[118] In each of these episodes, the disruptions to drinking were quick to pass.

Instead of prohibition, the lasting policy of the eighteenth-century Old Regime was to regulate and tax. A general division of labor persisted. Christians and Jews were responsible for the manufacture and sale of alcohol and operated nearly all the taverns.[119] As a consequence, these activities were far more likely to take place in neighborhoods that held large numbers of non-Muslims. The most famous location was the neighborhood of Galata in Istanbul, stretching up the hills from the northern shore of the Golden Horn toward Pera, where European states had long established their embassies. At the turn of the nineteenth century, it held about a third of the capital's taverns; another one-third were scattered along the villages of the Bosphorus, which also contained substantial Christian and Jewish populations.[120] The same correlations could be found in other towns. In eighteenth-century Cairo, Azbakiyya was the main pleasure ground, partly because of its taverns.[121] By no coincidence, it was the neighborhood where most of the local Coptic community had clustered. And in eighteenth-century Izmir, the taverns of the European quarter, located along the waterfront, kept their doors open "all Hours, Day and Night."[122]

The specialization of Christians and Jews only extended as far as the production and sale of alcohol. Although non-Muslims largely handled the trade and owned the taverns, their customers observed no such sectarian distinctions and hailed from all religious backgrounds. The numerous taverns of Galata bred a cosmopolitan demimonde, in which Ottoman subjects might easily bump into European visitors.[123] They drank together—or at least saw each other drinking. The same law of attraction applied in Izmir. In 1785, the authorities struggled in vain to reinforce the night watch and keep local Muslims and Christians from congregating in the taverns of the European quarter, notorious for its nocturnal disorders. The French consul complained that these thirsty visitors "carried themselves to all sorts of extremes."[124] In Damascus, the Egyptian authorities approved (1832) the construction of a tavern in a ruined caravansary—a real milestone since the Arab lands had not previously harbored a genuine tavern culture.[125] The new tavern had no shortage of customers, who came from all religious communities.[126] The appeal of such outlets, to be sure, was highly uneven among Muslims. The staunchest foes of alcohol were most likely to be found among the ulama and middling stratum of merchants and shopkeepers who ostentatiously sought to affirm their piety and respectability. Inhibitions tended to fade toward the margins of society: among soldiers, sailors, bachelors, and the poor and transient.[127] Only Balkan Muslims refused to follow this pattern. Though a mostly Muslim town, late eighteenth-century Sarajevo held twenty-one taverns, supplied by local distilleries that produced Bosnia's famous plum-brandy. Despite the formal prohibitions against alcohol, Bosnian Muslims drank freely.[128]

Outside the towns, the more tenuous hold of religious orthodoxy further weakened strictures against Muslim drinking. To take one bibulous outpost: In the western Anatolian village of Geyre, near Nazilli, the Muslim inhabitants manufactured, and consumed, their own wine. "The village is a poor place," testified one traveler. "The Turks here make a very strong well flavored white wine and drink of it very plentifully."[129] So a subculture of drinking persisted, and even thrived, thumbing its nose at formal legal restrictions. By the eighteenth century, moreover, it had grown more self-assured. In Aleppo, some contemporaries thought that drinking was actually on the rise, and that some of the old stigma had faded.[130] Assessing the local demand for wine in Mosul, one early nineteenth-century British traveler left little doubt: "The people of Mosul of all religions are much addicted [to it]."[131] So corrosive, then, were the cultural repercussions of the Old Regime's policies that they could loosen even the most powerful religious taboos.

Drinkers made the most of this latitude. Among the most avid and uninhibited were state officials and their entourages. Ahmed Paşa al-Jazzar, infamous governor of Acre (r. 1775–1804), for many years used to drink wine until he suddenly repented and stopped. Some observers swore that his savage temper grew much worse afterward.[132] In Istanbul, there was whispering (1807) about the heavy tippling of Atıf Efendi, the chief scribe (reisülküttab) and foreign minister.[133] The head secretary to Mehmed Ali, governor of Egypt, was Halil Efendi (d. 1810), who "was never sober" (if we can believe the ungenerous assessment of his biographer).[134] The same charge hovered over Süleyman Bey, chief scribe to the governor of Aleppo (1819): the stench of wine "never lifted from his head, night and day."[135] Back at Acre, al-Jazzar's successor, Süleyman Paşa (r. 1804–19), failed to check the carousing of Said Ağa, a eunuch sent as a gift (1809) for the governor's household. Fluent in Turkish and Arabic, strong and athletic, he soon became one of Süleyman's favorites, behaving like something of a dandy with his fondness for fine clothing. Succumbing to temptation as "Satan played with him," he became a habitual drinker who consorted with disreputable characters. His luck ran out under the next governor, Abdullah Paşa (r. 1819–31). Outraged at Said's antics, he had him beaten and jailed several times. The final scandal was Said's affair with a young man. "He loved him and got drunk with him." After carousing together one day, Said invited him up to his room in the harem chambers and let him stand in the window so that the young man could admire the women of the governor's household. Abdullah soon found out and had them both clapped in irons and steeply fined.[136]

The most active and unabashed drinkers unquestionably belonged to the Ottoman army.[137] This "military" revelry was most obvious in Istanbul (fig. 2.5), which held by far the highest concentration of soldiers, but

FIGURE 2.5. "Marines of the Ottoman Navy" by Jean-Baptiste Vanmour. Among the most enthusiastic partisans of Ottoman leisure culture, in all its facets, were soldiers. Here they have girded themselves for an evening of entertainment with ample stocks of wine and tobacco. To further enliven the proceedings, they have not neglected to supply themselves with feminine company. SOURCE: Rijksmuseum, Amsterdam.

would have resounded in any town where units were stationed. In Baghdad, some soldiers were rumored to drink "wine more than water." They drank so much, some said, that one could smell the wine from the street outside their barracks.[138] Officers, as well as common soldiers, helped to generate this thirst. In late eighteenth-century Cairo, Osman Bey Tamburi earned his nickname for playing the tanbour (a long-necked lute). Along with his love of music, he "was very much devoted to the use of intoxicating liquors, for a supply of which, it is said, he had in a few years become indebted."[139] Creating far more consternation was the drinking of troops. Urban lore spoke of taverns as the lairs of carousing soldiers and sailors, joined by "bachelors," "prostitutes," and all their sundry companions and acquaintances commonly dismissed as "riffraff" and consigned to a dangerous and seething underclass. In the taverns of Üsküdar, the Asian suburb of Istanbul, some unruly soldiers had long demanded free drinks. To ward off these parched ultimatums, tavern owners had to request, in 1808, that the authorities post guards.[140] This protection was not always reliable. The governor of Manisa in western Anatolia (c. 1720) learned that a detachment of Janissaries had not reported on time to escort a departing caravan. He discovered that they had gone out to nearby villages, ostensibly to gather intelligence about the state of the roads, but had instead stopped at a village where they were filling themselves with wine.[141]

Beyond alcohol, in the outer reaches of Ottoman leisure culture, lay the misty realm of opium and other psychoactive drugs like hashish. Eastern Mediterranean leisure culture had long experience with them, dating back to medieval times. Like alcohol, they provoked the hostility of Muslim jurists, who condemned them, with varying degrees of outrage, as illicit intoxicants; and like alcohol, they sprang back with the same tenacity against all moral and legal obstacles and carved out their own hedonistic subculture.[142]

By the eighteenth century, such drugs had found a new channel for consumption. Medieval connoisseurs had eaten them, usually in the form of pills or paste.[143] The advent of smoking, courtesy of tobacco, lent a new, distinctly "early modern" twist to this pastime. Aficionados would now mix tobacco into the paste, which they stuffed into pipes and smoked. As a consequence of smoking, instead of eating the various preparations, the use of such drugs became brazen and conspicuous. Whereas medieval opium-eating and hashish use had taken place entirely in private spaces, tobacco pipes could transport the new mixtures nearly anywhere. Some artisans were observed to puff themselves into long reveries in front of their shops.[144] In Cairo and other Egyptian towns, the smoking of hashish was quite popular among the poor. They could easily obtain their supplies, whether from disreputable coffeehouses or directly from hashish shops, where the intoxicated might linger for desultory conversation.[145]

Far more disturbing, in the eyes of moralists, was the entry of this unapologetic escapism into the coffeehouse, the flagship for early modern leisure culture. Opium was particularly galling. It quickly installed itself at the shady end of the coffeehouse trade, where owners had never objected to serving intoxicants. Some places became absolutely notorious. In Istanbul, everyone knew of the row of coffeehouses, close to the Süleymaniye Mosque, where opium addicts gathered and silently whiled away the hours.[146] One British traveler, echoing the verdict of his time, believed

(1839) that opium was an urban pastime, concentrated above all in Istanbul, and that villagers did not partake of it.[147] Still, we should not rush to proclaim the innocence of the countryside. At a village outside Izmir (1673), an earlier traveler, John Covell, had come across an opium addict who assured him that the habit of taking the drug every morning had made him fresher and more vigorous. The Englishman had his doubts: "He was very lean, the flesh, or rather the skin of his cheeks, hanging like Spanish leather; and he had very often (almost every minute) a strange kind of spasm in the muscles of his breast, or a jerking motion like those who have a strong hickock [hiccup]."[148] Ottoman opium production, most notably in western and central Anatolia, easily met domestic demand and had sufficient stocks left over for an active export trade that remained strong throughout the nineteenth century.[149]

Even though the recreational use of opium was neither legal nor respectable, it did not circulate, as one might assume, only among a kind of underclass. One indirect measure of its consumption was the extent to which it penetrated the Ottoman elite, who might either smoke or eat it. Hamevi Ali Efendi earned an exile (1703) to the Aegean island of Kos, allegedly for practicing astrology. Hastening his downfall was an unseemly addiction to wine and opium. He would sit up the entire night carousing with fellow "pleasure-seekers" (*ehl-i keyif*) and sleep during the day.[150] Addicts were to be found at the very top of the political order inside the palace. Racih Bey, one of Mustafa III's trusted courtiers, had the responsibility of carrying a censer before the sultan during Friday prayers. During one of these ceremonies, he suddenly fainted from the opium that he had earlier consumed. Instead of punishing him, the sultan took pity and offered him whatever he wished. The episode led to Racih's appointment to a financial office inside the artillery corps.[151] One European traveler was astounded by the amounts of opium that members of the bureaucracy could consume. "These, by constant use, become enabled to digest a quantity of force sufficient to destroy three other men."[152] Even in the early nineteenth century, some officials at the Porte might still find time to gather and mix administrative business with "opium fun" (*afyon keyfi*).[153]

Despite the horror that legal authorities reserved for all intoxicants, the biographical literature holds occasional references to judges, scholars, and Sufis who used opium or hashish. According to his followers, Abdullah Efendi (d. 1760), head of a Sufi lodge in Istanbul, resorted to opium—late in life, and rather reluctantly—as a treatment for "tightness of chest."[154] Others did not bother with medical pretexts and might slip into helpless addiction. Baron de Tott noticed that his Turkish teacher, a religious scholar, took opium (as well as brandy) quite regularly.[155] The Ottoman judicial establishment, in particular, seems to have harbored an opium subculture—or at least to have long been plagued by such rumors. One addict was Seyyid Kudsi Efendi (d. 1807), a former judge of Mecca, whose condition was known to his colleagues.[156] More embarrassing than such biographical details were public gaffes and lapses. No one could rescue the reputation of Ataullah Efendi (d. 1813), a judge who had risen all the way to the coveted post of chief judge (kadıasker) of Rumelia. An opium addict, he was attending a meeting one day when he dozed off in the middle of deliberations. Suddenly coming again to his senses, he thought for a fleeting moment that he was back home and clapped his hands for coffee. Laughter rippled through the room. Everyone understood that he had taken opium and become delirious.[157] Blatant intoxication was undoubtedly bad form for a member of the religious establishment, even if such opium use was an open secret in well-informed quarters.

These recreational habits seem to have been something of a social fashion that provincial jurists and scholars, settling in Istanbul or spending long intervals there, acquired through emulation of their Rumi peers. This was the fate of Mustafa al-Safarjalani (d. 1765), who made his way to Istanbul from Damascus. He proved so successful in networking at the capital that he was able to teach for a time in the imperial legal schools, which were responsible for training Ottoman judges. Though winning acclaim for his intelligence, contemporaries could not overlook his heavy use of opium. In the cutting appraisal of his biographer, "His knowledge was greater than his piety."[158] It is tempting to blame Istanbul for his addiction, as did many contemporaries. In Aleppo, reported Alexander Russell, the use of opium was not as prevalent as it was in the capital. This disparity is not surprising. In view of its outsized purchasing power, Istanbul undoubtedly held the largest share of the Ottoman opium trade at its disposal. Judges, bureaucrats, and other well-heeled connoisseurs merely tapped into this ready supply, which far exceeded that of provincial markets. A second reason for blaming Istanbul is that it played a role in "exporting" this taste for opium. To take the case of Aleppo again: The most receptive members of local society were the ulama, "owing probably to the influence of example" of Ottoman judges and their entourages, many of whom were known to bring their pastimes with them.[159]

But let us not oversimplify. Opium did not simply make its way out from the capital. The drug was long entrenched throughout the Arab lands prior to the Ottoman conquest. Needing no "Ottoman" introduction to such illicit pastimes was Ibrahim bin Sa`d al-Din, head of the Khalwati Sufi order in Damascus. He earned scorn and mockery for his habit of taking opium paste (*barsh*) and shamelessly sitting in coffeehouses or even shops in the marketplace.[160] Scion of a wealthy and prestigious Sufi lineage, he openly traduced religious law. Equally distressing to contemporaries were his sins against urban decency and respectability. As the careless antics of this Sufi reveal, the quest for amusement and good fellowship had long pushed beyond the confines of private recreation and now flaunted itself with an unsettling freedom.

Conclusion: The Eighteenth-Century Acceleration of Leisure Culture

Pleasure and escapism became more visible and assertive during the eighteenth century. No official could realistically believe that it would ever again be possible to close the coffeehouses. A few might try, like their seventeenth-century predecessors, to restrict smoking or drive it off the streets. But these efforts were plainly doomed, if they were ever more than passing puritanical poses. So, too, were fantasies about doing away with the taverns. Opium had meanwhile received a new boost from the introduction of tobacco, the new and less discreet platform for this medieval pastime.

The resilience of these drugs, old and new, rested on more than a crude hedonist appeal. They worked their way into social routines and became emblems of polite living—or at least the aspiration to achieve it. The prospects for alcohol and opium, circumscribed by moral taint, were always dimmer. Coffee and tobacco, which became respectable, tell the story more fully. Beyond their indubitable pleasures, these inseparable companions performed social functions that made them simply irreplaceable. To any household that had the means, the presentation of coffee and pipes to visitors was automatic; omission constituted a social slight. Coffee and tobacco also inserted themselves into common social ceremonies that could no longer be imagined or perhaps even endured without them. Seemingly omnipresent in homes, shops, and streets, the twin amenities had become indispensable accompaniments to greetings, meals, and even ordinary conversation. One Dutch traveler, taking a ship across the Aegean Sea, discovered the devotion of the crew: "The sailors, like the rest of the Turks, are very still on board, their sole delight being smoking and drinking of coffee."[161] These habits spanned the entire social spectrum. Arriving later in Cairo, he watched as grandees sat and whiled away the hours with their feet soaking in fountains as they sipped their coffee and puffed on pipes.[162] Such luxuries had become unassailable. More than commodities to be consumed, coffee and tobacco had generated new bodily disciplines that were now intimately bound up with the notion of a decent life.

Easing the way for this thriving leisure culture was the blessing of the state. Political or religious principle had nothing to do with it. Rather, it was fiscal necessity, driven by warfare, which furnished the most persuasive arguments. Even alcohol and opium won a relative acceptance that earlier generations, used to more precarious and furtive outlets, could not have foreseen. The war-making apparatus of the Old Regime had, quite ironically, multiplied and reinforced the possibilities for fun and recreation.

Ottoman culture thus joined the advance of pleasure over a long front. Across Eurasia, early modern urbanization and commercial expansion had spawned a more robust leisure culture that was coming defiantly into view and routing the opposition of moralists and scolds. From one region to another, the turning point was the eighteenth century. The big towns of East Asia created "floating worlds," pleasure districts full of teahouses, theaters, and other diversions. In Japan, it was the dawn of kabuki theater, while Chinese townspeople pursued their own infatuation with opera.[163] One finds a mirror image in Europe with the proliferation of coffeehouses, theaters, opera houses, and a noticeable rise in the production and consumption of alcohol.[164] This upwelling of cultural creativity and consumerist desire rode a more modern attitude toward pleasure. It left behind older attempts at the regulation of morality and authorized new forms of liberating idleness. Particularly in the towns of the eighteenth century, these temptations would win growing numbers of converts.

THREE
POLITE MANNERS

While serving as *mufti* of Damascus, Muhammad Khalil al-Muradi (d. 1792) wrote an idealized sketch about his office, whose main responsibility was to handle questions from ordinary petitioners about Islamic law.[1] The good mufti would, of course, have both a thorough education and expert command of legal matters. But in equal measure, he would carry himself self-consciously as a model of probity and propriety for all Muslims. He should be supremely civil and polite. In dealing with questions from petitioners, most of whom were uneducated, he should show patience and forbearance, treat them with kindness, and strive to help them with their perplexities about law and religion. He should never forget that erudition and manners were fundamentally intertwined.

The category under which al-Muradi placed all these qualifications was "etiquette" (*adab/edeb*).[2] This was not a neutral term, as if it encompassed gestures and cues that anyone could mimic as a mere external performance. It was part of a broader set of dispositions that connoted civility and sophistication, along with refinement of taste, whose main purpose was to better equip individuals to lead a moral and upright life. Hence etiquette manuals, the literary genre that discussed how a proper gentleman should act and think, showed far more concern for cultivating piety and goodness than listing the exact motions and words to be used in interpersonal communication. The real point was to temper and discipline the soul.

Like al-Muradi, the main spokesmen for these polite manners were the literate and educated, who comprised a small subset of urban society. Their cultural prestige far outstripped their numbers. They observed—or more accurately, were expected to observe—a more elaborate model of comportment that befitted their social dignity. Most were members of the Ottoman religious establishment, found mainly in the towns. A much smaller number were bureaucrats and literati, concentrated disproportionately in the capital. All distinguished themselves through facility with the written word, acquired from a lengthy education that stressed, above all, the religious sciences, together with a taste for poetry, the main literary vocation of the refined. By virtue of their training, this religious-bureaucratic stratum was most closely identified with the arts of urbanity.

The polite manners of the Ottoman Old Regime were part of a cultural legacy that long predated Ottoman rule. No royal court, as Norbert Elias thought, was needed to invent or disseminate them. Nor was there any movement to challenge this general conception of etiquette. It was so widely invoked, and so long regarded as natural and proper, that it hardly needed to be explained or justified. From one end of the empire to the other, Ottoman society practiced the same polite manners. Members of the social elite, in particular, used them to signal their status and gain entry to social and political networks across the Balkans and Middle East. This common code of politesse functioned as a long-term source of social and political stability. During the great Ottoman conquests of the sixteenth century, it helped to build bridges between Ottoman officials and provincial notables and facilitate the political integration of new territories.[3] It proved still more vital in reinforcing these links across a later period, amid the military misfortunes and political stresses of the long eighteenth century. The Ottoman imperial system would, in part, weather the shocks of the Great Crisis through polite defenses.

Polite manners revealed themselves in word and deed. Urban gentlemen took pride in demonstrating elevated patterns of speech, which they wielded both in everyday conversation and in the more rarefied and exclusive settings of intellectual salons. There were bodily aspects of politesse that they had to master as well. Proper etiquette required knowledge of correct or conventional gestures, motions, and postures to be used in different social situations. Equally essential was adherence to basic standards of decency in personal care and grooming. Especially in the towns, polite circles did not fail to note, or judge, individuals who had not acquired this social polish.

Polite Conversation

During his tour of Egypt and Syria (1783–85), the French traveler Constantin-François Volney could not hide his bewilderment at the conversational style of his Ottoman companions. Exhibiting a "grave and phlegmatic air," they spoke calmly and courteously, checked their temper, and held themselves with remarkable self-possession.

> Instead of the open and cheerful countenance, which we would either naturally possess or assume, their behavior is serious, austere, and melancholy. They rarely laugh, and the gaiety of the French appears to them a fit of delirium. When they speak, it is with deliberation, without gestures, and without passion; they listen without interrupting you; they are silent for whole days together and by no means pique themselves on supporting conversation.[4]

The tone of polite conversation, he marveled, was never hurried. No one felt the urgency to fill up the time with empty prattle. To another French traveler (1703) it seemed as though "they smoak [sic] much more than they talk in Turkey."[5] One British traveler, having passed through Egypt and Syria (1792), explained this comfort with silence as a matter of social ease and recreation: "It is with them, however, neither ridiculous nor irksome to be silent. They go into company to be diverted, not to labour, and they esteem effort in conversation a vain toil."[6] If their talk happened to die out, they would wait in the confidence that it would eventually resume. More than a few European visitors were put off by the long pauses, which were so different from the endless repartee favored in their own polite circles. Even as they acknowledged the civility of Ottoman manners, the extended silences and ruminations could sometimes seem like haughtiness.[7]

Were these impressions little more than "orientalist" delusions that the travelers had manufactured and then repeated to audiences in Europe? This is certainly not the case if we consult Mouradgea d'Ohsson, the Ottoman Armenian turned Swedish diplomat, who offers much the same sketch of Ottomans in conversation. They were orderly, he insisted, never interrupted one another, and always waited their turn to speak.[8] These generalizations were, of course, rather idealized. It is more accurate to see them as valid for public conversation, mostly in formal settings where the participants held themselves with a certain self-conscious reserve and propriety. This stiff talk resembled what Alexander Russell commonly heard in Aleppo at social visits among the refined and well-to-do, where "the conversation is made up of empty professions, and compliments often repeated. These are generally composed in a hyperbolical strain, and expressed with much solemnity. The 'how do you do?' is repeated several times; and after a long pause, they begin anew, 'and once more how do you do?' "[9] The pleasantries were a kind of verbal screen that allowed everyone to keep talking while not committing themselves to a false intimacy. Good friends might certainly enter into warmer and more familiar exchanges, but only when they gathered in private.

Russell further noticed how differences in social rank tended to suppress free conversation or intensify self-monitoring. In official circles, subordinates adopted a deferential attitude toward superiors; they were "attentive, silent, and submissive. No provocation almost whatever, can make them forget the respect they owe, or disconcert the seeming readiness of their temper: they feel, but conceal the emotion."[10] These skills were honed with particular diligence by those who had risen through the ranks of the Ottoman service or in elite households. This hierarchical modulation of speech was deeply ingrained in the culture of the Old Regime. From his Sufi lodge in Rusçuk (modern Ruse in Bulgaria), Ömer Zarifi (d. 1795) stressed this exact point in his own etiquette manual. He cautioned his readers to hold their tongues with social superiors. They should prefer to listen instead of brazenly opening their mouths, and they should say no more than absolutely necessary for an answer.[11] At the summit of the social order, this reserve reached an extreme. When Mustafa IV (r. 1807–8) toured the imperial mint, the Armenian staff were forbidden to address him directly; they spoke to the sultan's attendants, who then repeated what the sultan had already heard.[12] Thus social difference was very much built into ideals of comportment. Individuals had to be constantly attentive to various hierarchies that might come into play. Far from smoothing over these differences, the manners of the Old Regime preferred to underscore them and grant each person precisely the form of address and dignity that they were owed.

No social group more fully embraced these ideals of formality in speech than the members of the religious establishment. They were prickly about their public image, retained an air of solemnity, even pomposity, and held themselves somewhat aloof from fellow townspeople. Jesting and joking were out of the question. Small talk was beneath them.[13] Indecent references to intimate bodily functions such as sex, defecation, and urination were to be avoided at all costs, or at most to be signaled through the use of delicate and unobtrusive euphemisms.[14] In all settings, they were to maintain a serious demeanor and sense of purpose.[15] They ought to be mindful at all times that they were representatives of religious values and lived and worked in the public eye. They therefore ought to act as models of rectitude and dignity. In the advice manual that Sünbülzade Vehbi (d. 1809) left to his son, he stressed the distinguished bearing of the ulama who lived up to these ideals, to which their students and all others would have to pay homage.[16] Knowledge and erudition reinforced these social hierarchies. A strict decorum reigned, above all, in the professional settings where the ulama and their students mingled. In Cairo, the classes of Muhammad al-Hifnawi (d. 1767) were infused with such a heavy air of gravity that no one would ask any questions, so august was his presence. In conversation, he was patient and unhurried; he never betrayed annoyance when others rambled on or attempted dodgy arguments.[17] Learned opinion disapproved of scholars who were willing to pull down these barriers and minimize social distance. In Tunis, Hasan al-Sharif (d. 1819) startled colleagues with his style of teaching, which encouraged lively interaction with students.[18]

So a kind of remote and unruffled self-possession was central to the image that the upright and educated sought to project. But let us not form a one-dimensional impression of Ottoman sociability, whether from etiquette manuals or foreign travelers. A languid, taciturn air was the public face of urban gentlemen. It was the ideal that they emulated wherever they knew that others were watching. But the moment we turn our attention away from public sociability and consider more intimate settings with family and friends, these same gentlemen begin to present a very different face to us. Still conscious of their dignity, they nonetheless adopted less guarded poses and revealed a positive delight in the arts of banter and conversation.

This conviviality found its freest outlets in the salons of the towns. At these private gatherings to which urban gentlemen invited friends and colleagues, the mood was lighter than their public personas would ever suggest. Participants regaled each other with clever and learned conversation and might watch performances from poets, storytellers, or musicians. They treasured wit and levity and could not resist a good story. Every member of this smart set sought to present himself as a cultivated gentleman who made good company.

The urban sophisticates of the Old Regime all sought a place in the salons. They aspired not merely to join as spectators, but to work at making their mark and proving that they truly belonged among the ranks of the refined and cultivated.[19] Members of these gatherings relished displays of talent. And with the exact same gusto, they disparaged those whom they judged out of their depth or lacking proper education and breeding. Salons thus fostered social competition while providing a platform for it. One could not wander into the proceedings unknown and uninvited.[20] Selection signified a kind of passport into exclusive company. Even the relatively open salon of the Beşiktaş Scientific Society (Beşiktaş Cemiyet-i Ilmiyesi), which operated in Istanbul during the 1820s, insisted on this restricted access. It welcomed all students who showed an interest in the subjects that it debated—including the new European knowledge that was seeping into learned circles. But the members would, of course, have the final say about admission.[21]

Not all salons were the same. Some, usually managed by ulama, prided themselves on being sober and staid affairs. In Damascus, colleagues showered praise on the sedate gatherings held by ʿAbd al-Baqi al-Mughayzal (d. 1727), whom they acknowledged as an arbiter of good taste and respectability. Attendees remarked on the unfailingly high tone of his receptions, which were "spared nonsensical speech and calumny."[22] Other salons prized literary flair and elevated entertainment. They were the perfect venues for less conventional talents who gained fame for quick wit and spellbinding performance. Good fellowship became the calling card of ʿAbd al-Rahman al-Safaqisi (d. 1794/5), a well-traveled scholar. Originally from Ottoman Tunisia, he passed through Istanbul before settling in Cairo, where he became a pleasant companion to fellow scholars, a master of jokes and witticisms, and very much devoted to song and music.[23] Gracing the same social circuits in Cairo was Ismaʿil al-Khashshab (d. 1815), a down-and-out scholar who had to make a career as a lowly functionary at the courthouse. He salved this disappointment with the many friends whom he dazzled as a witty conversationalist. So agile was his speech, and deft his choice of words, that "his intellect brought about the same effect on minds as drink." Perhaps it was his rivals who griped that his tone was a little too unctuous and ingratiating.[24]

Most salons therefore combined elements of the serious and playful.[25] We should not imagine that polite society was so proper that it would forgo fun; or so eager for entertainment that it would entirely sacrifice its dignity and composure. It aimed, rather, at sophisticated amusement and unabashedly assumed that few townspeople would have the necessary credentials to participate. In Cairo, here is how the chronicler ʿAbd al-Rahman al-Jabarti remembered the recreations of his father Hasan (d. 1774):

> With his intimate friends he spoke in a relaxed manner, jesting or amusing them with anecdotes, bits of literary conversation, curiosities, lines of classical or popular poetry, risqué verses, charming stories, and witty jokes. They used to wander among the houses and promenading grounds of Bulaq, spending their time partly in learned discussion, partly in debating questions, and partly in exchanging jokes, pleasantries, and literary curiosities.[26]

Even scholars, then, might tire of the stiff formality of their learned circles and seek outlets for diversion and humor. But there was an art to it. The accomplished scholar would steer comfortably between levity and learning, mixing intellectual interests with amusing quips and tales. Absent was any trace of coarseness. The unspoken rule was that cultivated gentlemen, even when relaxing, would observe decorum, uphold a dignified demeanor, and not descend into unseemly buffoonery. To take one unexceptional example: The scholar and poet Erib died in office (1780) as judge of Tırhala (modern Trikala) and earned posthumous tributes not merely for his learning but for "being peerless in pleasant conversation and having good sense."[27] The first quality implied the second.

Urban gentlemen understood these ground rules. Whenever they opened their mouth, they sought to demonstrate that they were, in fact, gentlemen by the content of their conversation. To embellish this impression, they paid equally close attention to the way in which they spoke. Contemporaries were sensitive to variations in dialect, pronunciation, and choice of words, all of which placed individuals instantaneously on a social scale of prestige and respectability. One could immediately tell whether speakers were educated, where they lived or had originated, and perhaps whether they belonged to a particular religious or professional group. The ideal was to strive for a polished, soothing manner of speech. Refined gentlemen would cultivate a sonorous voice, both in conversation and the recital of texts. Pronunciation would be exact; the tone, clear and pleasant.[28] "If he spoke, the ears fell in love with listening to his anecdotes and eloquence," related the biography of Khalil al-Siddiqi (d. 1760), a Damascene scholar.[29] In Beirut, the Melkite patriarch Ighnatius Sarruf (d. 1813) won admirers for his mellifluous language and keen mind. Contemporaries recalled how he could speak eloquently for hours, without the slightest preparation.[30]

An elevated register of speech was one telltale attribute of the urban gentleman. Educated speakers of Turkish, for example, might lard their conversation liberally with loan words from Arabic and Persian. But this artifice could backfire. Sünbülzade Vehbi openly complained that it might quickly dissolve into unintelligible nonsense if, as was sometimes evident, one had not really studied those languages and was only pretending to know what the words meant.[31] Arabic speakers achieved the same effect through the use of literary Arabic. Normally reserved for writing or learned discussion alone, its intrusion into everyday conversation was jarring and dissonant. Only the most erudite scholars, like Ahmad al-Saydawi (d. 1752) in Damascus, could expertly move between registers of speech without making fools of themselves.[32] The very few who had honed this skill showed little tolerance for imposters.[33]

Among the educated, only a few plainspoken dissenters forswore this lofty style of conversation. Contemporaries were amazed by Ayn-i Ekber Mehmed (d. 1722), a Sufi who had moved from Bursa to Istanbul. He was so unpretentious that if one asked a question, his reply made him seem like someone who was entirely uneducated. As they explained it, he disliked showing off his spiritual grace (*keramet*).[34] In Cairo, Muhammad al-Dusuqi (d. 1815) disdained excessively ornate language. His classes were well attended and attracted the best students. They appreciated his easygoing personality and straightforward manner of speaking, which stood out in refreshing contrast to other teachers of his day.[35]

Verbal facility opened doors. It allowed members of salon society to win friends and patrons, who might then lift their careers. Shakir al-'Umari (d. 1780), a scholar and poet from Damascus, had a charming knack for finding the right turn of phrase. Seeking advancement, he set out for Istanbul, met the grand vizier Ragıb Paşa, and won his lasting gratitude for helping him compose a diplomatic letter to the sharif of Mecca. Having secured plum appointments in the provincial administration, he later returned to Damascus and continued to make a name for himself as a witty saloniste who dispensed poems, stories, and jokes as the occasion demanded. His literary nous paid further dividends when the Ottoman poet Tevfik was made chief judge of Damascus. The two of them got on well together, for Shakir "knew the way of the Ottomans" thanks to his seven years' residence in Istanbul.[36] Thus literary performance was not idle display. It constituted a social and professional qualification, which was convertible to material reward and social prestige. It was also highly portable. Ottoman towns harbored more or less the same salon culture and were used to welcoming talent from other parts of the empire.

Carrying the greatest prestige in these pan-Ottoman circuits was the command of poetry. Polite society expected that the polished gentleman would have committed hundreds and perhaps thousands of verses to memory. Better yet, he would sprinkle them into conversation whenever some particularly apt quotation came to mind and suited the topic at hand. Perfectly fitting this mold was ʻAbd al-Rahman al-Ghazzi (d. 1706), who had memorized large amounts of verse and relaxed in his spare time by preparing his own compositions. These feats, combined with a winsome personality, made him one of the literary stars of Damascus.[37] The most gifted poets might extend their range over several languages—usually some combination of Arabic, Persian, and Turkish. Particularly in the learned circles of the capital, knowledge of "the three languages," as connoisseurs habitually referred to them, was a commonplace.[38] Salih al-Halabi (d. 1764) was extraordinary to the point of straining credulity. A poet and self-proclaimed polymath from Aleppo, he not only knew "the three languages" but was hailed for composing verse in Kurdish, Greek, and Hebrew—albeit without knowing, as it transpired, what the words really meant.[39]

Poetic talent might arise from across the social order. Wealth and pedigree were optional ornaments.[40] Nor was an extensive education strictly necessary, although conscientious poets would strive to memorize as much poetry as possible, analyze the work of great predecessors, and explore the meanings and nuances of arcane words. Contemporaries were usually willing to judge poets on their literary merits. In Aleppo, ʻAbdullah al-Yusufi, (d. 1780), among the most inventive poets of his generation, was so poor that he had to make a living from a coffeehouse that he operated near the Umayyad Mosque. Compounding his hardship was the loss of hearing that afflicted him near the end of his life and plunged him into deep depression. To make himself understood, he had to resort to hand gestures. His final composition was a long poem in which he pleaded with God to restore his hearing.[41] The relative openness of the ranks of poets might extend to women, usually members of elite households who had the time and opportunity to pursue an education and literary vocation. One of these female literary lights was Fıtnat Hanım (d. 1780), the daughter of a *şeyhülislam* (head of the Ottoman religious establishment). She had studied Turkish and Persian literature as part of the education that her father had directly overseen. Her fame reached as far as Syria, where Muhammad Khalil al-Muradi took note of her accomplishments and included her under the name of "Zubayda al-Qustantiniyya" in his vast biographical dictionary of eminences.[42] She thereby took her place among a small number of female poets memorialized in Ottoman literary collections.[43] In intellectual formation and literary taste, they were no different from their male counterparts.[44]

All this poetry came together in books and collections, but was really meant to be performed. At salons and other social gatherings, poets graced the company as a matter of course.[45] The Ottoman court was the model, eagerly emulated by the grandees of the capital.[46] Poets were summoned to entertainments, where they hoped to win literary fame and patronage. The notables of the provinces needed no urging to follow suit. One of the wealthiest merchants of eighteenth-century Cairo, Ahmad al-Sharayibi, held regular salons in his mansion. Surrounded by honored guests, many of whom were high-ranking military officers, he used to receive poets who made sure to extol his name and generosity. They had learned not to apply to him directly but to head straight to his gatherings, where they could offer up their words before a suitably large audience. Al-Sharayibi was known to pay well for these poetic salutes.[47] He was no different from other wealthy patrons who held literary court across the towns of the empire. In Mosul, for instance, wealthy households eagerly sponsored poetry competitions at their salons, and awarded prizes for several different genres such as laudatory poetry (*madh*), friendship poetry (*ikhwaniyat*), wine poetry (*khamriyat*), and love poetry (*ghazal*).[48]

At the opposite end of these flattering tributes was defamatory poetry (*hiciv/hija'*). An old branch of literature that long predated the eighteenth century, it generated competitions among its own specialists.[49] Rivals aimed verses at each other as if they were slinging arrows or rocks. Spectators followed the duels and savored the feisty verbal sparring.[50] Poetic feuds could easily erupt. One expert satirist was Hamuda al-Sadidi (d. 1750), who amused his friends in Cairo with an extended rhyming composition (*maqama*) that targeted a fellow scholar.[51] In Damascus, Husayn al-Qasafi (d. 1711), a scholar and poet, spouted so much vitriol that he sometimes took aim at himself—that is, when he was not "mocking the old and young." The taunts extended beyond his death. As was customary under Islamic law, his estate was sold off after burial. Purchasers of his many books found defamatory verse directed at them personally.[52] But it would be a mistake to view this genre as nothing more than an outlet for personal invective. It could equally serve as a tool for managing rivalries or shaming those who had not honored their obligations. No infraction was too petty for poetic vengeance. `Abd al-Rahman al-Taji (d. 1704), a poet and scholar from Baalabek, once incurred the wrath of Rajab al-Hariri, a renowned expert in defamatory poetry. A wealthy man, `Abd al-Rahman's mistake was not sending a promised delivery of honey to the poet, who then broadcast his stinginess throughout Damascene salons.[53]

We should not imagine that poetic recitals were set up only as verbal jousts. Poets frequently turned to more intimate talk of love and sexuality. Nothing about these topics was particularly shocking for the salons of the Old Regime, which were heirs to a very old tradition of love poetry.[54] In the palace itself, officials and courtiers composed odes to a beloved who might, as part of this poetic convention, be either male or female. (Poetry in Turkish and Persian, which are gender-neutral languages, left this identity ambiguous.) One of the great poets of his generation, Enderunlu Fazıl (d. 1810) was the youngest son of the vanquished Palestinian chieftain Zahir al-`Umar (d. 1775). Brought to the palace after his father's defeat and raised with the pages, he blossomed into an outstanding poetic talent. In the *Zenanname* (Book of Women) he sang the virtues of the different women of the Ottoman Empire, sorted by ethnicity and religion. His verses were frank, sensual, and sometimes downright lascivious. He composed in the same spirit the *Hubabname*, a libidinous tribute to the young men of Istanbul. These tastes were by no means a peculiarity of the palace and appealed to listeners in provincial salons as well. One of the foremost poets of eighteenth-century Cairo was `Abdullah al-Idkawi (d. 1770), whose prolific verse was universally praised. Among the genres that activated his muse was erotic poetry, in which he proved his versatility, writing about both heterosexual love and attachments between men.[55] Like other poets who addressed the theme of love, he did not shy away from its physical aspects and knew that his listeners were not averse to this imagery.

Mingling with the poetry of the salons was the art of storytelling. No less than the poets, the great raconteurs ranked among the stars of polite society. They might move from town to town and win fame for their wit and skill, like Ahmad Shakir al-Hakawati (d. 1779), one of the most celebrated storytellers of the eighteenth century.[56] Born and educated in Hama, he soon turned to a footloose life, leaving first for Aleppo and then venturing on to Baghdad, Mosul, and Cairo before permanently settling in Damascus. Wherever he went, he was feted for stories and anecdotes spun from wide travels, which, as he liked to boast, had taken him as far as India and Iran. He had his greatest success at Cairo and Damascus, where he quickly inserted himself into salon society and composed poems honoring various notables. Literary fame earned him a small fortune that he squandered on a fruitless obsession with alchemy. Destitute and desperate for a regular income, he began to ply his literary talents in "the most wretched coffeehouses, in spite of his virtue and good breeding, which could not be denied." He then recovered from this reversal of fortune, turned to Sufism, and reappeared in polite society. After his death in Damascus, his books were scattered among secondhand dealers in local markets. An ambitious student discovered them and tried to pass off fragments of verse as his own work, which he dedicated to would-be patrons. He might have carried off the plagiarism if suspicious literati, veterans of the salons that al-Hakawati once charmed, had not uncovered the ruse. As we can see from this long career, practitioners did not necessarily specialize in storytelling; they might easily combine it with poetry and other pursuits. When making the social rounds, the real aim was to amuse and divert by whatever means imaginable.

Like poetry, storytelling encompassed a range of themes and styles. At one end was a rarefied, erudite manner that was entirely proper and conventional in its tastes and exercised its strongest appeal among scholars. Muhammad al-Ghazzi (d. 1782) conformed to exactly this model of sedate and respectable narration. Conversing with his colleagues in Damascus, he "possessed tranquility, gravity, and deliberation in his affairs. He had elegant conversations and a powerful memory, and [told] charming jokes and anecdotes."[57] Other storytellers played up tales of the exotic and mysterious, drawn from travels or reports from the far reaches of the world. In Cairo, Yusuf al-Dalaji (d. 1757/58) became a favorite of Emir Osman, leader of the Faqari military faction. The emir invited him frequently to his mansion and enjoyed al-Dalaji's seemingly endless supply of anecdotes and marvels.[58]

Perhaps the largest stock of stories, though, had to do with humor. Polite society could never get enough jokes, witty quips, and clever wordplay. Biographies fondly recalled the most gifted performers and lauded them for making such agreeable company.[59] A native son of Karaferye (today Veroia in Greece), the scholar Ramiz (d. 1759/60) later taught at Edirne and made a name for himself as a poet. Long after his death, fellow townsmen were still quoting his witticisms at literary gatherings.[60] In Cairo, Mustafa al-Khalifa (d. 1766/67) was a leading scribe, but won greater renown as an enchanting conversationalist and storyteller. He became a regular participant in local salons with his droll tales and hilarious pantomime.[61] Not everyone was at ease with his bodily gestures and theatrics. But only a few listeners, grumbling in the name of decency, seemed to object. The salon scene was much too preoccupied with its amusements to care very much.

Greetings and Salutations

If Ottoman conversational etiquette seemed somewhat disconcerting or even baffling to European travelers, they needed no interpreters for basic greetings. Reflecting on their own customs, which seemed entirely too laden with formalities, they thought that the Ottoman style was refreshingly simple and honest. As one Dutch traveler approvingly noted, Ottoman townsmen were "strangers to ceremonies and complaisance; for all the salutations consist in laying the hand on the breast; and the people of inferior rank, by dropping the hand a little."[62] Lady Craven, a British traveler passing through Istanbul (1786), added her own endorsement: "I assure you that if this kind of salutation is accompanied with a smile or a respectful look, it conveys to me more greeting than all our bonjours and how d'ye do's."[63] Despite these compliments, which testified mainly to the vexations of upper-class European etiquette, travelers conveyed an impression that was a little too straightforward and uniform. Some greetings mixed in little modulations. One might bow several times while making inquiries about health and the latest news. Pious Muslims might add, "Peace be upon you."[64] Further inflections might follow from differences in social status. To a superior, the correct gesture was to carry the hand to the mouth and then place it on the forehead. A true grandee would receive the most elaborate flourish: a deep bow, with the right hand sweeping downward toward the ground before being brought up to the mouth and then forehead.[65]

These ceremonies crossed ethnic and religious boundaries and formed a common vocabulary of motion. The same gestures and postures were recognizable throughout the empire. The result was not absolute uniformity but a general set of rules on which members of local communities might, here and there, place their own distinctive stamp. Alexander Russell remembered how the Jewish women of Aleppo had invented their own manner of greeting. "Instead of laying the hand upon the left breast, the person saluting presents both hands joined at the point of the fingers, which the other touches gently, sliding her fingers over them, and then each, by an easy motion, carries her hands, joined at the finger points, to her own lips."[66] Nothing about this variation was particularly scandalous or objectionable to anyone in Aleppo. It ought to be viewed, rather, as an expression of an urban "subculture" that had evolved its own telltale gestures. As we will later see, eighteenth-century towns were fertile ground for the formation of such subcultures and their corresponding codes and "insider" forms of communication. Religion was hardly the only source of such innovation.

Modulating all greetings was the respective status of the parties. Social inferiority carried with it a burden to show or reinforce deference: for instance, by greeting with a polite hand gesture but withholding the verbal salute.[67] Equals, on the other hand, could behave in a more relaxed fashion. They could more freely engage in demonstrations of friendship and affection. It was easier for them to reveal emotions and pass into a more unguarded informality. Friends and family did not hesitate to display emotional depth and attachment, which they signaled through closer physical proximity. The main target of attention was the hand. Most simply, one could clasp it as a sign of warmth, trust, and affection.[68] More effusive was a full-blown handshake (*musafahe*). In the Ottoman manner, one man would take the hand of his acquaintance, who in turn placed his own on top; the two men would then shake their joined hands gently up and down, repeating the motion "twenty to thirty times" as they exchanged greetings.⁶⁹ Combining the regular salutation with the handshake served as a double greeting that conveyed emotional emphasis.⁷⁰ Public holidays might further loosen social restraints. People became more expressive with their body language and were more willing to move beyond the usual salutations and shaking of hands. Friends might embrace on the streets, as townspeople were wont to do during Ramadan and other religious celebrations.⁷¹

During the rest of the year, a polite reserve hovered over social exchanges. The polished and genteel, in particular, frowned upon public displays of emotion and intimacy. Open embracing was discouraged. Social taboos demanded, moreover, that greetings not venture into private affairs. Well-bred men, unless they were very close friends, never asked about each other's wives or family. They addressed their inquiries about health and news strictly to each other; at most, they might ask about the "household," if they were on good terms and wished to broach the question with tact.⁷² Nor would they have had the opportunity for firsthand observation. Socializing largely proceeded on two tracks, which put men and women in separate homosocial worlds. Outside the family, polite society did not condone the mixing of the sexes. This was not a "Muslim" preference. Members of all religious communities honored these informal boundaries. When Mikha'il Mishaqa (d. 1888), a Christian chronicler from Syria, briefly passed over his own family history, he dropped a reference to his four brothers, but declined to say anything at all about his five sisters as there was "no need to mention them."⁷³ Like others who grew up under the Ottoman Old Regime, Mishaqa was content to cloak the women of his family behind a discreet barrier of propriety. Even inside the bosom of the family, polite society insisted on emotional composure. Among the well-bred of the capital, for instance, husbands and wives hailed each other with formal terms like "gentleman" (*efendi* or *çelebi*) or "lady" (*hanım*).⁷⁴ Their children dared not embrace their parents unless they were explicitly bidden. It was far better, they were taught, to kiss an elder's outstretched hand and raise it to their forehead.⁷⁵

These lessons about age and authority did not fade with childhood. The kissing of the hand was one of the universal gestures of deference. Men, women, and children used it for elders, dignitaries, and any personages held in special esteem.⁷⁶ Even members of the social elite would not hesitate to show this honor to some patron or eminent figure. Religious leaders were certain to command it. Visiting Istanbul in 1778, Muhammad Khalil al-Muradi, future mufti of Damascus, arranged for a meeting with the şeyhülislam. His host rose as a mark of respect for al-Muradi's family and greeted him in a friendly fashion, recalling how he had studied with his illustrious great-grandfather, Murad al-Muradi, and once had the privilege of kissing the great Sufi's hand.[77] In Cairo, Abu'l-Hasan al-Qal`i (d. 1785), a distinguished scholar, was held in such affection that people would approach him in the street and kiss his hand. The tribute became so common that "it was considered as a duty" among his many admirers.[78] The powerful Egyptian commander Ahmed Ağa al-Barudi (d. 1774) won acclaim for his polite ways and habit of mingling with scholars. His attachment to Hasan al-Jabarti was so deep and heartfelt that al-Barudi once halted a military procession through the streets of Cairo when he encountered the elderly scholar riding on the back of a mule. The officer dismounted, approached al-Jabarti, and kissed his hand in full view of bystanders.[79] These social niceties had nothing to do with religious identity and were not at all specifically Muslim. Members of all religious communities used more or less the same gestures in addressing elders and social superiors. The bishop of Salona (1819), from his see on the Gulf of Corinth, used to receive local peasants after dinner. They entered his room as he sat on a divan smoking from a pipe. The motions were well-rehearsed: they would first prostrate themselves, touching their forehead to the ground, and then plant the inevitable kiss on his hand.[80]

On the receiving end, these graces were taken as the due of one's social station, particularly by those who held high office. When the British traveler John Lewis Burckhardt toured the monastery of Mar Elias on Mt. Lebanon (1810), he offended the Maronite patriarch by refusing to kiss his hand. From Burckhardt's point of view, the incident exposed the prelate's "arrogance." For his own part, the patriarch could not understand the foreigner's reaction, which seemed like a snub to the entire social hierarchy.[81] In all social circles, refusing to kiss the hand of a dignitary was an obvious slight. When a Cairene scholar balked (1809) at taking the hand of the *naqib al-ashraf* (chief of the descendants of the prophet Muhammad), he created a commotion that was not easily quelled. For many onlookers, his refusal amounted to an affront not only to the official but to the entire lineage of the prophet.[82] Such negligence was an entirely different matter only if the person owed the salute willingly waived it. A "prodigy of his age," the Egyptian scholar Mustafa al-`Azizi (d. 1742) "was never willing to let people kiss his hands and abhorred it."[83] His impatience was attributed to an austere and pious lifestyle dedicated entirely to learning. His attitude was all the more conspicuous since so few of his peers would forgo the honor.

In official ceremony, the kissing of the hand was automatic. Men of state would extend their hand almost as a reflex whenever a petitioner approached; the latter would perform the gesture without thinking.[84] It was a moment in which officials and subjects achieved physical proximity—occasionally with tragic consequences. An Egyptian officer, Ali Kethüda al-Jalfi, lost his life (1740) when he allowed a soldier into his presence and awaited the perfunctory kissing of his hand. The soldier was actually an assassin, who seized al-Jalfi's hand and fired a pistol into his chest.[85] Having grown accustomed to Ottoman manners, the French general Jean-Baptiste Kléber, appointed as commander when Napoleon returned to France (1800), made the same mistake. An assassin pretended to kiss his hand, as if approaching with a petition, and instead plunged a dagger into him.[86]

To exaggerate deference, a subordinate or petitioner might perform a double gesture: kissing both the hand and hem of the robe. The model for this latter gesture (the *damen-bus*) was the Ottoman palace, which had long incorporated it into court ceremony.[87] In provincial society, the custom became the prerogative of high-ranking officials like governors or military commanders, who might also receive this homage.[88] When Ottoman soldiers finally captured the renegade Selim Paşa near the Georgian frontier (1815), they still treated him with courtesy and a certain gentleness. Before his execution, officers asked him to make his last ablutions and went so far as to kiss the hem of his robe.[89] Peasants would perform the same obeisance while presenting petitions or making pleas to officials. The British consul William Leake remembered the scene (1805) at the provincial court of Ali Paşa of Yanina in northern Greece:

> As policy obliges him to receive the lowest Albanian with familiarity and apparent confidence, to allow them to approach him, to kiss the hem of his garment, to touch his hand, and to stand near him while they converse with him, his dress is often covered with vermin, and there is no small danger of acquiring those companions by sitting on his sofa, where they are often seen crawling amidst embroidered velvet and cloth of gold.[90]

When making some particularly urgent appeal, petitioners might introduce extra gestures to emphasize their submission and respect. The

Tunisian scholar Ahmad Ibn Abi'l-Diyaf (1804–1874) remembered how, as a young boy, he sought permission to attend the lectures of a revered teacher, approaching the old man after a lesson and kissing his knees.[91] Grown men did not hesitate to do the same. In 1786, an imperial fleet arrived in Alexandria to chastise the leading mamluks of Egypt, who had ceased to forward tribute to Istanbul and become overmighty warlords. Getting the news in Cairo, Murad Bey, half of the ruling duumvirate in Egypt, made his way to the citadel for an audience with the governor. The mamluk "humbled himself," kissing not only the governor's hands but also his knees and the hem of his garment, while begging for his intercession with the expeditionary force.[92] To signify positive self-abasement, and thus utter helplessness, a supplicant might kiss the feet of a dignitary, as did two mamluks (1809) who secretly visited Mehmed Ali, governor of Egypt, to dissuade him from sending an expeditionary force against them.[93] At the very moment the power of the central state was forever waning in Egypt, officials still performed all the forms of Ottoman obeisance.

So routinized were these gestures of deference and reverence that officials would always take care to kiss letters and decrees sent from the sultan or grand vizier.[94] The personage might be absent, but the ceremony would have to be performed anyway. It was a way of vicariously kissing the hand that held power and could therefore send out commands. The same tribute might be extended to scholars, in acknowledgment of their moral and intellectual authority. In Egypt, the great scholar Murtada al-Zabidi received these symbolic genuflections from Kapudan Hasan Paşa, commander of the imperial fleet that arrived in Egypt in 1786. The admiral held him in such regard that he always yielded to al-Zabidi's requests. He would kiss the scholar's letters and place them on his head as a token of deep reverence for his learning.[95]

In conveying humility or submission, ceremonial kissing did not necessarily descend into groveling. It could equally denote respect, affection, or fidelity. One governor of Egypt held Ahmad al-Bakri (d. 1741), head of the powerful Bakriyya Sufi order in Cairo, in such reverence that he would kiss both his hands and feet whenever he received him.[96] Directed at the head or upper part of the body, kissing unambiguously functioned as a salute. To "kiss the hat," as one Ottoman soldier did to an officer's tall headpiece, was an obvious act of obeisance.[97] Such gestures performed around the face and head might also transmit trust and amity. A master of political ceremony, and renowned for his diplomatic touch, Süleyman Paşa of Acre once put an end to a feud at Nablus (1816) by bringing the leading antagonists together. He had them cement the truce by kissing each other's head and beard. As the final gesture, tantamount to a signature, they kissed the hem of Süleyman's robe.[98] The governor likewise knew how to manipulate the language of ceremony in the opposite direction, toward informality, as a means of putting clients at ease and winning their goodwill. He once invited Emir Bashir al-Shihabi, the main overlord of Mt. Lebanon, to a funeral and made sure to greet him personally, with extreme cordiality. When Bashir tried to kiss the hem of his robe, Süleyman demurred, clasped him warmly, and led him away to the council room for a private interview. The governor made a great show of taking him by his side, chatting amiably, even laughing.[99]

What was so remarkable about two officials carrying on in such a relaxed manner? Everyone in state service knew from long training and experience that they could not speak or move as they pleased during official proceedings. Even far-off administrative centers adhered, however loosely, to the protocol laid down in the imperial palace, which served as the model for all officialdom. Ceremony was strictest in the presence of the sultan. At royal audiences, attendees were not to speak unless explicitly bidden. Violations would create instant scandals. Mustafa al-Safarjalani (d. 1765), a scholar from Damascus who spent part of his career in the capital, once shocked the Ottoman court by breaching this decorum. Invited to the palace during Ramadan to deliver a lecture, he had the nerve to address the sultan personally and plead for the release of his brother, who had been imprisoned in Istanbul after the downfall and execution (1758) of As`ad Paşa al-`Azm, former governor of Damascus.[100] Only if the sultan was complaisant might the rules be bent. A popular Sufi from Bolu, Mustafa Safi-i Amedi gained an invitation to a reception at the court of Mahmud II (r. 1808–39). The sultan did not mind when Mustafa and his other Sufi guests addressed him in an informal manner.[101] Without the sultan's indulgence, this laxness was unthinkable.

Governors and other Ottoman grandees did not, of course, have the same standing as the sultan himself. But the general rules of ceremony still applied. Subordinates and petitioners approached with gestures of humility and deference, and were made to feel and act out differences in hierarchy. In Cairo, the formidable "Cloud-Catcher" (Bulutkapan) Ali Bey (d. 1773) had such an intimidating manner that "many men would tremble" in his presence. Aware of his imposing aura, and having achieved the desired effect, he would tell them to relax and help them regain their composure by turning their attention back to the matter at hand.[102] The first of the obstreperous provincial warlords, he nonetheless continued to hold himself very much in the image of a mighty Ottoman commander.

Magnifying ceremonial intimidation was social distance. High officials took special care to restrict accessibility and visibility. To return to Acre: Süleyman Paşa's patron and predecessor as governor of Acre, Ahmed Paşa al-Jazzar, had made a point of never mingling with anyone not holding the rank of vizier.[103] But Süleyman was flexible—and savvy. In welcoming Bashir al-Shihabi in the funeral scene mentioned above, he was not rejecting the principle of social distance, only adapting it as circumstances required. Süleyman wished to keep Bashir as a valuable ally, flattering him and showing personal kindness, as Bashir might have treated his own local allies. Bashir would have understood these gestures. At the very top of the political pyramid on Mt. Lebanon, he made a habit of conversing with his dependents and protégés. He positively sought out company, mainly as a means of acquiring political intelligence.[104] Within the social structures of rural society, where nearly all communication was oral and social relations were renewed with face-to-face contact, these laxer attitudes about hierarchy were to some degree inevitable. Rural gradations of status were not so steep as they were in the towns. Familiarity and proximity were tolerated, even encouraged. Süleyman, on the other hand, never forgot the code of manners in which he was socialized. Informality was a tactic, reserved for political initiatives. With ordinary subjects, he would still stand apart. During Ramadan celebrations, for instance, he made himself visible, but only from the tower of his treasury, where he held council meetings.[105] He would oversee the revelry, not join those who were making it.

Grooming and Bodily Deportment

Polite manners called for more than the mastery of social rules and rituals. The body itself had to exude refinement through cleanliness and neatness, which reflected an orderly, sober mind. The cultivation of the soul demanded proper care of its earthly vessel. Indispensable to good breeding, then, was good hygiene, which, in practice, really meant regular visits to the bathhouse.

Very much like the decorum of salons or the formal ceremony of social visits, all this attention to the body was yet another privilege of the towns, where bathhouses were long established and easiest to find. An emblem of urbanity itself, these public facilities were heirs to the ancient Roman legacy of bathing and hygiene, which, most notably in the eastern Mediterranean, had survived across the medieval period to Ottoman times. Every town had its own bathhouses, and new ones were still being built throughout the long eighteenth century. Although Istanbul had to ban further construction by 1768, owing to extensive deforestation that limited the nearby fuel supply, it was still the capital and could therefore count on the services of an unusually large number of establishments: perhaps three hundred by the early nineteenth century for its four hundred thousand inhabitants—i.e., about one for every thirteen hundred people.[106] By comparison, Aleppo, the third-largest city of the empire, had at least forty-nine bathhouses for a population of some one hundred twenty thousand, which created an average distribution of roughly one to every twenty-four hundred.[107] This latter ratio is a fairly good rule of thumb. It prevailed not only in the small towns of Greater Syria (Bilad al-Sham), like Tripoli, Beirut, and Jerusalem,[108] but also in the Balkans, where the Ottoman period witnessed the construction of numerous bathhouses.[109] Nearly all these premises were founded by wealthy donors, who set up religious endowments that would then rent to private operators. Entry was open to the public for a modest fee. Only the destitute could not afford to pay. Not much better off than the urban poor were peasants. Though some villages were able to maintain their own bathhouses, sometimes little more than sheltered hot springs, regular bathing was mainly an urban privilege (and preference).[110]

Bathing was more than a matter of hygiene. It was an opportunity for fun and recreation. Across urban society, visits to the bathhouse became the pretext for full-blown social outings with friends. At the best establishments, patrons could look forward to a steam bath, soaking, depilation, and massage as they lounged or chatted with friends, probably with coffee and pipes awaiting them at the end of their session. The avidity for regular washing surprised, indeed disconcerted, northern Europeans, whose cultures deplored bathing as harmful to the health.[111] Ottoman women embraced the call to hygiene with notable relish. So loyal was this clientele that most places would set aside specific days and hours for female customers.[112] The bathhouse thus became one of the major centers of female sociability. Some women were known to spend the entire day relaxing with friends. Lady Mary Montagu fondly recalled her introduction to these recreations while staying in Sofia (1717). Most striking to her newcomer's eye was the ease with which women strolled around the pools, entirely naked and unself-conscious. She was bashful at first, but was soon made to feel comfortable. "There was not the least wanton smile or immodest gesture among them."[113]

The imperative to keep the body clean was strictest with the basic bodily functions of urination and defecation. Ottoman townspeople harbored a deeply ingrained sense of propriety.[114] They were careful to hide away these physical requirements, which were always performed in private. In Ottoman towns, most homes had latrines. A rudimentary system of pipes flushed away the accumulated waste—albeit through public drains that created insalubrious quagmires, especially in summer or whenever water ran low. Mosques were routinely equipped with their own latrines and pipes as well, thereby ensuring general access to this infrastructure. It was only the uncouth, or uninformed European visitors, who would dare to relieve themselves in the open. If seen and apprehended, ignorance was no grounds for mercy. One unwitting British sailor, taking his first shore leave in Istanbul (1709), thought nothing of urinating against the wall of a building that turned out to be a mosque. In his own mind, he had done no wrong. After all, the residents of eighteenth-century European towns commonly urinated in the streets and ground floors of buildings, and emptied chamber pots from windows to gutters below. Unable to imagine these daily European scenes, a furious crowd seized him and administered a severe beating followed by a circumcision on the spot (symbolizing repentance and conversion to Islam).[115] Their violence had to do with more than the defiling of a mosque. It expressed horror and disgust at such a blatant violation of urban propriety.

The quest for good hygiene and cleanliness led to an unceasing battle against noxious odors. The mouth was a zone of particular concern. Ethical guides warned of the deleterious effects of garlic and onion on the breath. For the self-conscious, folk palliatives abounded. In the Aegean basin, women were fond of chewing mastic, which was praised for freshening the breath, whitening the teeth, and conferring other health benefits.[116] The entire supply originated on the island of Chios, for which it was a lucrative export, carefully monitored by the state. For the body, affluent women, and even some men, made ample use of rose water and other fragrances.[117] But excessive devotion, at least among men, seems to have been deemed an eccentricity. In Cairo, the scholar ʿAli al-Karimi (d. 1766) was able to live comfortably after a doting patron, an Algerian merchant, rescued him from poverty and furnished him with a house. Colleagues recalled his "strange habit" of washing at the bathhouse with rose water as he burned incense.[118] Few townspeople could contemplate such luxuries. It was enough to keep clothes neat and washed and to visit the bathhouse with a decent regularity. Rather than scenting the body, a more common solution was to use incense at home. Among the many domestic items recorded in probate inventories were censers, which could be effective since most houses were small and had few rooms.[119] Living spaces were cramped; ventilation, poor. In these tight quarters, where people were unavoidably thrown into close social contact, the use of incense was a little touch of elegance.

Accustomed from birth to these restricted dimensions, Ottoman bodies did not need much room for maneuver. Domestic space was devoid of clutter. Households had no bulky furniture like the dressers, bedsteads, tables, and chairs of Atlantic Europe. The affluent might have, at most, a low-slung sofa (*divan*), slightly elevated from the floor. Ordinary homes would have counted no belongings heavier than a wooden chest, used mainly for storing possessions such as textiles and carpets. Life was spent close to the ground. Entering any room or indoor space, people would remove their shoes at the door and sit cross-legged on the cushions, pillows, and carpets that constituted most of the domestic furnishings of any Ottoman home. Easily moved and rearranged, these lightweight objects were ideal for rooms that had to accommodate multiple uses. During the day, rooms might function as spaces for working, eating, or other activities as daily routines required. At night, people would then put down mattresses and blankets and sleep in the very same spot. Domestic interiors had yet to become specialized.

As a further concession to tight spaces, indoor life was sedentary. Ottoman townsmen eschewed unnecessary movement. To Ottoman witnesses, the European habit of pacing back and forth inside a house or garden was perplexing. They could not fathom why their Frankish acquaintances could not sit still, and assumed that something must be troubling them.[120] Europeans noticed the difference too. To the French traveler Volney, the Ottoman lifestyle seemed altogether too languid and impassive:

If they walk, it is always leisurely, and on business; they have no idea of our troublesome activity and our walks backwards and forwards for amusement. Continually seated, they pass whole days musing, with their legs crossed, the pipes in their mouths, and almost without changing their attitudes.[121]

They sat comfortably for long periods, whether they were working or idly conversing. As a matter of fact, this manner of sitting cross-legged was the global norm; only western Europeans stood out with their insistence on using chairs.[122] From this low-set posture, Ottomans were able to carry out all their daily routines. So skilled were they at holding themselves cross-legged that scribes had figured out how to write and smoke at the same time without the least inconvenience.[123] The only rule about sitting was that, in polite circles, the legs were to be kept tucked neatly away under the body.[124] Stretching or crossing them in front was permitted only among close friends. In all other settings, it was a social gaffe that conveyed excessive informality, even impertinence.[125] Mustafa Safi-i Amedi, a Sufi whom we saw earlier at the palace, once carelessly extended a leg while he was sitting in front of the tomb of ʿAbd al-Qadir al-Kilani. As he later swore, the spirit of the great medieval Sufi suddenly materialized and beat him so hard with his staff that Amedi could not stand on his feet for several days. He remembered thereafter to keep his feet primly stowed under his body.[126]

Only when greeting friends or guests would anyone bother to rise to their feet. This gesture was most obvious, and punctiliously performed, during formal receptions, whose ceremonies followed a predictable sequence. Guests entered the room and waited for the acknowledgment of the host. Social inferiors would not dare to sit unless the host was also sitting and had signaled his permission to do so. One French traveler watched the humiliation of a Christian headman (*kocabaşı*) who had accompanied him to the small Macedonian town of İştip (modern Štip). The headman had brazenly sat, unbidden, with a local official, who quite deliberately, in retaliation, made him kneel before him.[127] If, on the other hand, the visitors were social superiors, or even equals, the host would then rise and stand as a mandatory part of the greeting. In exceptional circumstances, guests wishing to magnify their homage might remain standing and altogether refuse to sit.[128] The host, too, had a part to play. Refusing to rise was either a social slight or an indication that the host regarded the guest as a social inferior who was not due this token of respect. Europeans understood all these rules perfectly well and were ever alert to affronts directed their way. Even at the beginning of the nineteenth century, they could not count on being cordially received. One British traveler saw (1801) how a "Frank," brought before an official or some other dignitary, would have to wait for the host's signal. Only then could he take a place nearby on a cushion or pillow (used instead of chairs) and join the rest of the company.[129] Seating was not automatic. Baron de Tott once grew furious at an Ottoman official who received him and then kept him standing even though he was an Ottoman military advisor. He correctly perceived it not as an oversight but as a deliberate snub.[130] Careless officials might needlessly create the wrong impression. Köse Ahmed Efendi and Manuk Bey Mirzayan, trusted lieutenants of the grand vizier Alemdar Mustafa Paşa (1808), used to visit the Porte frequently. On one occasion, they were playing backgammon in the treasury room when a delegation of high-ranking officials arrived, including the treasurer and chief scribe. Contrary to the expected niceties, they paid no attention and continued to chat until they had finished their game. The powerful visitors, who far outranked them, did not overlook this solecism.[131]

The wealthy Greeks of Istanbul, especially the so-called Phanariot families who served the Ottoman state, were the only members of Ottoman society who dabbled in new models of bodily deportment. During the eighteenth century, some of them began to acquire European-style furniture and make a show of eating with European cutlery (the latter of which, in Europe itself, had only recently come into vogue).[132] These fashions were likely absorbed from contacts at European embassies, for whom many of them served as translators and liaisons on behalf of the Ottoman state.[133] European table manners still remained very much foreign and ungainly. Baron de Tott watched in disbelief during a dinner with one such Greek family. He recalled how the meal "was served in the French style; a circular table with chairs around it, spoons and forks; in short, nothing was wanting except the habit of making use of them." A woman of the family openly struggled as she manually stuck olives on the prongs of her fork before eating them.[134] Not until the turn of the twentieth century would this dining etiquette gain a firm foothold in Ottoman society, as members of the emerging modern middle class, a new and disproportionately influential social group, set their minds to mastering it.[135]

De Tott's dinner was almost certainly a performance put on for his benefit. Under the Old Regime, nearly all of Ottoman society retained the prevailing etiquette handed down from earlier generations.[136] Diners sat cross-legged around a low table or tray. Food was put in common bowls from which everyone helped themselves. Except at the most sumptuous dinners, dishes were set out all at once. Cutlery was simple or altogether absent. A Frenchman accompanying Napoleon's army to Cairo (1798) recalled the many meals that he witnessed:

> There were neither chairs, plates, spoons, forks, drinking-glasses, nor napkins: each of the guests squatted on the ground, took up the rice in his fingers, tore the meat in pieces with his nails, dipped the bread in the ragouts, and wiped his hands and lips with a slice of bread.[137]

Elegant diners would have their own wooden spoon, particularly useful for handling stews; knives and forks belonged to the table, and were generally reserved for cutting and serving meat. Up and down the social order, the most common implement was the hand, which conveyed food directly to the mouth (fig. 3.1). Pieces of bread, the next best solution, were equally effective in cradling food or sopping up plates. Once everyone had eaten, guests might drink from a common cup. As a final courtesy, the master of the house might then circulate a basin of water for the company to clean their hands and mouth.

In nearly all households, dining followed the same tempo: quick meals, little chatter. Even in polite society, conversation over food was not the regular custom. A little light banter before the meal might suffice at a grand banquet and was considered the only obligatory social grace. Failure to exchange at least a few pleasantries was an unmistakable snub. When İbrahim Paşa, son of the Egyptian governor Mehmed Ali, held a celebration for his nephew's circumcision (1820), he invited the leading notables of Cairo to a banquet. Contrary to their expectations, not to mention the normal rules of etiquette on such occasions, he refused to rise for them as they entered the room and returned none of their greetings. The servants brought out the food, and the guests ate without his taking the slightest notice of their presence. Once they had finished, they left in silence.[138] It was impossible to overlook the calculated coldness, which told them that they had fallen from favor.

FIGURE 3.1. "Ottoman ladies at a banquet." Painting by Jean-Baptiste Vanmour (c. 1720–37). The ladies in the painting demonstrate the proper manner of Ottoman dining. Everyone sits cross-legged on cushions at a low table. The servants set out common dishes of food. The elegant diners help themselves to the feast with that most popular Ottoman utensil, their hands.
SOURCE: Rijksmuseum, Amsterdam.

Only at smaller, more informal gatherings might polite diners briefly address each other during a meal. Though they did not drink toasts in the European style (as European travelers had to explain), they might wish good health to the host or fellow guests as they took a drink from the common cup. The recipients would raise two fingers to their right temple and return the benediction.[139] Taking somewhat greater liberties was an Ottoman governor stationed at the small town of Tripolitsa in the Morea. An English traveler, who was quite fond of him, nonetheless recalled (1813) how his host had "elegantly belched" toward the end of the meal.[140] A surprise to his guest, the noise was accompanied by enough self-control to keep it well within the bounds of proper Ottoman etiquette. We might more broadly conclude that decorum did necessarily require the complete muting of the body. What most irked polite sensibilities were careless and slovenly gestures that betrayed a lack of breeding and regard for others. Respectable diners were neat and clean. They suppressed gestures or sounds that might provoke outright disgust. Within these general guidelines, good manners did not demand overly rigid self-monitoring.

Most remarkable about all these bodily dispositions was their wide application across Ottoman society. The wealthy could no doubt set out more lavish meals, graced with many more dishes than the poor, urban or rural, could ever contemplate. But they ate with the same kinds of implements and observed dining manners that were completely recognizable to everyone (fig. 3.2). Travelers found the same etiquette wherever they ate—or to put it more exactly, described dining scenes that did not differ very much across the length and breadth of the empire.[141] Ottoman sources do not dis-

FIGURE 3.2. "Dinner at Chrisso." A depiction of a meal at the village of Chrisso in central Greece. The home almost certainly belongs to a local (Christian) dignitary, who sets out a table in the style of respectable Ottoman society, no different from any other part of the empire. The diners will help themselves from common dishes, and have only long-stemmed spoons as implements. One guest is washing his hands with the help of a servant. Shoes have been neatly left at the entrance.

SOURCE: Edward Dodwell, *A Classical and Topographical Tour of Greece during the Years 1801, 1805, and 1806*, 2 vols. (London: Rodwell and Martin, 1819).

agree. Nor do they suggest that anything about this etiquette was undergoing revision. Diners observed more or less the same customs, for example, that manuals from the sixteenth century had laid out.[142]

By the eighteenth century, the most notable difference was that a polite host would conclude the meal with cups of coffee (or perhaps sherbets made from fruit) and tobacco pipes. Each had become inseparable from the rites of hospitality and were the automatic accompaniment to any social visit. Anyone making a call on a friend could expect to be received in this manner, and would have interpreted their omission as a social slight. Declining these polite gestures was difficult, even if one did not like to drink coffee or smoke.[143] For the abbot of an Athenian monastery, this pressure carried heavier consequences. Invited for an interview (1795) with Haci Ali, the ruthless governor (*voyvoda*) of central Greece, he acquiesced against his better judgment, fearful that his host was plotting against him. When the customary cups of coffee came at the end of their meeting, he could not refuse. His suspicions were soon confirmed. Despite taking only the smallest sip, the poison was so strong that it later caused his beard to fall out and left him bedridden for weeks.[144]

Coffee and tobacco had long become part of a social code that regulated the pace of interviews and visits. After an exchange of greetings and pleasantries, the host and guest would get to the business at hand. The arrival of coffee cups would signal that the meeting had come to an end. In the most elegant farewells, available only to the wealthiest households, the host would then have servants perfume the guest's beard.[145] Women performed their own version of this gesture. After having dinner with the wife of the Ottoman grand vizier, Lady Mary Montagu knew that the conversation was drawing to an end when coffee was served and then slaves came to her side and perfumed her hair, clothing, and handkerchief.[146] All these ceremonies were conducive to a certain efficiency that Europeans had no difficulty appreciating. At the end of the eighteenth century, one British traveler found this choreography quite refreshing and rated it favorably to the social customs of his homeland: "In visiting, as is well known, the common but absurd practice which obtains among ourselves, of urging those to stay longer, of whose company one is already tired, is obviated by the simple use of a little scented wood in a censor."[147] The signals were so simple and lucid that any visitor could learn them in a short time.

Conclusion: An Imperial Code of Manners

Whether in public or private, the same set of polite manners extended throughout the Ottoman Empire. Or to put it a little differently, this formal etiquette marked out an Ottoman cultural zone that stood secure and intact across the long eighteenth century. Wherever one traveled in the sultan's domains, this code of verbal and bodily communication represented an unassailable ideal. The urbane and cultivated would know how to conduct themselves, whomever they met and wherever they might be, from the Balkans to the North African and Iraqi frontiers.

The biggest divergence in politesse lay not between different parts of the empire but between town and countryside. To extend this observation a little further: the biggest towns nurtured the most elaborate manners. Even as cultural outsiders who often spoke little or nothing of the local language, European travelers instantly recognized gradations along this register of bodily expression. One British traveler reminisced (1797) how the residents of Aleppo carried themselves with "an air of affected polish," which was attentive to all social niceties. But when he arrived in the small southeastern Anatolian town of Elbistan, which was not used to seeing Europeans, he got a different reception. The residents, he complained, "form a striking contrast to the more polished natives of Syria. They inspected us with stupid curiosity and without the usual tokens of salutation practiced by the Arabs."[148] Ethnicity had nothing to do with their respective reactions, which corresponded instead to the size of the population and overall depth of integration into networks that reached out far beyond their locality, determining the relative density and diversity of social traffic. Nor would the inhabitants of eighteenth-century Aleppo have disagreed with the traveler's appraisal. They surveyed their hinterland with an undisguised sense of cultural superiority and placed their own urbanity at the top of a pecking order that descended steeply to villagers and nomads.[149] One cannot say that the latter thereby lacked manners, only that they contented themselves with simple, unaffected courtesies, whereas towns, by their nature, promoted complexity and hierarchy in social communication.

Ottoman subjects had no thought of discarding their inherited notions about manners and adopting alternatives. Imperial cultural prestige remained undiminished. Across the Balkans and Middle East, Ottoman norms and conventions retained their luster. The durability of these cultural habits and affinities testified to the deep penetration of the imperial order. Even as the empire began to shed more territory with the onset of the Great Crisis, these cultural attachments were difficult to shake. It would therefore be entirely wrong to imagine that Ottoman political weakness produced a comparable cultural retreat, as if politics and culture directly and instantly mirrored each other. On the contrary, the Ottoman model of politesse, as the next chapter will show, was still winning new adherents across the long eighteenth century.

FOUR

THE EXPANSION *of* POLITE SOCIETY

Near the end of the eighteenth century, the British traveler William Browne could not hide his surprise at the lifestyle of leading mamluk officers in Cairo. Having accumulated great fortunes, they openly went about their amusements and felt no compunction about pursuing them. "They are rather gay and thoughtless, than insolent; fond of show and unprincipled in the means of obtaining it."[1] Most Egyptians, he thought, viewed them "as little strict in the principles or duties" of Islam. As soldiers, he continued, the mamluks were brave and stalwart. He rated them "by far the best troops in the East" and acknowledged their skill as swordsmen and mounted warriors. "But in a regular battle, conducted by maneuvers, and large or rapid movements, they are equally inferior to European troops." This last judgment could later claim vindication in Napoleon's rout of the Egyptian garrisons in 1798. But what of this image of the opulent soldier? Browne's eyes did not deceive him. By the eighteenth century, a new figure, the urbane warrior, had arisen in Ottoman society.

The urbane warrior was the product of social trends that unfolded across the seventeenth and eighteenth centuries. Throughout the empire, high-ranking military officers were turning increasingly into urban notables. Wherever the state had planted a Janissary garrison or sizable military barracks, local units settled down and evolved into political blocs. Their commanders thereafter became key contestants in politics, whether in the capital or the provinces. Acquiring a nose for business, they entered into commerce and built alliances with merchants. By the eighteenth century, many of them were amassing large fortunes, as indicated by soaring levels of inequality within the ranks of the Ottoman military.[2] The most successful built their own military households.[3] Their models were the Istanbul grandees who filled the highest offices of state. In imitation of the imperial palace, though on a far reduced scale, they surrounded themselves with numerous clients, retainers, servants, and assorted flunkeys. And like their counterparts in the capital, provincial military officers recruited and equipped their own troops.

This accumulation of "military" wealth would have insidious cultural consequences. Affluence and access to consumer comforts would seduce leading officers and remake their manners and self-presentation as they came to cultivate the ideals of urban sociability. While they retained an outward attachment to the old martial values of strength and virility, they would slowly succumb to the charms of urban leisure culture and assume the suave affectations of urban gentlemen. Spurred by these "military" conversions to urbanity, the circle of polite society would noticeably widen over the course of the long eighteenth century. Older ideals of military virtue did not fade away, but were becoming less relevant to the actual lifestyle of urban officers. These ideals persisted partly as a historical legacy, fondly treasured though not necessarily practiced, and partly as folkloric adulation for the rough-hewn warriors of the mountains, steppes, and deserts around the Ottoman lands.

The Old Ideal of Martial Virility

The first step in tracking this trend toward politeness is to identify the earlier self-imagery that "men of the sword" were so fond of cultivating. Once a page in the Ottoman palace, the famous traveler Evliya Çelebi (1611-1682) offers glimpses of these enduring poses in reminiscences about Murad IV (r. 1623-40), the last great warrior to sit on the Ottoman throne, who personally led the campaign to take back central and southern Iraq (temporarily held by the Safavids, 1623-38). In Evliya's account, the sultan is the very model of physical vitality. He wrestles for fun with courtiers—always winning, of course—and expertly hurls a javelin and shoots arrows. Evliya inserts himself into one scene. Fresh out of the bathhouse, Murad grabs him, effortlessly spinning him over his head; dizzy and nauseous, Evilya pleads with the sultan to be let down. Reflecting on the monarch's military accomplishments, the author hails him for his "heroism" (*yiğitlik*) and "bloodletting" (*kan dökücülüğü*).[4] As late as the seventeenth century, this raw projection of strength very much comported with broader expectations about rulers. They should show bravery, even ferocity, and embody all the martial virtues necessary to keep the realm in good order. A generation after Evliya Çelebi, the historian Naima (d. 1716) could still elevate these virile qualities in Murad IV and declare that his firmness and physical vigor redeemed him as a ruler in spite of his many shortcomings of character. He drank wine habitually, and would in fact die at a young age from liver failure. He could be cruel, as when he conducted nocturnal patrols in Istanbul and randomly executed townsmen for public smoking, which he had recently outlawed. These excesses, the defense went, were the product of his youth, which was the very basis of his dynamism. And if he did commit grave errors and fall short in his ethical conduct, no one could deny his commitment to "justice, state law (*kanun*), and Islamic law (*şeriat*)."[5] His warrior athleticism and sternness of purpose were an indispensable means to these exalted ends.

The ideal monarch was a model to all officials, who ought to be energetic soldiers, well-versed in all the military arts. They ought to govern with unbending resolve, not shrinking from measures that might be pitiless but necessary. Official opinion admired the hardened servants of the Ottoman state, like Duçe Mehmed Paşa (fl. 1638), a fearless and determined soldier who, it was said, had lost all his teeth and fingernails from cold, hunger, and other privations.[6] Battlefield ferocity and skill, perhaps the baseline attributes that contemporaries expected from officials and soldiers, were viewed as essential to keeping order and putting down brigandage and rebellion. Every member of the Ottoman elite paid homage to these ideals. Following suit, Evliya Çelebi styled himself as a gallant swashbuckler, and spun tales of his own physical daring. In one episode, undoubtedly embellished, he braved gunfire and rode with a party of cavalrymen to the rescue of a ship that had run aground off the coast of Egypt and come under attack from "infidel" pirates.[7]

This older warrior pose was highly seductive and retained a certain allure across the eighteenth century. It was a gateway to legend and verse. The most dashing warriors were sure to make an illustrious name for themselves as well as their families. The father of Hasan al-Daftari, a provincial treasurer of Damascus, had personally slain (1635) the powerful Lebanese Druze emir Fakhr al-Din ibn Ma`n, cutting off his head but accidentally dropping it on the field of battle. When the commander of the Ottoman force asked him for proof, Hasan impatiently pointed at his sword and exclaimed, "Look at the blood!" (*Kana bak!*). Rendered into Arabic as "Qanbaq," it would thereafter become the family name and endure as a testament to his bravery.[8] In the eighteenth century, officials were still eager to prove their mettle—or at least to have stories about it circulating far and wide. Ahmed Paşa, governor of Baghdad, astounded his entourage (1733), it was said, when they encountered a lion during a hunting trip. His men fled in terror, but the governor stood his ground and subdued the animal single-handedly with a sword.[9] Throughout the Ottoman military, prowess with gun and sword still won plaudits and esteem. The exploits of Mustafa Ağa (d. 1777), a Kurdish gallant cut down at the young age of twenty-five, were more conventional in occurring on the battlefield. A lieutenant of the governor of Acre, he cemented his memory as "a great war hero" who possessed "courage, cunning, and deception and loved to shed blood.... He was enamored of hunting and equestrian games."[10] The most athletic warriors might become legends for their skill with weapons. One Egyptian mamluk became a sensation (1707) for his extraordinary strength. He was able to draw a bow that no one else could budge. Admiring chatter among the Egyptian garrisons eventually circulated as far away as Istanbul, where it came to the attention of the sultan. The mamluk was at once summoned for a royal audience. He exceeded expectations in dazzling form. Not only could he draw the famous bow; he demonstrated superb equestrian skills, wielding a heavy gun and hitting a distant target while riding at full gallop.[11] This appreciation for martial skill persisted through the end of the Old Regime. Emir Ali (d. 1791), who eventually became provincial treasurer of Egypt, was a mamluk of Anatolian origin. He rose through the ranks, thanks partly to the sponsorship of his patron, who saw to his education. Beyond his administrative talents, he acquired fame as the finest archer of his generation.[12]

This warrior creed achieved its fullest apotheosis in sketches of rough soldiers from the desert and mountain zones, recruited into military service for the empire. Their communities were accepted as the living repositories of timeless warrior ethics on account of their rude lifestyle and familiarity with horsemanship and physical combat. A Circassian veteran who never learned to speak proper Turkish, Ketağaç Paşa served much of his career against Arab tribes who prowled the edges of the desert in central Syria. As Evliya Çelebi recalled, this seventeenth-century commander was savage in repelling them, and used to leave behind heaps of his enemies' bones that his comrades called "the hills of Ketağaç Paşa." One scene commemorates his heroic strength: when Arab tribes gathered near Antakya, he summoned his men for action at his palace. No one could find the gatekeeper to undo the chains and let the squadron out. Ketağaç Paşa would not wait. He rode up and personally sundered them with his sword, and for years afterward left them hanging in pieces as a token of his wrath.[13] Since the same warrior ethos prevailed on both sides of the frontier, the very tribesmen hunted by officials like Ketağaç Paşa might later, by official invitation, take up Ottoman arms. From the sixteenth to the eighteenth century, bedouin leaders received numerous provincial appointments throughout Syria and Palestine.[14] These sons of the inhospitable frontier were viewed as perfect candidates for keeping order on the distant fringes of the empire. Some of them would pass back and forth from official service to banditry, as opportunities beckoned.

The most charismatic frontier warriors were renowned for their horsemanship and stamina, and were celebrated in legend and verse for simplicity, hospitality, and probity. To take one figure from the gallery of Syrian commanders: Muhammad ibn Turkoman (d. 1660/1) was the finest equestrian in Damascus, and once proved it in a public riding contest that lasted an entire day on the edge of town. Contemporaries extolled his bravery, which he displayed while fighting against the Safavids, as well as his intelligence and integrity.[15] Though enemies of the provincial soldiery, the bedouin might earn the same respect for their military ardor. They could also incite emulation. Salih Bey al-Qasimi (d. 1768), a highly capable Egyptian commander, was posted to Upper Egypt, where he and his soldiers regularly socialized with the Hawwara bedouin tribe. This social mingling was so free and routine that they began to speak Arabic in the local bedouin dialect.[16] The lingering imagery of the fortitude and courage of desert warriors explains why İbrahim Paşa, commander of the Egyptian forces invading Ottoman Syria (1831), would ask a bedouin rider, Shibli al-`Urban, to show off his skill with a spear "like the deeds of `Antar," the great pre-Islamic poet and warrior. The performance delighted the general.[17]

Did these rugged poses belong strictly to the soldiery? In fact, they were widely esteemed throughout Ottoman society, far beyond military units.

Before falling from grace and being exiled from the court of Ahmed III, the poet Vahid (d. 1732) distinguished himself as a *saz* (long-necked lute) player who wrote songs under the separate pen name Mahtumi. Completing the dashing portrait, he was also a first-rate horseman, accomplished in the use of arms.[18] A scribe from Damascus, `Umar al-Nabulsi was fluent in Arabic and Turkish and supremely skilled at calligraphy, at least until the governor ordered his hand to be amputated (1730). In spite of having earlier lost a leg, he made a name for himself as a superb horseman.[19] Most improbable—and therefore fascinating, from the perspective of Ottoman society—were the equestrian gifts of a young girl from Acre, daughter of a British merchant. She became an expert at trick riding, which made her (1757) something of a local celebrity. Only her marriage to a French merchant brought an end to the performances.[20]

Members of the religious establishment were no less susceptible to the lure of soldierly poses. Among the advice imparted to his son, Sünbülzade Vehbi spoke glowingly of horsemanship as a "pleasant and beautiful skill" which was very much in keeping with the attentiveness that one ought to show to outward appearances.[21] In the case of Muhammad Emin Efendi (d. 1744), a Sufi and disciple of the great sage Ismail Hakkı of Bursa, the passion was archery, even though it had nothing to do with the mystical life of contemplation.[22] The most enthusiastic representatives of the religious establishment might participate in military campaigns. Mystics sometimes joined expeditions to boost morale and exhort troops to ever greater feats of courage in the name of Islam. Ali Fenai Efendi (d. 1745) was a Celveti Sufi who fought with the Ottoman army against Russia during the victorious Pruth campaign (1710–11). Having seized an enemy banner in battle, he took it back to his lodge in Istanbul as a trophy.[23] No one should suppose, though, that Islam itself was responsible for the militant zeal of these religious figures. On Mt. Lebanon, Maronite priests were quite willing to take up arms, roam the battlefield, and exhort soldiers to bloodshed.[24] Demonstrating his skills at hand-to-hand combat was the priest who saved the Druze leader Bashir Jumblat from an assassination attempt. The doughty prelate tackled the assailant and brought the struggle to an end by squeezing the man's testicles.[25]

Some religious warriors owed their fighting spirit to previous careers as officials or soldiers. One should not imagine, then, a rigid boundary separating these different career paths. It was always possible, though not necessarily common, to cross over. Born in the small town of Izmit, east of Istanbul, Mustafa Aczi Ağa (d. 1866) eventually settled into a career as a Sufi in Istanbul. His father was a warlord, one of the notorious "lords of the valley" (*derebey*) near Izmit. An expert horseman and marksman, Mustafa nearly followed in his father's footsteps until a Sufi mentor pulled him into a religious vocation.[26] Süleyman Rüşdü Efendi (d. 1834) took a more direct route to a religious career. He was himself a "lord of the valley" in western Anatolia, near the small town of Nazilli. He later became a Sufi affiliated with the Uşşaki order, but did not quite give up his older proclivities. He hung his weapons in his lodge and would summon local bandits (*efeler*) and demand that they submit to him as their religious guide. It was said that if any of them strayed, he would take up arms and frighten them back into line. Aware of his local charisma, and speaking with the confidence of a former warrior, he was unafraid to feud with the farmer general of taxes (*muhassıl*) of Izmir, who was, in the words of his biographer, the "pharaoh to his Moses." For his fearlessness, he was sent several times into exile at Kayseri.[27]

The culture of the Old Regime frankly and unreservedly admired physical strength. It was a world in which most men still earned their livelihood from the sweat of their brow. If this was true in the towns, where most men had to labor in the trades or at various menial tasks, it was far more obvious in the countryside, the land of tilling and reaping and endless toil in the fields. Tales of daring young braves abounded.

One Lebanese peasant, Hanna Baydar, turned himself into a local legend when he helped to spring three sons of the powerful Nakad family of Druze chieftains from the citadel of Sidon, located at the end of a long spit of land extending into the harbor. He used to bring kindling to the guards, who so prized his supplies that they refused to let anyone else purchase them. From the familiarity of this trade, he won their confidence and was able to pull off a bold jailbreak, against long odds, which was still recounted years later.[28] Participants long recalled the Egyptian siege of Acre (1831), where the warlord Abdullah Paşa (r. 1819-31) vainly tried to hold out. Interrupting the tedium of the besiegers, resigned to weeks of waiting, was a sudden sortie from a band of reinforcements, horsemen from Nablus, who rushed the lines, broke through, and galloped into the fortress. "Every night they could be heard on the walls chanting victory for Abdullah Pasha."[29] Serving on the other side was Ibrahim Agha al-Rishmani, a Maronite hired as an equestrian instructor for Mehmet Ali's Egyptian army. He assured himself of countless tributes when he became the first soldier to go over the walls as Mehmed Ali's forces finally stormed the town.[30] Even in defeat against this same Egyptian army at the battle of Konya (1832), the Ottoman grand vizier, Reşid Mehmed Paşa (d. 1836), could cut the right figure as "one of those brave types who rode his steed among his soldiers, encouraging and stirring them to fight." Amid fog and confusion on the battlefield, his valor did not prevent him from being taken prisoner.[31] Displays of courage against stronger or more numerous foes elicited particular admiration. A combat-hardened veteran of the northern frontier, the grand vizier Alemdar Mustafa Paşa had originally earned his nickname, "Standard-Bearer" (*alemdar*), for carrying his unit's standard into battle against Russian forces. To the end, contemporaries conceded, he was the same fearless warrior who had first emerged from the small Danubian town of Ruse. Surrounded in his residence during a Janissary counter-coup (1808), the grand vizier lured his attackers to a warehouse where he stored munitions. As "several hundred" rebels descended on this last redoubt, he ignited the powder and blew everyone to pieces, including himself.[32]

In recognizing such do-or-die courage, however cunning or desperate, bards and storytellers did not discriminate in ladling out praise. Courageous deeds would earn their own credit. The Ottoman court long remembered Cevri Kalfa, a Georgian concubine who had come to the rescue of the future Mahmud II (r. 1808–39) during the very same events (1808) that had brought Alemdar Mustafa to power. As an army of provincial warlords descended on Istanbul, the reigning sultan, Mustafa IV (r. 1807–8), sent executioners to find and kill his brother. Only the quick-witted actions of the concubine saved Mahmud. In a scene worthy of a Turkish soap opera, she barred the door and held off the attackers, repeatedly flinging hot coals into their eyes as the prince clambered to safety on the palace rooftop.[33] Contemporaries would not have overlooked her Georgian origins. As Ottoman stereotypes would have it, the people of the rugged Georgian lands were hardy and courageous. In the *Zenanname*, or *Book of Women*, the court poet Enderunlu Fazıl praised Georgian damsels as "merciful and brave"; they were, he declared, "raging lions of the desert."[34]

The Folk Mode: Heroic Manners

The culture of the Old Regime always venerated a combination of martial vigor and noble character, which would come together in the ideal hero. Folk poets exalted warriors who were both brave and generous, virile and gentle, daring and pious. In the cycle of tales built around the legendary hero Köroğlu, which had gained recognizable form by the seventeenth century, the protagonist is not simply adept at fighting and killing. He takes the side of right and opposes oppression, often against great odds. His exploits represent the triumph not of might but of justice and morality.[35] In the Balkans, folk poetry similarly elevated the *klepht*, or mountain bandit. More than a fearsome warrior, indifferent to danger and pain, he was also chaste and honorable in his treatment of women, even if they were captives being held for ransom; neither did he blaspheme nor otherwise show the slightest disregard for religion.[36] In Janissary lore, too, soldiers sang verse that celebrated courage, brotherhood, and chivalry. They were expected to embody a code of masculinity and honor, reinforced by the teachings of the Bektaşi Sufi tradition that was closely associated with the corps.[37]

Within Ottoman society, rural commanders and chieftains bore the greatest affinity to this model of folk heroism. They lived in the mountains, plateaus, deserts, and other remote places where lifestyles, it was imagined, were simple and honest.[38] By necessity, they were active and courageous, and inured to danger and hardship. They were expert horsemen, and wielded sword, bow, and gun with an aptitude that was a virtual birthright. They might serve as officials and soldiers, or maintain a proud, stiff-necked independence toward all authority. Or more unpredictably still, they might drift back and forth between the two social states, as opportunity and self-interest dictated.[39] They were impossible to tame, and never submitted fully to any ruler beyond their own communal leaders.

One of the most revealing figures in this mold was the warlord Zahir al-'Umar (1690?– 1775), who remains a hero in Palestinian folklore to this day. He had become the paramount tax-farmer in northern Palestine by the 1740s and thereafter dominated the politics of the region. He wasted little time in establishing himself in the port of Acre, which he rescued from ruin, and built a thriving economy in which the most lucrative sector was the export of cotton to western Europe.[40] Local bedouin and their rural clients became the backbone of his small military force, supplemented by mercenaries whom he hired with proceeds from the cotton trade. Contemporaries acknowledged his talents as an able administrator, deft in handling the demands of the imperial bureaucracy and managing relations with provincial rivals. Author of a flattering biography, and grandson of Zahir's Christian chief scribe, Mikha'il al-Sabbagh praised Zahir's skill, sagacity, and chaste lifestyle. His account contains all the character traits that Palestinian folklore would later burnish in its own legends.

By birth, Zahir was not necessarily destined for military or political leadership. His father was a trader whose clan had attached themselves to the Banu Asad, a bedouin tribe who made their home near the small town of Ma'arat Nu'man in northern Syria. He was successful in commerce and accumulated a fair amount of wealth in the markets of Aleppo and Damascus. Because of social friction with tribesmen, attributed to "envy," he took his family southward and settled near the small town of Tiberius on the Sea of Galilee, where, by the late seventeenth century, he had established himself as a regional tax-farmer.[41] Here Zahir would come of age, but without losing the virtues expected of a good young warrior. Under the tutelage of local bedouin, he became a skilled horseman and liked to go hunting.[42] Equally noteworthy, he could not abide injustice. In one of the stories told about his youth, he rescued a maiden who was being raped and killed her assailant. Zahir's brother worried about a possible blood feud, but Zahir insisted that he had taken the only honorable course of action.[43] The heroic feat most responsible for launching him (c. 1728) to a wider career was a raid on a prison in Tiberius where a military officer, deputy of the governor of Sidon, was committing abuses. He had just jailed a townsman, whose father appealed to Zahir for help. Averse to using force without good reason, Zahir tried to use moral suasion with the officer, but his exhortations about doing the right thing had no effect. He returned soon afterward with a small band of horsemen; they stormed the jail and freed all the prisoners. After apprehending the officer, whom he treated with kindness and sent back to Sidon, he convened a council of leading townsmen, who signed a letter to the governor backing Zahir's raid. Note that the story emphasizes at every turn how Zahir was on the side of morality. He further made the point of patching up relations with the governor of Sidon, who was furious about the jailbreak, by sending a fine steed as a gift. He included a note suggesting that the governor make him his deputy at Tiberius, which, as he assured him, only needed more order and security to prosper. Delighted, the governor acceded to the request.⁴⁴

Subsequent accounts reinforce the image of an upright ruler, never deviating in his pursuit of justice, even when it might serve his own self-interest. In one episode (1738), a man in his service had committed a crime and fled to the commander of a nearby fort for sanctuary. Zahir got nowhere with demands for the man's return, and the correspondence "coarsened." Careful not to exceed his authority, he sought and received permission from the governor of Sidon to attack the commander and won a complete victory. Again, he did not overplay his hand. Having killed his adversary and evicted the latter's family from the fort, he took no plunder and pensioned them off instead of shedding more blood.⁴⁵ This magnanimity became one of his trademark virtues, fortified by an incorruptible sense of honor. In 1773, he captured Beirut from Ahmed Paşa al-Jazzar ("the Butcher"), who was then a lieutenant of Yusuf al-Shihabi, the leading emir of Mt. Lebanon. Weary of al-Jazzar's constant intrigues, Zahir secretly wanted to kill him, and now had the opportunity. Holding him back, however, was a pledge of safe passage that al-Jazzar had secured for himself and his troops before surrendering the town. Arresting his dangerous adversary would have meant breaking his word, which was unthinkable. He hit upon a different idea: he would appoint al-Jazzar as lieutenant-governor (*mütesellim*) of Jerusalem and thereby make him a "prisoner of his favor." Only al-Jazzar's treachery scotched this plan. Marching to his new appointment, al-Jazzar ambushed a caravan carrying supplies and ammunition in northern Palestine. He and his troops hauled the booty to Damascus and sold everything. He then made his escape to Istanbul, soon returning to Syria with heavy consequences for the entire region.⁴⁶

Matching Zahir's sense of honor was a commitment to upholding public morality. On this subject, too, his probity was unshakable. After settling in Acre, he once ordered the expulsion of a woman who had tried to flirt with him from an open window. Zahir insisted on an interview with the woman's husband, and confirmed his suspicions that the two were not originally from Acre but the much larger town of Damascus, where manners, as many believed, were much looser.⁴⁷ Zahir would not exempt anyone from his strict code of chastity and morality. He exploded in rage after discovering that one of his sons had tried to seduce a Christian woman. Zahir had to remind his son how this misconduct threatened his own honor (*sharaf*). He scolded the youth: "Have I made you a shepherd so that you would be a wolf?"[48] Still, he could recognize when he had overstepped or needed to show mercy and understanding. Toward the end of his life, he fell in love with a maiden from Nazareth. He asked her family for her hand and received their consent. While staying with his new wife, he happened to notice a young man who was hovering in the area from a distance. Not long afterward, Zahir apprehended him as he was secretly trying to leave the house. In the subsequent interrogation, the youth swore that he had done nothing improper. Pressed for more information, he finally admitted that Zahir's wife had been his beloved and that he had once hoped to marry her. Zahir sent the young man off with a warning not to tell anyone what had happened. He then went into the house and spoke with his wife, who also protested her innocence and further admitted that she was still in love with the young man. Recognizing that he had unwittingly walked into a love triangle, Zahir drew on his famous forbearance. He would divorce his wife and arrange for the two young lovers to be married, donating a patch of land and regular allowance to them.[49] He would not force himself on the woman; and since her lover had not behaved dishonorably, he would receive honorable treatment too, as long as he did not bring scandal to Zahir, who had not known the full truth about their relationship.

In stressing the positive moral qualities that Zahir represented—and would have to represent in any folk-telling of his career—we should not overlook the part of his character that was worldly, cunning, and downright ruthless. Pitiless revenge was the prerogative of the virile warrior. He should take it as quickly and decisively as possible and was free to spill as much blood as he pleased. After learning of the death of his grandson in battle against the Saqr bedouin, Zahir was so disconsolate that he gave himself up to wailing, weeping, and rending his clothes. The next day his grief turned to rage as he rode out with his men and unleashed retribution on the defeated tribesmen, hunting down stragglers and survivors and mercilessly killing them, even children and the elderly.[50] For other enemies, particularly powerful state officials, wilier tactics were advisable, and would demonstrate, against the odds, the daring and resourcefulness of the true hero. One of the tensest encounters of Zahir's career pitted him against Sulayman Paşa al-'Azm, governor of Damascus, who laid siege twice to Tiberius. On the second occasion, in 1743, one wrong turn of events could have easily toppled Zahir. He rescued himself primarily through intrigue. He and his brother Sa'd pretended to have a public quarrel. Sa'd stormed out of town and approached Sulayman's camp, where the governor graciously received him. It proved to be a fateful mistake. The governor invited Sa'd to the bathhouse, where the latter feigned an aversion to bathing, protesting that it was not the custom of his people. As witnesses later surmised, he was able to poison one of Sulayman's sherbets and slip away before the governor drank it and died that same afternoon.[51] With this devious stratagem, celebrated in later folklore, Zahir's clan had collectively outwitted the might of the Ottoman state.

Having followed several highlights from Zahir's career, we can now step back and try to place him on the social scale of the Old Regime. An urban sophisticate he was not, and never pretended to be. This lack of polish, however, was part of his appeal. Aloof from the ways of great towns like Damascus, Zahir represented, at least in the folk-telling, the honest virtues of bravery, probity, and generosity that oral folk culture had long treasured. Though neither learned nor refined, he kept up an unvarnished example of piety and dignity that was the main model of comportment in the small towns and villages where few members of polite society ever set foot. He respected religion and heeded the basic teachings of Islam, which is why his son 'Uthman, fond of wine, was so disappointing to him. He was eloquent and had such a love of poetry that he held his own unpretentious salons, which were hailed for their sedate and unblemished tone.[52] Within this rudimentary literary scene, the accent fell on simplicity of manners and entertainments. To visitors from the great towns, used to a more convivial tone, these gatherings would have seemed dull, insipid, and boorish. They had little trouble picking out the little solecisms and differences in etiquette that set the two cultural worlds apart. Mehmed Bey Abu'l-Dhahab, commander of the Egyptian invasion of Syria (1771), reflexively "felt disgust" when 'Ali, one of Zahir's sons, barged into his own salon. 'Ali was entirely too informal, first entering without seeking permission and then sitting with an overly relaxed posture. He did not recognize the more pronounced social hierarchy and elaborate manners of the Cairene elite and conducted himself "as if he were among his own people, like one of the bedouin, not in a royal salon (*majlis sultani*)."[53] What passed as reasonable and familiar in the countryside provoked only scorn among the polite set.

This plainer, bluffer style of self-presentation continued to thrive in small towns and villages and was by no means destined to go out of fashion. Across the nineteenth century, most of Ottoman society—which remained overwhelmingly rural—still had to make do with the cultural resources at its disposal. The martial virility identified with Zahir al-`Umar and other heroic warriors had lasting appeal and relevance. Only a few decades after Zahir's death, Süleyman Paşa "the Just" (r. 1804–19) became governor of Acre. By origin, he was a Georgian Mamluk who had entered the service of Ahmed Paşa al-Jazzar, who had, in 1775, taken Zahir's place in Acre. After the harsh rule of al-Jazzar, Süleyman won the gratitude of the peasantry for his clemency and moderation. He cancelled the onerous monopoly policy, which had placed the sale of export crops like cotton under the strict supervision of al-Jazzar's officials. And repulsed by al-Jazzar's brutality, he ended arbitrary confiscation and abolished the cruel tortures to which al-Jazzar had put so many of his prisoners, including some of his own unfortunate officials. Though not a native of Palestine, Süleyman became expert in its local politics.[54] Part of his success came from fitting himself into folk models of the just ruler, very much as Zahir had done earlier. "He hated tyranny, oppression, and aggression. He was courageous and had a strong heart which did not fear anything." At the same time, "his face was laughing, and he inclined towards leniency."[55] He practiced self-restraint, kept an orderly council, and adopted the pastimes of a proper warrior in his fondness for hunting and other physical games.[56]

These images of the heroic warrior were central to the political language of the countryside. The peasantry knew little of the Ottoman court. The sultan was a remote figure. Whatever praise bureaucrats and poets in the capital might lavish on dynastic power, and whatever they might say about individual rulers or officials, their debates created only the faintest echoes within the overwhelmingly local world of rural society. The state came to them in the guise of provincial administrators and tax-farmers; more common still was contact with low-level retainers and soldiers who dealt with matters of taxation and security when they were not pursuing the local feuds and stratagems of their patrons. Hence from the perspective of village and field, the exercise of power often looked very much like combat or some kind of martial exertion. But victory of arms was never tantamount to legitimacy, which had to be earned through demonstrations of justice, morality, and generosity. Though a mere villager from Burj al-Barajina, near Beirut, Yusuf al-Khuri attained celebrity as "one of the bravados" of Mt. Lebanon, which in the Ottoman imagination held an inexhaustible supply of sturdy warriors, fit for battle and accustomed to hardship.[57] Yusuf excelled in horsemanship, and was such a formidable figure on the battlefield, it was said, that he could drive off entire parties of attackers single-handedly. He had no sooner entered the service of Bashir al-Shihabi (r. 1789–1841), paramount notable of the Lebanese highlands, than he quickly made himself a trusted lieutenant. His appeal lay in his incorruptible sense of honor as much as his martial ardor and skill. "He was sociable and of good character, generous as an Arab, and never refused a beggar."[58] Thus the moral caliber of the ideal warrior had to match the daring exploits of gun and sword. One measure of character to which observers repeatedly returned was chivalry. Among the military commanders who found regular employment on Mt. Lebanon at the turn of the nineteenth century was Jirjis Baz, "a man renowned for nobility and moral rectitude, as well as for his chivalry and bravery." On the battlefield, he was "reckoned the equal of about five hundred cavaliers"; but equally admired were his "generosity and good nature."[59]

But can we assign such images entirely to the countryside? Consider the fate of Selim Ağa, one of the most trusted retainers of Ahmed Paşa al-Jazzar—at least until he became one of the ringleaders in a failed palace revolt (1789). He fled for his life. Abandoning his wife and daughter and all his household possessions, he settled in Istanbul. More fortunate than most of his fellow political outcasts, he found employment at the palace. "In view of his horsemanship, beauty, and intelligence, he gained great favor and advanced until he became the stirrup-holder (rakıbdar) of sultan Selim [III]."[60] Even at the end of the eighteenth century, the palace did not hide its admiration for a man of the sword who could embody such heroic poses. The ideals of manhood and valor would retain their luster across the society of the Old Regime.

The Urbane Warrior

In spite of these lingering attachments to older images of martial virtue, the political leadership of the Old Regime had begun to nurture a new self-conception that revolved around the arts of civility. By the eighteenth century, we can begin to measure this shift in sensibility in the lifestyle of the sultans themselves. Reduced to symbolic potentates, they had, since the late sixteenth century, ceased to receive administrative training as princes, and after ascending the throne, left the actual business of government to bureaucrats and soldiers. After Murad IV, the only sultan to accompany an army fully into battle was Mustafa II (r. 1695–1703), who presided over the Austrian rout of his troops at Zenta (1697).[61] Living in gilded confinement in the private quarters of the palace, sultans might still involve themselves in political affairs or throw their weight behind one faction or another, but the center of Ottoman government had, from the mid-seventeenth century onward, definitively moved to the Porte, where the grand vizier managed the day-to-day affairs of the empire. The palace now stood at the apex of a network of political households in which it was merely the wealthiest and most prestigious. Under Ahmed III (r. 1703–30), who returned the court permanently to Istanbul after several decades of residence in Edirne, the dynasty expressed its leadership increasingly through cultural patronage and royal pageantry, symbolized by the new pleasure palace, Sa'adabad, built on the northern shore of the Golden Horn at Kağıthane.

Although the Patrona Halil rebellion (1730) toppled Ahmed III from the throne and razed the complex at Sa'adabad, it did nothing to curtail the opulence of the royal family.[62] With all its glitter and spectacle, the court retained its role as the preeminent salon of the empire. Poets, musicians, and performers had long participated in private entertainments. Shorn of their military duties, the sultans could now turn to these aesthetic pursuits with few distractions. In the person of Selim III (r. 1789–1807), one can observe the full development of the sedentary sultan (fig. 4.1), so very different from the temperament for which Murad IV was famed. During Selim's youthful confinement in the palace, he passed the time in literary pursuits, reading dynastic histories and composing poetry. A man of refined tastes, he became a talented musician whose compositions remain among the earliest pieces of Ottoman court music that have survived in written form. As the young prince acquired an interest in affairs of state, his energies sought a bureaucratic, not a military, outlet. He conversed with high officials and even began a correspondence with the court of Louis XVI.[63] After taking the throne, he took an active interest in intellectual life and liked to stage religious debates among scholars during the month of Ramadan.[64] He governed as a highly engaged bureaucrat, presiding regularly over councils of state and scribbling frequent orders and notations into the margins of official reports.

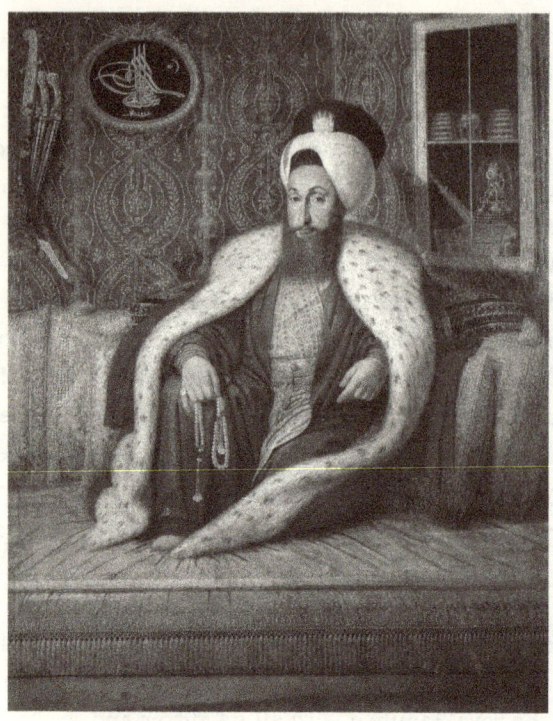

FIGURE 4.1. Portrait of Selim III (r. 1789–1807) by Konstantin Kapıdağlı, a Greek painter at the Ottoman court. A tragic figure, Selim III launched the New Order, the Ottoman Empire's first attempt at large-scale military and administrative modernization, only to be overthrown and murdered by the Janissaries and their allies. His pose here epitomizes the transformation of Ottoman sultans into the courtly equivalent of sedentary urban gentlemen by the late eighteenth century. SOURCE: Topkapı Palace Museum.

That the last sultan of the eighteenth century should assume such a bureaucratic manner was utterly befitting a state in which the most powerful officials increasingly rose from the bureaucracy. After 1700, the chanceries became the main recruiting ground for grand viziers as Ottoman statecraft came to depend more on diplomacy than arms, a strategy made unavoidable by ebbing Ottoman military fortunes.[65] Valor on the field of battle was therefore not a likely distinction for members of the scribal service. They instead presented themselves as cultivated gentlemen who had polished manners suitable for any salon. Across the length and breadth of the empire, there were at most two thousand of them (leaving the Ottoman domains with a relatively low ratio of bureaucrats to imperial subjects for the eighteenth-century world).[66] In cultural outlook, they were not much different from the ulama, a few of whom might enter bureaucratic careers themselves. Their schooling followed the same curriculum; and if they applied themselves, they might very well engage in advanced scholarship and win recognition for their attainments in learning and literature. At the summit of the administration, the grand vizier Ragıb Mehmed Paşa (d. 1763) had risen from the scribal service and could plausibly pose as a man of learning himself. He had many friends within the religious establishment and could comfortably debate with scholars.[67] One chief scribe, Mustafa Efendi (d. 1749), was a master of etiquette and conversation. He impressed the Syrian and Egyptian scholars with whom he comfortably chatted in formal Arabic.[68] Still other bureaucrats shone for their literary talents. Among the best known was Mustafa Sami Arpaeminizade (d. 1734), a versatile administrator who produced a collection of highly regarded poetry and served toward the end of his life as court historian.[69]

The vast majority of bureaucrats, though, were humble scribes who worked in the capital and served in the financial bureaus, where they handled tax receipts and other correspondence. They learned their trade in an almost artisanal milieu, having been initiated as young apprentices into the intricacies of reading and drawing up documents.[70] As they gained command of different scripts, they became the chief adepts in the art of calligraphy, which was the calling card of their profession.[71] Proficiency was taken as a sign of talent and good breeding and could open doors. Rising to governor of Bosnia, Ismail Paşa (d. 1785) was born in Istanbul, the son of a tradesman. As a young man, he entered Galatasaray, then a palace school (*mekteb*), and began working as a scribe. He excelled and came to the attention of the sultan himself, who praised his fine script. His ascent within the imperial service was thereafter assured.[72]

As bureaucrats gained prominence inside the state, so too did their models of deportment. Officials who could not live up to them became more glaring in their deficiencies. Since many viziers and military commanders remained poorly educated or downright illiterate, the social judgments against them were hardening. Illiteracy, in particular, could create embarrassing situations. Having arrived in Cairo as the new governor (1697), Hasan Paşa tried unsuccessfully to hide this blemish. Sitting in front of the local advisory council (*divan*), he vainly pretended to inspect the account books.⁷³ In 1703, Kiblelizade Ali Bey, having recently returned to Istanbul, got into trouble for bringing back "a strange almanac" from Egypt. Probably used for astrology, it came to the attention of the *şeyhülislam*, who had him condemned to death for its contents. That Ali Bey was utterly illiterate and needed others to read and explain the manuscript, which he may still not have understood, proved no defense.⁷⁴ So power was not everything. Lack of refinement and education, whether perceived or demonstrated through blunders and solecisms, tended to undermine the projection of status and authority.⁷⁵

By the eighteenth century, the attributes of the urban gentleman were increasingly in demand, precisely because they smoothed the way through elite circles. Those who could move comfortably among the educated and participate in learned salons would immediately turn heads and acquire extra social cachet. Among these glad-handing sophisticates was Mustafa al-Arna'ut (d. 1813), a mamluk at the bey's court in Tunis. Lauded for his impeccable manners, he became a trusted emissary who handled delicate missions to Istanbul and European capitals.⁷⁶ In Istanbul, even a mid-level translator like Bogos Sepastyan, right-hand man to the Armenian financier Manuk Mirzayan (d. 1817), could make a small splash. An expert performer on the *keman* (a stringed instrument), he became a favorite of salons in the capital.⁷⁷ He compared favorably with Alemdar Mustafa Paşa, patron of his own patron Mirzayan. From the vantage point of the refined and educated, Alemdar would always remain an outsider. Though climbing to the rank of grand vizier, he never shook off the damning impression that he was little more than a rough soldier, an upstart from the Balkans who was notorious for his uncouth language and hair-trigger temper.⁷⁸ In one memorable scene (1808), Alemdar and his men discovered the body of Selim III, whom they had come to restore to the throne. The deposed sultan had fallen victim to the machinations of his brother, Mustafa IV (r. 1807–8), who was desperately trying to cling to power. Outraged by the treachery, Alemdar "began to growl like a wounded lion. He let loose terrible screams, shouted, and roared like a thunderhead."⁷⁹ Fits of unbridled ferocity had become downright unseemly and were treated as ever more damaging to the dignity attached to the highest offices of state. Officialdom had, in effect, adjusted itself to a different social milieu. As the administration and economy of the empire became more elaborate and complex, so too did manners. Social expectations correspondingly rose. Ottoman officials sought to demonstrate social finesse, now recognized as an absolute asset. In responding to these incentives, senior officials and soldiers were more likely to disdain conduct deemed vulgar or brutish. There may have been no worse an offender than the brother of Kaid Ağa (d. 1801), an Egyptian emir. Cruel and sadistic, the brother was known to turn his sword on donkeys for sport, decapitating them, he boasted, with a single blow.[80] His biographer holds him up as a morally defective figure, utterly wicked and repulsive. By the eighteenth century, such judgments were exerting a stronger hold over the military and administrative leadership, who now aspired openly to urbanity. Those who ignored these social judgments left themselves diminished in the sight of urban society.

Under the Old Regime, the towns were thus better able to remake the military elite in the image of urban notables. In the biographical dictionaries written by members of the religious establishment, recognition of learning and education was handed down as a great compliment to military officials and soldiers. A vizier who briefly held the post of grand admiral, Ratib Ahmed Paşa (d. 1756/57) nonetheless distinguished himself as a poet who was "famous among the viziers for his knowledge and virtue."[81] More remarkable was Arabacılar Şeyhi İbrahim Efendi (d. 1775), head of the wagon-drivers (*arabacılar*) in the Ottoman army. More than a soldier, he was a talented scholar who first studied the Qur'an and then went on to compile an addendum (*zeyl*) to the famous seventeenth-century index of Islamic manuscripts, *Kashf al-Zunun*, which would have been a sterling feat for any member of the religious establishment.[82] Among the training grounds for such figures were the political households that leading officials of state had, since the late sixteenth century, been forming directly on the model of the palace. And like the imperial household itself, these "pasha households" might very well sponsor the education of promising recruits, grooming them both as candidates for state office and as future clients in their own political networks. Even in the eighteenth century, many officials were slaves by origin, and owed their social ascent to this training and acculturation. To take one such career: Süleyman Feyzi Paşa, a Georgian slave, climbed through the Ottoman service to the rank of vizier and was serving as governor of Aleppo at the time of his death in 1794. His education was so thorough that he had mastered Arabic, Persian, and Turkish. Having received this cultural formation, he naturally took care to oversee the daily instruction of his closest protégés.[83]

By the eighteenth century, what is most striking is that, as military households entrenched themselves across the empire, the same cultural aspirations took root everywhere. Military grandees now sought, very much like Ottoman pashas, to educate subordinates. In Cairo, İbrahim Kethüda al-Barkawi (d. 1784) was one of the military commanders who distinguished himself for his learning and passion for buying books. He made sure that his own mamluks could properly read and recite the Qur'an, and that they had studied literature.[84] Another Egyptian officer, Emir Ridvan (d. 1803), earned his own flattering portrait. A brave soldier, he could nonetheless read and write. More to the point, he positively enjoyed the company of jurists, held discussions with them, and showed an "inclination" toward them. His biographer presents him almost in the image of an exemplary scholar: dignified, modest, eloquent, even-tempered.[85] Along distant Ottoman frontiers, where governors founded dynasties of slave-soldiers, they built political households that fostered the same training and acculturation of top recruits. The last Georgian mamluk to serve as governor of Baghdad, Daud Paşa (r. 1816-31) had received an extensive education under his patron, Süleyman the Great (r. 1780-1802), who had him instructed in both the military and literary arts. Daud Paşa was so accomplished that, like an expert poet, he wrote and spoke with ease in "the three languages" of the curriculum: Arabic, Persian, and Turkish.[86] In Tunis, too, the beys (hereditary governors) of the Husaynid dynasty, founded in 1705 by a Janissary officer, routinely saw to the education of their mamluks.[87] In the profiles of these officials, and in the tendency of military households, like those of Egypt, Iraq, and Tunisia to educate young retainers, we can detect the diffusion of an imperial model of deportment that stressed civility and politesse.

Some soldiers took learning so deeply to heart that they switched career paths. Sadiq ibn al-Nashif (d. 1732) started his career as a soldier in Damascus. He followed his father and grandfather into the local bureaucracy as inspector of local religious endowments (*awqaf*) and later took charge of the collection of the religion tax levied on non-Muslims (*cizye*). He made a name for himself as a pious man, joined the Khalwati Sufi order, and twice led the pilgrimage caravan (as *serdar*) to the Holy Cities. Contemporaries saluted his character. He was sagacious and restrained; and like the most principled scholars, he resisted the blandishments of the powerful and therefore refrained from mixing more than was necessary with officials.[88] His was a rapid reinvention of the self. More likely was a switch that would play out in slow motion over two or three generations.[89] Mustafa al-Tarzi (d. 1747) was the son of an imperial Janissary posted to Damascus. His older brother returned to Istanbul and lost all his wealth, whereas Mustafa stayed in Damascus and remade himself as a scholar and poet.[90] Son of a cavalryman (*sipahi*) who served in Damascus, Muhammad al-Jawish (d. 1777/78) showed an early inclination for religious study and became a highly respected scholar.[91] All families of incoming officials and soldiers felt, to some degree, the allure of learning. Placing sons and grandsons in the religious establishment conferred the ultimate seal of respectability and assured their full integration into local society.

This tendency of provincial officials and soldiers to move into more "civil" professions found an easier path in the bureaucracy. Turning their back on campaigns and battlefields, the sons and grandsons of such families took refuge amid the dusty ledgers of state chanceries. Very different from Amir Qanbaq, whom we met earlier cutting off the head of the Druze chieftain Fakhr al-Din, was his son Hasan al-Daftari (d. 1694/95), who never wielded a sword. Raised in Hama, Hasan began his studies at a young age. After the death of his father, family connections allowed him to serve in the palace and central bureaucracy in Istanbul. He then returned to Syria and finished his career as provincial treasurer of Damascus, where his own son also served in the same post.[92] The historian Naima (d. 1716) followed much the same path, departing from it only in forsaking his provincial origins altogether. Born and bred in Aleppo, where his father was the Janissary commander of the citadel, he chose a bureaucratic career that removed him permanently to the capital.[93]

Unlike Naima, many bureaucrats making the move directly from a "military" background were never quite able to shake off the values and attachments of the soldierly milieu. Earning a backhanded compliment was Salih Efendi (d. 1790), secretary to an artillery unit in Cairo, who gained much attention simply for his love of reading. His real talent, fitting for a scribe, was calligraphy. So adept was his penmanship that he became widely acknowledged as one of the experts in this field.[94] Bringing together martial and bureaucratic virtues was Ali Agha, a treasury scribe in Damascus who was much beloved "because of his good character and kind dealings with all." He delighted the chronicler Mikha'il Mishaqa, who called him (1831) "one of those robust bravados who was formidable with the sword and the pen and could wield his left hand as well as his right. I saw him do it with my own eyes when I asked him to show me, and he was kind enough to do it. He split a reed with a blow of the sword with each hand and wrote a line in beautiful script, half with his right hand and half with his left."[95] As bureaucratic posts passed to later generations, these athletic poses quickly disappeared.

The most ambitious bureaucrats were never content with merely keeping accounts. They worked at turning their skill with the pen into a mark of social distinction. An outgrowth of their official duties, the art of calligraphy was the most obvious outlet. But in vying to prove their talents, they reserved their deepest passion for literature—which meant, above all, poetry. It was the main channel of expression for all educated gentlemen and far overshadowed the other literary arts. Most of its practitioners, of course, were members of the religious establishment, who were almost synonymous with literate society itself. As the biographical dictionaries from the period amply confirm, even very staid scholars would learn and compose verse. Poetic skill won the approbation of peers and flaunted the verbal mastery to which all educated men aspired. Taking this passion to the extreme was 'Abd al-Latif al-Kurani (d. 1737/8), head scribe at the main courthouse of Aleppo. He annoyed colleagues by refusing to do any work, preferring to stay at home and compose poetry.[96]

But poetry was more than a private avocation. It was redolent of a broader set of dispositions that urban culture associated with civility itself. Poetic learning and appreciation thus served as a testament to good breeding and rendered the urban gentleman ever fitter for genteel sociability. Officials were becoming more eager to acquire this sheen. The Damascene mufti and biographer Muhammad Khalil al-Muradi praised one eighteenth-century Ottoman vizier for having a flair for poetry. It was not accidental, he intimated, that these literary gifts accompanied a refined and pious character which all his peers acknowledged.[97] Hence men of state who wished to pass as sophisticated townsmen hoped to show off their literary talent and taste. Surpassing this exacting standard was 'Ali al-Daftari (d. 1740), who rose through the Ottoman bureaucratic ranks, first in Homs and then Istanbul. A political casualty of the "Edirne Incident" (1703), he was sent away to Damascus as head of the provincial treasury. He was devoted to learning, excelled at conversation, and charmed company with his flawless bearing, which extended not only to the recitation of poetry but expertise in music as well.⁹⁸ The social esteem attached to this range of talents acted as a spur to further emulation among soldiers and scribes.⁹⁹ The commander of the local Janissary faction (*yerliyya*) in Damascus was Darwish Ağa (d. 1758), who, even amid the tumult of local politics, garnered tributes as a perfectly well-mannered gentleman. The capstone to his reputation was skill in composing poetry in Turkish and Persian.¹⁰⁰

The same social tides flowed across the towns of the empire, from the capital to the provinces. More officials sought to become poets, or at least professed admiration for this ideal. Such figures had long turned up in the capital, whose immense patronage attracted literary talents of every description.¹⁰¹ Far more striking, especially in the provinces, was the infiltration of soldiers into the honor roll of poets. Some were the scions of local military families who had become assimilated over several generations into the social elite; others had abandoned their military careers, acquired learning, and entered literary circles. They appear rarely in the sixteenth century, and become more noticeable by the seventeenth, as the Ottoman army began to swell and soldiers embedded themselves in urban life.¹⁰² With each generation, more of them were likely to assume the airs and lifestyle of their fellow townsmen.

No one fits this portrait of social and cultural mobility better than the poet Amir Manjak (d. 1670/71). Stationed in Damascus, his father had been a soldier who ascended the ranks and entered the provincial bureaucracy, ultimately attaining the post of provincial treasurer.¹⁰³ This success was not repeated in the next generation. After his father's death, Amir Manjak soon squandered his inheritance and set out for Istanbul to rescue his fortunes. He languished for a time, until his poetry came to the attention of the sultan, who summoned him for a personal recital. He never looked back after this triumph, which allowed him to return as a literary star, thereafter acclaimed in his hometown as the greatest poet of his generation.¹⁰⁴ His biographer was Muhammad Amin al-Muhibbi (1651–1699), a scholar who was himself a leading Damascene poet. Years after Amir Manjak's death, al-Muhibbi remembered how the old poet would sometimes emerge from his house, which he rarely left late in life, and visit his father. He personally oversaw al-Muhibbi's literary education, making him memorize and explicate poems and obscure words, the latter of which were the true test of every literary expert. Amir Manjak had thus acquired remarkable fame and had an open invitation into the homes of the educated elite, who were happy to receive him. A commander (*amir*) only in name, he had transcended the soldierly origins of his family and entered the rarefied heights of literary celebrity.

By the eighteenth century, the soldier-poet had become a familiar figure in urban society. Some left the barracks altogether and slowly migrated to other professions. One of Amir Manjak's associates, Muhammad Efendi al-Sinti (d. 1702/3), was hailed as "one of the amirs of the sword and pen" and won a teaching position at a local religious school.[105] In Damascus alone, others followed this path.[106] But abandoning a military career was not a prerequisite for literary fame. Scion of a line of soldiers and provincial administrators, and himself a member of the local Janissary barracks (*yerliyya*), Ahmad al-Kiwani (d. 1759) became the most celebrated Damascene poet of his generation, equally feted for his mastery of calligraphy and composition. He used to hold literary sessions with fellow poets at his shop in Suq al-Darwishiyya, where he also pursued an infatuation with chess.[107] ʿAbd al-Razzaq al-Jundi (d. 1775), another talented poet, hailed from a line of bedouin leaders. His father had entered Ottoman service at the behest of the ʿAzm family, who supplied many of the governors of Damascus in the eighteenth century. His versifying did not keep him from active duty as commander of a desert fort between Homs and Hama in central Syria. He ended his days at the hands of bedouin raiders, who defeated his small detachment and then cruelly executed him.[108]

The cultivation of literary tastes was part of a broader pursuit of refinement and connoisseurship through which the urbane warrior sought entry into the smart set. Completing the package was an aptitude for repartee and banter, which proved that one really belonged with distinguished company in salons. İsmail Paşa (d. 1780), governor of Egypt, was recognized for his sophistication. A botched operation had deformed his neck, leaving it twisted. His chin rested on his chest, and he could turn his head only by turning his entire body. All observers nonetheless hailed him as a wise official of irreproachable character. Further confirming this good opinion was his lively disposition and skill in conversation.[109] More soldiers craved this social cachet and came to value it as integral to the life of leisure and comfort that they were now more openly emulating. The leaders of the military households in Cairo gathered the equivalent of their own salons. Mehmed Ağa al-Barudi (d. 1791), a powerful mamluk, sought out boon companions with whom he could pass the night, drinking wine and making jokes and interesting conversation.[110] More unpredictable was the conversation of Ahmed Kethüda (d. 1787). He became a favorite guest of the Egyptian warlord Mehmed Bey Abu'l-Dhahab, with whom he used to chat away the evening hours. His trademark banter was to switch suddenly between serious topics and lighthearted joking. His mercurial wit so disconcerted contemporaries in Cairo that they branded him "the crazy one" (al-majnun). His mixing of high and low themes was a version of the word games and love of diversion that shone in the best salons of the empire. Ahmed Kethüda's only fault was to take this eclecticism to an idiosyncratic extreme.[111] Most essential to social gatherings was wit. Participants liked to see minds at play, able to give and take in the heat of verbal exchange. A guest might know many anecdotes and try to tell them; but if he lacked the requisite skill to charm and entertain, the judgment of leading salonistes could be unsparing. This crushing verdict was the fate of Osman Ağa al-Jalfi (d. 1791), a powerful Janissary officer who collected books and made himself agreeable in polite society. He knew many wondrous stories and loved to introduce them into conversation. His biographer still found him "somewhat dim-witted" and very much out of his depth in learned company.[112]

Intensified contact with salon culture was one factor in the taming of "military" manners. Accelerating this shift in self-presentation was the military embrace of urban leisure culture. A new social figure arrived on the scene: the warrior and bureaucrat who lived as a bon vivant. The vibrancy of eighteenth-century Ottoman towns easily accommodated this lifestyle. Wherever there were substantial military barracks, officers entrenched themselves in local politics and trade, while their men infiltrated the guilds, and one way or another, earned a living in the marketplace. This integration into the urban economy, which dated at least as far back as the seventeenth century, nurtured military acculturation to the towns. The rank-and-file settled down, married, and had families. Their officers took their place among the urban notables and acquired the same tastes and pastimes as the rest of the social elite. They turned their backs willingly on older customs that no longer seemed consonant with their station or self-image. In 1743, Osman Bey Dhu'l-Faqar invited the incoming governor of Egypt to a banquet at his mansion. The original protocol had required the leading amirs of Cairo to construct pavilions in open fields near the Nile.[113] The welcome now became a more domesticated affair, away from the tents and canopies redolent of campaigning on distant frontiers. By the eighteenth century, the leading officers had created their own households, furnished themselves with finely appareled mansions, and would now insist on more sedentary gestures, as befitted their new social models.

Having amassed fortunes from trade and tax-farming, military notables did not deny themselves the sumptuous lifestyle that beckoned to them. No pleasure was too delicate or costly to be refused. In Cairo, İbrahim Bey Abu'l-Shanab (d. 1718), an otherwise fearsome officer, hired his own musicians who played at home in his mansion. They were one of his great consolations. When he heard of the dismissal of a governor who had been plotting his downfall (1707), he was so elated that he had them strike up a tune, even though it was close to dawn.[114] Such immediate access to music, available at the merest whim, was one of the most extravagant status symbols that an Ottoman grandee could seek. Head of the provincial treasury in Damascus, ʿAbd al-Muʿti al-Falaqansi (d. 1711) accumulated great wealth, built a bathhouse near the Umayyad Mosque, and constructed a mansion for himself. Not content with stocking his home with fine food, he kept a band permanently on staff. They played constantly throughout the day for his amusement and entertained the sparkling salons that he was so fond of organizing. Townspeople remembered him as a supremely cultivated host, who never lost his temper and addressed everyone in the same poised manner, whether he was calm or secretly enraged. These epicurean pastimes were marred only by the recurring headaches that no doctor could cure.[115] At a time when there were very few professional musicians at work, hiring a personal band was obviously an extreme luxury. Only the military bands (*mehter*) kept by the highest-ranking dignitaries like governors were comparable (fig. 4.2).[116] The one alternative to hiring musicians was for households to make their own music. Even the powerful and wealthy were not averse to home entertainment for guests. Elite women, normally barred from formal gatherings, might participate as well. In eighteenth-century Cairo, a few were known to sing for "select company," though always from behind a screen.[117]

Having embraced the delights of urban culture, officials and soldiers did not temper their appetites. If others objected to their high living, they gave no hint of caring. In Istanbul, the grand vizier Alemdar Mustafa Paşa, a native son of the small Danubian town of Ruse, was accused (1808) of drinking too much. Enemies whispered that he had uncertain morals and lived like a voluptuary.[118] These charges became something of a trope as the

FIGURE 4.2. Depiction of a military band (*mehter*) by Abdülcelil Levni, an Ottoman court artist. Here a band is playing as part of a grand circumcision festival thrown in 1720 by Ahmed III (r. 1703–30) for his sons. Besides the sultan, only the highest officials of state would have the prerogative of keeping their own military band, typically composed of horns and percussion.

SOURCE: Topkapı Palace Museum.

finery and ease of many officials helped to stimulate invidious gossip that condemned them as overly fond of worldly diversions and insufficiently attentive to religion.[119] One decree issued by the Porte (1808) openly blamed the craze for extravagant fashions not only on women, who frequently bore the brunt of official ire, but on the reckless spending of officials and soldiers (*askeri taife*), none of whom could restrain their love of luxury.[120] In Cairo, the powerful emir Ridvan Kethüda al-Jalfi (d. 1755) entirely lived up to this prodigal image. Though a connoisseur of poetry, he became better known for a carefree lifestyle in which he abandoned himself to the pursuit of pleasure in his mansion at Azbakiyya Pond, where many leading officers built their homes. He caroused, it was said, with young women and men alike, and drank wine without the least compunction. So unabashed was his cultivation of these hedonistic pastimes that, as the gossip of Cairo would have it, he forbade the police from suppressing prostitution, pederasty, and alcohol.[121]

By the eighteenth century, the taste for the good life pervaded the entire political establishment and reached into the most unlikely quarters. The filaments of the Ottoman fiscal system extended far into the countryside, generated new wealth, and quickly seduced whomever they touched with the possibilities of consumer culture. The upwardly mobile quickly grasped these opportunities. Even if they made their careers far from the main administrative centers, they sought grander lifestyles. Among the most incongruous beneficiaries was Humam al-Hawwari (d. 1769/70), chief bedouin shaykh of Upper Egypt. He had grown enormously wealthy as a tax-farmer, and managed extensive sugar and date estates. He could easily have stridden through polite society in Cairo. Suave and politic, he never forgot a name and face, and was famous for his hospitality to travelers. People sought him out for mediation and brought petitions to the public audiences that he regularly held. A certain unease began to overcome him. While receiving guests, he made sure to have a small container of rose water at his side. Whenever a peasant or someone "uncouth" approached, he would afterward daub a cotton swab and wipe his eyes so as to repel any noxious odors.[122] His delicate manners were a far cry from the mobile lifestyle of horseback and tent known by his forbears. His spectacular fortune testifies not only to the economic possibilities opened up by state office but to the spread of a new set of indolent attitudes that affluence encouraged and flattered.

We might even say that officials and soldiers were becoming more self-conscious. They worried about looking awkward and out of place, or worse still, rustic and ill-bred. In Cairo, Salih Bey (d. 1768), an experienced officer praised for his dignity and modesty, became a somewhat awkward practitioner of what Erving Goffman famously called "impression management." One of his front teeth was missing, and whenever he spoke, he put a finger in his mouth to hide the gap. So intense was his embarrassment that the gesture became something of a tic.[123] The gruff indifference of the battle-hardened warrior, scarred and perhaps disfigured in combat, had given way to the vanity and primping of the dandy. Blemishes and other unsightly features were to be covered up. The urbane warrior would make himself handsome, pleasing, debonair.

So far had this "domestication" of officials and soldiers proceeded that many had grown slack or downright unqualified in the use of arms. Many Janissaries drew salaries but no longer reported for campaigning or could hardly be mustered at all. They were now townsmen, absorbed in their own affairs and committed to defending their own interests. Particularly by the eighteenth century, the weapons of many soldiers were more likely to be deployed in factional rivalries on the streets of Ottoman towns than along the frontier against the sultan's enemies. Training and discipline had become lax. In Cairo, one governor called (1669) for the restoration of the old custom of launching decorated boats, which would carry parties of notables on the occasion of the Nile flood. Part of the entertainment had consisted of games of horsemanship and lance-throwing (*cirit*). He was informed that the spectacle had fallen into disuse for "years" because the exercise was "meaningless in these days."[124] The lapsing of the festival carried a double significance. It revealed a decline in military training among much of the rank-and-file, albeit with a weapon that mattered more on medieval battlefields than those of the seventeenth century. More ominously for Ottoman arms, it also exposed urban "soldiers" as shopkeepers more than warriors. Most had sedentary lives.[125] In eighteenth-century Aleppo, where soldiers were no more assiduous about riding and drilling, many members of local units were unprepared for the rigors of campaigning. In their daily routines and inclinations, they were indistinguishable from other townsmen. Only core regiments, who regularly patrolled and saw combat, would bother with military exercises. In 1824, one of these competitions claimed the life of the new Janissary commander in Aleppo, Mehmed Ağa ibn al-Qattan, who was accidentally killed in a lance-throwing competition.[126]

As the prospect of combat receded, except perhaps in local engagements, officers cultivated an ostentatious fondness for hunting. Murad Bey, half of the duumvirate who effectively ruled Ottoman Egypt at the end of the eighteenth century, whiled away his days at a pleasure palace in Giza, across the Nile from Cairo. He spent much of his time hunting, which was his favorite pastime.[127] These sporting fashions were for play, and now functioned as little more than a ceremonial relic of an older warrior ethic.[128] Were they perhaps taking their cues from the palace? By the early eighteenth century, the frequency of royal hunting parties had begun to decline as well.[129] The hunt no longer held the same appeal or relevance for sultans, who had withdrawn completely from active campaigning. For their officers, too, hunting was no longer preparation for battle. Especially in the towns, it had merely become a pastime for the well-to-do. Stripped of its original purpose, it gained a second life as a kind of genteel status symbol. By the early nineteenth century, any townsman of modest means might play the part of a seasoned hunter. In Aleppo, the schoolteacher Na'um Bakhkhash (d. 1875)—whom we only know about because of the chance survival of his diary—regularly ventured into the nearby gardens with his gun.[130] The advent of such figures, who would become more numerous in the following generations, heralded the first tentative appearance of the modern sportsman.

Conclusion: The New Urban Gentleman

If we adopt a more global framework for the questions that we have been pursuing, multiple parallels immediately spring up. In the sedentary tastes of grandees like Murad Bey, who might hunt but much preferred their domestic amusements, we find a social figure who had become far more common by the eighteenth century. One might think first of Louis XIV's domestication of French nobles at Versailles.[131] A few of them still served in the military; most lived at the palace and passed their time as polite courtiers. A more compelling parallel is the fate of Qing bannermen, most of whom, after the initial Qing conquest of China during the 1640s, settled into local garrisons away from the frontiers.[132] Within decades came the same murmuring from Chinese commentators that one could easily recognize from Ottoman sources. The bannermen were getting soft and losing their martial ardor. Civilian outsiders were infiltrating their ranks. They were succumbing, in short, to the temptations of urban life and consumer comforts. In Japan, the samurai had virtually completed, by 1700 or so, their own wholesale transformation along the same lines. From a warrior status group, ready for battle, they had eased into their new role as bureaucrats and literati.[133] They were now trend-setters and taste-makers in one of the most commercialized societies of the early modern world. We might think, too, of late eighteenth-century India. The pajama-clad operatives of the East India Company did not flinch from indulging their own tastes in luxury and comfort.[134] Though merchants by origin, the most successful had by necessity become military commanders as the EIC evolved from a mere trading company into a fiscal-military state in its own right by the 1770s. Despite their fabulous wealth, the officers of the company met with the scorn and indignation of British society. The corrupt and dissolute "nabob" would become an invidious refrain in British politics.

In all these different cases, we are not taking stock of some conscious state policy. It was not simply, as the great sociologist Norbert Elias would have it, the outward and downward diffusion of politesse from the great courts to their aristocracies, who then transmitted this social code to other sectors of society. Nor was it, as he also maintained, an internalized bodily discipline, driven by a more alert sense of shame and disgust. With all his talk of the muting of bodily urges and instincts, we might say that Elias's views are entirely too bourgeois for the early modern world. They smack of the anxieties of the twentieth century, racked by the searing experiences of two world wars. The advance of civility, then, did not inevitably lead to festering neuroses. Instead of narrowly conceptualizing it as the interiorization of self-denial, we would do better to recognize it as something more appealing: a kind of seduction. It held out the promise of pleasure and refinement, in both hedonistic and aesthetic forms.

Perhaps the question of civility looked different for the populations of northwest and central Europe—the implicit standard for Elias—because large-scale urbanization was so recent in the history of those regions. Until early modern times, its urban culture had been comparatively weak, frail, and stunted.[135] Other parts of Eurasia had a much longer experience with urbanity. In places like the Ottoman Empire, a deeply rooted urban culture extended back to medieval times, and for that matter to antiquity. Notions of civility were already well developed. For the Ottomans, and most other Eurasian societies, the "early modern" centuries had a different significance. They opened up the pursuit of new forms of everyday pleasure and recreation to more and more townspeople. Viewed in this broader Eurasian perspective, we should learn to recognize the advance not so much of repression and self-regulation but of further sensual liberation and refinement.

FIVE
HONORABLE MANNERS

Hakkı Efendi, a Sufi from nineteenth-century Trabzon, once entered a coffeehouse and found a certain Kazancızade Ahmed Ağa. He immediately swore at him, declaring, "I won't sit while this son-of-a-bitch is here!" (*Bu köpek oğlu köpek burada iken oturamam!*), and then bolted from the coffeehouse. Stunned and infuriated, Ahmed Ağa later went out and tried to find the Sufi, but had no luck. That same night, three times in succession, he had the same dream, in which Hakkı Efendi rode on a horse as passersby kissed his hands and feet. The next day he sought out the Sufi and found him at a coffeehouse. Wishing to patch up their differences, he tried to kiss his hand. Hakkı Efendi relented and forgave him. He spoke soothingly to the young man, explaining how he had not actually called him a "son-of-a-bitch" the previous day. His true words, he assured him, were much tamer: "son-of-a-belly" (*göbek oğlu göbek*).[1] Hakkı Efendi, we gather, would have preferred that everyone forget the earlier scene, which was completely unbecoming a man of his status. It was bad enough to stomp and shout. He had gone further and uttered coarse insults that one might hear from ordinary townspeople on the street.

Such incidents might seem like little more than a momentary breach of manners from someone who knew (or ought to know) better. But at the height of his fury, Hakkı Efendi clearly thought that his victim was getting what he deserved. The vulgar taunt came a little too readily to his lips, as if he had an ample stock of insults at hand and knew quite well how to sling them. The scene reveals him not so much "forgetting" who he was as invoking a parallel etiquette that might sometimes override the social dignity expected of scholars. In other words, politesse was not the only set of manners that Ottoman society recognized. Operating alongside it was a separate code that expressed itself through notions of honor. Neither urban nor rural, nor confined to any single social group, it came into play whenever people sought to protect reputation, family, or property. But just like the code of politesse, this second set of manners was hardly egalitarian. Some had (or claimed) more status than others; they therefore had more honor to protect (or assert).

The two sets of manners proved—in practice, if not in theory or spirit—functionally compatible. At the top of the social order, members of the social elite certainly acted as if they saw no contradiction between them. Brazen challenges to honor, they accepted, might require answers that violated the rules of polite comportment. In these moments, reputational self-defense would take precedence and authorize a loss of self-control—or rather, as was often the case, a deliberate outburst that was regarded as legitimate and justified.[2] If the threat to honor were severe enough, it could lead to full-blown physical violence. Committing such violence was not necessarily a failure of character; it was, rather, the last resort for dealing with unendurable provocations that could not be ignored. This veering between different ideals of conduct helps to explain the reaction of one French traveler, to whom Ottoman sentiments seemed "extreme."[3]

To better shield themselves from the uncouth and impertinent, those in Ottoman society who possessed the most honor—the wealthy, the powerful, scions of prestigious lineages—resorted to various forms of ceremonial self-defense. They sought to maintain a certain social distance, surround themselves with servants and other loyal subordinates, and reinforce a constant deference to social hierarchy. This communication of status through speech, gesture, and space pervaded everyday social exchange and constituted a kind of public etiquette that had as much to do with the history of manners as the cultivation of politesse.

The Limits of Self-Restraint

No social group reveals the tension between polite and honorable manners better than members of the religious establishment. Not merely the custodians of religious law and teaching, they presented themselves—and were expected to present themselves—as the very models of urbanity that others should emulate. Ranking among their most cherished ideals was a combination of emotional self-government and imperturbable poise. These virtues came together in a biographical tribute to Kasımzade Efendi (d. 1718), a leading Sufi in Istanbul, whose "silence and serenity" (*samt u sükut*) were taken as the external projection of an inward equanimity and spiritual grace.[4] Creating much the same impression was Husayn al-Muradi (d. 1774), mufti of Damascus, who won admiration in learned circles for his unwavering self-control, mildness, and kindness, which were the very portrait of a proper gentleman.[5] Scholars were aware of the difficulties in practicing this calm self-mastery. Others, more loosely bound to the norms of etiquette or altogether vulgar and rude, might frequently test them. But they should never willingly sacrifice this tranquil and composed demeanor. In his etiquette manual, Sünbülzade Vehbi recommended a cheerful forbearance: "Even if you would silence your enemy, strive to deal with him amiably."[6]

And yet this carefully cultivated veneer of civility might unexpectedly shatter and give way to sudden emotional convulsions. Like other townsmen, members of the religious establishment had their own honor and dignity to defend and were prey to sensitivities about their public reputation and good name. Insults had to be answered. Polite words, though always the ideal, might abruptly dissolve into tirades. To consider it from another perspective: their collective image as the guardians of Islamic tradition did not insulate them from the pull of other values and norms.[7] They were fully immersed in the wider culture around them, of which religion represented only one strand and did not necessarily serve as the preeminent source of guidance for all or even most social occasions.

These worldly entanglements were most obvious among the religious notables—that is, the leaders of the religious establishment, many of whom were officeholders and therefore schemed and bargained like other men of state. In asserting their authority, they might easily turn to the same dramatic displays of pique and wounded honor as any other official. The political character of religious posts helps to explain how, in 1774, the head of the Ottoman Muslim religious establishment (*şeyhülislam*) created an unseemly spectacle at the grand vizier's tent, where he had flown into a rage after one of his clients was denied an appointment. So deeply shaken was his normal self-possession that he barged out of the interview without his shoes, in full view of everyone, and rushed back to his mansion. It was "heavy conduct" for which he soon afterward lost his office. Trying to make sense of this breach of decorum, one biographer conceded that he was a "dreadful and strange personage" whose hot temper made him unsuited for imperial office.[8] Perhaps he was more careless than his peers. But he was surely aware of the polite gentility that the şeyhülislam and other high religious officials were supposed to model for others. In reality, the scene is puzzling only if one projects an idealized standard of conduct onto the ulama simply because they were men of religion. They had to protect their social standing as much as any other member of the social elite. This social vigilance helps to explain the disturbance that gripped Damascus in the middle of Ramadan in 1743. A member of the provincial treasurer's retinue had insulted two leading scholars inside the Umayyad Mosque and then drawn a pistol on them. The outrage was so egregious, agreed local ulama, that they convened an emergency meeting and drew up a religious opinion authorizing the soldier's execution. Only the protection of the provincial treasurer, who did not abandon his client, kept the uproar from getting out of control.[9] The same prickly self-regard applied to representatives of other religious traditions. In Damascus (1818), a dispute between the Orthodox leadership and local defectors to Catholicism so enraged the patriarch that he threw a screaming tantrum in public. The chief judge of Damascus tried to act as a mediator and at one emergency meeting was soon reduced to shouting at the patriarch to mind his manners.[10] Nothing about this intemperate exchange happened because of any "Muslim" peculiarities. Both Muslim and Christian representatives were responding to perceived assaults on their honor. Sensitivities peaked precisely at moments when their social authority seemed to be melting away.

To anyone passing within distant earshot of such scenes, it might not have been immediately evident that members of the religious establishment were creating the furor. Deep in their tantrums, they drew on the same repertoire of abuse as any of their fellow townspeople. A scholar from Edirne, Kiyamizade Efendi held a stipend from a religious foundation and went (1806) to the house of another scholar who managed it. To his utter surprise and indignation, he was driven out with "coarse invectives."[11] Only the delicacy of the chronicler prevents us from learning exactly what he heard. Occasionally, though, a few details do spill into the open. In 1720, the chief judge of Cairo got into a quarrel with an official, became enraged, and called his adversary a "dog" and "wretch."[12] But indecent language was certainly not limited to moments of fury. In regular conversation, all but the most scrupulous ulama might slip into plainer and more relaxed speech that carried salty bits of slang and dialect. In an unguarded moment, one Istanbul scholar made a sneering reference to enraptured dervishes as "a bunch of shit-assed lunatics" (*bir alay götü boklu delidir*).[13] The ulama were different only in facing greater pressure not to descend into such vulgarity. Crude language undermined their collective image as guardians of religion and morality and models of upright conduct.

Members of the religious establishment knew perfectly well how they ought to behave. They were to set a higher example to which they would strive to draw others. Heeding the ideals of their religion, some scholars pretended to have chaste ears and would simply leave whenever they heard abuse and profanity.[14] By instinct, they were discreet and politic; they were averse to confrontation and resorted to indirect gestures, whether of approval or condemnation. Withdrawal and ostracism were the preferred forms of criticism for anyone who stepped out of line and trampled on the norms of civility and decency. When Ahmad al-Tahtawi was forced into resigning as mufti of Cairo (1809), he immediately returned the fur-lined robe that he had received at his appointment. This gesture deeply offended the *naqib al-ashraf* (head of the recognized descendants of the prophet Muhammad), the official who had originally bestowed it on him. The latter began to grumble openly with colleagues and complained that al-Tahtawi wanted him to look like "a dog who takes back what he vomits."[15] Meanwhile, al-Tahtawi refused to engage in recriminations. Having walked away from the office, he confined himself to home, going out only to pray at his neighborhood mosque. In his own way, he would send an indirect message. He would show his former colleagues how he would retain his dignity and not stoop to open quarreling, while, in stark contrast, they resorted to low gossip and innuendo.

Even breaches of decorum tended to assume an oblique character among the religious establishment. Instead of confrontation, they found outlets for spleen and bickering through something more akin to passive aggression. As they honored the outward forms of politesse, they might pursue a more underhanded agenda in plain sight. Durun Efendi arrived in Cairo (1764) as chief judge, preceded by an unassailable reputation for learning. Some of the scholars at al-Azhar resolved to undermine and discredit him. They attended a lecture that he was invited to give, and began to pepper him with questions until he lost his composure. In vain did the judge protest about the proper rules of debate that his adversaries were blatantly violating. Durun Efendi was so offended by their persistent quibbling, which was obviously meant to disconcert him, that he got up from the chair where he was lecturing and left the mosque altogether. His adversaries were elated. Overlooking their own spiteful tactics, they proclaimed that they had vanquished him.[16] They boasted that he had run away from their questions and that his sudden withdrawal only raised questions about his learning. Through such sly maneuvering, they could disguise their real intentions, which were hardly innocent or civil.

Not all violations of scholarly etiquette necessarily concealed rotten or devious motives. Momentary loss of self-control might occur for entirely meritorious reasons that only confirmed piety and virtue. Mystics might gain notice for suddenly slipping into trances, for which they were, of course, universally forgiven.[17] `Abd al-Rahman bin Ja`far (d. 1758/9), a Kurdish scholar who eventually settled in Damascus, was so devout that he would tremble whenever anyone mentioned the name of God. He would soon return to his senses and murmur, "I have glorified the greatness of my Lord."[18] These spiritual fits were fully compatible with his religious vocation and were thus easily explained as flutterings of intense faith and feeling.

Very different from these mystical and contemplative ecstasies, but deemed equally permissible and perhaps even laudable, were diatribes directed at corrupt or tyrannical officials. Though unseemly in principle, such emotional outbursts might earn respect, rather than criticism, if religious figures were seen as speaking on behalf of the common good against injustice. In the most dramatic scenes, scholars in high dudgeon lost themselves in the most outrageous invective. `Ali al-Sa`idi (d. 1775) once rallied to the defense of a fellow Cairene scholar. The latter had composed a legal opinion that enraged Yusuf Bey al-Kabir (d. 1777), a military commander renowned for his short fuse. When Yusuf Bey threatened to have the scholar killed, al-Sa`idi immediately spoke up for his colleague, defended his integrity, and insisted that only the ulama could fathom the intricacies of Islamic law. His words rose to a frenzy, and he began swearing at Yusuf Bey, "God curse you and curse the slave dealer who brought you here, and the man who sold you, and the man who bought you, and whoever made you an emir!" Al-Sa`idi was making a direct and highly indelicate dig at Yusuf Bey's background as a slave-soldier of low social origins. It took the intercession of other emirs, watching the exchange with growing consternation, to soothe tempers and restore a semblance of decorum.[19] On a previous occasion, al-Sa'idi had exploded into a rant against the warlord "Cloud-Catcher" Ali Bey (al-Kabir). Witnesses could not help noticing how al-Sa'idi, in the midst of his tantrum, became so consumed by his fury that he slipped into his native dialect from Upper Egypt instead of using a more learned register of Arabic.[20] The commander bore the scolding patiently, for he deeply respected al-Sa'idi. He also understood that the tongue-lashing was being delivered in the name of religion. Though impassioned and perhaps coarse, the heated words rested on moral principles that absolved al-Sa'idi of any accusation of impropriety. The emir would leave himself in an awkward predicament if he had any thought of raising a hand against him.

This confrontation seemed brave to onlookers precisely because an official's forbearance could not be taken for granted. The eighteenth-century spread of civility among military notables did not erase older images of a martial virility that was quick to anger. A man of the sword might still use wrath as an extension of his power, to be wielded like a weapon.[21] However tame he might seem to have become, the older warrior was still assumed to lurk inside and might suddenly play his old "role" again. Enmities could boil into view without warning. When a leading bey objected (1697) to the jailing of the commander of the annual pilgrimage caravan, the governor of Egypt immediately escalated the exchange: "Are you trying to impede my order? God willing, I will dye your beard with blood!"[22] It seems to have been a formulaic threat. A few years later, a quarrel erupted in the governor's divan. One officer drew his dagger and swore at his enemy, "I will dye your beard with your blood!"[23] İbrahim Bey, another Egyptian officer, used plainer language with a rival, informing him (1719): "You are my enemy; it is inevitable that I kill you."[24] In the midst of an altercation among military commanders (1721), one officer vowed that he would kill another "in the place where you sit."[25] Thus the older model of military comportment did not disappear across the eighteenth century and continued to circulate within Ottoman culture.[26] Officials could seemingly activate it at any time, and spectators were not necessarily surprised when impassive exteriors yielded to intemperate outbursts.

But we cannot conclude that nothing had changed. Though the ideal of martial virility did not disappear, it no longer had the same purchase. Urban politesse and its accompanying lifestyle had made progress among military officers and other state officials. They more consistently strove to present a civil front. Impetuous conduct became more obviously an embarrassing defect of character. A Georgian slave by origin, Kapudan Hüseyin Paşa (d. 1803) eventually rose to the position of grand admiral (1792–1803) and married an Ottoman princess. He owed much of this success to his master and patron, a high-ranking courtier who first presented him to Mustafa III (r. 1757–74). Despite these fortunate connections, which would have ensured socialization in an elite household, it was said that he experienced unnecessary setbacks and made numerous enemies because of his petulant and quarrelsome disposition.[27] Governor of Baghdad, Ali Paşa (r. 1802–7) was courageous, but struggled with an explosive temper that, sighed contemporaries, needlessly embroiled him in disputes and complications.[28] Among the Egyptian emirs of his day, Osman Bey Zülfakar (d. 1776; fled Egypt in 1743) was "one of the best." Talent and ability, however, did not necessarily foster civility. He was so free with invective that colleagues shunned him and preferred not to interact. No one knew when he might lash out. One of his fellow officers, Derendeli Ali, once arrived for an administrative meeting only to face the sudden wrath of Osman Bey, who began to roundly insult him. Another officer who happened to be present received the same abuse, and almost fell prey to a beating.[29]

So the man of the sword ought to summon up the old martial swagger only if he had a very good reason for doing so. In Aleppo, as Alexander Russell recalled, civility had become a kind of social reflex among men of state. But in the face of impertinence or insubordination, they could very quickly switch tone:

> The Osmanli, though rather solemn in their ordinary deportment, may justly be reckoned courteous and polite. In conversation with inferiors, even with Christians and Jews, they can assume an easy, affable manner; but when irritated by contradiction, they are impetuous in their gesture, they elevate their voice, and indecently descend to the most scurrilous language.[30]

They were acutely attuned to hierarchy and could not bear any infringement of rank or office. When the governor of Egypt convened a meeting with a group of notables (1788), he demanded to know why merchants returning with the pilgrimage caravan paid so few customs dues. A Cairene merchant had the nerve to speak up and explain that it was an accepted "usage" and that merchants would always get away with not paying. The governor was incredulous. Was the merchant mocking him and his authority? His hands began to shake, and members of the audience could not calm him. His exasperation rising, he asked out loud how anyone could talk to him in such a fashion and swore that he would have done terrible things if he did not fear God.[31] Note that he did not come close to striking anybody. Though the anger was genuine, he knew how to convey it without really losing control and compromising his dignity. He had, in effect, dramatized a challenge to his office and underscored the gravity of the insult.

Whether officials actually lost their temper, they had license to open up their emotional register. The hold of civility was not absolute. To cow resistance or compel obedience, they had leeway to engage in displays of hostility and intimidation, which functioned, in essence, as a complement to guns and swords. Landing at Sidon with the imperial fleet (1775), the grand admiral Cezayirli Hasan Paşa (d. 1790) learned that Ahmed Paşa al-Jazzar had been appointed governor without his knowledge. He immediately summoned the new governor for an interview. Al-Jazzar tried to offer an apology for the backhanded bureaucratic maneuvering by kissing the admiral's hands. Hasan Paşa "checked him in the face" with his dagger, leaving a small wound.[32] It was a calculated act of fury that he allowed for a single instant. In lashing out for that split second, the admiral nonetheless retained full self-command. The flick of the blade was a political message for al-Jazzar, whose wiliness had already undermined part of the naval mission as well as the admiral's own authority. At the head of a later expedition to Egypt (1786), Hasan Paşa conducted the same close management of his emotions. His main aim on this second campaign was to bring to heel the various Egyptian military factions who had grown so obstreperous that they had suspended payment of the provincial tribute to Istanbul. As the leading mamluks were retreating in haste to Upper Egypt, he found out that the governor of Egypt, his ostensible ally, had failed to forward letters that the admiral had asked him to deliver to local officials. Hasan Paşa erupted into a rage and cursed the governor, calling him "a treacherous hypocrite." His frustrations had by no means ended. When several emirs later gained an interview, only to plead for more time in gathering taxes, his patience cracked again. He thundered at them in Turkish (the main language of the Egyptian military elite), warning them, "Your faces are like a wall!"[33] Hasan

Paşa knew the effect that he was creating. He was not a rough soldier who had come up through the barracks with no social polish, saying whatever came to mind. A Georgian slave by origin, he had received his early training in the household of a merchant from the Thracian town of Tekirdağ (Rodosto).[34] Service in the upper echelons of the state would have further impressed on him the imperative of self-possession. The real purpose of his tirade was to reinforce his authority and impose his will through a kind of verbal violence.

Officials were freest in directing this emotional energy toward clients and underlings. Networks and households depended on hierarchies that could not be questioned. If officials suspected foot-dragging or insubordination, tantrums and threats became their prerogative. In Aleppo, the master political operator Muhammad Efendi Tahazadeh (d. 1786) had made himself supreme boss of the entire province by the last years of his life. A local notable and tax-farmer, he had maneuvered through countless quarrels and factional conflicts. He thereby became an expert in the arts of administrative intrigue and duplicity, and built a sprawling portfolio of properties and investments. He was, in short, used to getting his way. When on one occasion local Christians protested against new imposts and financial demands that he had levied, the tough old boss would have none of it. He summoned them and uttered "foul curses and rebukes about their honor and religion."[35] His choice of words, even if not exactly reproduced in the chronicle, were intentional and precise, and were meant to put the Christians in their place—not only as "protected" and therefore subordinate subjects in the Ottoman political order but as his own clients who should know when he had made up his mind.

Far more intolerable than disputes within political networks were affronts to the dignity of the state itself. Political authority demanded deference. Lèse majesté was the symbolic equivalent of rebellion; it would have to be put down and punished. After Ottoman forces landed at Acre and killed the Arab chieftain Zahir al-`Umar (1775), they soon rounded up his many sons. One of them, the "hot-tempered" `Ali, made the fatal mistake of insulting the Ottoman state in front of Hasan Paşa, the grand admiral. It was, at best, a foolish act of bravado that a seasoned official, in shackles and under arrest, would never contemplate. Zahir's clan had already caused a great deal of trouble and expense to the Porte, and the admiral was in no mood to show lenience. `Ali's execution followed forthwith.[36] And as one approached the summit of power and addressed the highest officials, heavy measures were to be expected. But for officials of lower rank, mired in purely local affairs and causing no direct complications for Istanbul, bureaucratic retribution would likely be sufficient. One lieutenant-governor (*mütesellim*) of Nablus earned dismissal from office (1819) when he failed to master his emotions. Presented with a state edict to which he objected, he rebuked the imperial messenger, threw the document on the ground, and trampled it under foot.[37] There was no excuse for such an extreme loss of composure, which displayed contempt not only for the messenger but for the state itself. Once the news was carried up the chain of command, his removal became inevitable.

Interpersonal Violence

When did words go beyond talk and set off acts of aggression? Every altercation had its own dynamics. Some individuals, whether by disposition or social position, were more inclined to aggression; some disputes, whether personal or communal, were more sensitive than others and therefore more prone to escalation. We should remind ourselves, too, that appearances could be deceiving. Vehemence of tone and gesture was not necessarily a prelude to violence or even a sign of anger. The language of the streets and markets was frequently boisterous as townspeople jostled, hailed each other, and noisily bargained. Arriving in Alexandria (1777), one French traveler was taken aback by the stridency of much street talk:

> They bawl also rather than speak. I often stopped near persons who appeared to me incensed with rage: they gave their voice all the force it could derive from a strong and ample chest; their countenance bore all the marks of passion; their eyes sparkled; and violent gestures accompanied words which seemed still more violent. I approached, expecting to see them cut one another's throats in a moment; and was perfectly astonished to find, that nothing was in question but a bargain of small importance; that not one of their expressions was of a threatening tenor; and that all this uproar was nothing than their usual manner of cheapening any thing they meant to buy.[38]

Especially among the uneducated majority, Ottoman society made allowances for more demonstrative styles of communication. Only among the self-consciously polite, as we have already seen, did the regulation of outward emotion place greater demands on individuals and encourage a more measured style of self-presentation. On some occasions, of course, vehemence really did express antagonism. But it did not automatically give way to violence. We have to look more deeply for the triggers that would set off physical blows.

One factor that made the resort to physical violence more likely was a difference in social status. Wherever there was rough parity, a quarrel could more easily fizzle out. Each person could walk away without fear of diminished honor and standing. From the streets of eighteenth-century Aleppo, we can get some notion of the ease with which verbal sparring could flare up, but without tipping over into a full-blown brawl:

> The common people, when unawed by the presence of superiors, are apt on the slightest provocation to grow obstreperous and abusive; so that one can hardly walk the street without seeing some noisy broil. The contending parties approach each other, they appear at every moment to come to blows, terms of bitter reproach and execration are reciprocally lavished, accompanied by the utmost vehemence of voice and gesture. But the fray rests there; they are less disposed to fight than to scold.[39]

Each side created the loudest possible scene, mainly for the purpose of broadcasting their accusations before the largest possible audience. Regardless of the legal implications of their dispute, they would quickly open the equivalent of a hearing in the court of public opinion, often the first forum of adjudication.[40] Having little inclination for fisticuffs, the rivals would secretly count on spectators to keep them apart and maintain peace. Notice too how the approach of the powerful and wealthy acted as a brake on the worst wrangling. Their presence was a reminder of the wider social order that ought not to be disturbed. All these calculations, made in the heat of the moment, rested on a pronounced sense of hierarchy.

Since there was obviously more than one hierarchy in which Ottoman subjects took their place, the next step is to determine how the different forms of identity and status came into play in triggering violence. Across the eighteenth-century world, the societies of the Old Regime believed in nothing like equality, and imagined that hierarchy was the inescapable norm. Ottoman subjects were used to placing both themselves and others on ladders of prestige and power that, in combination, would dictate the terms of social interaction.

One axis of hierarchy that authorized the use of violence was seniority. Parents and elders had the right to discipline children and were expected to give them their first lessons about deference to age, religion, and authority. If a parent—or any adult in the community—administered a beating to a child, it never raised eyebrows as long as the child had truly committed some act that communal opinion regarded as wrong or disobedient. These lessons carried over to schooling. Teachers had the right, even obligation, to discipline wayward students and were allowed to use various forms of corporal punishment. This right was operative both at neighborhood schools, where young children learned bits of religious tradition, and at advanced religious schools where more mature students prepared for a career in the religious establishment. The mother of Muhammad La`li el-Fenayi (d. 1700) was later recognized as an ecstatic saint (*meczube*), who would have her sons' teacher punish them whenever they committed some "fault" (*kabahat*). Never speaking with him directly, it was said, she merely mumbled to herself the number of times that he should beat them. The teacher never failed to administer exactly that number of blows.[41] More startling was the scene created by `Umar al-Misri (d. 1724/25), an Egyptian scholar who had settled in Aleppo. A former student could still recall years later how he had personally tried to deceive al-Misri, pretending to recite a passage from the Qur'an by heart as he secretly read from a small copy concealed in his hand. Having caught on to the ruse, al-Misri "jumped" on him and delivered a beating on the spot.[42] Only if the "correction" was obviously disproportionate might witnesses object and step in. In Tunis, `Ali al-Jaziri (d. 1800) was a soldier known not only for his courage and quick temper but for a sensitive heart as well. Friends remembered how he had once intervened when a neighborhood teacher had beaten a young student too hard. He asked the teacher how he could hit a mere child so pitilessly, and hearing that it was only because the boy had not memorized something, he promptly thrashed the teacher, to the cheering approval of onlookers.[43] Leaving aside such blatant excesses, the use of corporal punishment was regarded as fully justified throughout Ottoman society, wherever adults and juniors took their place in the equivalent of a master-apprentice relationship. In this sense, it was part of a wider "social" education that everyone would receive, whether or not they had ever attended a school.

Occupying the same subordinate position, almost like children, were the dependents of a household. Officials and notables often treated their servants and retainers as extensions of their family network and might train and promote them as valued lieutenants. In return, underlings bore the brunt of their household's social privilege, which lay in the unquestioned prerogative to discipline and beat them. They had to be careful about not exceeding their rank. If their master struck them, it was better to bear the indignity without protest.[44] Those who fought back risked harsh retaliation. An altercation between a wealthy Cairene merchant and one of his servants once led to ferocious street brawling (1768). The servant had lost his temper and raised his hand against the merchant, who gathered his friends in the marketplace and formed a search party. The merchant tracked the wayward servant to the house of a shaykh, a neighborhood elder, and forced his way inside. One of the men in the posse opened fire on the servant, but mistakenly hit, and fatally wounded, a relative of the shaykh. Now it was the turn of the shooter to flee, as the people of the neighborhood united behind the shaykh's household. Street fighting erupted around the market of Khan al-Khalili, and soon spread to other neighborhoods over the next week. As markets closed, reports of fatalities reached the ears of "Cloud-Catcher" Ali Bey, who took the initiative and worked out a settlement at the main courthouse.[45] As respectable opinion would have it, the impertinence of a single servant had upended the order of the entire city.

From the standpoint of the head of a household, members of his retinue were an extension of his personage. They were his men, doing his bidding. Anyone who interfered with their work or committed offenses against them dishonored the household itself. To take one incident from Cairo (1716): The slave of a military officer was sent to buy meat during a time of privation and high prices. He exchanged unpleasant words with a neighborhood watchman (*nöbetçi*), who summoned the constable (*odabaşı*). An altercation ensued. The constable had the slave jailed for "insolence" and swore that he would "teach him manners"—not the kind, obviously, that one found in etiquette manuals. Whatever the slave had actually said, he undoubtedly drew confidence from his master's social status. Treating the arrest as an affront to his own dignity, the officer came running to the jail, had his own words with the constable, and wound up inside as well, held alongside his slave. By the very same social logic that placed individuals in multiple networks, the jailing of the officer touched upon the honor of his entire unit, who assembled at the jail and forced his release. Only the intervention of Janissary commanders prevented the incident from getting entirely out of hand.[46] The same tense complications might arise whenever servants or retainers from different households got into quarrels or full-blown brawls with each other. Their actions had potential implications for the honor of their patrons and could therefore flare up into much larger disturbances if mediation was not quick to calm passions and assuage wounded dignity.[47]

Wives and concubines, though members of the household as well, were subject to different rules, which, in most cases, conferred protection and kept them safe from such unseemly imbroglios. Among the social elite, they were not to appear in public unless they had an escort, whose purpose was to ensure (as the patriarchal ideal optimistically imagined) that they would have neither the opportunity nor incentive to enter into unmonitored social interactions. Though dependent, wives did not entirely subsume their identity under their husbands. They had rights that were recognized in law and custom (at least in the towns). Property that a wife brought into a marriage remained her own under the terms of Islamic law; and if any woman acquired property or wealth during marriage, her husband had no legal claim to it.

Aware of these legal provisions, the state and its agents were careful to distinguish which members of a household owned which possessions. During the mayhem of the "Alemdar Event" in Istanbul (1808), which brought down the grand vizier Alemdar Mustafa Paşa, rebel Janissaries sacked the home of the reformer Mustafa Refik Efendi; their looting entirely spared the women's quarters.[48] The same exemptions applied elsewhere too. After the murder of an Egyptian bey in 1701, soldiers plundered his mansion. But they touched nothing in the rooms assigned to the women as they went about seizing "things related to men." Their restraint momentarily faltered only when another bey ordered the soldiers to break open the door to the women's quarters, from which they brought out a chest full of jewels and money that "belonged to the *sancak* [local administration]." All other items they left undisturbed.[49] Their search was not entirely unreasonable. It was common knowledge that wives could act as savvy political advisors, particularly if they came from elite families, in which they would have learned a great deal about administrative intrigue and maneuvering through firsthand observation and gossip. A leading Sufi in Cairo, `Abdullah al-Sharqawi (d. 1812) completely depended on his wife, who "managed his affairs and took care of everything he brought in and amassed. He did not come or go without consulting her."⁵⁰ Concubines, too, could exercise great influence as confidantes and advisors. In elite households, they might become the equivalent of politicians who kept secrets and maintained back channels to other households or clients. In Damascus, the provincial treasurer Fathi al-Daftari naturally assumed that the women of the household were privy to all the secrets of the deceased governor Sulayman Paşa al-`Azm (d. 1743), whose estate he was charged with registering and confiscating on behalf of the imperial government. His zeal caused him to overstep legal and customary boundaries. He threatened Sulayman's wife with torture, until she paid him off with a quantity of gold. With Sulayman's favorite concubine, whom the deceased governor had adored "as if she were the full moon on the horizon of the evening sky," the treasurer tried to use the same tactics. She denied knowing anything, and kept her silence even as the treasurer had her beaten unconscious.⁵¹ The new governor, Sulayman's nephew As`ad, got word of the brutal interrogations only after returning to Damascus with the pilgrimage caravan. He quietly vowed vengeance and bided his time for three years until he could finally bring down the treasurer who had so heedlessly violated the honor of his family. If the rough handling of male servants and slaves was an intolerable affront to members of the social elite, the consequences were far graver when it concerned female members of the household. Only suspected sexual transgressions provoked more fury. In Cairo (1788), a military officer, Hamza Kaşif, abducted a Christian goldsmith, whom he accused of committing improprieties with his wife, and had him brutally tortured to death over several days. His wife managed to escape with her life to another household, where she took shelter.⁵²

As long as servants and slaves submitted to the hierarchy of the household, they too, like wives and concubines, could generally count on the protections afforded by power and property. Social privilege thereby acted as one of the most effective shields against interpersonal violence. But this protection was not absolute. Lower social status always left individuals at greater risk of being beaten or harassed. Whenever questions of honor or precedence were at stake, custom allowed members of the social elite greater leeway in the use of physical force against the poor and dependent. In contrast, social equals mostly spared each other, provided they had not behaved in an unseemly or overly provocative manner. And striking at social superiors, as everyone knew, was unthinkable and tantamount to rebellion. In Istanbul, these differentiated standards played out in the furor caused (1775/76) by a scholar, son of a former şeyhülislam, who once ordered the beating of a groom and palace guard. The palace could not tolerate this transgression, which led to a two-month exile in Gallipoli.[53] The real source of official outrage was that the hot-headed scholar had overreached himself. Striking a lowly groom might be permissible if the circumstances truly justified it. Having a palace guard thrashed was an altogether different matter, which infringed on the dignity of the palace itself.

Custom was especially emphatic about the right of the high and mighty to seek satisfaction against acts of effrontery. Almost as a judicial exercise, Ottoman officials would detain individuals who had offended them and order them beaten. At the beginning of the eighteenth century, one traveler witnessed an English merchant being pulled over on the road to Edirne for insulting an Ottoman official, who immediately had him seized and subjected to a severe bastinadoing.[54] Aggravating the offense was the merchant's identity as a foreigner, who had no business addressing a representative of the sultan with such impudence. European visitors to the empire would have to watch their words until the balance of military power tipped definitively against the Ottomans during the late eighteenth century; thereafter, the sultan's officials would act with much greater circumspection. But no one should imagine that earlier visitors, such as the insolent English merchant, could ever protest their innocence upon getting such rough justice. They were completely familiar with this hierarchical etiquette, which was common, in one version or another, throughout the eighteenth-century world. Indeed, Europeans who entered Ottoman service had no trouble grasping the unspoken rules of rank and deference. While serving as an officer in the Ottoman army, Baron de Tott once struck a state messenger on the chest for addressing him too informally.[55] As anyone from this period could have explained, hierarchies were not to be tested. Even personal familiarity was not sufficient grounds for ignoring them. A neighbor and fellow officer once came to ask for a favor from Mehmed Bey al-Alfi (d. 1806), the last serious rival to Mehmed Ali in Egypt. When Mehmed Bey agreed, but then failed to act on his promise, his neighbor returned and rebuked him. Mehmed Bey was indignant. Renowned for a volatile temper, he began to curse and ordered his servants to seize him. They flogged the neighbor with cudgels as Mehmed Bey looked on, and did the job so viciously that their victim died two days later.[56]

As one descended the social hierarchy, the leeway for verbal impertinence rapidly shrank. Slaves had to be the most careful about observing the boundaries of propriety. Both law and custom demanded their submission. During an encounter on the streets of Istanbul (1812), an officer of the palace guard (*bostancıbaşı ağa*) cursed at a slave of the Grand Admiral for singing loudly after nightfall. The slave made the mistake of cursing back, as if he could address him on the same social footing. When the officer determined who he was and referred the incident to official channels, the slave's execution followed swiftly.[57] His affiliation with the Grand Admiral's household was not enough to save him. The sentence spoke on behalf of the entire social order, which could not tolerate such a steep transgression against rank and honor.

The most senior men of state might assume responsibility for discipline themselves, taking matters directly into their own hands without bothering to delegate. We should first recognize that punishments might vary widely, depending on the circumstances of the offense. At one end of this spectrum of corporal violence lay the mild or ceremonial forms that were meant to express displeasure more than punishment and which were unlikely to do much physical harm. One Egyptian bey (1741/42) became so exasperated with a deputy (*kethüda*) that he struck him with a fly whisk and knocked off his turban.[58] Though the swatting must have been somewhat energetic, it aimed more to humiliate than to inflict pain, putting the subordinate in the same position as flies, the normal quarry of the whisk. The gesture seems to have become something of a trope, conveying contempt mixed with extreme irritation or impatience. The most famous fly whisk in history was undoubtedly the one wielded by the governor (*dey*) of Algiers in 1827 against the French consul during an official interview. His fit of pique over unpaid French debts for Algerian grain—shipped to France as far back as the 1790s—would become the pretext for the French invasion and conquest of Ottoman Algeria (1830–48).

The most severe cases of physical violence culminated in fisticuffs or worse. In 1781, the incoming governor of Aleppo displayed unusual vehemence in rooting out corruption. During a heated interview, he personally stabbed an extortionate military officer, who was then hacked to death by the pasha's lieutenants.[59] But it was not only officials and soldiers who might raise their hand. The same sensitivities about rank and office prevailed throughout the social elite. Even members of the religious establishment might, if badly provoked, commit acts of aggression, though these lapses were highly damaging to their public image. An embarrassing scandal engulfed Abu'l-Hasan al-Qal`i (d. 1785), a distinguished scholar in Cairo, after he got into an unseemly spat with a fellow scholar, who claimed that al-Qal`i had slapped him in the face.[60] In Damascus, the chief judge discovered (1818) that the mufti's assistant (*amin al-fatawa*) had drafted a religious opinion invalidating the conversion of a local Christian to Islam, which he had personally overseen at the courthouse. The judge denounced it as a subversion of his authority and took such deep umbrage that he scolded and then beat the unfortunate assistant. The outburst was truly shocking to observers, and quickly cost the judge his appointment.[61]

Hidden within many of these physical assaults were symbolic messages. Assailants did not necessarily lose themselves or commit random violence. Despite their obvious rage, they would still manage to draw on a set of gestures that were instantly recognizable to fellow townspeople. Take the chain of events unleashed by a legal dispute in Cairo (1790). A Bosnian litigant had acted insolently toward the chief judge, who then complained to the governor. Summoned to the governor's council, the Bosnian antagonized the governor himself, and then went a little further in declaring that both officials were liars. The governor ordered him imprisoned, with the guards beating him as they took him away. The self-inflicted plight of the Bosnian grew worse. The mufti leaked a letter to the governor. The Bosnian had mocked the latter as "that wretched warrior" and used much the same language for leading military officers. The governor's agitation was now brimming over. He had the Bosnian hauled out of his cell and showed him the letter. The Bosnian stammered a few words before begging for a pardon. The governor slapped him in the face, began plucking out his beard, and threatened to stab him with his dagger. The members of the council rose to their feet and had to restrain him physically from doing more harm.[62] In the midst of this scuffle was one act that all Ottoman townspeople would have immediately understood: the plucking of the Bosnian's beard. In figurative terms, the governor was trying to unman someone who had mocked him and trifled with his power.

The growing of a beard was, as we have already observed, one of the main rites of passage for youths entering adulthood. Once they had acquired a beard, they would never willingly shave it off, for it would be tantamount to losing manhood itself. For precisely this reason, depriving a man of his beard became a favorite folk punishment. Before executing Haci İbrahim Efendi, one of the leading officials in the New Order, mutinous soldiers in Istanbul (1807) mocked him, and as an extra measure of spite, cut off his beard.[63] The same rituals were put into motion in Damascus following news of the death of Ahmed Paşa al-Jazzar (1804), who at the time was serving his fourth term as governor of Damascus, very much feared and loathed as ever. Simultaneously jubilant and vengeful, residents poured into the streets to hunt for his henchmen and soldiers. Most detested were his Kurdish mercenaries. The furious townspeople managed to seize three of them. As they beat their prisoners, they did not neglect to pluck out their beards and moustaches before dragging them away to be killed.[64] In Alexandria (1785), a retainer of the military commander (serdar) killed a local resident and provoked an uprising. A crowd seized the commander himself, seated him backwards on a donkey, and paraded him through the town as they slapped his face and beat him with sandals. The crowning humiliation was to strip him of his turban and shave half his beard.[65] So deep-seated was this rough folk justice that the state had long incorporated the shaving of the beard into its own rituals of public shaming. To take one scene from the streets of Cairo (1697): A crier paraded a forger, seated backwards on a camel and shorn of his beard, after the latter was convicted of falsifying the foundation deed for a religious endowment.[66] This fate awaited all counterfeiters and anyone who would dare to tamper with coins, weights, and other market regulations.

Pomp and Status

No spectacle signified the presence of power as strikingly as a public procession. More than a ceremonial tool of the political establishment, it was one of the most coveted prerogatives of the social elite. Those who held high posts or commanded large households did not simply walk casually or unaccompanied through the streets. They quite deliberately surrounded themselves with an entourage—ideally one that was armed and mounted—to open the way and magnify their honor and importance (fig. 5.1). One eighteenth-century Dutch traveler was impressed by these supernumerary displays of rank. "The Turks are remarkably well attended by their servants, though they have generally no wages, especially if the master be possessed of some grand post."[67] At the head of one such entourage was Mehmed Hayri

Efendi (d. 1789/90), chief scribe (*reisülküttab*) of the imperial bureaucracy, who was riding through the streets of Istanbul when his horse suddenly fell over. The many servants at his side were unable to extricate him as he lay dying underneath.[68] Yet they had still done their job. Recruited from among the poor, lackeys and attendants had few responsibilities apart from conveying, through their superfluous presence, the wealth and prestige of their employer. Nothing about their role was an Ottoman peculiarity. Across the early modern world, social dignitaries would not have dreamed of moving through the streets without a proper escort. The Old Regime of the eighteenth century merely brought older patterns of patronage and household politics to new and outsized proportions.

In Istanbul, the model for these displays of pomp and status was, of course, the imperial court. Though largely reduced to a symbolic head of state, the sultan still had to show himself before his subjects with suitable pageantry. From the early seventeenth century onward, the first public ceremony of every reign was the girding of the new sultan with a sword at the

FIGURE 5.1. The grand vizier crossing Atmeydanı (the old Hippodrome) in Istanbul (c. 1720–37). Painting by Jean-Baptiste Vanmour. High officials like the grand vizier always entered the streets with an escort of servants and retainers.   SOURCE: Rijksmuseum, Amsterdam.

shrine of Eyüp Sultan, just outside the city walls.⁶⁹ After this coronation, his public appearances followed a fairly predictable schedule. The imperial chronicles are replete, above all, with royal cavalcades to Aya Sofya Mosque for Friday prayers. It was impossible to leave the palace unannounced—unless the sultan was conducting an incognito tour of the markets and streets, as several sultans, like Abdülhamid I (r. 1774–89) and Selim III, were wont to do in the company of guards. In fact, the sultan and his retainers could not enter the streets without setting off a cascade of ceremonial salutes. Every departure triggered a vast train of courtiers, eunuchs, soldiers, and servants, all of whom helped to project the dynasty's presence in the capital. Glittering processions also made their way along the waters of the Bosphorus. The sultan and members of the court periodically rode out in convoys of elegant oared boats, whose sumptuousness proclaimed a royal passage.⁷⁰

Augmenting the pageantry of the capital were the ceremonial processions of foreign emissaries, who were entitled to their own displays of pomp. European ambassadors were by no means excluded from these privileges. Whether presenting their credentials to the court, or simply setting out from their embassies in the district of Pera, they made their way through the streets with an escort of Janissaries. Most magnificent were the processions that accompanied emissaries from the Safavid and Mughal emperors, great Muslim sovereigns in their own right who would not have passed up the sumptuous trappings of state.⁷¹ Mughal ambassadors made the most unforgettable impressions with the elephants that lumbered along their route.⁷² Within the Ottoman Empire itself, protocol allowed the privilege of an embassy only to the ruler of the Crimean khanate, who was simultaneously a vassal of the sultan and head of a venerable Muslim dynasty whose origins extended back to the fifteenth century. When Selim Giray arrived in Istanbul (1747), his entourage dutifully paraded in solemn procession to the palace.⁷³

Away from the capital, ceremonial entries were mainly the privilege of governors and chief judges (*kadı*), the two highest offices in the Ottoman provincial administration. By the eighteenth century, these positions had to be purchased from the state at auction and were generally held as one-year appointments. Governors shouldered the added expense of having to maintain a substantial household, essentially carrying their own staff and soldiers from one appointment to another in long columns that contained scores of pack animals.⁷⁴ In the absence of any municipal government or rural gendarmerie, they bore responsibility for keeping order and conducting patrols wherever they went. Their entry into the towns was therefore a spectacle designed to awe and reassure the population. Cairo extended the most extravagant welcome. The longtime custom was to receive the incoming governor of Egypt with fireworks as his barge moved down the Nile. The culmination of the festival was a parade through town, with further fireworks, as he and his troops made their way up to the citadel.⁷⁵ Every province had its own protocol for greeting high officials. In Damascus, the governor entered with his troops to general fanfare, whereas the chief judge, in this proud center of Islamic learning, had his route illuminated by torchbearers in a special nighttime parade.⁷⁶ The welcome at smaller towns was correspondingly scaled back. Before reaching Diyarbakir, the new judge might receive a mounted escort sent out by the governor. At Manisa, as well as the towns of Herzegovina like Mostar, it was enough for local officials and notables, and perhaps a few of the leading guild members, to greet the judge as he entered the town.⁷⁷

In large provincial centers, local notables were not to be outdone. The biggest households easily rivaled, and might surpass, those accompanying governors. İsmail Bey, the commander of the Azeban military corps in Cairo, possessed such a large entourage (1723) that the troops at the head of it, having filed through the streets, would enter his nearby house before he and his personal guard had even left the barracks, where he was just setting out.⁷⁸ Long trains of retainers were not the sole prerogative of military officers. When a leading *sharif* (recognized descendant of the prophet Muhammad) got into a legal dispute in Damascus (1703), he decided to appeal to the governor of Tripoli for assistance. Head of a wealthy household, the sharif left Damascus amid a noisy procession of music and banners.⁷⁹ Even Europeans might tap into the same symbolic repertoire. Finally allowed to set up a mission in Damascus (1833), the British consul entered in extraordinary pomp, complete with "a thousand soldiers marching to music."⁸⁰ This escort constituted a European version of an Ottoman political household, marching in ceremonial order through the streets. And how could European consuls resist this grand style? As Albert Hourani shrewdly noted, they were already becoming the equivalent of provincial notables by the middle of the nineteenth century.⁸¹

Many of the principal families in the religious establishment joined other urban notables in building large households. In their wealth, prestige, and official honors and appointments, they resembled other members of the urban elite, with whom they intermingled and routinely intermarried. It is no surprise, then, that they held themselves with much the same pomp and hauteur. A successful jurist in Cairo, Hasan al-Kafrawi (d. 1788) leveraged his position as mufti into a more informal role as a popular arbiter for legal and financial disputes. Favors immediately flowed his way. He built up a fortune, began to dress in the best clothes, and was soon riding mules in the street surrounded by retainers.[82] Best equipped for urban spectacle were the heads of Sufi lodges, who had households of disciples and servants. In Damascus, for example, the Sufis of the Taghlibi family were renowned for their stately processions of banners and drums during religious holidays and other special occasions.[83] Like other notables, leading Sufis were protective of their social dignity. The head of the Wafa'i Sufi order in Cairo, Shams al-Din ibn al-'Arifin (d. 1813) was so quick to take offense at perceived slights that everyone who approached him was careful to speak in measured phrases and flatter his vanity. He surrounded himself with an extensive retinue who answered his every whim. If he suspected anyone of even indirectly criticizing him, he would send followers to beat them. He once heard that youths from well-to-do families had held a nighttime gathering and amused themselves by performing imitations of various personages around town. When he confirmed that he was one of their satirical targets, he summoned them one by one to his presence and had them flogged.[84] There was no authority to which they could appeal. Ibn al-'Arifin was too eminent a religious leader and had his own retinue who were ready to administer more beatings. He could, moreover, count on sympathy from fellow members of the urban elite, who were equally sensitive about their own reputations and had no patience for ridicule from any source, especially from within their own social set.

In the countryside, public processions were much harder to muster. Communities were smaller, and such ceremonies were capable of mobilizing comparatively fewer participants and spectators. Yet on this smaller social stage rural notables might still conduct their own versions of the grand entry. In 1792, the victory of Emir Bashir al-Shihabi's troops over Druze rivals prompted communal celebrations ('*arada*), first in Dayr al-Qamr, the seat of his administration, and then "all over the mountain."[85] In 1806, Jirjis Baz, Emir Bashir's commander, led another triumphal procession through Dayr al-Qamr.[86] Ceremonial revelry did not arise from military events alone. In 1802, Zahle saluted the patriarch of Damascus with a clamorous welcome.[87] It was not the first occasion. The patriarch would occasionally make tours of Mt. Lebanon and visit monasteries. The monks came out to greet him in festive order every time.[88]

Wherever an entourage passed, it would insist on deference. Soldiers and retainers would freely wield cudgels and rarely drop their stony glare for some fleeting wink of familiarity.[89] Bystanders and pedestrians would yield, or the entourage would rain down blows. One cavalry commander, freshly departed from Adana (1785), was fording a stream with his troops when two caravan attendants veered into his path. Overcome with rage, he promptly cut them down with his battle axe. He took their carelessness as impertinence. This defense proved inadequate once the incident was reported to Istanbul, which ordered him arrested and executed.[90] The risk of violence was highest in processions that carried some extra symbolic charge. In 1811, the butchers of Istanbul, who were aligned with the Janissaries, were bringing a load of meat from the slaughterhouses to Etmeydanı, where Janissaries would receive their customary share. This was a regular, and to them virtually sacrosanct, passage through the streets that they would allow no one to interrupt. When a man absent-mindedly crossed in front of the pack animals, the butchers warned him to stop. He did not listen, or perhaps had not heard. It did not matter: the master butchers would not overlook the moment of inattention. They immediately seized the man and had him whipped on the spot. Retainers in the service of Su`ada Bey, a former judge of Medina, happened to be watching the scene nearby. They confronted the procession, shouting, "Hey dogs! Why are you beating this man?" They fell upon the butchers with clubs and chased them away. Meanwhile the butchers had no intention of letting this challenge pass. They rallied their comrades at Etmeydanı and returned for vengeance. The judge's retainers were arrested, taken to the Janissary headquarters (Ağakapısı), and murdered. The affair was shocking, and nearly became a full-blown political scandal, which was only snuffed out by the dismissal of the lieutenant commander of the Janissaries (*segbanbaşı*) and exile of Su`ada Bey.[91]

Status had to be continually reaffirmed. Even the smallest concession or moment of inaction might be perceived as a symbolic downgrading. In every ceremonial entry, both officials and local notables were touchy about matters of rank and precedence, which were bound up in notions about the larger social hierarchy. In Damascus, Nasuh Paşa had to issue an apology (1708) for disregarding protocol and allowing the chief judge to walk ahead of him during his procession into town.[92] The bad blood between Gürcü Osman Paşa, governor of Damascus (r. 1761–72), and Mehmed Bey Abu'l-Dhahab, Egyptian military commander, long preceded the Egyptian occupation of Damascus (1771), a rebellion against the sultan that quickly fizzled out, but ultimately led to the flight and deposition of Gürcü Osman. Both had memories of an earlier encounter in Mecca when Osman commanded the pilgrimage caravan from Damascus and Mehmed Bey the one from Cairo. They arrived at the same time and quarreled over who should have the right to enter first.[93] It was not a superficial question. Not only the leading officers, but all their men, were attentive to these points of ceremony, and would have taken any concession to the other column as a collective slight and admission of inferiority in rank and honor. In the rough politics of the Ottoman administrative system—particularly as rivalries between provincial officials turned more venomous in the second half of the eighteenth century—such symbols became ever more contentious.

So ingrained was this predilection for pomp and parade that voluntary renunciation of these status symbols could cause a sensation. Refusing to keep up appearances created the perception of downward mobility, which to this way of thinking, was almost as bad as the actual loss of power and privilege. In Cairo, Afranj Ahmad Bey stunned his fellow soldiers (1711) when he resigned his rank in the Janissaries and took the post of başodabaşı, putting him in charge of urban policing. They viewed the appointment as demeaning. He had condemned himself to an inferior position, which required its occupant to assume ordinary "civilian" garments. Worse still, he would ride a donkey instead of a horse, and no longer have "runners and riders with swords as well as retainers escorting him." No one in Egypt could remember a soldier making such a switch in his career or accepting a symbolic reduction of such steep proportions.[94] Even at lower social levels where it was not really possible to finance a grand household or hire many servants, the ambitious townsman would still try to evoke some small measure of grandeur. Najm al-Din al-Tamurtashi (d. 1786), a jurist, lived in comfort and liked to ride through the streets of Cairo on horses, a privilege normally reserved for state officials.[95] This high perch would both literally and symbolically elevate the rider in the eyes of townspeople, most of whom did not own any animals at all and had to walk about town. Riding a mount automatically opened up social distance and made it harder for bystanders to approach. Bishop of the Bulgarian town of Vratsa, Sofroniy Vrachanski (d. 1813) once hit upon a ruse to escape while Ottoman troops were quartering themselves in local homes for the winter (1798). Donning a turban and putting a whip in his hand, he rode into the street with a groom leading the way. Since he looked like an Ottoman postal rider (*tatar*), and had his own servant, no one thought of questioning him as he departed.[96]

For members of the religious establishment, the fondness for public ostentation came at a higher price than for officials and soldiers. It undercut their professed image as moral leaders who would uphold the highest values of religion and not succumb to material temptations and distractions. Hence excessive fanfare and display might ignite criticism, particularly if it betrayed a preoccupation with worldly fame. Ibrahim al-Jabawi (d. 1723), head of the Sa'diyya Sufi order in Damascus, was faulted for his excessive attachment to "magnificence," which led to his squandering a large part of the family fortune.[97] Better conforming to the modesty and probity expected of the men of religion was Muhammad al-'Azizi (d. 1785), a dignified and unassuming jurist. He had no interest in worldly affairs, it was said, and would never ride a horse through the streets of Cairo or eat at the house of an emir.[98] Kuşadalı İbrahim Efendi (d. 1846), a revered and yet unpretentious Sufi originally from the Aegean coast, renounced extravagant ceremony and showed little interest in adorning himself with the apparel of his order.[99] Most widely admired were scholars who dispensed with servants, took care of their own business, and had no aversion to carrying out basic chores in full view of everyone. A fine scholar, Muhammad al-Jinaji (d. 1786) would ride through the streets of Cairo on a donkey. He would buy clover, place the load on the animal, and return atop the pile. With the same indifference to majestic poses, he would carry a bowl full of dough to the baker himself. Friends recalled that he would sometimes run errands on their behalf.[100] This simplicity, however, was not license to forget social dignity. Scholars still had to hold themselves with the necessary gravity and self-possession. No matter how austere or self-denying their lifestyle, they had to refrain from habitually socializing in the markets, frequenting coffeehouses, or otherwise mingling with those who were unworthy of their company. In the name of respectability, even the modest and self-effacing would have to safeguard the honor of the religious establishment.[101]

Conclusion: The Eighteenth-Century "Inflation" of Honor

The humility of such scholars made a striking impression within eighteenth-century Ottoman society. Displays of pomp and honor were becoming more frequent and extravagant due to the prosperity of provincial notables. A distinct "downward" and "outward" diffusion in public ceremony is observable. Grand gestures like festivities to accompany the marriage of a family member or circumcision of a son had once been the prerogative of the palace or high-ranking officials of state, overwhelmingly in Istanbul or Edirne (where the imperial household resided throughout the late seventeenth century).[102] As late as 1700 or so, provincial townspeople could still expect that only a governor or chief judge would have the financial means to organize such celebrations.[103] In the following decades, provincial notables would begin to accumulate so much wealth, mainly from tax-farming, that they too could stage their own grand spectacles. Their outsized fortunes allowed the most ambitious to enter brazenly into social competition with high officials. In Damascus, the provincial treasurer, Fathi al-Daftari, turned the marriage of his daughter into an advertisement of his wealth and power. He organized a week-long celebration (1743), with each day dedicated to a particular social group whom he feted. It was a direct answer to his local rival, the governor Sulayman Paşa al-`Azm, who had just organized a lavish circumcision ceremony for his son.[104] This expansion of pageantry was taking place in all the large Ottoman towns, where more notables now had the resources to indulge in social ostentation. In Egypt, military officers could now contemplate throwing celebrations that would have astonished earlier generations. The redoubtable "Cloud-Catcher" Ali Bey oversaw a month-long gala for his deputy, İsmail Bey, who had married the daughter of İbrahim Kethüda, his former patron. Ali Bey built a stage on Birkat al-Fil, the great pond toward the southern end of Cairo, so that people could promenade and watch musicians, acrobats, buffoons, and other entertainments. Lamps illuminated the homes of notables nearby as they sponsored concurrent feasts in honor of the occasion. At the close of the festivities, a winding train of soldiers and servants escorted the bride, who rode in a carriage through Cairo to her new home.[105] No one had seen anything like it—even in Cairo, where these rivalries were acquiring an eye-popping sumptuousness. Military office was not a prerequisite for this grand style. Ahmad al-Mahruqi (d. 1804), chief of the merchants (*shahbandar*) in Cairo, was a wily operator whose career survived the French occupation of Egypt. He nimbly switched alliances between French and mamluk commanders and retained his magnificent fortune. One of the lasting memories that he left to Cairenes was the enormous wedding celebration that he sponsored for his son.[106]

The Old Regime of the eighteenth century was slowly transmitting ceremonies of power and prestige down the social ladder. Among the biggest beneficiaries were the governor-princes (*hospodar*) of Wallachia and Moldavia, appointed (1711–1829) from the great "Phanariot" families of Istanbul, wealthy and well-connected Orthodox Greeks who had long served the Ottoman dynasty as administrators, fixers, and diplomatic liaisons with European embassies. Arriving at the Porte for formal investiture, each new hospodar received military salutes and robes of honor in the presence of the sultan before departing in pomp to their frontier capital, Bucharest or Jassy, with a long column of soldiers and retainers.[107] During the height of the Great Crisis, warlords arrogated political symbols without waiting for the blessings of the state. In Cairo, Mehmed Bey earned his sobriquet, Abu'l-Dhahab ("the Gold Bearer"), from his habit of scattering gold coins before the poor. He first made the gesture after winning promotion to the rank of emir and immediately gained notoriety, for no other emir had previously done anything like it. When he later became aware of the nickname that townspeople had conferred on him, he always made sure to carry gold in his pockets. He would tell companions, "I am Abu'l-Dhahab. I never touch anything but gold."[108] Normally associated with a ruler, this flourish was a barometer of the wealth that was accruing to provincial magnates throughout the eighteenth century. The political overtones of such gestures were not lost on Ottoman officialdom. Upon his elevation as governor of Egypt (1805), Mehmed Ali sought to activate this memory on his own behalf. After donning the ceremonial robes of office, he rode back to his mansion in Azbakiyya and scattered gold coins among the bystanders.[109] The real and symbolic ambitions of the governor did not go unnoticed. In 1810, the Chief Eunuch of the Harem (*Kızlar Ağası*) arrived in Cairo with an order for Mehmed Ali to campaign against Wahhabi forces and recapture Mecca and Medina. As his entourage made its way to the citadel, the sultan's emissary tossed gold and silver coins to the waiting crowds, as if he were reclaiming this royal prerogative on behalf of the palace.[110]

Beneath the grandees in eighteenth-century society were parvenus who stood ready, in increasing numbers, to grasp at the new opportunities for display. More individuals were gaining access to symbols of prestige and favor. Public opinion generally resented these pretensions. Whenever it caught wind of social climbers, it retaliated with invidious gossip. We can take the case of İbrahim Kethüda, head of the porters' guild in Üsküdar in the early nineteenth century. He had accumulated a handsome fortune and liked to flaunt it. He dressed extravagantly and held himself with an arrogance that befitted a member of the palace entourage. He most blatantly overstepped his station in traveling along the Bosphorus in his own procession of magnificent boats.[111] It was obvious mimicry of the grand passage of the sultan and other grandees on the waters of Istanbul. Contemporaries immediately noticed, and clucked about it incessantly. Rivals could not contain their glee when his downfall finally came (1811) after he became implicated in a financial scandal.

This broader diffusion of pomp and ceremony did not signal the rise of a new kind of society. Whether in Istanbul or the provinces, the composition of the Ottoman elite did not significantly shift during this period. The officials and notables who disproportionately shared the benefits of the eighteenth-century fiscal state were figures who would have been fully recognizable to earlier generations. What was novel, beyond their greater share of wealth, was the wider distribution of status symbols. As leading families became more affluent, they were tempted into more stately and magnificent poses. Grandeur had become easier to purchase and assume. This "inflation" of social distinction was most conspicuous in the towns, where, after all, most grandees and notables lived. The expansion of polite society thus had its counterpart in the dispersal of trappings of rank and honor, which now began to circulate more extensively and promiscuously across the eighteenth century.

SIX
ROUGH MANNERS

The so-called "Galata Event" (Galata Vakası) of February 1772 began as a personal affair. Two sailors from the imperial fleet, an Albanian and a Christian named Gavur Haci, murdered the proprietor of a coffeehouse in Galata, the northernmost neighborhood of Istanbul, and looted his shop. Not content with their bloody deed, they marked their triumph by hanging his corpse at a nearby grocer's stall. The street patrol (*kolluk*) soon arrived and ordered the body to be taken town. The officers smelled trouble. Like many coffeehouse owners in Ottoman towns, the victim was probably affiliated with the Janissary corps, who would inevitably hear about the murder.[1] The two sailors refused to comply and became belligerent. As word about the incident got out, comrades from the imperial fleet rushed to their side. And just as the patrol had feared, the Janissaries were beginning to gather. The confrontation quickly escalated into a gunfight, which lasted three entire days and at its height brought cannon fire from ships in the Golden Horn into the streets, where the two sides continued to shoot at each other. It took the intervention of high officials to finally arrange a truce and halt the factional mayhem that had grown out of a single act of violence.[2]

In the larger view of Ottoman history, this "event" foreshadowed the troubles that would beset the Ottoman state during the long decades of the Great Crisis covering the late eighteenth and early nineteenth centuries. The Ottoman-Romanov war (1768–74) was entering its final stages, with Ottoman defeat already on the horizon. Staggering under mounting financial and military losses, the Ottoman war machine was revealing new frailties and giving hints of larger disorders to come. The Galata Event was merely a microcosm of these difficulties. Janissaries and sailors were brawling and shooting in the streets of the imperial capital itself, making a mockery of military discipline. The tide of events was turning distinctly ominous.

Disturbances like the Galata Event exposed not only the brittleness of the Ottoman military but also the extent to which a defiant paramilitary subculture had taken root. By the eighteenth century, Ottoman towns were full of soldiers, whether Janissaries or members of other units, most of whom were rural migrants. They actively intermingled with the urban population and sought out the amenities of urban life. From the other direction, more and more townspeople searched for connections or outright membership in military networks, which promised "protection" and other social and economic advantages. The resulting paramilitary complex—simultaneously military and "civilian," imperial and local—bred a rough and refractory social milieu. Its distinctive manners paid little heed to the codes of conduct espoused by polite gentlemen and instead invoked the values and poses of "heroic manners." This cultural transplant from the countryside was ill-suited to its new urban environment. Paramilitary culture was thus caught in an impossible bind. Although it craved the basic comforts and dignities of an urban lifestyle, its rough manners turned it into an unruly presence that inspired fear and revulsion among "respectable" townspeople.

The Social Consequences of the Ottoman Paramilitary Complex

By the eighteenth century, military recruitment had become the most significant avenue of social mobility in Ottoman society as the exigencies of early modern warfare brought ever larger armies to the battlefield. Two sources of Ottoman manpower were most critical.

The first was the Janissary corps. Originally recruited, during the fifteenth and sixteenth centuries, as slave-soldiers from the Balkan Christian population (through the *devşirme*, or "levy of youths"), the early Janissaries had served as the sultan's personal guard and fought as musket-wielding shock troops, universally feared by the empire's enemies. But by the seventeenth century, the corps had come to look very different. From about five thousand highly trained soldiers around 1500, to some twelve thousand in the mid-sixteenth century, their ranks had swollen to nearly forty thousand by the 1630s, at which point the state ceased using slave-soldiers, who were, in fact, no longer necessary.[3] Though they technically remained "slaves" (*kul*) of the sultan, Janissaries had become freemen, able to marry and bequeath their status and property to sons, since at least the late sixteenth century. Meanwhile, by the early seventeenth century, members of the corps were beginning to infiltrate urban markets as the purchasing power of their salaries steadily dwindled with the global onset of severe inflation (c. 1570s–1640s). Soldiers bargained or muscled their way into partnerships with local tradesmen, some of whom, in turn, became members of the corps.[4] The Ottomans thereby "socialized" the costs of military expansion, which they achieved on the cheap.[5]

The number of Janissaries continued to soar. By the 1690s, enrollments stood at around seventy thousand. A century later, Mouradgea d'Ohsson offered a stunning estimate of some one hundred twenty thousand soldiers (about a fifth of them stationed in Istanbul), combined with another one hundred fifty thousand who held Janissary pay-tickets but performed no real military service. Surrounding these two groups was a third and more nebulous category of "pretenders" (*taslakçı*), usually young laborers and migrants who hoped to gain formal membership; their loose affiliation and uncertain status made it impossible to gauge their true size.[6] Oversight had become almost entirely unmanageable, especially since Janissary pay-tickets were freely bought and sold outside the corps. So diffuse had membership become that even most Ottoman officials did not know exactly how many Janissaries were on the muster rolls. Military discipline correspondingly slipped. Most of the troops were poorly trained, little more than artisans and laborers attached to urban guilds. Indifferent or downright derelict as soldiers, they nonetheless prized Janissary status as a means of obtaining imperial tax exemptions and access to military networks. The least scrupulous imposed themselves as unsavory racketeers, making threats and flexing muscle against the unwilling and uncooperative in the marketplace.[7]

Sporadic efforts to restore the separation of townspeople and soldiers faced active resistance. When the new chief judge arrived in Cairo in 1709 and introduced plans for keeping Janissaries out of the guilds, the reply from guild masters was startling. Most tradesmen were either soldiers or sons of soldiers, they explained, and therefore the order could not be enacted. Sizing up the hopelessness of the situation, the judge dropped his project.[8] Paramilitary networks could stretch far beyond the marketplace. To one European observer, it seemed that more than half the population of Mosul had ties to one of the five local Janissary regiments.[9] In the Balkans, where the urban population was disproportionately Muslim, Janissaries were an especially conspicuous element in garrison towns. At Vidin, a Bulgarian town that became a key fortress along the western frontier during the eighteenth century, local Janissaries numbered more than five thousand by 1750 and dominated the provincial economy.[10] In such circumstances, the line between full-time soldiers and tradesmen could be difficult to draw. It is more helpful to think of the Janissaries as a political faction. Wherever they were stationed, they kept a watchful eye on their interests and were ready to defend them, if necessary, in street skirmishes against rivals—or even, in the case of the Balkan garrisons, against reforms proposed by the central state.

Alongside the Janissaries, the second main source of military manpower consisted of provincial levies and mercenaries (*sekban, deli,* or *başıbozuk*). Most were rural youths with no prospects at home.[11] A military career beckoned as the most accessible path to social advancement and regular employment. Recruitment was piecemeal and opportunistic, and drew men from the farthest reaches of the empire. Accelerating this hunt for manpower during the eighteenth century was the formation of large political households in the provinces. Governors, commanders, and contractors scoured the empire for the poor and unemployed. Particularly favored were the denizens of the mountains, remote plateaus, and deserts, all of whom were easy to lure away from the harsh penury of their native lands.[12] There was no single policy or pattern for hiring them. But across the empire, military recruitment tended to produce a hodgepodge of what Virginia Aksan has called "ethnic warrior bands": Bosnians, Albanians, Kurds, Anatolians, Circassians, North African and Lebanese highlanders.[13] Augmenting these mercenary forces were slave-soldiers, primarily Circassians and Georgians who were purchased from the long-established slave markets of the Caucasus. They turned up most conspicuously in the powerful political households of the Arab provinces, where they often took their place in hybrid "mamluk" forces alongside freeborn Muslims, recruited both locally and from across Anatolia and the Balkans, together with a smattering of European converts.

With so many men thrown together from diverse origins, soldiers' most intense loyalty tended to revolve around their own military unit. They had an interest in cultivating an inner solidarity that would encourage members to look out for each other. Sometimes this identity would be obvious if they were fielded from the same region. The governors of Damascus, for instance, frequently hired mercenaries whom locals could instantly name by ethnic or regional background: Kurds, North Africans, Albanians, Turkomans (*dalatiyya*), Baghdadis, Mosulis.[14] They had become a far larger and more obtrusive presence by the eighteenth century, and their rivalries with Janissary forces contributed to the turbulence of local politics. But not all units had such a ready-made identity. In the absence of some regional or ethnic bond, they might have to manufacture a symbolic fraternity. Among barracks stationed in Egypt, soldiers commonly turned each other into "blood brothers." They would cut each other with knives and take turns licking the blood, making them thereafter bound to each other's defense.[15] Heightening the sense of mutual dependence and loyalty was the sheer fact that so many Ottoman soldiers were outsiders to local society, as a matter of ethnic and/or linguistic difference. Further alienating them from the local population, at least in the large urban garrisons, were their origins in villages from distant parts of the empire. Having arrived in unfamiliar settings, they were therefore taught, by social and material necessity, to turn to each other for support.

The vast paramilitary complex bred a lively subculture. Soldiers and their confederates split into cliques and devised secret "insider" codes for themselves. Known as "the crazy one" (al-Majnun), Mehmed Bey ibn Ivaz (d. 1723) formed his own gang of retainers and dependents; they had their own argot, and used to "play ball" with local boys outside his palace in Old Cairo.[16] Members of units might further declare their military status through the use of outlandish nicknames, which often functioned as a kind of wry social commentary.[17] One common custom was to take some physical peculiarity or defect of character and turn it into a kind of personalized "tag." Such labels tended toward exaggeration, which, however crude or distorted, always preserved some kernel of truth (at least as their comrades saw it). From the turmoil of the Patrona Halil uprising (1730), contemporaries could recall soldiers such as "Black Snake" (Karayılan) Ahmed, "Short" (Küçük) Muslı, "Bald" (Keleş) Halil Ağa, "Wrestler" (Pehlivan) Halil Ağa, "Blind" (Kör) İbrahim Ağa, and "Tall" (Uzun) Abdi.[18] Since soldiers lived and worked in urban communities, and might even attain a certain local celebrity, townspeople immediately recognized nicknames. When elements of the Twenty-Fifth regiment of Janissaries started a brawl in Üsküdar (1810), residents could readily identify two well-known participants: "Jackal" (İt) Ömer and "Drunk" (Sarhoş) Arif.[19] Within Janissary regiments, soldiers took a perverse, almost subversive pride in such nicknames, which evoked extreme bravado and aggression, and suggested that they lived at the margins of the law, accountable only to themselves.

This fierce esprit de corps expressed itself in the use of tattoos. By the eighteenth century, perhaps earlier, Janissaries had begun to mark themselves with the insignia of their units. Whenever any soldier had to prove that he belonged to the corps, he might simply display his tattoo if no comrades were nearby to testify on his behalf.[20] After the abolition of the Janissary corps, the arms of several detained soldiers were found to have tattoos, not only of their former unit's insignia but of Christian crosses as well.[21] It is possible that these men were converts who had later joined the corps. More plausible is a link to the Bektaşi Sufi order, which had been closely affiliated with the Janissaries for centuries and had long incorporated elements of Christian ritual and iconography.[22]

Like the tattoos imprinted on their bodies, membership in units was meant to last. Soldiers recognized each other and knew at a glance who belonged and who did not. They did not casually welcome newcomers; nor did they forgive betrayals and defections—condemned as "throwing down the saddle" (semer devirmek) in Janissary slang. One former member of the Azeban barracks in Cairo left Egypt and became an Ottoman naval officer. When he later returned (1706) and tried to reclaim his former place, he got a chilly reception from his erstwhile colleagues, who would not allow it. As doors closed in his face, he joined a rival unit, the müteferrika corps. The defection of such a prominent member initiated a cycle of attacks and reprisals between the two units. The feud spilled into the streets. Soldiers accosted their rivals, pulled them down from horses, and subjected them to beatings.[23] In Istanbul, the defection of a member of the Twenty-Seventh regiment (orta) to the Twenty-Sixth prompted a gunfight (1811) at the Rose Mosque (Gül Camii). The battle left six dead and did not cease even when the sultan happened to pass nearby.[24]

Since dueling was unknown in Ottoman culture, members of the military tended to resolve disputes, whether individually or collectively, through assassinations and ambushes. Common soldiers and sailors were most likely to confront one another with weapons, though not in anything like a ritualized fashion.[25] Casual encounters might quickly turn violent. Contemporaries preserved scattered reports of brawls, knifings, and murders committed in the streets, sometimes in broad daylight. Any mishap could become the explosive pretext for fisticuffs or worse.[26] In 1824, the servants of Yannis Makriyannis, the rebel Greek commander, carelessly threw bathwater out of the window and splashed a passing sailor, who immediately charged up the steps of his house and attacked them. Only the general's personal intervention, together with reimbursement for the sailor's clothes, restored order.[27] The root cause of this particular fray was obvious. But in most cases, observers say little about what ignited altercations or why they might suddenly escalate to violence.

Acting as a constant irritant were rivalries and grudges between military factions. Perhaps the main fault line lay between Janissaries, who regarded themselves as the sultan's true soldiers, and units of mercenaries and provincial levies. The latter groups often felt mistreated. They received lower and/or less regular pay, served under uncertain terms of employment, and chafed under the scorn of the Janissaries.[28] Introducing an extra element of tension was the ethnic organization of some units, which could heighten long-simmering questions about status and prestige. In Damascus, As'ad Paşa al-'Azm was put in a difficult bind (1753) when a North African retainer in the household of his cousin (a daughter of the former governor Sulayman Paşa al-'Azm) got into a dispute with a member of the imperial Janissary garrison (*kapıkulları*) and stabbed him to death.[29] The governor hastily executed him, knowing that the imperial Janissaries would not tolerate any lesser sentence and would likely accuse him of trying to protect his larger kinship network at their expense. The murder of a soldier was most explosive when a quarrel had taken place in the open and the community knew who the combatants were. Unless a unit was prepared to lose face, any offense to their collective dignity would have to be put right. But when violence was committed without witnesses, or without any ostensible political motives, the stakes were lower, or at least more manageable. For precisely this reason, the discovery of a dead Albanian soldier in one of the markets of Damascus (1750) created no disturbances.[30] The body was found around evening prayers, and no one could determine who might have committed the crime. The assumption was that the matter was personal.

Adding plausibility to this verdict was the truculent demeanor of soldiers. They drew guns and knives easily and were susceptible to brawling. So the body was buried, and Damascenes thought no more of the affair.

Rivalries bred by paramilitary culture often expressed themselves in struggles over urban property and territory. In its broadest sense, this "turf" might encompass entire neighborhoods. In Damascus, for example, everyone knew that the imperial Janissaries, one of the two local factions of Janissaries, were heavily concentrated in the neighborhoods to the north and west of the citadel, whereas the "local" Janissaries (*yerliyya*) had their stronghold in al-Midan along the southernmost quarters.[31] During the long Janissary-*ashraf* rivalry in Aleppo (c. 1770s–1810s), the division of territory was broader: Janissaries held Banqusa and the other extramural quarters while the ashraf drew their strength from inside the city walls.[32] In Istanbul, merchants, captains, and sailors all understood that different Janissary units had placed the wharves under their "protection." If ships wanted to land goods, they would have to hang the shield of the regiment in charge and share the profits with its officers.[33] At the turn of the nineteenth century, for instance, the Fifty-Sixth regiment held the wharf at Yemiş İskelesi, where they edged their way into the fruit trade and forced up prices. They quickly extended their racketeering to olive oil, honey, and other goods bound for grocers' shops.[34] Any trader would have known in advance about this informal partition of urban space. Failure to pay off or involve the right military officers would lead to seizures of property or sudden exclusion from neighborhood markets, caravansaries, and shops.

Most emblematic of this division of urban space was the paramilitary presence within coffeehouse culture. One of the stock figures in eighteenth-century towns was the soldier lounging inside a coffeehouse. The notorious thug ʿAli al-Shammaʿ was a soldier attached to the warlord Ahmed Paşa al-Jazzar, whom he represented in Damascus. ʿAli used to take his coffee and pipe every morning at the "Royal Coffeehouse" (without paying, of course). He enjoyed this routine until the news of al-Jazzar's death (1804) reached Damascus and jolted him into a panic one morning as he was sitting in his accustomed place.[35] Easy access to the delights of the coffeehouse was thus one of the great rewards that all soldiers sought. But it was particularly gratifying for those of humble background to whom these consumerist satisfactions had once been either difficult to obtain or altogether unavailable. Conspicuous lounging in a coffeehouse performed a symbolic elevation of their status. To a passing audience on the street, they could now pose as townsmen who were able to partake of the good life.

So powerful was this consumerist allure that most military units had their own coffeehouse, declared to all visitors with a shield bearing their regimental number, often emblazoned with "a weapon, an animal, a plant, [or] some object" and hung over the hearth.[36] In Istanbul, Janissaries spoke of such coffeehouses as being "under their sword."[37] From this inner sanctum, officers would recline and hold the equivalent of court, adjudicating disputes within their regiment and showering gifts and favors on subordinates and dependents.[38] Soldiers would pass their time inside, chatting and drinking, just like other townspeople. More than social haunts, coffeehouses could also act as the urban equivalent of military stations. If anyone wanted to contact a soldier in a particular unit, they would know to ask at its coffeehouse. In Aleppo, it was common knowledge that the "Agha's Coffeehouse," located in the neighborhood of Banqusa, was the informal headquarters for local Janissaries.[39]

Coffeehouses linked to the paramilitary complex participated in a kind of urban demimonde, full of marginal, rootless, or downright disreputable social types. In Istanbul, these were the haunts that welcomed, above all, the workers of the waterfront, which harbored its own restive subculture and absorbed a constant flow of migrants who eked out a living as porters, boatmen, and sailors. Many of them gained membership in Janissary units and quickly entered this bawdy social world.[40] From the larger cast of paramilitary characters, we can select Deli Şerif, a Janissary and rowdy boatman who used to lounge in Istanbul coffeehouses, where he would sometimes play the *saz*. More often, he was a public nuisance. He drank alcohol openly during Ramadan, squeezed passing Christians for money, and committed "various other crimes."[41] Among the most legendary toughs was Laz Küçük Ali, a soldier who ran his own coffeehouse on a wharf (at Yağkapanı İskelesi) in Galata. After he killed two men (1800), a warrant was issued for his arrest. No one could apprehend him. An entire squad of Janissaries surrounded his coffeehouse and began a gunfight. Though entirely alone, Laz Ali repelled the assault and killed several soldiers. The Janissaries then fell back and hatched a new plan. They mined the ground beneath the coffeehouse and blew it to pieces, together with its heavily armed proprietor.[42]

These characters all sought to project a warrior front. They presented themselves as true men of the sword, instantly ready to meet every challenge and redeem their honor personally, man to man, in combat. We get a glimpse of this mentality in the martial bluster of Jackal Ömer, whom we briefly met earlier. Once, as his fellow Janissaries were in a tense standoff with a rival unit, several soldiers attacked him. He goaded the latter with an invitation: if they wanted a "manly fight" (*merdane gavga*), he swore, they should first let him retrieve his sword. His point was that guns could be fired at a distance. A sword put combatants in close proximity where they could truly test each other as warriors.[43] This ideal of swashbuckling gallantry pervaded the Ottoman ranks. At the opening of the Ottoman-Romanov war in 1768, reported Baron de Tott, Ottoman troops had the same complaint against their Russian rivals, whose artillery bombardments kept them at a frustrating distance. If only the Russians would allow hand-to-hand combat, they declared, Ottoman sabers would cut them to pieces.[44] With the same exasperation, they would deplore the hit-and-run tactics of Greek rebels in the 1820s.[45]

All this martial swagger was an outgrowth of ideals of physical courage that members of the paramilitary complex were ever eager to enact. But these ideals had a far larger resonance within Ottoman society and did not amount simply to a cult of masculinity. Women, too, might partake in spectacles of courage, with a doughty few exposing themselves directly to the dangers of battle. Particularly in remote parts of the countryside, they might have to take up arms for the sake of family and community. Tepedelenli Ali Paşa, the Albanian warlord who ruled from Yanina (r. 1788–1822), freely admitted the debt that he owed to his mother, the formidable Esmihan Hamko, who brought him up after his father's death, and as he later swore, "made me a man and a vizier." Before he came of age, she sometimes led their mountain clan's fighters personally into combat.[46] High status was not a prerequisite for such valor. When the governor of Baghdad attacked an Arab tribe (1738), many of its women joined their menfolk in picking up guns and firing back.[47] In towns, too, the same loyalties might persuade urban women to place themselves in danger and wield arms. Getting wind of an assassination plot against him (1768), İsmail Ağa barricaded himself in his mansion in Cairo. At his side was his wife, who reloaded his gun while he held off attackers for two whole days until they tricked him into a false parley and killed him.[48] Virtually the same scene played out in Damascus after the death of the detested warlord al-Jazzar (1804). A jubilant crowd, bent on vengeance, surrounded the home of his chief henchman ʿAli al-Shamma', whom we last saw lounging in a coffeehouse that same morning. As his sister dutifully reloaded his weapons, he fired at them for half the day until they were both overwhelmed.[49]

The bravery of women was nowhere more evident than in street protests, such as demonstrations against grain shortages or official abuses of power. During riots in Istanbul (1758), touched off by the soaring cost of rice, a crowd of women drove away the owner of a storehouse and plundered its stocks. At their head was a woman fearlessly waving a dagger to show that they meant business.[50] During a protest against high prices in Bursa, a crowd of women armed with rocks and clubs rampaged through the main marketplace, smashing the windows in Sırmakeş Han and driving out customs officials. Their actions came to the notice of Selim III, whose call for law and order arrived days after the furor had subsided. With ironic approbation, the folk poet Aşık Halil declared that the "women's faction had unfurled their banner" and become the real men of the town.[51] In Cairo, women turned out alongside men (1806) to protest a proposed tax on the poor. They were conspicuous among the demonstrators for their singing and playing of tambourines.[52] Several years later (1814), a crowd of female tax-farmers, reacting to Mehmed Ali's confiscation of these grants, stormed al-Azhar Mosque in Cairo and caused so much havoc that scholars cancelled classes and fled to their homes. After occupying the mosque for most of the afternoon, the women warned that they would return if their stipends were not properly paid.[53]

Most of the population, even in the towns, remained wedded to ideals of physical valor. In other words, they embraced the "heroic manners" of strength, chivalry, and nobility. Under the Old Regime, these values retained their relevance. Especially below affluent and "respectable" society (ehl-i ırz/ahl al-'ird), townspeople worked with their hands. They performed various kinds of manual labor and did not cultivate excessive refinement. It went without saying that, in working with their hands, they should know how to use their fists as well. Physical strength conferred status. Every neighborhood promoted the memory of its own braves. Admired for more than their muscle, they embodied decency and honor, and were ready to defend their community. In Damascus, Ibn Kannan scribbled a couple of lines (1715) about a local youth who was so strong that he could split a rock with a single blow of his hand.[54] But he did not praise him for anything more than this extraordinary feat. The true champion, most worthy of local legend, had to battle for the communal good: hence the tribute that the same author reserved for a local hero (*shija'*), Muhammad al-Mughassil, who had led his neighborhood (1730) in bringing down a corrupt headman. His victory was short-lived. The headman had been friendly with the local garrison of imperial Janissaries, who began a manhunt, surprised the neighborhood hero as he was relaxing in a coffeehouse, and shot him down.[55] The mantle of noble heroism, rooted in the community, was precisely the legitimizing aura that rebellious Janissaries in Aleppo (1784) wished to invoke for themselves. Members of the corps marched to the courthouse and informed the chief judge of the deposition of the governor and then forbade Friday prayers. As the soldiers prepared to fight, they selected from among their ranks a neighborhood youth of high moral repute and made him their symbolic leader. "The merits of youth, virility, courage, generosity, and gracefulness of character were united in his personality."[56] Behind him they could present themselves as so many neighborhood braves—and were happy to assume this pose precisely because most of them were recruited straight from the countryside.[57]

The same cult of physical strength and valor found a home inside the guilds, many of which had links to the Janissaries. Even after the abolition of the corps, this imagery was still very much alive. As the troops of Mehmed Ali, governor of Egypt, approached Damascus in 1831, a makeshift militia went out to meet the invaders. They were no match for the highly disciplined conscript army of peasants that the Egyptian administration had ruthlessly built. In a brief skirmish, ten Damascenes were killed. One of them was a butcher, Sa'ud, who was "famous for manliness."[58] In this admiration for martial virility, paramilitary culture merely reinforced values that were already deeply embedded in urban society and would outlive the Old Regime itself.

Further flattering these heroic poses was the acquisition of firearms, which, since the sixteenth century, had diffused widely across Ottoman society in both town and country. Prohibitions proved absolutely futile. To take one measure: Christians and Jews were not supposed to own guns, but only in the towns did this restriction have any force. Rural society had long ignored it. On Mt. Lebanon, members of all religious sects went about armed, and made no attempt to hide their weapons.[59] The towns meanwhile were awash with firearms. Periodic campaigns to confiscate them made no appreciable difference. To take one futile effort in Cairo (1664/65): Leading officers gained permission from the governor to conduct searches and seizures of weapons from civilians on the grounds that there were now too many firearms in circulation. The scale of the problem quickly became evident as they combed caravansaries in the markets and fanned out to nearby villages. They turned up "indescribably" large caches and redistributed them to the regiments of Cairo.[60] The population quickly rearmed, as if nothing had happened. They could easily afford to do so since pistols and muskets were cheap and cost much less than sturdy swords, which remained the ceremonial weapon of choice. To cite one telling example: By the eighteenth century, roughly a quarter of the male population of Damascus owned firearms.[61] Townsmen carried them mainly for status. As they knew, few of them would see action in battle on distant frontiers. The real attraction was not military service but association with local political factions, who might at most summon them to the streets as a kind of supplemental militia. During the extended tumult of 1723, the governor of Cairo received a petition from terrified townspeople, who begged him to do something about all the armed men who were swarming through the streets. He announced that anyone caught entering a home or a coffeehouse while carrying a firearm would be summarily executed.[62] The latter warning, aimed specifically at coffeehouses, suggests the extent to which guns now permeated the social life of the towns. In Istanbul, the imperial government, determined to restore order following the deposition of Selim III (1807), issued a decree forbidding anyone from carrying weapons in the streets. A military officer who heard the ferman being read aloud immediately foresaw the difficulty of enforcing it. Nearly all men, he observed, kept at least a gun or knife on their person as they wandered through the markets.[63]

The prevalence of firearms created dangers for urban populations. Most obviously, townspeople might become caught up in the crossfire of factional battles whose frequency was rising across the eighteenth and early nineteenth centuries. On the day that Alemdar Mustafa Paşa immolated himself (1808), a contingent of Janissaries chased former members of the New Army into Aya Sofya Mosque in Istanbul. The protracted exchange of gunfire helped to ignite a conflagration that devastated the surrounding neighborhood.[64] Even when factions were not actively fighting, guns introduced new hazards into street life. Ill-trained soldiers, bristling with weapons and subject to a loose discipline, roamed about town with an undisguised swagger. Alert to snubs and challenges, and forever watchful of rivals, they harbored hair-trigger sensitivities that could all too easily find outlets from the barrel of a gun. During one altercation in the streets of Cairo (1814), a driver was leading camels carrying gunpowder destined for the citadel. He got into a dispute with a nearby soldier, who became so incensed that he drew his gun and fired. A bullet randomly hit one of the sacks and set off an enormous explosion that claimed the lives of more than one hundred people.[65]

Street Talk

Reviewing such an incident, we might wonder: what exactly did the cameldriver say to the soldier that so enraged him? The narrative sources at our disposal do not often furnish such details, mostly passing over them in silence without even pausing to blush. If authors deigned to consider such questions at all, they preferred polite or neutral evasion. In 1784, a mercenary seized a camel from a Janissary auxiliary who had "mocked" him in the streets of Aleppo. Janissaries immediately rushed to their protégé's defense. Gunfire crackled in the streets as shops closed.[66] Which words had goaded him beyond endurance? We will never know. Or we can take the account of the boatmen of Ayazma Wharf in Istanbul, who once hired (1810) a Janissary to steal customers from their rivals. A watchman (*bekçi*) found out about their scheme and confronted them. Words soon escalated into fisticuffs, and the melee spread along the docks, dragging in Janissary units.[67] What had the watchman said? We learn only that he had used a "coarse insult" (*şetm-i galiz*).[68]

Complicating our efforts to make sense of these reactions are questions about what exactly constituted offensive speech. We cannot be sure which words might have crossed the line and turned a verbal exchange into a physical attack. One scribe found out the hard way (1812) as he sat in an Istanbul shop with a neighboring shopkeeper, a former Janissary, and teased him about having gained his money from illegal plunder during the overthrow of the New Order. He had teased him before; little did he realize that he was now going too far. A moment later, the neighbor struck without warning, knifing him to death.[69] Even if we knew exactly what the victim had said, we cannot assume that every soldier, let alone every townsman, would have felt the insult as keenly or immediately turned to physical aggression as the only remedy for wounded honor. Rather than trying to pin down exact expressions, we should first try to establish the range of "coarse insults" to which soldiers resorted.

Once again, the first step is to recognize how paramilitary subculture was embedded within a larger urban culture, where the same insults were in constant circulation. Although the surviving historical sources from the Old Regime do not provide many examples of such speech, we can still get a fairly good idea about the bounds of decency and honor. Affording interesting clues about this verbal register are the surviving traces of Ottoman leisure culture, which fostered forms of coffeehouse entertainment that deliberately and unabashedly mimicked the language of the streets.

The two that tell us the most about patterns of speech were shadow puppet theater (*karagöz* or *khayal al-zill*) and theatrical storytelling (*meddah*). From its first appearance in late medieval times, shadow puppet theater had become an entertainment known and loved throughout the Balkans and Middle East. The setup was simple. Hidden behind a platform, a puppeteer manipulated figurines behind a backlit screen. Complete with accents and other verbal cues, the "cast" represented various ethnic and neighborhood stereotypes, straight out of contemporary urban lore.[70] Every part of the empire had its own version and used local variations of names and characters. Puppeteers performed stock scenarios in which the emphasis lay on satire and earthy humor. The plot usually revolved around characters' pursuit of pleasure and self-interest and had nothing to do with high-minded ideals. The puppets rained down blows and kicks on each other and committed gratuitous violence. Shameless and uninhibited, they spoke frankly about bodily drives and functions. No more diffident was *meddah*, an entertainment especially popular in the capital. Unlike minstrels (*aşık*), who set their stories in faraway times and places, meddah entertainers drew on contemporary urban life and narrated romps and adventures through the very cityscape in which the audience lived.[71] Like the shadow puppeteers, they peppered their speech with street slang and wit. They had little patience for sanctimony and hypocrisy and took free aim at officials deemed corrupt or tyrannical.[72]

As essentially oral forms of entertainment, neither of these genres has left an extensive documentary record. Manuscripts of a few *meddah* tales have survived from the eighteenth century—mainly bare storylines that performers could use to refresh their memory.[73] The earliest transcripts of shadow puppet performances date from the first decades of the twentieth century and can therefore offer little guidance about precise patterns of speech from the Old Regime. But contemporary accounts leave little doubt that shows were irreverent, rough, and lascivious. Particularly revealing is the prudish recoil of European observers, who deplored the indecent antics and gestures that they watched—as well as the audience's gleeful reaction.[74] Their professed disgust had to do mostly with cultural shifts in North Atlantic societies, where the bourgeois cult of prim respectability was ascendant and rapidly distancing itself from folk forms of expression by the late eighteenth century.[75]

The Ottoman Old Regime was not so buttoned up. It did not necessarily insist on polite entertainment. Audiences were relaxed about bawdy performances. Even members of the social elite might delight in prurient banter. If children were in attendance, no one tried to cover their eyes or shoo them away. Ottoman leisure culture treated sex and the body with a frankness that saw no need to blush or apologize. One eighteenth-century traveler came across dancing girls in the streets of Cairo, where their "libidinous postures and actions exceed all imagination."[76] No spectators tried to protest or interfere. The stigma attached only to the profession, not the performance. Hence female dancers were recruited mostly from the lowest ranks of society; only a small number of them, trained in poetry and music, were able to escape this taint.[77] The alternative was to hire men who impersonated women. These dancers performed throughout the Ottoman Empire, and helped to compensate for the reluctance of Ottoman culture to put women "on stage." They wore women's clothing and assumed female mannerisms. There were no campaigns to outlaw or restrict them. Despite this blurring of gender roles, which Ottoman society blithely tolerated in this particular social space, these dancers occupied a fully acceptable role in public as well as private entertainment. When Balkan troops entered Cairo in 1809, they had already endured many tribulations on campaign and looked exhausted and shabby. Even in this battered state, they still made sure to keep their own troop of cross-dressing dancers, who affected female speech and had drums and tambourines to accompany their movements.[78] The soldiers had the same taste in entertainment as the rest of Ottoman society.

So if soldiers used "coarse insults," they had plenty of company. In filling their speech with obscenities and rough expressions, they were repeating expressions that one could hear on nearly any street, where the hurling of vulgarities was commonplace. Among the most reflexive taunts were comparisons with animals regarded as unclean, especially dogs or pigs.[79] On the island of Syros during the 1820s, Orthodox Christians mocked their Catholic neighbors as "dog-Franks" on account of the consular protection that they received from France, as well as their reluctance to join the anti-Ottoman revolt.[80] After rebel soldiers in Istanbul hacked to death Ahmed Bey (1807), a "very fat" courtier to Selim III, unsympathetic spectators sneered that he was "a pig, but a fatty one" as his intestines spilled out.[81] Across the entire social order, to the very top, donkeys took perhaps the most routine verbal abuse. Reading correspondence from officials who had somehow mishandled affairs, Selim III himself would occasionally vent his spleen at the "jackass of a guy" (*eşek bir herif*) who was responsible for bungling some matter or other.[82]

The heaviest insults invoked religious, scatological, and sexual imagery, the same verbal triad that has consistently appeared in most societies as the core repertoire of abuse and vilification.[83] Ottoman usages were by no means peculiar.

Religious oaths and imprecations were among the favorite verbal salvos. Of most practical concern, because of the potential legal consequences, were conditional oaths of divorce (set to go into effect, that is, if some stipulated event ultimately happened or came true). Muslim men, drawing on a long-standing pattern of "Islamic" swearing, were known to utter them during moments of rage or frustration.[84] If the premise of the oath had actually come to pass, and witnesses could testify to the man having pronounced it, Islamic law viewed the marriage as instantaneously dissolved. In the interest of stabilizing marriage as an institution, jurists worked hard at rescuing rash husbands from the fallout of their own verbal thunderbolts.[85] Beyond the thickets of these legal complications, into which only the most impetuous hotheads would stumble, lay the true mainstream of religious invective. Only the polite and educated worked at keeping their tongues pure. Among the unlettered majority—and for that matter, even among those who in theory knew better—this vituperation made itself heard nearly everywhere. The streets of Istanbul, for instance, rang with a chorus of oaths: "irreligious" (*dinsiz*), "faithless" (*imansız*), "infidel" (*gavur*), "heretic" (*kızılbaş*), "son-of-a-priest" (*papasoğlu*).[86] All these words were too common to retain any shock value.

Along with religious taunts, Ottoman society spewed a torrent of carnivalesque language that openly and exultantly conjured up lower bodily functions. The worst imprecation, as Mouradgea d'Ohsson recollected, was uttered by men and women, young and old alike: "Let me fuck his/her mother" (*anasını sikiyim*).[87] Scatological references were ubiquitous and littered the speech of workers. During the Kabakçı Mustafa rebellion (1807) in Istanbul, boatmen tried to buck up the courage of an Ottoman officer who had taken refuge with them. Cowering in one of their rowboats, and fearful of the strong currents, he was afraid to make a dash and enter the main channel of the Bosphorus for a quick escape. They lectured him: "All the waters of Büyükdere are treacherous with currents. Hey, efendi, don't eat shit! If we don't enter the current and take the Istanbul route, the fortress soldiers following us by land and sea will certainly engage now and shit in your dear mouth!"[88] In Mosul, a military commander could openly mock a local butcher as "son of shit," even though the latter was a *sayyid*, or recognized descendant of the prophet Muhammad.[89] The streets of Egyptian towns were equally used to hearing such talk. To take one saying from Damietta: "A man ... sinks as low as a sheatfish searching for excrement. They also say of someone who speaks of what is not his business that he is as persistent as a sheatfish in eating shit."[90]

There was nothing particularly "soldierly" about profanity. Paramilitary culture merely took a more gleeful and unapologetic delight in invoking it and more readily garnished its speech with crude gibes and insults.[91] The entry of more townsmen into the ranks of the military, together with rural migrants whose speech was no more delicate and perfumed, meant that this foul-mouthed patois was ascending in pitch and volubility during the long eighteenth century. Officers resorted to it as freely as the men under their command. When cavalrymen in Cairo protested that their salaries and grain allotments had fallen into arrears (1746), blame fell on Ibrahim Bey Katamiş, who defiantly responded, "Let the soldiers eat shit!" His fellow officers were appalled—not by the swearing, but by his indifference to the plight of the unpaid troops, who finally got their wages after hurried negotiations.[92] Coarse language was particularly likely to erupt in moments of military bravado. It could act as a means of shaming comrades who were vacillating in the midst of battle; or more reassuringly, it could summon up a kind of rough courage that would pull them together. During the revolt that brought down Selim III in Istanbul, Janissaries were busy in Etmedyanı dismembering the body of İbrahim Kethüda (İbrahim Nesim Efendi), one of the top reformist officials whom they detested. When rumors reached them about troops loyal to the sultan preparing for a counterattack, some soldiers in the crowd began to waver. One of the ringleaders sought to stiffen their resolve and shouted, "Hey shits! What are you running from? It's as if you're a bunch of crows!"[93] The Janissaries would keep their nerves intact that day. So, too, would Greek rebels at the battle of Lerna (1825). As the fighting got under way, their commander, Yannis Makriyannis, privately worried that "all the feeble troops we were saddled with would shit themselves with panic and push off to Nauplion."[94] Decades later, as an honored general of the Greek kingdom, he still resorted to the pungent language of the battlefield in recollecting his emotions that day.

With its attachment to martial virility, paramilitary culture nursed an extreme sensitivity to any imputation of cowardice or even the slightest hesitation in battle. When an Ottoman officer mocked the irregular cavalry (*delibaşları*) in his force as "chicken-hearted" for their reluctance to go on the attack, the words carried more weight and vitriol than any casual reading of the insult might convey.[95] Many officials and soldiers were conscious of public opinion and feared being labeled as weak or indecisive. Soldiers in Cairo, bent on toppling Çerkes Mehmed Bey al-Kabir, a regimental commander, were certainly aware of this pressure. As they were rumored to have told each other (1728/29), "If we don't challenge him, the people of Cairo will mock us."[96] Far more cutting, and intolerable to masculine sensibilities, was any insinuation about fearing women, held up as the very antithesis of the rugged warrior. During the final Faqari-Qasimi showdown in Cairo (1730), three upper-class women from the vanquished Qasimi faction were implicated in a murder plot. Osman Kazdağlı, a Faqari leader, intervened and had their sentence commuted. He chided the officer who had obtained the decree against them: "You idiot! Do you want the central government to say that the warriors (*ghuzz*) of Egypt were so frightened of three women that they had to exile them to Istanbul? I'll guarantee the three. If they get involved in anything, I'll be responsible."[97] Ever vigilant about honor and reputation, the proper soldier would create an aura of grim and unflinching valor.[98] If the mask slipped even slightly, he would expose himself to the mockery of wagging tongues. As`ad Paşa al-`Azm, governor of Damascus, was for a time (1745) unable to stop the depredations of local mercenaries, who began to call him "Lady Sa`diyya (the feminine form of his name) who sleeps with the sleepers." Irritated by his inaction, local Janissaries soon took up the refrain, also taunting him as "Sa`diyya."[99] Worst of all was the charge that an official or soldier was so weak and helpless that he had openly succumbed to tears. Deposed from the governorship of Damascus after major defeats against Egyptian and regional forces (1771), Osman Paşa traveled north in disgrace and reportedly "wept like the women" after being barred entry by the small Syrian town of Ma`arat Nu`man. In the voice of Ibn al-Siddiq, the soldier who related this episode, the words conveyed contempt, not pity.[100] Only during the deep emotional shock caused by the death of a loved one, or perhaps a patron, might a hardened man of state freely give way to tears.[101]

One step down from this feminizing imagery was a demeaning repertoire of sexual slurs. Utterly commonplace, they ranked among the heaviest assaults on honor—not only against the individual, but potentially an entire family or household. In Istanbul, street banter was full of gibes about "pimps" (*pezevenk* or *kerata*) or "catamites" (*puşt*). As his enemies would have it, Feyzullah Efendi, the disgraced officer in charge of the Dardanelles fortifications (1807), "came into the world as the son of a shameless, dishonorable womanizing pimp."[102] Bursting into an imperial stable in Istanbul (1811), guards demanded that the steward hand over a fugitive who had taken shelter there. They swore and made threats. The steward was defiant. "Who are you to come and swear at me and call me a pimp? I am a member of the palace guard!" He yielded only after being shown an order from Janissary headquarters.[103]

Sexual innuendo had the further function of symbolically expressing domination. Within sexual relations, the culture of the Old Regime thought in terms of male and female roles, even when sexual partners were of the same gender. The male role was active; the female, submissive.[104] Taunts about sex—like the frontier soldiers who boasted about "the infidel whose grandmother I fucked"[105]—therefore served as imagery for conquest or subordination. More than the woman, the man was the target of the mockery: that is, the man who was unable to protect the women of his household. This protection was the cornerstone of a household's honor. Casting doubt on another man's ability to provide it was an intolerable provocation. Amid a wave of monetary turbulence in Istanbul (1809), officials could only seethe as Janissaries went about shaking down shopkeepers and money-changers. With feigned horror, some soldiers asked what they had done to antagonize "the higher-ups" (*paşalılar*): "Did the Janissaries fuck their women?"[106] In the language of the street, it was the most unbearable humiliation.

The symbolism of domination worked in reverse as well. Scabrous insults that put rivals in the "female" sexual position rendered them submissive or overpowered. During the "English Event" (Vaka-i İngiliz) of early 1807, a brief Anglo-Ottoman war, British ships bombarded hastily constructed defenses near Istanbul, causing local units to flee in a panic. A hostile chronicler has the routed troops exclaim: "Mercy brother! The ass cannot take the infidel's buggering!" as they ran away to hide in their villages in the mountains.[107] The ignominious retreat in the military engagement carried, at least for the author of the account, the equivalent of a sexual humiliation at the hands of other men. A steadfast posterior, on the other hand, was an indisputable sign of bravery and masculine sternness of purpose. This is the point that Georgios Karaiskakis (d. 1827), a rebel Greek commander, was literally trying to prove (1821) in the early months of the Greek war of independence. During a skirmish with Ottoman forces, he "was wounded in his cock; he stuck his arse out to make mock of the Turks and got hit" in a hail of gunfire.[108]

Most provocative were demeaning references to mothers, wives, or sisters. No affronts touched so directly on the honor of a family or proved so hard to ignore. We can take them as a part of a larger pattern, also found in early modern Europe, whereby the honor of women was a paramount social concern and thus a perennial target for slander and vilification.[109] These sensitivities were on full display one evening (1810) at a tavern in the Istanbul neighborhood of Galata. After five sailors got drunk and became unruly, the owner sent for a Janissary patrol. The two responding officers tried to usher the sailors out gently: "Comrades, you've had a good time" (*Keyfiniz tamamdır yoldaşlar*). The sailors shot back, "Get out of here!" (*Hayda şurdan!*), and chased them away. The officers came back with reinforcements, and received "coarse insults" from the sailors. Sensing the growing danger, three of the sailors now thought twice about their defiance and left. In a fit of drunken bravado, the two who remained swore that they would rather die than leave. As it so happened, everyone in this standoff belonged to the same Janissary unit, and so the officers called their commander to the tavern. The sailors' tantrum did not subside. They "swore about the mother and wife" of the commander and pulled their weapons. Perhaps aware that they had now gone too far, they decided to leave. The commander followed them anyway, and as he later claimed, saw them assault a Christian in front of a church. He intervened and met with a second round of curses from the two sailors. Having reached the breaking point, the patrol now opened fire and killed them.[110] The words aimed at the women of the commander's family were no doubt ringing in his ears. He had found a pretext for avenging the offense, which had become intolerable once they repeated it. Some insults could not be allowed to stand.

The "Etiquette" of Factional Violence

Just as individuals who committed violence often performed gestures that carried some deeper meaning, so too did groups or units of soldiers. They might well feel rage against some enemy and set about attacking them in the most pitiless manner. But exactly how would they express this rage? Even at the peak of ferocity, violence was never entirely blind or random; it had an underlying coherence, if not complete predictability or forethought. It contained some ritual element that conveyed a latent message, aimed both at enemies and spectators and presented as a rationalization or coded appeal for legitimacy. As the anthropologist Anton Blok memorably put it, there is no "senseless violence."[111] The most vicious deeds use a shared set of symbols and signals that witnesses, though gripped by fear and horror, can still interpret. Ottoman society was familiar with this otherwise hidden "system" of communication, which the political unrest of the late eighteenth and early nineteenth centuries would bring to the fore with a disconcerting frequency.

Since so many soldiers were drawn straight from the countryside, their actions have to be related, first and foremost, to the social idioms of village and clan. This vast influx of recruits quite naturally transplanted the informal "rules" of rural conflict to the streets and markets of even the largest towns. Most conspicuous was the resemblance of factional struggles to the customs of feuding and raiding. Amid regimental vendettas and street skirmishes, soldiers did not simply commit random violence; they observed a hidden set of conventions that helped to determine the rhythms and targets of their attacks. Units acted like fictive clans and reproduced many of the same tactics and maneuvers of the rural honor system.[112]

All factions were highly conscious of the "turf" that they controlled. Members of different units knew not to cross the invisible—and yet well-known—territorial boundaries that separated them. Any intrusion represented a potentially explosive challenge that would not go unanswered. Perhaps nothing was more provocative than an assault on a unit's coffeehouse, which acted as its informal headquarters and housed its insignia. In Aleppo, the *ashraf* opened prolonged skirmishes against local Janissaries (1797) by seizing and plundering several of the latter's coffeehouses. When the tide of battle later turned, the Janissaries visited identical retribution on their foes, who watched the invasion of their own coffeehouses.[113] During both phases of these disturbances, nearly everyone could have predicted this selection of targets, which were treated almost as military bases. Possession, even if temporary, could be held up as a tactical victory that both factions, in "keeping score," would not have failed to tally. Coffeehouses fell prey to the same sequence of sally and reprisal in Istanbul during the period of disorder that followed the overthrow of Selim III. One evening in 1809, troops from the Sixty-Fourth regiment shattered the windows of a coffeehouse in Karaköy, which, as they well knew, belonged to the head of the Twenty-Fifth regiment, who had earlier sealed shut a coffeehouse owned by a member of the Sixty-Fourth, implicated in a scandal.[114] The Twenty-Fifth regiment had another coffeehouse, which not long afterward became the target of an attack from the Fifty-Ninth. The raid ignited a long struggle, which only ended when troops of the Twenty-Fifth, together with allies, landed in Üsküdar and routed the Fifty-Ninth in their Asian stronghold. The victors immediately went on a rampage, burning shops and breaking the shields (*nişan*) of the Fifty-Ninth wherever they found them.[115] As strategic objectives, coffeehouses lent direction and purpose to urban warfare that might otherwise seem chaotic and senseless. Two years after this skirmish, Janissary units mobilizing for campaign began a fierce gun battle that raged throughout the day and paralyzed much of the capital. With smoke still hanging in the air, the lieutenant commander of the corps (*segbanbaşı*) was amazed to learn that no one had died, quipping that "with all those gunshots, how is it there aren't a hundred dead?"[116] He snorted that it was like watching "dogs fighting under a tray of pastries." One of the sparks for the clash was a Janissary turf war over coffeehouses in Esirpazarı and Tavukpazarı.[117]

The *segbanbaşı* was taking an overly professional view of the matter. The entire battle had no doubt seemed like an absurd military pantomime that, amid all the din, had not followed any discernable plan. But it was not empty theater. For the troops firing in the streets, the rules of engagement obeyed the protocol of rural feuding and raiding.[118] Honor was paramount.[119] A detachment might well set out to kill a rival, but could easily settle for an attack on property or any symbol associated with the enemy. Whichever target they chose, they would have to mount a kind of public performance in which they ostentatiously stood their ground and proved their mettle.[120] The noise and smoke must have rightly seemed terrifying to spectators, but left behind relatively little damage—even though the soldiers had paralyzed the capital for an entire day. As far as the soldiers were concerned, they had achieved their objective. In accordance with the rules of rustic frays, each side took turns in a series of managed retaliations.[121] Saving face did not require them to spill excessive blood. Instead of raiding fields and pastures like rural combatants, they sought out urban landmarks where they could stage the equivalent of an ambush. The resemblance becomes still more obvious in the symbolic targeting of property. In laying claim to urban territory, soldiers commonly hung regimental insignia to specific buildings and equipment.[122] Rivals would try to deface this property. Hence an officer from the Faqari faction in Cairo (1713), wishing to infuriate rival Qasimis, knew exactly how to get at them: by conducting a secret raid in which he and his men cut off the tails of Qasimi horses, put out to pasture.[123] The scene could have been easily transported to the countryside.

Unlike inter-factional struggles, organized around the rituals of feuding and raiding, factional revolts took a different form: rituals of vengeance inflicted on individual officials who had enacted some detested measure or policy. To illustrate, we can take several episodes from the turbulent months in 1807 and 1808, which witnessed first the overthrow of Selim III, then Mustafa IV, and finally the grand vizier Alemdar Mustafa Paşa. Punctuating this unrest were moments in which the victorious Janissaries of the capital, having killed or captured high-ranking enemies, perpetrated symbolic violence on their corpses.[124] Each of these acts was deliberate, not spontaneous, and communicated through a repertoire of formulaic gestures. Some mirrored official pronouncements and punishments; others were purely transgressive in spirit. All were broadly understood by participants and witnesses.

In the bloody purge that followed the dethronement of Selim III (1807), Janissary rebels took their revenge on the leaders of the New Order with a brutality and glee that unnerved many onlookers. They seized and beheaded several senior officers, placed their heads in a basin (*leğen*), and then hauled these trophies to Etmeydanı. They took out the decapitated heads in the square and began to kick them around; they taunted the lifeless skulls, and cut at the faces with knives. Much of their fury was directed against the body of İbrahim Kethüda, whose grisly execution we encountered earlier. The Janissaries did not stop with simply killing him; one of the soldiers took his corpse and shoved a piece of wood into his anus. This last gesture recalled, in rough form, the punishment that the Ottoman state commonly meted out to those condemned as outlaws, forcing them to sit on sharpened stakes that pierced them from the buttocks up through the midriff. As the Janissaries' agitation grew, they sliced his body apart with swords, hacking it into small fragments until "each piece was about the size of a piaster [*kuruş*]." The horrifying culmination of this scene, which took place in plain view, was undoubtedly the ritual licking of the very swords that they had used to carve up the corpse. Other Janissaries, watching from a distance, bellowed that they too should have the privilege of licking the blood, and demanded their turn.[125] These acts bore a strong resemblance to the bonding rituals that created blood-brothers, who licked each other's blood off the same blade. Here, too, the Janissaries asserted solidarity. Equally manifest was a second symbolic gesture, in which they absorbed the strength and vitality of their vanquished foe.[126] One soldier, explicitly invoking this imagery, insisted on cutting out İbrahim Kethüda's liver. "He destroyed my family and made my liver suffer anguish. So I shall bake and eat his liver!"[127] The cannibalistic meal would confirm both the defeat of his victim and the restoration of his own potency.

Nothing about this gruesome scene was particularly novel—or by the standards of early modern societies, uniquely Ottoman—in character.[128] Rebellious Janissaries had hacked other officials to pieces during earlier uprisings in Ottoman history. The soldiers would have known these stories and could enact them as part of an older Janissary lore, in which the corps had defended itself and quite literally obliterated enemies who had threatened it.[129] The selection of Etmeydanı was very much part of this ritual procedure. It was the place in Istanbul where Janissaries received their allotment of meat and where they gathered whenever they wished to declare grievances against officials. Since the seventeenth century, several Janissary rebellions had begun there.[130] It was therefore the same place where they would visit retribution on hostile officials and, if necessary, march on the palace itself. We can see this same reflex being activated in a separate incident that very same day. While one group of Janissaries was tearing apart the body of İbrahim Kethüda, a second was looking for "Gizli Sıtma" Hacı İbrahim Efendi, director of the imperial arsenal, who was hiding at his waterside mansion. Betrayed by a boatman, Hacı İbrahim soon fell into the hands of his pursuers, who showed no mercy. As if following some official directive, they marched him, barefoot and bareheaded, toward Etmeydanı along the royal procession route (Divanyolu). They began to insult and beat him. In a mock salute, some soldiers called out to their comrades to stand at attention while others pretended to present a petition. Still others cut off "the finger that held his pen" (and thus wrote out decrees) and threw it, in a cannibalistic gesture, into a Janissary cauldron as punishment for oppressing the poor.[131] As the group passed Beyazit Mosque, their prisoner collapsed from exhaustion. At once, the Janissaries hacked him to bits. "Each piece they threw to a part of Sultan Beyazit Square." No one was allowed to remove any portion of the body. The Janissaries were determined to inflict the final revenge, not merely of denying him a proper funeral, but of leaving his scattered remains to the dogs, who came at night to devour their grisly meal.[132]

The same acts appear over and over as part of a vocabulary of revenge. The victim's body would bear the fury of soldiers in public spectacles of humiliation designed to play out in front of the largest possible audience. To take the death of Alemdar Mustafa Paşa: After a Janissary uprising toppled the grand vizier in 1808, the rebels took his corpse, attached ropes to the legs, and pulled him through the streets, conveying him in a sort of cadaverous tour to underscore his downfall and utter defeat. When the soldiers reached Etmeydanı—again chosen quite deliberately—they hung him upside down from a tree and put a pipe (*çubuk*) in his mouth. Once they had finished this mocking of the corpse, they set to work, exactly as with Hacı İbrahim, carving it up with swords and knives. His "meat and fat" were left for the dogs. Many of Alemdar's allies were executed in the following days along with a number of officers from the New Order who had survived the first purge. Their bodies, too, were dumped in the streets for the dogs; and for good measure, a few of them were burned until only "ashes" remained, as if to extinguish their memory forever.[133] The soldiers had no need to invent any of these macabre reprisals. Janissary lore could look back to the example set during the Patrona Halil revolt. After the dismissal of Nevşehirli Damad İbrahim Paşa (1730), the grand vizier's body was dragged through the streets and left for the dogs at the gates of the palace. On that earlier occasion, rebels varied only in their method for defiling the corpse: gouging out his eyes with tulips and placing candles in the empty sockets. They mocked their victim twice over. A craze for tulips had overtaken the Ottoman court during the 1720s and become a symbol of the imperial extravagance that the rebels accused Damad İbrahim of promoting. The candles recalled the numerous nighttime festivities that the fallen grand vizier had organized at court.[134]

So the dragging of the corpse through the streets was a central ritual of revenge in Ottoman political culture. Practiced far beyond the capital, it was a fate that might overtake any fallen official, wherever factional contests turned deadly. In Damascus (1746), Fathi al-Daftari, the powerful provincial treasurer, lost a power struggle with the governor, As'ad Paşa al-'Azm (r. 1743–57), who had for several years been quietly plotting his removal. As'ad Paşa personally presented the imperial death sentence to Fathi, who vainly pleaded for his life, offering all his property and accumulated wealth for a reprieve. After the beheading, the governor's troops pulled the corpse, headless and naked, through the streets of Damascus for three days.[135] This posthumous shaming of the treasurer was completely calculated. As we earlier had the opportunity to observe, Fathi had mistreated women in the household of As'ad's uncle, the previous governor, and set As'ad on a course to avenge his family's honor and literally strip his rival of his own. In exposing the body, As'ad branded him as deviant and impious, as if his victim were as indecent in death as he was in life. But stripping was egregious, and not strictly necessary for the vindictive and delegitimizing functions of the spectacle. During the overthrow of the New Order in 1807, Janissaries took hold of the hapless corpse of Sırkatibi Ahmed Efendi, close advisor to the sultan, who had tried to make a desperate escape over the rooftops of the capital. He did not get very far. As a detachment of Janissaries pursued him from below, he slipped and fell to the street, where they cut off his head. The soldiers were not content with this summary execution alone. They made local Christians and Jews, shoemakers in the market of Şehzadebaşı, pull his corpse along the nearby thoroughfare.[136] The delegation of the insult was doubly demeaning insofar as they delivered a dead Muslim to Christians and Jews, who would now handle the body instead of co-religionists. In denying Ahmed Efendi a prompt and dignified burial, they further emphasized his exclusion from the community of Muslims, retrospectively damning him as unfit and unqualified for high office.

This attachment to Muslim symbols merely legitimized political interests and claims. It did not imply anything like absolute reverence for religion itself. When a Janissary in the central Anatolian town of Amasya (1824) quarreled with a religious student over a debt, the dispute boiled over into the streets the next day. Reinforced by a contingent of armed townsmen, both Muslim and Christian, the Janissaries staged a raid on the religious school (*medrese*) where the student was staying. The attackers killed the student and several of his friends before binding their feet and dragging the corpses into the streets. The final gesture of contempt was to stomp publicly on their turbans, whose association with Islamic learning offered no protection.[137] Why the homicidal violence? It was undoubtedly a moment of factional vengeance. Despite their vocation, religious students were perfectly capable of organizing their own armed gangs. In Istanbul, they occasionally clashed with Janissaries and affiliated artisans. During one bloody melee in Istanbul (1787), students brought knives and guns and scuffled with members of the belt-makers' guild; the two groups rampaged from Sultan Mehmed Mosque all the way to a nearby bathhouse.[138] Thus at street level, the difference between armed students and other factions would have easily blurred and made them subject to the same reprisals that other combatants suffered.

Whoever the victims might be, paramilitary violence did not flinch at the public display and mutilation of dead rivals. It took its cues partly from official rites of punishment reserved for criminals, brigands, and other enemies of the state. In Istanbul, the bodies of disgraced officials or captured rebels were still being hung in public places, either at Topkapı Palace or one of the main city gates, well into the nineteenth century.[139] Outlaws—or to put it more accurately, anyone whom the state branded with this term—were a special target of official wrath. Military expeditions strove to send back tangible proof of their victories in the field. In 1798, an Ottoman ambush took the lives of sixty-three brigands in Serbia. Heads and ears were duly cut off and carried to Istanbul.[140] These mutilations were, in fact, an old procedure. Sacks of heads, stuffed with salt and straw, functioned as a kind of forensic addendum to official dispatches bearing news of the latest military exploits. In battle, too, Ottoman soldiers—as well as their peers in other societies, then and now—commonly took bodily trophies from fallen enemies.[141] After repulsing a Russian attack on the fortress of İsmail (1806), the Ottoman commander sent back six hundred prisoners, fifteen hundred heads, and several wagons full of "the horsetails that the infidels attach to their heads."[142] Though in rebellion against the sultanate, Greek rebels very much conformed to the same practices in collecting the heads of fallen enemies or offering bounties for them.[143] Even in leaving the empire, they retained their Ottoman formation.

In provincial towns, these gruesome rites were adapted to local power struggles. The display of human trophies furnished the same incontestable proof of one side having prevailed over another and symbolically subjected it to domination and dishonor. When two military officers were assassinated in Cairo (1720), their skulls were skinned, stuffed with hemp, and fitted with glass eyes.[144] In the tumultuous politics of the Egyptian barracks, such ghoulish souvenirs ranked among the spoils of combat. In 1768, a struggle among the beys of Egypt ended at the town of Tanta. The leaders of the losing faction were killed and promptly beheaded. A procession carrying six heads "in a silver case" entered Cairo. As the soldiers paraded through the streets, attendants cried, "Blessings upon Muhammad!" One of the victorious commanders, Salih Bey, rode with a ferocious scowl on his face, warning of the same fate for anyone who would oppose his will.[145] Why did the severed heads receive so much care and attention? If they were to be kept as trophies, it was necessary to preserve them from decay. Fresh from a punitive expedition to Upper Egypt (1807), where the last of the Mamluks were waging an insurgency, Mehmed Ali's troops forgot this cardinal rule in transporting severed heads. As onlookers quickly deduced, the victors had neglected to take the precaution of skinning and salting the skulls, which had begun to decompose and "stink."[146] In view of all these complicated preparations, some officers simply dispensed with them, content either to place decapitated heads atop lances and parade them through the streets, or to haul sacks of heads at their side.[147] A variation on this theme was to leave the head of the executed outside his residence, where passersby would take note of his fate.[148]

We might wonder in passing: were these gestures peculiar to Ottoman political culture? Not if we are to judge from the actions of French commanders during the occupation of Egypt (1798–1801). They were ready to take the same measures and parade the severed heads of defeated Mamluks around the streets of Cairo.[149] These scenes were not very different from the political theater staged by the tribunals of revolutionary France, which had never blanched at placing heads on pikes or exhibiting them to gawking crowds after the guillotine had done its work.[150]

All these violent rituals were not simply a manifestation of state or factional power. In the mountain feuds of the Balkans, the taking of heads served as both a humiliation of the vanquished enemy and a badge of bravery for the battle-tested warrior.[151] Townsmen, too, were not necessarily averse to the practice. During the Janissary uprising against the governor of Aleppo (1784), many locals joined the fighting. In the full flush of victory, they cut off the heads of fallen retainers and mercenaries and paraded them through the streets.[152] In fact, the line between soldiers and townspeople was not so easy to draw; they recognized the same gestures of vengeance and retribution. When troops attached to Ahmed Paşa al-Jazzar ambushed and killed a son of the recently executed Zahir al-`Umar, they made haste with his head to Damascus, where townspeople greeted the trophy with an impromptu celebration (1776).[153] They had fresh memories of Zahir's role in supporting the Egyptian invasion of 1771, which had caused much hardship.

If there were general rituals guiding factional violence, townspeople knew that they could not count on anything like firm rules that would shield them from the fallout of full-blown street fighting. Battles could erupt nearly anywhere; no space was off-limits. Even houses of worship such as mosques, supposedly sacrosanct in "Islamic society," were no guarantee of safety. In the middle of Ramadan in 1808, a religious student, a "fanatical Laz," murdered a romantic rival from the Janissary corps. The student took refuge in Sultan Mehmed Mosque, one of the great Ottoman monuments in Istanbul, where he fired on his pursuers from inside. Wounded, his ammunition exhausted, he staggered into the streets, where Janissaries quickly subdued and executed him.[154] In Cairo (1714), soldiers skirmishing with rival units chose Sultan Hasan Mosque as their base. They had no hesitation about interrogating and executing captured enemies inside.[155] During factional clashes in Aleppo (1798), Janissaries did not shrink from butchering ashraf who had surrendered in al-Utrush Mosque.[156] From a strictly military perspective, the occupation of mosques conferred undeniable tactical advantages. Amid street battles in Damascus (1739), Albanian mercenaries took up perches on the minarets and roofs of two mosques and freely sniped at enemies below.[157] During the uprising in Aleppo that would lead to the expulsion of the governor (1784), Janissaries also had no compunction about firing on the governor's palace from nearby minarets, which commanded a superb line of sight.[158]

If troops could turn mosques into battlefields, it was certainly no more difficult to rampage through churches. Emir Yusuf al-Shihabi sent his North African troops to the village of Antelias, north of Beirut, seeking payment of back-taxes (1776). When they met resistance, they wrecked the village church, pulling down its walls and belfry in retribution.[159] This demolition did not represent the release of some pent-up hostility felt by Muslims against Christians on account of sectarian antagonisms. Across Mt. Lebanon, as well as many other parts of the Ottoman Empire, some churches had long served as places of pilgrimage for members of all religious communities and were universally recognized as sacred grounds.[160] The message that the raid delivered to the delinquent villagers was entirely political. Enfolded within it was a second message reminding subjects that, in the grim calculus of political struggles, no refuge was perfectly secure or untouchable.

Can we pin all this profane violence, which did not heed the sanctity of mosques and churches, on the actions of ill-disciplined soldiers? On this question, too, it is wrong to view soldiers differently from subjects. Urban rioters might themselves convert mosques or churches into theaters of vengeance. After the death of Ahmed Paşa al-Jazzar (1804), townspeople poured into the streets to hunt for his henchmen and retainers. They dragged three to Sinaniyya Mosque, where they killed them inside.[161] Christians were no less willing to turn churches into crucibles of political struggle. In the turbulent aftermath of the Greek war of independence, rivals had no hesitation (1831) about assassinating Yannis Kapodistrias, the first Greek head of state, at the Church of St. Spyridon in Nafplio.[162]

Conclusion: The New Urban Warrior

The blurring of the boundaries between Ottoman military and "civilian" society created an extensive paramilitary subculture. Firmly entrenched in the Janissary corps, many of whom were indistinguishable from artisans and laborers, lay a segment of urban society that had acquired military status but without necessarily performing military service or gaining the requisite training for it. They had joined the ranks mainly to qualify for exemptions from imperial taxes and to gain access to political networks and their accompanying forms of protection. Flooding into the ranks of the military during the tumultuous decades of the Great Crisis was a further infusion of recruits, lured overwhelmingly from among the poor, who became the main beneficiaries of the state's desperate search for manpower. The growing number of men placed under arms, whether for real or nominal terms of service, ensured that they would leave a deepening footprint in Ottoman society, particularly in the towns, where they integrated themselves into local markets. Thus a set of new figures appeared on the urban scene. Of lowly birth, and mostly of rural origin, they pressed for social advancement with few resources of their own. To urban observers, they seemed like little more than a seething rabble, who, owing to their humble station, held no share of the honor to which urban gentlemen believed themselves entitled.[163] In other words, they suffered from a mismatch between their self-perception and wider social reception. Despite having gained new status as soldiers of the sultan, they earned only contempt from established townsfolk, who regarded them as boors and ruffians whose presence was becoming ever more disruptive to urban life.

As military units expanded and absorbed men of disparate social origins, their precise social standing became more indeterminate. Insecure, their expectations unfulfilled, they became more truculent. The modest social mobility that they had gained from military affiliation and service had produced benefits which were hard to measure or had delivered less than they had hoped for. Their disappointments would mount during the economic and monetary crisis of the late eighteenth and early nineteenth centuries, which ate away at their precarious earnings. Much of the social turbulence during this period flowed directly from the discontents of the paramilitary "underclass," which had made itself both more feared and despised by the final decades of the Old Regime in the early nineteenth century.

Viewed from a global perspective, these troubles amounted to a uniquely Ottoman social problem. Unable to generate revenues comparable to its main western Eurasian adversaries, the Ottoman state continued in the eighteenth century with increasingly threadbare financial expedients that vastly enlarged its sprawling paramilitary complex, but without shaping it into a more disciplined or effective fighting force. By the decades of the Great Crisis at the turn of the nineteenth century, the terms of this social and fiscal bargain had become more obviously unsustainable as perceptions of urban insecurity became more rampant and acute. The fall of the Ottoman Old Regime thus proceeded from more than a struggle over political and military interests. It owed as least as much to a cultural reaction from the towns, which, as we will see, ultimately repudiated the intractable paramilitary underclass in their midst.

CONCLUSION

The Great Urban Backlash

Across the late eighteenth and early nineteenth centuries, the political and economic difficulties of the Great Crisis became progressively more destabilizing. Most glaringly, the empire suffered repeated defeats on the battlefield against European powers. Demoralizing and exhausting, these failing military campaigns drained the Ottoman treasury. A series of currency devaluations followed. Inflation took off and proved even more severe than the more famous episode of the late sixteenth and early seventeenth centuries. Like so many other places across Eurasia, the Ottoman Empire experienced these decades as a long period of demographic and economic stagnation.

The Ottoman paramilitary complex aggravated these stresses. As the state brought larger numbers of soldiers into its service, it struggled to adequately pay and supply them. Urban society watched with growing unease. It mistrusted the new recruits, most of whom arrived as outsiders, immediately recognizable from their rustic clothes and manners. Most unsettling was their evident lack of training and discipline. To many townspeople, they appeared downright threatening—"men of different types and deviant natures," as ʿAbd al-Rahman al-Jabarti assessed the new recruits of İsmail Bey (1788), briefly the most powerful official in Egypt, who had lured them from Albania and other parts of the Balkans. "He employed them from the first moment in horsemanship, and did not train them in manners or knowledge of religion or writing, all in the desire to fight his enemies and increase his army."[1] These men were to receive none of the social polish that, as we have already observed, eighteenth-century political households had increasingly applied to their recruits. Neither refined nor educated, the newcomers were destined only for the battlefield. As unattached outsiders, they were unfamiliar with local language and culture and were slow to acquire urban manners.

Urban society did not hide its fear and revulsion. Most aghast at the disorders unleashed by the paramilitary complex were "respectable people" (ehl-i ırz/ahl al-ʿird), who began to look upon Ottoman soldiery, especially the Janissaries, as an unruly rabble whom the sultan himself could no longer control. The most negative stereotypes about Janissaries flourished precisely among this sector of the population, who would transmit their judgments to nineteenth-century Ottoman historians. These voices came not merely from the comfortable and affluent but from townsmen who hovered at the lowest rungs of respectability: the shopkeepers and petty tradesmen who earned a precarious living and yet proudly nurtured their urban identity. They were pious and God-fearing, confidently took their place among neighborhood elders, and, above all, craved law and order.

Throughout the decades of the Great Crisis, concerns were mounting over reports of crimes and offenses committed by Janissaries and other soldiers, who seemed to move about the streets like unaccountable thugs and bandits. In 1788, as military units were marching to the front from Istanbul, men dressed as soldiers reportedly robbed homes while sailors in Galata started deadly brawls.[2] This unruliness was not a mirage or an expression of some "discourse" that contemporary authors would repeat and parrot. The crumbling discipline within Ottoman ranks was obvious to European officers who served on Ottoman campaigns.[3] And it seemed just as undeniable to Ottoman military reformers: hence their obsession with instilling "order" throughout the army.[4] Provincial garrisons seethed with the same unrest. In Aleppo, townspeople came to fear the mobilization of local Janissaries as a convenient pretext for the latter to shake down merchants and shopkeepers.[5] With equal trepidation, they bore the occasional quartering of soldiers in local homes, which imposed the same hardships as elsewhere in the eighteenth-century world.[6] In Belgrade (1793), the predations of the local Janissary garrison had become so intolerable that Istanbul ordered their expulsion from the province. After the exiles launched repeated raids from Vidin, the governor authorized local Serbian leaders to form a Christian militia (1799). It was the first time that the Ottoman state had ever armed Christian subjects on such a scale.[7] In Cairo, Mehmed Ali, though an Albanian by origin, eventually got rid of his refractory Albanian mercenaries, who had conspired to assassinate him after he subjected them (1815) to European-style drilling and uniforms. By the 1820s, he would turn to the Egyptian peasantry to fill the ranks of his army with conscripts.[8]

All this instability would reach the heart of the empire with the overthrow of Selim III and his New Order in 1807. Military discipline was thereafter harder to enforce. In Istanbul, rumors abounded about nefarious plots hatched by Janissaries and other soldiers. Suspicions fell most heavily on rank-and-file troops, whose salaries were meager and poverty was obvious, especially at the fringes of the paramilitary complex, where membership might be little more than notional. Fears mounted among the "respectable." Destitute soldiers would stop at nothing to wring wealth from townspeople and had little respect for the law. As they departed for the front, they might try to exact "gifts," "loans," and "contributions" to the war effort.[9] Among other opportunities for extortion, Istanbulites warned each other, were the firefighting teams on which Janissaries served. Since nearly all of Istanbul's buildings were made of wood, fires were a perennial threat and could wipe out entire neighborhoods in only a few hours. Some fires, it was said, were being deliberately set. The folklore of the capital would later mythologize men "in the guise of firemen" who would appear amid the flames to rob helpless bystanders.[10] Another rumor (1810) had the porters of Istanbul secretly plotting to set fires so that desperate homeowners would beg for their help; once hired, the porters would simply abscond with their possessions.[11] Soldiers seemed to flaunt their lawlessness, and acted with impunity. Sailing up the Bosphorus (1812), one flotilla of Janissaries randomly fired guns at passing mansions and threatened boatmen, who withdrew to the wharves and began discharging passengers for their own safety. Reports alleged that these same Janissaries later robbed villagers at Yeniköy, further north on the Bosphorus, and requisitioned goods at low prices.[12] Inside the Ottoman state, officials confronted a more disturbing problem. They could not assume that officers would enforce discipline. Violent feuds were left to rage until they burned themselves out. In 1819, two Janissary regiments engaged in a three-day gunfight along the wharves of Galata. One unit went so far as to seize a Greek ship and train its fire along the waterfront. As soldiers plundered nearby shops, the commander of the

Janissaries tried unsuccessfully to mediate. Meanwhile, the grand admiral watched from the opposite shore "like a spectator"; for his inaction, he was banished to Izmir.[13]

Unchecked over several decades, the prevailing sense of disorder was politically damaging. Low-level street violence had become one of the unintended consequences of the eighteenth-century fiscal state. By the early nineteenth century, the accompanying social frictions had created precisely the right conditions for toppling the Old Regime, which could no longer manage the problems that it had unwittingly brought into existence. It was not merely failure on the battlefields of the Morea that swept away the Janissaries in 1826. Nor was it sheer cunning and ruthlessness which allowed Mahmud II and his allies to finally crush their foes and begin implementing their program of military reform and administrative centralization. Crucial to their success, and to the legitimacy of the entire Tanzimat project, was tacit popular assent. In Istanbul and other towns, Ottoman subjects had wearied of the exactions and disruptions of the paramilitary complex. They were ready for its abolition.

The coarseness and indiscipline of paramilitary culture had made townspeople deeply apprehensive about social order. They watched as soldiers scoffed at urban respectability and openly trampled on social and moral norms. When Ottoman marines docked on the Nile near Cairo (1788), they were brazen about drinking and consorting with prostitutes—in the middle of Ramadan, no less. Nearby Moroccan pilgrims could not endure the sight. They demanded that the soldiers put an end to their carousing at once. The marines' answer came with pistol shots, which touched off a massive melee in which the pilgrims overwhelmed the defenders and chased them off the ship. Brawling continued for most of the night and left at least two dozen dead.[14] With its unbridled hedonism, paramilitary culture had never been very attentive to religious mores. But as soldiers grew bolder and discipline slackened, this indifference to public opinion curdled into outright insolence. While mustering in Cairo for the next campaign in the Hijaz (1814), soldiers sat in coffeehouses throughout the daylight hours of Ramadan, sipped their cups, and smoked wherever they liked.[15] Urban opinion could do nothing to stop or even shame them. Only the worst excesses might lead to reprisals. In 1800, the governor of Damascus left town to lead the pilgrimage caravan to Medina and Mecca. In his absence, the remaining members of the garrison went on a binge of daylight drunkenness and thieving from shops and homes. So many outrages were committed that he ordered the execution of their commander, the lieutenant governor, upon his return.[16]

Since Istanbul held the largest concentration of soldiers, anxieties about social order came into sharpest focus there. The respectable set wrung their hands about threats to public security, both real and perceived. They reserved their greatest misgivings for poor and unattached newcomers who arrived from villages and small towns across Anatolia and the Balkans. The eighteenth-century state shared these suspicions and set up makeshift monitoring networks. Migrants were forbidden to settle in the capital unless they could produce a "guarantor" (*kefil*)—that is, an established resident who could vouch for their employment and good character. This dragnet proved highly ineffective. Some newcomers were able to bypass it and assimilate fully into neighborhood life thanks to chain migration, which linked up new arrivals with earlier immigrants who hailed from the same town or region.[17] Many others simply slipped in, both unnoticed and unwelcome. Most were young men who, once settled down, made their way in urban society through casual labor or military service. These "bachelors," as officials loosely referred to them, were unattached, but only in the sense that they were either literally young men who had yet to marry, or perhaps villagers who had left behind their families to seek employment in the capital. The flotsam and jetsam of Istanbul society, they numbered at least seventeen thousand by the end of the eighteenth century.[18] Having no permanent residence, they tended to gravitate toward makeshift lodgings in caravansaries, boathouses (*kayıkhane*) along the waterfront, or coffeehouses and shops. Most notorious were the numerous "bachelor rooms" (*bekar odaları*) located in many different parts of the capital. Built to various dimensions—from small collections of rooms to enormous structures capable of holding hundreds of lodgers at a time—these shabby tenements created their own social underworld, which defied conventional notions of morality and became the backdrop for lurid urban legends about vice and crime.[19] Their rootless denizens became anathema to the polite and pious, who, from a wary distance, fulminated against the rowdy subculture of drinking, smoking, and illicit sex.

Though many soldiers were bachelors, they did not necessarily live without female companionship. Among the residents of the "bachelor rooms" were many women, who were themselves unattached and indifferent to conventional morality. Respectable opinion condemned them as shameless "prostitutes" (*fahişe*). Many of them no doubt worked in the sex trade; others seem to have inhabited a gray zone in which, unmarried and pursuing an indeterminant livelihood, they partook in the drinking and carousing as much as the soldiers, boatmen, porters, and other members of this rough counterculture whose privations they consoled. In the bachelor rooms of Balaban İskelesi in Üsküdar, on the Asian shores of the Bosphorus, the occupants had a habit of shooting firearms randomly from their windows. The surrounding streets, it was said, were regularly littered with aborted fetuses and the corpses of women and infants. Men openly consorted with women in their rooms or brought back youths, such as apprentices from nearby shops, whom the women (or men) desired. The rules of public conduct were completely inverted. Women openly walked the streets without bothering to cover their faces. They strolled "like a patrol," often in large groups of eight or ten, without any thought of bowing to urban norms of modesty. So notorious was the area that even the owners of the bachelor rooms had no objections to demolishing their own property whenever the authorities insisted. Indeed, amid reports of rampant immorality and kidnapping of local women, imperial officials twice (1808 and 1811) ordered the tenements torn down.[20] Soon afterward (1812), imperial officials sent soldiers into the neighborhoods of Galata and Kasımpaşa, also home to large numbers of migrants and drifters, and ordered them to drive out the "lowlifes and prostitutes."[21]

The kidnapping of "prostitutes" became one of the recurring themes in the struggle over urban space among the different military units of Istanbul. Respectable society sneered that these clashes were nothing more than "woman quarrels" (*avret gavgası*) waged by the deviant and debauched. Though undeniably hostile to the Janissaries, these reports were nonetheless right about the new scale and frequency of ambushes in which soldiers vied for control over unattached women.[22] The attacks were an extension of larger power struggles over turf and property in which military units had become embroiled. The deposition of Selim III in 1807 seems to have inflamed these rivalries by upsetting earlier understandings about informal "boundaries" and encouraging factions to test their strength in the streets. When palace guards tried (1809) to take away several "prostitutes" from the village of Beşiktaş along the Bosphorus, Janissaries and porters intervened, almost certainly because of their own claims on the women. The confrontation quickly turned violent.[23] That same year a dispute over women ignited a gunfight between two Janissary regiments in the streets of Galata. Several people died in the exchange of fire.[24] Yet another melee in 1809 began with Janissaries and palace guards quarreling over a woman, and escalated into wider violence as the guards raided a coffeehouse belonging to the Fifty-Ninth regiment, where they broke windows and pulled down the unit's insignia.[25] In 1811, it was the turn of sailors to quarrel over women. Their brawl on the wharves in front of Yeni Camii, right on the Golden Horn, prompted tradesmen to call in the Janissary patrol. Shopkeepers caught one of the sailors and began beating him with poles.[26] From their customary skirmishing grounds along wharves and markets, soldiers were willing to carry their rivalries into the most restricted social sanctuaries. When a clash over a "prostitute" left one Janissary dead (1819), members of the victim's unit rallied and chased his killer into the women's section of a bathhouse, where they paid no heed to the bathers and ruthlessly "cut him to pieces."[27]

All the demeaning talk about "prostitutes" conceals a large category of women in early nineteenth-century Istanbul who were poor and unattached. Although some eked out a living by working from home, many more lived outside the conventional social arrangements of marriage and family.[28] The price of this dangerous rootlessness—which represented nothing like self-affirming personal autonomy anywhere in the pre-industrial world—was a loss of protection that they had to restore through affiliation with paramilitary culture. Everyone in Ottoman society recognized the necessity of social networks, which provided security and furnished individuals with a crude social safety net, whether through family, clan, neighborhood, guild, Sufi lodge, or other groups. Paramilitary culture acted no differently. Its networks created a curious mirror image of respectable society in attaching and protecting women and reasserting patriarchal controls. The women who lived in the orbit of soldiers and their auxiliaries became their consorts and dependents. Soldiers recognized these social bonds, which were always a matter of informal knowledge on the streets. When soldiers from the Twenty-Sixth and Twenty-Seventh regiments started an argument (1809) over a "prostitute," officers could not restore calm. Complicating their mediation was the woman's attachment to the Thirty-First regiment, which meant that she was not really available. Talks dissolved into a general brawl.[29] Soldiers would never give up "their" women.

Respectable townspeople looked on in horror. They were not, of course, thinking of the plight of the "prostitutes," whom they despised, but of their own women. The factional tumult enveloping the capital made a mockery of the moral and political order. It led urban gentlemen to wonder whether they could protect the women of their household—and by implication, their own honor. In Istanbul, the most lurid reports whispered of women being dragged out of bathhouses and raped.[30] A variation on this theme had soldiers or "lowlifes" (*erazıl*) raiding women's picnics on the outskirts of town and violating their victims.[31] During the "Beşiktaş Incident" (1808), drunken soldiers spilled out of taverns and began to harass women who happened to be passing by.[32] The streets were becoming so unsafe, it was said, that—another stain on male honor—women were having to take the initiative in protecting themselves. One young Janissary made the mistake (1811) of trying to abduct a young "lady" (*hatun*) as she walked in the street. She rescued herself by screaming and drawing a crowd. Vigorously protesting her innocence, she swore that she was a virgin, and explained that she had become separated from her companion. The Janissary was detained and executed.[33] Confronting much the same danger was a woman escorting two slave-girls through the streets. Two youths met them with lascivious stares and catcalls. The woman warned them against "impertinence" (*edepsizlik*) and suggested that, if they wanted the girls, they should bring enough money to buy them. Enraged at her words, they stabbed the slaves. The youths were later captured and sentenced to death.[34]

Each incident that came to the ears of merchants and tradesmen helped to fan new images of women in peril from roaming thugs who attacked in broad daylight. To arouse horror and panic, transgressions did not have to be violent. Stories circulated about soldiers and assorted ruffians engaging in low-level harassment. To take one scene from Istanbul (1811): Two boatmen from Üsküdar had been physically forcing patrons into their rowboats. Among their victims were "respectable types of women" (*ehl-i ırz makulesi haremi*), whose hands they squeezed during the ride.[35] These unseemly advances were a flagrant violation of social boundaries. Unrelated women were not to be addressed in familiar terms, let alone touched. Such reports of unwanted attention, escalating to the point of actual physical contact, scandalized respectable opinion and appeared threatening to all notions of urban order. Casual social contact, not only with women but even young men, often seemed like little more than the prelude to sexual seduction and corruption.[36]

Insults to everyday propriety, directed at women, helped to spur a burgeoning crisis of confidence inside the Old Regime. Officials could no longer keep effective order. The honor of respectable households had been rendered precarious in public spaces. Worse still, these transgressions were occurring not in distant rural hamlets, which popular lore (not to mention official records) had long filled with marauding "bandits" ready to abduct local women, but in the heart of the sultan's capital. It was a veritable crisis in patriarchy that the Old Regime seemed helpless to redress.[37] From such cultural insecurities sprang a powerful backlash against the Ottoman paramilitary complex. Anxieties about women's safety made this patriarchal reaction qualitatively different from eighteenth-century attempts by the authorities to regulate women's clothing and access to public space. Those campaigns aimed to reduce women's visibility and were initiated by the state. By the early nineteenth century, concerns about women's safety were arising from urban society itself and had to do with questions of physical and reputational danger, not ideological musings about the nature of an ideal moral order. Even after modernization regimes had installed themselves in Istanbul, Cairo, and Tunis, subjects might measure political success simply from the state's capacity to protect property and honor. Having invaded Syria and occupied Damascus (1831), the revamped Egyptian army won praise for committing no offenses against the population. Meanwhile, Ottoman troops stationed in Homs were raiding grain stores and committing, it was whispered, outrages against local women.[38]

The cause of political reform thus owed its victory not merely to political and military calamities; it drew strength from cultural fears and sensitivities as well. By the early nineteenth century, a large segment of urban society had decisively turned against the paramilitary complex, which would have few allies at its side when the modernizers finally moved against them.

Myths of "Westernization"

In the first wave of reforms enacted after the elimination of the Janissaries, one of the most visible symbols of order was the new uniform stipulated for Ottoman bureaucrats and soldiers. Announced in 1829, the clothing regulations required European-style jackets and pants.[39] The only distinctively "Muslim" touch was the fez, the cylindrical hat originally worn in the Mediterranean region. In "de-turbaned" form, it would remain the official Ottoman headgear until the end of the empire after the First World War. The rationale for this reform was to create a uniform class of state servants, shorn of all social and religious distinctions. In pursuing wholesale military modernization and administrative centralization, the state wanted army officers and bureaucrats who not only had the requisite training and discipline for these policies; they also had to look the part of modern officials, nearly identical in appearance to their European peers.

For many decades across the nineteenth century, the fez and jacket had little appeal outside officialdom. Some of this aversion to the new uniforms undoubtedly sprang from opposition to political reform. There was, in fact, already a precedent for such a reaction. In 1807, Albanian auxiliaries began the revolt that would topple Selim III when they caught wind of rumors that the Ottoman government would soon force them to adopt the uniforms of the New Order, which, in turn, were modeled on the berets, jackets, and breeches of the French army.[40] After the abolition of the Janissary corps (1826), the issue again came to the fore. It was most glaring in the rebellions that swept through the towns of Bosnia during the first years of the Tanzimat (c. 1828–32). Local notables, many of whom had ties to the Janissary corps, feared for their old privileges and resented the new taxes and administrative measures that Istanbul was imposing. Their opposition found sartorial expression as well. In 1826, only a few weeks after the suppression of the Janissaries in the capital, soldiers in Sarajevo were already protesting that the new military uniforms were an "insult" to Islam, grumbling that the cords fastened to the front resembled the figure of a cross.[41] At the height of the unrest, in 1831, crowds sacked Bosnian military depots and burned consignments of new uniforms in the streets. In Travnik, they led out the Ottoman governor, whom a rebel detachment had earlier captured; removing the fez from his head, they replaced it with a turban. Janissary bands, as though never outlawed, defiantly marched through the streets to public jubilation.[42]

Did such hostility to the new official fashions express wider popular support for the Old Regime? One version of this argument presents the Janissaries as champions of artisans and laborers, helping them to fend off the encroachments of the state through the Janissaries' participation in the guild system.[43] Shorn of this protection after 1826, workers experienced immiseration as state reformers signed commercial treaties (first with Great Britain in 1838 and then in quick succession with all the Great Powers) that lowered import tariffs and exposed urban markets to waves of cheap factory-made goods that undermined local production. The urban poor thus signaled an abiding loyalty to the Old Regime by clinging to inherited fashions, which symbolized better times in which they had worked in better conditions. But were these relationships really so simple and straightforward? The argument surely romanticizes the Janissaries, who, first and foremost, looked after themselves and were highly selective about which trades they infiltrated and "protected." They never assumed anything like leadership of the entire working population, many of whom, unaffiliated with the corps, regarded the Janissaries and their confederates as little more than thugs and extortionists. The activities of the Janissaries thus evoked many different responses across the urban social order. Only those townsmen who benefited from these networks directly would have felt any allegiance or gratitude; others, who bore the brunt of the Janissaries' exactions, could hardly hide their loathing and resentment. During skirmishes in the streets of the capital (1811), many tradesmen were heard to grumble that the combatants were not even pursuing a proper "Janissary quarrel." Their true aim, rather, was to "set fire to Istanbul, pillage it, and return to the provinces," where so many of them, now dressed as the sultan's soldiers, had originated.[44]

An equally tempting, and problematic, argument is to imagine that ordinary Muslims despised the new uniforms because of specifically "Muslim" objections. The fez, as the emblem of reform, was too egalitarian. It would visually erase all the social and religious hierarchies that both state regulation and religious law had always upheld as proper and natural. This prospect, it is said, was too galling for Muslims, who wished to retain the old distinctions, which reinforced the politically subordinate status of Christians and Jews.[45] Artisans therefore refused to wear the fez or insisted on modifications that better suited inherited fashions. In Istanbul, workers hit upon the solution of wrapping it with pieces of cloth in the style of the turbans that they were used to wearing.[46] But was this resistance to official fashions really such a "Muslim" reaction? Take the question of military dress: Greek fighters during and after the Greek war of independence showed an identical disdain for European-style uniforms (as well as modern military discipline). As a concession, the Greek army allowed many units to keep their familiar peasant garb throughout much of the nineteenth century.⁴⁷ The customs of the Old Regime continued to shape popular thinking, whether in the Ottoman Empire or its "Christian" successor states.

Putting aside faulty assumptions about religion and culture, we can easily recognize a more prosaic factor in the lack of enthusiasm for the new uniform. The jacket and pants were obviously borrowed from Europe, whose fashions, as we noted earlier, had long looked ridiculous and felt uncomfortable to Ottoman tastes.⁴⁸ The fez, too, would have seemed somewhat peculiar and "foreign." After all, it originated from a particular Ottoman fashion zone along the Mediterranean coastlines, which would have made it cumbersome and unfamiliar to Muslims who lived elsewhere. Not surprisingly, they balked at this "cap" fashion. In 1829, thousands of recruits were hastily mobilized from the working population of Istanbul for the defense of Edirne, which faced imminent attack from the Russian army. Many refused to put on fezzes and simply kept their turbans.⁴⁹ To put the matter more plainly: How could the state expect to get its way? It could no more impose new sartorial habits, whenever it pleased, than it could dictate cuisine, residential architecture, or any other customs embedded in material culture. Identifying the fez as "Muslim" was true only in the sense that Tunisia, the main manufacturing center for it, possessed an overwhelmingly Muslim population; and that the Ottoman court, speaking in the name of an "Islamic" political order, had elevated it to the status of official headgear. Educated Ottoman opinion had the same broad view of the question and never thought of it in strictly sectarian terms. By the middle decades of the nineteenth century, affluent townsmen of all religious communities, Muslim or not, were donning the fez.⁵⁰ Wealth and high status always made this switch easier.

For the vast majority of the population, state reform made little difference to bodily habits and routines. In both town and country, ordinary subjects essentially preserved their inherited lifestyles. They kept wearing the same clothes, and retained all the familiar postures and gestures of work and home. Among the social elite, too, old ways proved durable. The bodily movements imposed by European-style protocols and regulations were an uncomfortable graft that most learned, at best, to accommodate and bear during official duties. The largely military and administrative aims of modernizing reform ensured that, at least among the first generation of Tanzimat reformers, the state expected little more. As a sign of these enduring mentalities, we can take the etiquette manual (*Risale-i Ahlak*) written by

Mehmed Sadık Rifat Paşa (1807–1856). President of the supreme judicial council (Meclis-i Valâ), former ambassador to the Austrian Empire, and one of the leading lights of the early Tanzimat administration who served in many other posts, he was a wholehearted partisan of modernizing state reform. Yet his etiquette manual for the modern Ottoman gentleman differed little in its thinking, organization, and choice of topics from the writers of the Old Regime.[51] Like these earlier figures, he laid heaviest emphasis on the cultivation of piety and morality. Moreover, he betrayed no hint of any anxiety about a foreign moral order that threatened to corrupt and undermine the empire. In tone and content, his book dealt with familiar themes and references. It answered, in fact, to a presumed audience of literate Ottomans, who likewise saw no need to break with their cultural heritage. Inherited manners and values retained their appeal.[52]

Only in the final decades of the nineteenth century did bodily deportment undergo a more substantial reworking. State ceremony began to lose much of its old stiffness and exaggerated deference. By the 1830s, European diplomats had freed themselves from the old Ottoman court etiquette, with its requisite signals of supplication and obeisance. In greeting them, the sultan became less distant and imperious.[53] For Ottoman subjects, official protocol took longer to thaw. Unlike his predecessor Abdülaziz (r. 1861–76), who still insisted that subjects entering his presence should prostrate themselves and kiss the ground, Abdülhamid II (r. 1876–1909) was, by comparison, downright casual. He discouraged them from kissing the hem of his pants, which so many Ottomans, by upbringing and expectation, continued to regard as obligatory. In a break with earlier ceremony, his manner with high-ranking officials was relaxed and understated. Shortly after taking the throne, he brought two powerful viziers, Midhat Paşa and Rüşdü Paşa, for an interview. Instead of making them stand, as the old protocol would have demanded, he immediately had them seated and personally gave each one a cigarette. Midhat Paşa (1822–1883), the great administrative reformer and champion of constitutionalism, began to smoke right away. More reticent despite (or perhaps because of) several terms as grand vizier, Rüşdü Paşa (1811–1882) kept the cigarette in his hand, still conscious of the pervasive social etiquette that forbade smoking in the presence of superiors. The sultan had to order him directly before he would light up.[54]

Away from the palace, the true revolution in lifestyle had already begun to put down roots. Taking hold among the emerging modern middle class—

small but dynamic and influential beyond their numbers—it looked unapologetically to European models of comportment. The most enthusiastic devotees to the new ways were graduates of modern state and missionary schools, whose curriculum exposed them—most critically for manners and sociability—to European languages and cultures. They would increasingly eat with forks and knives, sit on chairs at tables, sleep in bedsteads, and decorate with all the bulky furniture, such as bureaus and dressers, with which their European peers were accustomed to filling their homes. Well-to-do townswomen would walk about in petticoats done up in all the latest fashions from Paris and Vienna. In the most elegant households, their daughters would learn to play piano. Middle-class men of all religious communities—not only bureaucrats and military officers but members of rising professions like lawyers, doctors, teachers, and journalists—dressed in jackets and pants and kept only a fez atop their head as an emblem of Ottoman modernity. For the most flamboyant, a walking-cane, cigarette holder, or monocle might mark them out as a European-style dandy. All these innovations in material culture and self-presentation, we should remember, arrived comparatively late.[55] Not so long before, in Mehmed Sadık Rıfat Paşa's time around the middle of the nineteenth century, the adoption of such exotic customs would have been inconceivable, or at best unconventional, for polite Ottomans, who could still believe that keeping up with the times was a matter best left to the state.

In fact, Tanzimat officials had no wish to remake Ottoman culture. Their policies were entirely technocratic. They wanted to build a stronger military so that they could keep the European powers at bay and impose order and security evenly across the full breadth of the empire. To better manage the sprawling imperial territories, they dreamed of a stronger, larger bureaucracy that could instantly and obediently transmit the will of the central government, without having to rely on intermediaries—i.e., the indispensable provincial notables, who were loyal but self-interested. They had no illusions about the models for these plans. They knew that they were engaged in the wholesale borrowing of policies that, in one version or another, their European adversaries had already put into practice. As one Tanzimat propagandist freely confessed, the Ottoman state was merely following the path of Peter the Great (r. 1694-1725) who had overhauled the Russian Empire with foreign knowledge and expertise and trained home-grown cadres of bureaucrats and officers. The Ottomans would do the same.⁵⁶ The fundamental problem with the empire lay not in its culture but in the disorder and feebleness of the state.

Hence both the New Order and the Tanzimat regime pursued self-consciously limited aims. Or to put it a slightly different way: the Ottoman Empire would embrace *conservative* reform.⁵⁷ Viewing modernizing reform in this light helps us to better place the outlook of the Ottoman leadership within the broader sweep of early nineteenth-century history.⁵⁸ For the Ottoman state was not the only imperial system that was trying to renovate itself. After the Napoleonic wars, the Romanov administration pushed ahead with plans to overhaul state administration with the aim of making it more centralized and efficient. It likewise pursued military reform and sought to expand and reorganize its new state system of schools. As formulated by the arch-conservative Nicholas I (r. 1825–55), these initiatives advanced under the banner of dynasty, nationality (i.e., imperial identity), and religious orthodoxy.⁵⁹ With varying degrees of enthusiasm, Prussia and Austria, which along with Russia formed the "Holy Alliance" after the Congress of Vienna, heeded the same call for state-led reform, also under the auspices of an autocratic administration.⁶⁰ In acting on a common belief not merely in the compatibility of reform with empire but in its necessity as well, the Ottoman Empire loomed as the unacknowledged fourth member of this coalition. Imperial thinking in the early nineteenth century was thus broadly similar within all the large Eurasian empires. They all saw reform as essentially military and technocratic, and had no intention of extending it to cultural affairs. On the contrary, they were hostile to anything, political or cultural, which smacked of revolutionary agitation. They mounted a steadfast defense of religion, which they celebrated as the indispensable bulwark of stability and order. In this pragmatic, piecemeal statecraft, harnessed to an ideology that looked for assurance to the past, the agrarian empires of western Eurasia embraced a common conservative agenda. Only the Ottomans' relative weakness within the European political system, coupled with an Islamic identity, made them seem different and alien.

Since state reform was so controversial—mainly because it threatened so many entrenched interests—it had to engage in a continuous ideological struggle for legitimacy, which always proceeded through appeals to Islamic tradition. Opponents of reform decried it as the "work of the infidel" (*gavur işi*), due to its obvious borrowing of knowledge from Europe.⁶¹ "Westernization" thereafter became a dirty word lobbed by those who feared that the new policies would diminish their power and status.⁶² Particularly suspicious were members of the religious establishment, who quickly foresaw how the new administrative models would not require their legal and educational expertise. Sensitive to accusations of cultural betrayal, advocates of reform insisted that there was nothing wrong with borrowing technical knowledge from non-Muslims and that the earliest Muslims, including the prophet Muhammad himself, had resorted to this expedient. Any knowledge that made an Islamic state stronger had to be beneficial. This argument, repeated with formulaic regularity across the nineteenth century, would become one of the key ideological defenses of state reform.

Debates over cultural matters such as fashion erupted at the end of the Old Regime in the early nineteenth century precisely because of their symbolic usefulness. Partisans could discuss questions of political legitimacy in indirect and coded fashion. Opinions about clothing, furniture, greetings, gestures, and bodily habits could instantly identify a person's political affiliations. Most interesting was the fidelity that all participants in these nineteenth-century discussions showed to religion, which they imagined as the foundation of culture. But as we have repeatedly observed, manners hardly differed by religious community. In nearly all aspects of self-presentation, etiquette, and sociability, differences sprang mainly from long-standing regional variations, not religious identity. The strenuous insistence that religion somehow stood at the center of culture was merely the birth cry of modern conservatism, which emerged at the very moment that the Old Regime began to crumble—or more accurately, reinvent itself. Like other agrarian societies, the Ottoman Empire retained a conservative cultural outlook across the nineteenth century. Some imperial conservatives were reformers, trying to import technocratic knowledge and thereby preserve the social order, which, in their view, was fundamentally sound and just; others were reactionaries, who comprehensively despised reform and saw it as nothing less than a corrosive threat to stability and morality (as well as their own interests). In either case, ideologues argued from nostalgia and revered a social order that had never really existed. In the imaginary struggle to defend "Islamic" norms and values, this veneration of "tradition" would, over the course of modern history, prove as novel, fanciful, and disruptive as the schemes of the most starry-eyed revolutionaries.

NOTES

Introduction

1. Baron de Tott, *Memoirs of Baron de Tott* (London: G.G.J. and J. Robinson, 1785 [reprint, New York: Arno Press, 1973]), 2:18–19. De Tott was not always the most reliable narrator, and so one cannot discount the possibility that the story was heavily garnished. On the challenges of reading de Tott, see Virginia Aksan, "Breaking the Spell of the Baron de Tott: Reframing the Question of Military Reform in the Ottoman Empire, 1760–1830," *International History Review* 24 (2002): 253–77. On the other hand, the antics of a talking bird may have become something of a staple in Ottoman folk stories by the late eighteenth century. See the unfortunate end of a Christian grocer, a "lady's man" (*zen-dost*), whose amorous pursuits were betrayed (1788) by a "canary" that he kept at his shop; Taylesanizade Hafız Abdullah Efendi, *İstanbul'un Uzun Dört Yılı: Taylesanizade Hafız Abdullah Efendi Tarihi*, ed. Feridun Emecen (Istanbul: Tatav, 2003), 253–54.

2. Norbert Elias, *The Court Society*, trans. Edmund. Jephcott (New York: Pantheon Books, 1983); Norbert Elias, *The Civilizing Process*, trans. Edmund Jephcott (Oxford: Blackwell, 1994). For an overview of Elias's main ideas, see Robert van Krieken, *Norbert Elias* (London: Routledge, 1998); Helmut Kuzmics, "The Civilizing Process," in *Civil Society and the State*, ed. John Keane (New York: Verso, 1988), 147–76; Stephen Mennell, *Norbert Elias: An Introduction* (Oxford: Blackwell, 1989); Stephen Quilley and Steven Loyal, "Towards a 'Central Theory': The Scope and Relevance of the Sociology of Norbert Elias," in *The Sociology of Norbert Elias*, ed. Steven Loyal and Stephen Quilley (Cambridge: Cambridge University Press, 2004), 1–22; Dennis Smith, *Norbert Elias and Modern Social Theory* (London: Sage, 2001).

3. Jacques Revel, "The Uses of Civility," in *A History of Private Life*, Vol. 3, *The Passions of the Renaissance*, ed. Philippe Ariès and Georges Duby, trans. Arthur Goldhammer (Cambridge, MA: Belknap Press, 1989), 167–205.

4. For research on early modern France that has drawn inspiration from Elias, see in particular Orest Ranum, "Courtesy, Absolutism, and the Rise of the French State, 1630–

1660," *Journal of Modern History* 52 (1980): 426–51; Roger Chartier, *Cultural History: Between Practices and Representations*, trans. Lydia Cochrane (Ithaca: Cornell University Press, 1988), 71–94. On early modern England, see Anna Bryson, *From Courtesy to Civility: Changing Codes of Conduct in Early Modern England* (Oxford: Clarendon Press, 1998); Peter Burke, Brian Harrison, and Paul Slack, eds., *Civil Histories: Essays Presented to Sir Keith Thomas* (Oxford: Oxford University Press, 2000); Keith Thomas, *In Pursuit of Civility: Manners and Civilization in Early Modern England* (Waltham, MA: Brandeis University Press, 2018). An older view identified a key pre-Victorian turning point for manners in the late eighteenth and early nineteenth centuries; see Maurice J. Quinlan, *Victorian Prelude: A History of English Manners, 1700–1830*, 2nd ed. (Hamdon, CT: Archon Books, 1964).

    5. Roger Chartier, "Introduction," in *A History of Private Life*, Vol. 3, *The Passions of the Renaissance*, ed. Philippe Ariès and Georges Duby, trans. Arthur Goldhammer (Cambridge, MA: Belknap Press, 1989), 16.

    6. See for example Patrick Jory, *A History of Manners and Civility in Modern Thailand* (Cambridge: Cambridge University Press, 2022).

    7. See Hans Peter Duerr, *Intimität* (Frankfurt am Main: Suhrkamp, 1990); Hans Peter Duerr, *Nacktheit und Sham* (Frankfurt am Main: Suhrkamp, 1988). For an overview and critique of Elias's views about medieval culture being more childlike and naïve in self-expression, see Barbara H. Rosenwein, *Emotional Communities in the Early Middle Ages* (Ithaca: Cornell University Press, 2006), esp. intro. For a general overview of critiques aimed at Elias, see van Krieken, *Norbert Elias*, esp. chap. 4; Mennell, *Norbert Elias*, chap. 10.

    8. Jack Goody, "The 'Civilizing Process' in Ghana," *European Journal of Sociology* 44 (2003): 68.

    9. For an overview of violence in early modern European culture, see Julius R. Ruff, *Violence in Early Modern Europe, 1500–1800* (Cambridge: Cambridge University Press, 2001).

    10. For stinging critiques of Elias's treatment of non-European cultures, see Jack Goody, *The Theft of History* (Cambridge: Cambridge University Press, 2006), chap. 6; Goody, "The 'Civilizing Process' in Ghana," 61–73; Jack Goody, "Elias and the Anthropological Tradition," *Anthropological Theory* 2 (2002): 401–12. Goody and Elias actually crossed paths in Ghana when the latter briefly held a teaching post there. They did not hit it off. See Katie Liston and Stephen Mennell, "Ill Met in Ghana: Jack Goody and Norbert Elias on Process and Progress in Africa," *Theory, Culture, and Society* 26 (2009): 52–70.

    11. For one classic rejoinder to Elias's assumptions, see H.U.E. van Velzen, "The Djuka Civilization," *Netherlands Journal of Sociology* 20 (1984): 85–97.

    12. Nicole Pepperell, "The Unease with Civilization: Norbert Elias and the Violence of the Civilizing Process," *Thesis Eleven* 137 (2016): 3–21.

    13. See for example the work of Mehmed Birgivi and Gelibolulu Mustafa Ali. On Birgivi's writing, which touched on manners mainly as an extension of Islamic ethics, see Katherina Ivanyi, "*Adab, Akhlaq*, and Early Modern Ottoman Parenesis: Birgivi Mehmed Efendi's (d. 981/1573) *al-Tariqa al-Muhammadiyya*," in *Adab and Modernity: A "Civilizing Process"? (Sixteenth-Twenty-First Century)*, ed. Catherine Mayeur Jaouen (Leiden: Brill, 2020), 49–62. Mustafa Ali more explicitly addressed the question of manners in a guide that he wrote about etiquette at Ottoman salons. His assumed readers were fellow Ottoman gentlemen; the targets of his sneering prose, social upstarts and imposters. For an English translation of this guide, see Mustafa Ali, *XVI. Yüzyıl Osmanlı Efendisi Mustafa Ali:*

Meva'idü'n-Nefais fi Kava'idi'l-Mecalis (Tables of Delicacies Concerning the Rules of Social Gatherings), trans. Douglas Scott Brookes (Cambridge, MA: Department of Near Eastern Languages and Civilizations, Harvard University, 2003). For an overview of Mustafa Ali's thought, see Cornell H. Fleischer, *Bureaucrat and Intellectual in the Ottoman Empire: The Historian Mustafa Ali (1541-1600)* (Princeton: Princeton University Press, 1986).

14. For an attempt to apply Elias's model to the sixteenth-century Ottoman court, see İrem Özgören Kınlı, "Principal Elements of the Ottoman State-Formation Process through an Eliasian Perspective," in *Norbert Elias and Empirical Research*, ed. Tatiana Savoia Landini and François Dépelteau (New York: Palgrave Macmillan, 1974), 161-78.

15. In France, for example, the initiative for cultivating new forms of sociability arose from the upper ranks of both Parisian and provincial society, not Versailles. See Jeroen Duindam, *Myths of Power: Norbert Elias and the Early Modern European Court*, trans. Lorri S. Granger and Gerard T. Moran (Amsterdam: Amsterdam University Press, 1994); Daniel Gordon, *Citizens without Sovereignty: Equality and Sociability in French Thought, 1670-1789* (Princeton: Princeton University Press, 1994); Emmanuel Le Roy Ladurie with Jean-François Fitou, *Saint-Simon and the Court of Louis XIV*, trans. Arthur Goldhammer (Chicago: University of Chicago Press, 2001).

16. For an overview of the declensionist version of eighteenth-century Ottoman history, see Jane Hathaway, "Rewriting Eighteenth-Century Ottoman History," *Mediterranean Historical Review* 19 (2004): 29-53; Cemal Kafadar, "The Question of Ottoman Decline," *Harvard Middle Eastern and Islamic Review* 4 (1997-98): 30-75; Dana Sajdi, "Decline, Its Discontents, and Ottoman Cultural History," in *Ottoman Tulips, Ottoman Coffee: Lifestyle and Leisure in the Eighteenth Century*, ed. Dana Sajdi (London: Tauris Academic Studies, 2007), 1-40.

17. Mehmet Genç, "18. Yüzyıla Ait Osmanlı Mali Verilerinin İktisadi Faaliyetin Göstergisi Olarak Kullanılabilirliği Üzerinde Bir Çalışma," in *Osmanlı İmparatorluğunda Devlet ve Ekonomi* (Ankara: Ötüken, 2000), 153-85; Şevket Pamuk, "The Ottoman Empire in the Eighteenth Century," *Itinerario* 24 (2000): 104-16; André Raymond, *Artisans et commerçants au Caire au XVIIIe siècle* (Damascus: Institut Français de Damas, 1974), chap. 3.

18. Donald Quataert, *The Ottoman Empire, 1700-1922*, 2nd ed. (Cambridge: Cambridge University Press, 2005), 112; Şevket Pamuk, "The Evolution of Financial Institutions in the Ottoman Empire, 1600-1914," *Financial History Review* 11 (2004): 8. On the various estimates proposed for the eighteenth-century population, see Bruce McGowan, "The Age of the Ayans, 1699-1812," in *An Economic and Social History of the Ottoman Empire*, Vol. 2, *1600-1914*, ed. Halil İnalcık and Donald Quataert (New York: Cambridge University Press, 1997), 646-47. On sixteenth-century estimates, see Halil İnalcık, "Introduction: Empire and Population," in *An Economic and Social History of the Ottoman Empire*, Vol. 1, *1300-1600*, ed. Halil İnalcık (New York: Cambridge University Press, 1997), 26-29.

19. For a brief overview of the main features of the Ottoman Old Regime, see Ariel Salzmann, "The Old Regime and the Ottoman Middle East," in *The Ottoman World*, ed. Christine Woodhead (London: Routledge, 2012), 409-22.

20. On the fiscal evolution of the Ottoman state during the seventeenth and eighteenth centuries, see Yavuz Cezar, *Osmanlı Maliyesinde Bunalım ve Değişim Dönemi: XVIII. Yüzyıldan Tanzimat'a Mali Tarihi* (Istanbul: Alan Yayıncılık, 1986); Murat Çizakça, *A Comparative Evolution of Business Partnerships: The Islamic World and Europe, with Specific Refer-*

ence to the Ottoman Archives (Leiden: Brill, 1996), chap. 5; Linda T. Darling, Revenue-Raising and Legitimacy: Tax Collection and Financial Administration in the Ottoman Empire, 1560-1660 (Leiden: Brill, 1996); Mehmet Genç, "Osmanlı Maliyesinde Malikane Sistemi," *Osmanlı İmparatorluğunda Devlet ve Ekonomi* (Ankara: Ötüken, 2000), 99–152; Halil İnalcık, "Military and Fiscal Transformation in the Ottoman Empire, 1600–1700," *Archivum Ottomanicum* 6 (1980): 283–337; Erol Özvar, *Osmanlı Maliyesinde Malikane Uygulaması* (Istanbul: Kitabevi, 2003); Şevket Pamuk, "Institutional Change and the Longevity of the Ottoman Empire, 1500–1800," *Journal of Interdisciplinary History* 35 (2004): 225–47.

21. On the transformations overtaking the Ottoman state during the seventeenth and eighteenth centuries, see Rifa'at Abou-el-Haj, *Formation of the Modern State: The Ottoman Empire, Sixteenth to Eighteenth Centuries*, 2nd ed. (Syracuse: Syracuse University Press, 2005); Virginia Aksan, *Ottoman Statesman in War and Peace: Ahmed Resmi Efendi, 1700-1783* (Leiden: Brill, 1995); Norman Itzkowitz, "Eighteenth-Century Ottoman Realities," *Studia Islamica* 16 (1962): 73–94; Baki Tezcan, *The Second Ottoman Empire: Political and Social Transformation in the Early Modern World* (Cambridge: Cambridge University Press, 2010); Fatih Yeşil, *Aydınlanma Çağında Bir Osmanlı Katibi: Ebubekir Ratib Efendi (1750-1799)* (Istanbul: Tarih Vakfı Yurt Yayınları, 2010).

22. On the proliferation of these "pasha households," see in particular Rifa'at Abou-el-Haj, "The Ottoman Vezir and Paşa Households, 1683–1703: A Preliminary Report," *Journal of the American Oriental Society* 94 (1974): 438–47; Rifa'at Abou-el-Haj, *The 1703 Rebellion and the Structure of Ottoman Politics* (Leiden: Nederlands Historisch-Archaeologisch Instituut te Istanbul, 1984).

23. For the original proponent of this term, see Halil İnalcık, "Centralization and Decentralization in Ottoman Administration," in *Studies in Eighteenth-Century Islamic History*, ed. Thomas Naff and Roger Owen (Carbondale: Southern Illinois University Press, 1977) , 27–52.

24. For one account of the eighteenth century that has put the notables at the center of Ottoman history, see McGowan, "The Age of the Ayans." For an overview of eighteenth-century notables, see Jane Hathaway, *The Arab Lands under Ottoman Rule, 1516-1800* (New York: Pearson Longman, 2008), chap. 5; Albert Hourani, "Ottoman Reform and the Politics of Notables," in *The Beginnings of Modernization in the Middle East: The Nineteenth Century*, ed. William Polk and Richard L. Chambers (Chicago: University of Chicago Press, 1968), 41–68; Yücel Özkaya, *Osmanlı İmparatorluğunda Ayanlık* (Ankara: Türk Tarih Kurumu Basımevi, 1994); Ehud Toledano, "The Emergence of Ottoman-Local Elites: A Framework for Research," in *Middle East Politics and Ideas*, ed. Ilan Pappé and Moshe Moaz (London: IB Tauris, 1997), 145–62; Deena R. Sadat, "Rumeli Ayanları: The Eighteenth Century," *Journal of Modern History* 44 (1972): 346–63.

25. Dina Rizk Khoury, *State and Provincial Society in the Ottoman Empire, 1540-1834* (New York: Cambridge University Press, 1997); Ariel Salzmann, "An Ancien Régime Revisited: 'Privatization' and Political Economy in the Eighteenth-Century Ottoman Empire," *Politics and Society* 21 (1993): 393–423; Jean-Pierre Thieck, "Décentralisation Ottomane et affirmation urbaine à Alep à la fin du XVIIIe siècle," in *Mouvements communautaires et espaces urbains au Machreq*, ed. Mona Zakariya (Beirut: Centre d'études et de recherches sur le Moyen-Orient contemporain, 1985), 117–68; Gilles Veinstein, "Ayan de la region d'Izmire et la commerce du Levant dans la deuxième moitié du XVIIIe siècle," *Études Bal-*

kaniques 1 (1976): 71–83. On the urban face of the Old Regime, see Nora Lafi, *Esprit civique et organization citadine dans l'Empire ottoman (Xve-XXe siècles)* (Leiden: Brill, 2018), chap. 2.

26. See the critique in Ariel Salzmann, *Tocqueville in the Ottoman Empire: Rival Paths to the Modern State* (Leiden: Brill, 2004), esp. intro.

27. See for example Antonis Anastasopoulos, "Crisis and State Intervention in Late Eighteenth-Century Karaferye (mod. Veroia)," in *The Ottoman Balkans, 1750-1830*, ed. Frederick Anscombe (Princeton: Marcus Wiener, 2006), 11–33; Karen Barkey, *Empire of Difference: The Ottomans in Comparative Perspective* (Cambridge: Cambridge University Press, 2008), esp. chap. 7; Khoury, *State and Provincial Society*, esp. chaps. 4–5; Christine M. Philliou, *Biography of an Empire: Governing Ottomans in an Age of Revolution* (Berkeley: University of California Press, 2011), chap. 1. For a general overview of eighteenth-century provincial administration, see Yücel Özkaya, *18. Yüzyılda Osmanlı Toplumu* (Istanbul: Yapı Kredi Yayınları, 2007).

28. For the origins of this expression, see Halil İnalcık, *The Ottoman Empire: The Classical Age, 1300-1600* (New York: Praeger, 1973).

29. K. Kıvanç Karaman and Şevket Pamuk, "Ottoman State Finances in European Perspective, 1500-1914," *Journal of Economic History* 70 (2010): 593–629; Karaman and Pamuk, "Different Paths to the Modern State in Europe: The Interaction between Warfare, Economic Structure, and Political Regime," *American Political Science Review* 107 (2013): 603–26; Şevket Pamuk, "Fiscal Centralisation and the Rise of the Modern State in the Ottoman Empire," *Medieval History Journal* 17 (2014): 1–26.

30. Yavuz Cezar, "18. Ve 19. Yüzyıllarda Osmanlı Taşrasında Oluşan Yeni Mali Sektörün Mahiyet ve Büyüklüğü Üzerine," *Toplum ve Ekonomi* 9 (1996): 89–145; Christoph Neumann, "Ottoman Provincial Towns from the Eighteenth to the Nineteenth Century," in *The Empire in the City: Arab Provincial Capitals in the Late Ottoman Empire*, ed. Jens Hanssen et al. (Beirut: Ergon Verlag Würzburg, 2002), 131–44; Şevket Pamuk, *A Monetary History of the Ottoman Empire* (New York: Cambridge University Press, 2000), chap. 11.

31. On soaring Ottoman expenditures for eighteenth-century warfare (e.g., jumping 200 percent from 1760 to 1800), see Mehmet Genç, "18. Yüzyılda Osmanlı Ekonomisi ve Savaş," in *Osmanlı İmparatorluğunda Devlet ve Ekonomi* (Istanbul: Ötüken, 2000), 211–25.

32. For an introduction to debates about early modern fiscal-military states, see for example Richard Bonney, *The Rise of the Fiscal State in Europe, c. 1200-1815* (New York: Oxford University Press, 1999); Bartolomé Yun Casalilla and Patrick O'Brien, eds., *The Rise of Fiscal States: A Global History, 1500-1914* (Cambridge: Cambridge University Press, 2012); Stephen Conway and Rafael Torres Sánchez, eds., *The Spending of States: Military Expenditure during the Long Eighteenth Century: Patterns, Organization, and Consequences, 1650-1815* (Saarbrücken: VDM Verlag Dr. Müller, 2011); Jan Glete, *War and the State in Early Modern Europe: Spain, the Dutch Republic, and Sweden as Fiscal-Military States, 1500-1660* (New York: Routledge, 2002); William D. Godsey and Petr Mata, eds., *The Habsburg Monarchy as a Fiscal-Military State: Contours and Perspectives, 1648-1815* (Oxford: Oxford University Press, 2022); Aaron Graham and Patrick Walsh, *The British Fiscal-Military States, 1660-c. 1783* (London: Routledge/Taylor and Francis Group, 2016); Alfani Guido and Matteo di Tullio, *The Lion's Share: Inequality and the Rise of the Fiscal State in Preindustrial Europe* (Cambridge: Cambridge University Press, 2019); Wenkai He, *Paths toward the Modern Fiscal State: England, Japan, and China* (Cambridge, MA: Harvard University Press,

2013). For an argument about why the Ottoman Empire was not a fiscal-military state, see Gabor Ágoston, "Military Transformation in the Ottoman Empire and Russia, 1500–1800," *Kritika: Explorations in Russian and Eurasian History* 12 (2011): 281–319. For a more sanguine assessment (at least for the sixteenth century), see Erol Özvar, "Transformation of the Ottoman Empire into a Military-Fiscal State: Reconsidering the Financing of War from a Global Perspective," in *The Battle for Central Europe: The Siege of Szigetvár and the Death of Süleyman the Magnificent and Nicolas Zrínyi (1566)*, ed. Pál Fodor (Leiden: Brill, 2019), 21–63.

33. For studies that have begun to explore these decades as a turning point, see for example Butrus Abu-Manneh, *Studies on Islam and the Ottoman Empire in the 19th Century (1826–1876)* (Istanbul: Isis Press, 2001); Albert Hourani, "The Changing Face of the Fertile Crescent in the XVIIIth Century," *Studia Islamica* 8 (1957): 89–122; Hülya Canbakal, "Preliminary Observations on Political Unrest in Eighteenth-Century Ayntab: Popular Protest and Faction," in *Political Initiatives "From the Bottom Up" in the Ottoman Empire*, ed. Antonis Anastasopoulos (Rethymno: Crete University Press, 2012), 33–58; Dina Rizk Khoury, "Political Community in the Age of Reform: Rebellion and Empire, 1780–1820," in *Arabic Thought beyond the Liberal Age: Towards an Intellectual History of the Nahda*, ed. Jens Hanssen and Max Weiss (Cambridge: Cambridge University Press, 2016), 101–20. On the economic side of the Great Crisis, see Pamuk, *A Monetary History*, chap. 12; André Raymond, "The Economic Crisis of Egypt in the Eighteenth Century," in *The Islamic Middle East, 700–1900*, ed. Abraham Udovitch (Princeton: Princeton University Press, 1981), 687–707; Aysel Yıldız, *Crisis and Rebellion in the Ottoman Empire: The Downfall of a Sultan in the Age of Revolution* (London: IB Tauris, 2017).

34. On the ideological preparation for these reforms, see Virginia Aksan, "Ottoman Political Writing, 1768–1808," *International Journal of Middle East Studies* 25 (1993): 53–69.

35. Engin Akarlı, "Provincial Power Magnates in Ottoman Bilad al-Sham and Egypt, 1740–1840," in *La Vie sociale dans les provinces Arabes à l'époque Ottomane*, ed. Abdeljelil Temimi (Zaghouan: Centre d'Études et de Recherches sur les Provinces Arabes à l'Époque Ottomane, 1988), 3:41–56; Ali Yaycıoğlu, *Partners of the Empire: The Crisis of the Ottoman Order in the Age of Revolutions* (Stanford: Stanford University Press, 2016).

36. For an overview of the political climate of this period, see David Armitage and Sanjay Subrahmanyam, eds., *The Age of Revolutions in a Global Context, 1760–1840* (New York: Palgrave Macmillan, 2010); C.A. Bayly, *The Birth of the Modern World, 1780–1914* (Malden, MA: Blackwell, 2004), esp. chap. 3.

37. For an analysis of population estimates for eighteenth-century Istanbul, see Betül Başaran, *Selim III, Social Control, and Policing in Istanbul at the End of the Eighteenth Century* (Leiden: Brill, 2014), 60–62. For a longer set of estimates across the Ottoman period, see Cem Behar, *Osmanlı İmparatorluğunun ve İstanbul'un Nüfusu (1500–1927)* (Ankara: Türkiye Cumhuriyeti Başbakanlık Devlet İstatistik Enstitüsü, 1996).

38. Elena Frangakis-Syrett, *The Commerce of Smyrna in the Eighteenth Century (1700–1820)* (Athens: Center for Asia Minor Studies, 1992); Daniel Goffman, *Izmir and the Levantine World, 1550–1650* (Seattle: University of Washington Press, 1990).

39. Antoine Abdel-Nour, *Introduction à l'histoire urbaine de la Syrie ottomane (XVIe–XVIIIe siècle)* (Beirut: Université Libanaise, 1982); André Raymond, *Grandes villes arabes à l'époque ottomane* (Paris: Sinbad, 1985); Jean Sauvaget, *Alep: Essai sur le développement d'une grande*

ville syrienne, des origins au milieu du XIXe siècle (Paris: Libraire Orientaliste Paul Geuthner, 1941).

40. Nikolai Todorov, *The Balkan City, 1400-1900* (Seattle: University of Washington Press, 1983).

41. See for example James Cracraft, *The Petrine Revolution in Russian Culture* (Cambridge, MA: Harvard University Press, 2004); Lindsey Hughes, "'The Crown of Maidenly Honor and Virtue': Redefining Femininity in Peter I's Russia," in *Women and Gender in 18th-Century Russia*, ed. Wendy Rosslyn (Burlington, VT: Ashgate, 2003), 35-49; Nancy S. Kollmann, "Etiquette for Peter's Time: The Honorable Mirror for Youth," *Russian History* 35 (2008): 63-83; Yuri M. Lotman, "The Poetics of Everyday Behavior in Eighteenth-Century Russian Culture," in *The Semiotics of Russian Culture*, ed. Yuri M. Lotman and Boris Uspenskii (Ann Arbor: University of Michigan Press, 1984), 231-56; Elizabeth Clara Sander, *Social Dancing in Peter the Great's Russia: Observations by Holstein Nobleman Friedrich Wilhelm Von Bergholz, 1721 to 1725* (Hildesheim: G. Olms, 2007).

42. On this general point about early modern war-making and the necessity of granting internal political concessions, see Charles Tilly, "War-Making and State-Making as Organized Crime," in *Bringing the State Back In*, ed. Peter Evans, Dietrich Rueschemeyer, and Theda Skocpal (Cambridge: Cambridge University Press, 1985), 183-4.

43. Sünbülzade Vehbi, *Lütfiyye: Metin Tespiti, Özet, Yorum, ve Açıklamalar*, ed. Süreyya Beyzadeoğlu (Istanbul: Milli Eğitim Bakanlığı Yayınları, 2004). For published editions of etiquette manuals written from the late seventeenth to early nineteenth century, see Nabi, *Hayriyye*, ed. İskender Pala (Istanbul: Bedir Yayınevi, 1989); Ömer Zarifi, *Pendname-i Zarifi*, ed. Mehmet Arslan (Sivas: Dilek Matbaacılık, 1994); Sarı Mehmed Paşa, *Zübde-i Vekayiat: Tahlil ve Metin (1066-1116/1656-1704*, ed. Abdülkadir Özcan (Ankara: Türk Tarihi Kurumu Basımevi, 1995). For an overview of this genre in Turkish across the entire Ottoman period, see Bursalı Mehmet Tahir, *Ahlak Kitaplarımız* (Istanbul: Necm-i İstikbal Matbaası, 1909).

44. Overreliance on prescriptive manuals is, in fact, one of the biggest criticisms leveled at Norbert Elias, who, as we have seen, built his model about the "civilizing process" mainly from etiquette guides. See in particular Bryson, *Courtesy*, 8-18.

45. See Jürgen Osterhammel, *Unfabling the East: The Englightenment's Encounter with Asia*, trans. Robert Savage (Princeton: Princeton University Press, 2018). To speak more broadly: new scholarship on eighteenth-century orientalism has come to question the direct link to colonialism that Edward Said famously imputed to it. See also Urs App, *The Birth of Orientalism* (Philadelphia: University of Pennsylvania Press, 2010).

46. For a fresh assessment of Edward Lane's work, freed from the polemical excesses of the orientalism debate, see Paulo Lemos Horta, "Heterotopia as a Site of Cross-Cultural Collaboration: Ibrahim al-Dusuqi and Edward Lane," *Middle Eastern Literatures* 15 (2012): 273-85; Suha Kudsieh, "Beyond Colonial Binaries: Amicable Ties among Egyptian and European Scholars, 1820-1850," *Journal of Comparative Poetics* 36 (2016): 44-68; Jason Thompson, "Edward Lane in Egypt," *Journal of the American Research Center in Egypt* 34 (1997): 243-61.

47. The anthropologist Julian Pitt-Rivers regarded these complementary registers of comportment as characteristic of "Western civilization"; Julian Pitt-Rivers, "Postscript: The Place of Grace in Anthropology," in *Honor and Grace in Anthropology*, ed. J.G. Peristiany

and Julian Pitt-Rivers (Cambridge: Cambridge University Press, 1992), 242–43. But as we will soon see, there was nothing about them that was foreign to the societies of the Ottoman Empire.

Chapter 1

1. Ignatius Mouradgea d'Ohsson, *Tableau général de l'empire ottoman* (Istanbul: Isis, 2001), 4:159. For a study of d'Ohsson's life and career, see Carter Findley, *Enlightening Europe on Islam and the Ottomans: Mouradgea d'Ohsson and His Masterpiece* (Leiden: Brill, 2019).

2. Aaron Hill, *A Full and Just Account of the Present State of the Ottoman Empire in All Its Branches* (London: Cengage Gale, 1709), 92.

3. Carsten Niebuhr, *Travels through Arabia and Other Countries of the East*, trans. Robert Heron (Edinburgh: R. Morison and Son, 1792), 1:118. On Egyptian women as more willing to expose the breasts than the face and head, see also Edward Lane, *An Account of the Manners and Customs of the Modern Egyptians* (London: John Murray, 1860), 52.

4. Alexander and Patrick Russell, *The Natural History of Aleppo*, 2nd ed. (London, 1794), 1:246.

5. Richard Pococke, *A Description of the East* (London: Cengage Gale, 1745), 3:13.

6. Charles Colville Frankland, *Travels to and from Constantinople in the Years 1827 and 1828* (London: Henry Colburn and Richard Bentley, 1830), 1:53. See also Ami Boué, *Turquie d'Europe* (Paris: Arthus Bertrand, 1840), 2:204–5.

7. François-Réné Chateaubriand, *Travels in Greece, Palestine, Egypt, and Barbary*, trans. Frederic Shoberl (London: Henry Colburn, 1812), 1:263. This fashion was popular in many parts of the southern Balkans. One traveler observed (1621) how Bulgarian women decorated their hair in the same way; Louis des Hayes, *Voiage du Levant par le commandement du roy en l'année 1621* (Paris: Adrian Taupinart, 1632), 75–76.

8. Russell, *Aleppo*, 2:63.

9. Lane, *Manners*, 52.

10. Lane, *Manners*, 52. For similar verdicts about the state of dress in the countryside, see also de Tott, *Memoirs*, 4:74; Benoit de Maillet, *Description de l'Egypte* (Paris: Louis Genneau and Jacques Rollin, 1735), 2:230; Niebuhr, *Travels*, 1:118; Jean de Thévenot, *The Travels of Monsieur de Thévenot into the Levant*, trans. Archibald Lovell (London: Gregg Farnborough, 1971), 1:248; J. Aegidius van Egmont, *Travels through Part of Europe, Asia Minor, the Islands of the Archipelago; Syria, Palestine, Egypt, Mt. Sinai*, trans. John Heyman (London: Cengage Gale, 1759), 2:57–58.

11. van Egmont, *Travels*, 2:368.

12. John Lewis Burckhardt, *Travels in Syria and the Holy Land* (London: John Murray, 1822), 294. In the Balkans, veils were hardly to be seen outside the towns, except in parts of Albania; Boué, *Turquie*, 2:461.

13. Serkan Delice, "The Janissaries and Their Bedfellows: Masculinity and Male Friendship in Eighteenth-Century Ottoman Istanbul," *Gender and Sexuality in Muslim Cultures*, ed. Gül Özyeğin (Burlington, VT: Ashgate, 2015), 125.

14. d'Ohsson, *Tableau*, 4:159; de Thévenot, *Travels*, 1:30. See for example the Greek women working in the gardens outside Edirne who only bothered to veil when they entered town; Lady Mary Wortley Montagu, *Letters from the Levant during the Embassy to Constantinople, 1716-1718* (New York: Arno Press, 1971), 137.

15. Aubry de la Mottraye, *Travels through Europe, Asia, and into Part of Africa* (London: T. Woodward, 1732), 1:171.

16. For observers making the explicit comparison, see Girolamo Dandini, *A Voyage to Mount Libanus* (London: A. Roper and R. Basset, 1698), 46; Cornelis de Bruyn, *Voyages de Corneille le Bruyn au Levant* (The Hague: P. Gosse and J. Neaulme, 1732), 1:130; d'Ohsson, *Tableau*, 4:160-61; Thévenot, *Travels*, 1:30; C.-F. Volney, *Travels through Egypt and Syria in the Years 1783, 1784, and 1785* (Dublin: Cengage Gale, 1793), 2:458.

17. Volney, *Travels*, 1:244.

18. Michel Febvre, *Théâtre de la Turquie* (Paris: E. Couterot, 1682), 285.

19. Hüseyin Vassaf, *Sefine-i Evliya* (Istanbul: Kitabevi, 2006), 4:415.

20. Hill, *Account*, 92.

21. Edward Brown, *A Brief Account of Some Travels* (London: Benjamin Tooke, 1673), 60; Edward Dodwell, *A Classical and Topographical Tour through Greece* (London: Rodwell and Martin, 1819), 1:133; Henry Holland, *Travels in the Ionian Isles, Albania, Thessaly, Macedonia* (London: Longman, Hurst, Rees, Orme and Brown, 1815), 157. In the Aegean basin, the custom seemed to vary between this tonsure and the freer option of letting the hair grow long; d'Ohsson, *Tableau*, 4:161; John Galt, *Letters from the Levant* (London: T. Cadell and W. Davies, 1812), 244. In northern parts of the Balkans, such as Albania and Serbia, custom seems to have followed the general Ottoman preference for leaving a tuft of hair at the top of the scalp; Margaret Hasluck, *The Unwritten Law in Albania*, ed. J.H. Hutton (Cambridge: Cambridge University Press, 1954), 229-30.

22. Brown, *Brief Account*, 60.

23. Muhammad Khalil al-Muradi, *Silk al-durar fi a`yan al-qarn al-thani `ashar* (Beirut: Dar Ibn Hazm, 1988), 3:32.

24. al-Muradi, *Silk*, 3:118-19.

25. Dodwell, *Tour*, 1:133; Niebuhr, *Travels*, 1:114.

26. Van Egmont, *Travels*, 2:35.

27. Markos Antonios Katsaites, *Dio Taxidia ste Smyrne, 1740 kai 1742* (Athens: Ekdoseis "Henoseos Smyrnnaion," 1972), 103-4.

28. Radu Florescu, *Essays on Romanian History* (Portland: Center for Romanian Studies, 1999), 176; Constanta Vintila-Ghitulescu, "Constructing a New Identity: Romanian Aristocrats between Oriental Heritage and Western Prestige (1780-1866)," in *From Traditional Attire to Modern Dress: Modes of Identification, Modes of Recognition in the Balkans (XVIth-XXth Centuries)*, ed. Constanta Vintila-Ghitulescu (Newcastle upon Tyne: Cambridge Scholars, 2011), 122-25.

29. Mikha'il al-Dimashqi, *Tarikh Hawadith al-Sham wa Lubnan, 1782-1841*, ed. Ahmad Ghassan Sabbanu (Damascus: Dar Qutayba, 1982), 33.

30. d'Ohsson, *Tableau*, 4:161.

31. Hasan Agha al-`Abd, *Tarikh Hasan Agha*, ed. Yusuf Nu`aysa (Damascus: Wizarat al-Thaqafa wa al-Irshad al-Qawmi, 1979), 143; Mikha'il Mishaqa, *Murder, Mayhem, Pillage, and Plunder: The History of the Lebanon in the 18th and 19th Centuries*, trans. Wheeler M. Thackston (Albany: State University of New York Press, 1988), 62-63. See also the order by the patriarch of Damascus (1819) to arrest all Catholic Orthodox priests. They were to have their beards shaven and then to be sent into exile (Mishaqa, *Murder*, 118).

32. Yusuf al-Halabi, *Hawadith Halab al-yawmiyya, 1771-1805* (Aleppo, 2006), 189. He was

a "Franco"—that is, a Jew of Italian lineage—and was known to Europeans as Raphael Picciotto; Abraham Marcus, *The Middle East on the Eve of Modernity: Aleppo in the Eighteenth Century* (New York: Columbia University Press, 1989), 46.

33. See for example the biography of Muhammad al-Maliki (d. 1771/72), a North African scholar who migrated to Damascus. He went so far as to shave his beard, mustache, and even eyebrows; al-Muradi, *Silk*, 4:61.

34. 'Abd al-Rahman al-Jabarti, *'Aja'ib al-athar fi al-tarajim al-akhbar*, ed. Hasan Muhammad Jawhar, 'Abd al-Fattah Sirinjawi, Ibrahim Salim, and 'Umar Dusuqi (Cairo: Lajnat al-Bayan al-'Arabi, 1958–67), 1:262. See also W.G. Browne, *Travels in Africa, Egypt, and Syria* (London: Cengage Gale, 1799), 55; Vivant Denon, *Travels in Upper and Lower Egypt*, trans. Arthur Aikin (London: T.N. Longman and O. Reese, 1803; reprint: New York, Arno Press, 1973), 2:254.

35. Febvre, *Théâtre*, 285.

36. This was the debate, at any rate, in eighteenth-century Aleppo; Russell, *Aleppo*, 1:112–13.

37. al-Dimashqi, *Tarikh*, 39.

38. In eighteenth-century Aleppo, men who used antinomy were considered "effeminate"; Russell, *Aleppo*, 1:111–12. On the other hand, it may have enjoyed an earlier fashion in official circles. Sürmeli Ali Paşa (d. 1695) was a grand vizier who was originally from Dimetoka in Thrace. He got his nickname from the habit of putting antinomy (*sürme*) around his eyes; Osmanzade Taib, *Hadikat ül-Vüzera* (Istanbul: Ceride-i Havadis Matbaası, 1854), 122.

39. Chateaubriand, *Travels*, 1:236.

40. See for example Elizabeth Craven, *A Journey through the Crimea to Constantinople* (Dublin: H. Chamberlaine et al., 1789), 225–26; J. Griffiths, *Travels in Europe, Asia Minor, and Arabia* (London: T. Cadell and W. Davies, 1805), 88; Lane, *Manners*, 35; van Egmont, *Travels*, 1:225; Russell, *Aleppo*, 1:109–11.

41. Van Egmont, *Travels*, 1:93. See also d'Ohsson, *Tableau*, 4:170. In eighteenth-century Aleppo, the use of rouge was associated with prostitutes; Russell, *Aleppo*, 1:109.

42. 'Abd al-Ghani al-Nabulsi, *Al-Hadiqa al-nadiyya: Sharh al-Tariqa al-Muhammadiyya* (Lyallpur: al-Maktaba al-nuriyya al-ridwiyya, 1977), 2:452–53. On the wearing of rings in Damascus, see James Grehan, *Everyday Life and Consumer Culture in Eighteenth-Century Damascus* (Seattle: University of Washington Press, 2007), 207–8.

43. Lane, *Manners*, 31.

44. See for example Boué, *Turquie*, 2:206; van Egmont, *Travels*, 1:225.

45. Niebuhr, *Travels*, 1:118–19.

46. Montagu, *Letters*, 117. For this custom among Greek women, too, see Dodwell, *Tour*, 1:140–41.

47. Paul Lucas, *Voyage au Levant* (Paris: Nicolas Simart, 1714), 1:215. See also van Egmont, *Travels*, 2:315.

48. As reported for eighteenth-century Aleppo; Russell, *Aleppo*, 1:108.

49. See for example Edmund Chishull, *Travels in Turkey and Back to England* (London: W. Bowyer, 1747), 74; Dodwell, *Tour*, 1:140–41; J.C. Hobhouse, *A Journey through Albania* (New York, 1817), 1:123–24; Frankland *Travels*, 1:53.

50. See for example Russell, *Aleppo*, 1:224; Lane, *Manners*, 32.

51. For the full description, see Montagu, *Letters*, 124–27.

52. For images of these ornaments, see Griffiths, *Travels*, 87; Richard Chandler, *Travels in Asia Minor and Greece* (London: Joseph Booker, 1817), 74–75; Hill, *Account*, 95, 175; Craven, *Journey*, 225. As John Covell observed (1675), "Here you must understand that every woman must have girdles, bracelets, and topazes, or else they are not gentle women, as in England they are not without a black bag"; John Covell, "Extracts from the Diaries of John Covell," in *Early Travels and Voyages in the Levant*, ed. Theodore Bent (London: Hakluyt Society, 1893), 229.

53. For other accounts of the outer cloaks (*ferace*) worn by Istanbul women, see Thévenot, *Travels*, 1:56; Hill, *Account*, 95; de Bruyn, *Voyages*, 1:129; Antoine-Laurent Castellan, *Lettres sur la Morée, l'Hellespont et Constantinople* (Paris: A. Nepveu, 1811), 2:297.

54. For other accounts of upper-class female headwear, see de Bruyn, *Voyages*, 1:130; van Egmont, *Travels*, 1:224–25. Having studied the pictorial evidence, one historian of Ottoman fashion believes that the *yaşmak* may have been a seventeenth-century innovation; Nureddin Sevin, *Onüç Asırlık Türk Kıyafet Tarihine Bir Bakış* (Ankara: Kültür Bakanlığı, 1990), 94–95.

55. See for example the "thin translucent veil of muslin" popular in eighteenth-century Izmir; Chandler, *Travels*, 75.

56. Muslim and Christian women of the capital wore the same fashions; see Hill, *Account*, 175.

57. D'Ohsson, *Tableau*, 4:167.

58. Craven, *Journey*, 225. For other accounts of fashions favored by upper-class ladies, ranging from the mid-seventeenth to the early nineteenth century, see Thévenot, *Travels*, 1:56; d'Ohsson, *Tableau*, 4:162–71; van Egmont, *Travels*, 1:224; Griffiths, *Travels*, 87–88. For an overview of female fashion in Istanbul, see Jennifer Scarce, *Women's Costume of the Near and Middle East* (London: Unwin Hyman, 1987), chap. 4.

59. de la Mottraye, *Travels*, 159. On Izmir, see also Jean Dumont, *A New Voyage to the Levant* (London: M. Gillyflower et al., 1696), 271–72; Chandler, *Travels*, 74–75.

60. Van Egmont, *Travels*, 1:173.

61. Van Egmont, *Travels*, 1:227–28; William Wittman, *Travels in Turkey, Asia Minor, Syria, and Egypt* (London: Richard Phillips, 1803; reprint: New York: Arno Press, 1971), 455–56.

62. Craven, *Journey*, 245.

63. Wittman, *Travels*, 429. See also van Egmont, *Travels*, 1:275–76. Some elements of island fashion seemed to have been borrowed or partially transmitted. On Cyprus, the female fashions were not much different from Rhodes, "except that in Cyprus they wear no veils. Their hair is covered before, but hangs down behind in curls. They also wear those large white plaited gowns that I have already mentioned at Scio [Chios]"; ibid., 1:286. For more on Chios, see also Dumont, *New Voyage*, 192–93; de Bruyn, *Voyages*, 1:169–70; Thévenot, *Travels*, 1:101; van Egmont, *Travels*, 1:244. On the island of Simi, both men and women had won the privilege of wearing turbans. According to the local legend, they had greeted Süleyman I with turbans on their heads as he returned from conquering Rhodes (1522). The sultan was so gratified that he authorized the fashion on the island; van Egmont, *Travels*, 1:244. On fashions in Crete, see Joseph Pitton de Tournefort, *Voyage into the Levant* (London: D. Midwinter et al., 1741), 1:91–92. On Patmos, Wittman, *Travels*, 113.

64. See for instance the reaction of visitors to the fashions of Chios: Thévenot, *Travels*, 1:101; Dumont, *New Voyage*, 192–93; de Bruyn, *Voyages*, 1:169–70; van Egmont, *Travels*, 1:244; Griffiths, *Travels*, 241.

65. Dodwell, *Tour*, 1:140. See too the same recognition about Aegean fashions by a Greek observer (1740); Katsaites, *Dio Taxidia*, 107.

66. Hobhouse, *Journey*, 1:407, 409.

67. Dodwell, *Tour*, 1:140–42; Holland, *Travels*, 171.

68. Hobhouse, *Journey*, 1:123–24.

69. Lane, *Manners*, 43, 45; de Maillet, *Description*, 2:232–33. On the prevalence of local styles for veils in the Arab lands, see Yedida Stillman, *Arab Dress: A Short History* (Leiden: Brill, 2000), 148–49.

70. Russell, *Aleppo*, 1:113–15. See also Mehmed Haşim Efendi, *İma-yi Törehat-ı Büldanan*, ed. Feridun Emecen and İlhan Şahin (Ankara: Neyir Matbaacılık, 2022), 96.

71. Niebuhr, *Travels*, 1:118–19.

72. Frankland, *Travels*, 1:339–40.

73. Mehmed Haşim, *İma*, 109.

74. Boué, *Turquie*, 2:200. For a seventeenth-century reference, see Evliya Çelebi, *Evliya Çelebi Seyahatnamesi*, ed. Yücel Dağlı et al. (Istanbul: Yapı Kredi Yayınları, 1999–2006), 5:130. On the tall caps of gold and silver that he saw women wearing in Bitlis, Diyarbakir, and Van, see ibid., 5:31, 70.

75. Boué, *Turquie*, 2:211–12. For an overview of fashions in the Ottoman Balkans, see Charlotte Jirousek, "Ottoman Influence in Balkan Dress," in *Resplendent Dress from Southeastern Europe: A History in Layers*, ed. Elizabeth Wayland Barber and Barbara Belle Sloan (Los Angeles: Fowler Museum at UCLA, 2013), 143–76.

76. Browne, *Travels*, 493–94. For evidence of this fashion in the seventeenth century, see Evliya, *Seyahatnamesi*, 4:15. On similar headdresses that he saw in Erzincan and Kayseri, see ibid., 2:108; 3:109.

77. Russell, *Aleppo*, 1:104. See also Niebuhr, *Travels*, 1:114–15.

78. al-Jabarti, *'Aja'ib*, 4:167.

79. For two North African scholars who settled in Cairo and adopted the local dress, see al-Jabarti, *'Aja'ib*, 4:258–59, 261–62.

80. Here is the ceremonial headpiece of the grand vizier during an audience: "a small white turban, decorated with feathers, and fastened in the middle with large diamonds"; van Egmont, *Travels*, 1:193. For late seventeenth-century views, see for example Antoine Galland, *Journal d'Antoine Galland*, ed. Charles Schefer (Paris: Ernest Leroux, 1881), 1:73–74; 2:107–9. See also Madeline Zilfi, *Women and Slavery in the Late Ottoman Empire* (Cambridge: Cambridge University Press, 2010), 79–81. On the exclusive shops that catered to the sartorial needs of courtiers and high officials in seventeenth-century Istanbul, see Robert Mantran, *Istanbul dans la seconde moitié du XVIIe siècle* (Paris: Librairie Adrien Maisonneuve, 1962), 409–10.

81. In Tunis, for example, the ceremonial turbans of scholars differed according to their affiliation with either the Hanafi or Maliki legal school; André Demeerseman, *Aspects de la société Tunisienne d'après Ibn Abi'l-Dhiyaf* (Tunis: Institut des Belles Lettres Arabes, 1996), 237–38.

82. Compare Cairo and Aleppo: Niebuhr, *Travels*, 1:115; Russell, *Aleppo*, 1:104–5.

83. See for example van Egmont, *Travels*, 2:35.

84. In one scene from 1774, the imperial camp knew immediately that a contingent of Kurds had entered on account of their signature *kalpak*; Ahmed Efendi, *III. Selim'in Sırkatibi Ahmed Efendi Tarafından Tutulan Ruzname*, ed. Sema Arıkan (Ankara: Türk Tarih Kurumu, 1993), 66. For the kalpak worn by Kurds in Aleppo, see Russell, *Aleppo*, 1:104.

85. Boué, *Turquie*, 2:189. This is probably the same "Bosnian kalpak" (*boşnak kalpağı*) that caught the eye of Evliya Çelebi, who encountered it again in Belgrade and Serres; Evliya, *Seyahatnamesi*, 5:198, 227; 8:59. The poor of Varna, he tells us, preferred a variation that he called "*Tatar kalpağı*"; ibid., 5:51. On the tall kalpaks favored by Romanian boyars, the landed elite, see William Wilkinson, *An Account of the Principalities of Wallachia and Moldavia* (London: Longman, Hurst, Rees, Orme, and Brown, 1820), 134–35. For a brief attempt to require flat-topped kalpaks in Istanbul (1807)—perhaps because some now towered to extravagant heights—see Georg Oğulukyan, *Georg Oğulukyan'ın Ruznamesi 1806-1811 İsyanları: III. Selim, IV. Mustafa, II. Mahmud ve Alemdar Mustafa*, trans. Hrand D. Andreasyan (İstanbul Edebiyat Fakültesi Basımevi, 1972), 18.

86. al-Jabarti, `Aja'ib, 2:201.

87. By 1800, their numbers were rapidly growing. There were some fifteen hundred non-Muslim consular agents in Aleppo alone; Marcus, *The Middle East*, 46.

88. Dodwell, *Tour*, 1:134. See also Chateaubriand, *Travels*, 1:271. On the trade in fezzes, manufactured mainly in North Africa, see Suraiya Faroqhi, "The Adventures of Tunisian Fez-Sellers in Eighteenth-Century Istanbul," in *Travel and Artisans in the Ottoman Empire* (London: IB Tauris, 2014), 143–55; Lucette Valensi, "Islam et capitalism: Production et commerce des chéchias en Tunisie et en France au XVIIIe et XIXe siècles," *Revue d'Histoire Moderne et Contemporaine* 17 (1969): 376–400.

89. Dodwell, *Tour*, 1:286. On the prevalence of turbans in the towns of Cyprus, a cap-wearing island, where members of the urban elite generally dressed in the Istanbul style, see Euphrosyne Rizopoulou-Egoumenidou, "From Oriental (Ottoman) to European (Frankish) Dress: Dress as Key Indicator of the Lifestyle and Role of the Elites of Cyprus during the Eighteenth and Nineteenth Centuries," in *From Traditional Attire to Modern Dress: Modes of Identification, Modes of Recognition in the Balkans (XVIth-XXth Centuries)*, ed. Constant Vintila-Ghitulescu (Newcastle upon Tyne: Cambridge Scholars, 2011), 134–35.

90. Angela Jianu, "Women, Fashion, and Europeanization: The Romanian Principalities, 1750–1830," in *Women in the Ottoman Balkans*, ed. Amila Buturovic and İrvin Cemil Schick (New York: IB Tauris, 2007), 201–30; Vintila-Ghitulescu, "Constructing," 104–28.

91. Hobhouse, *Journey*, 1:406. See also ibid., 472; Hill, *Account*, 174–75; Holland, *Travels*, 169; Thomas Smart Hughes, *Travels in Sicily, Greece, and Albania* (London: J. Mawman, 1820), 1:301.

92. Hananiya Munayyir, *al-Durr al-marsuf fi tarikh al-Shuf* (Beirut, 1984), 79. See also the reaction of Damascenes to the "strange dress" of Ottoman troops who had arrived to defend Syria after the French invasion of Egypt. Many were recruits from the Balkans, recognizable from the tall caps to which they had attached bells; al-Dimashqi, *Tarikh*, 23.

93. For other references to the distinctive clothing of Balkan troops, see al-Jabarti, `Aja'ib, 3:341, 349.

94. Dumont, *New Voyage*, 192. See also Thévenot, *Travels*, 1:100.

95. Rizopoulou-Egoumenidou, "From Oriental," 134. On the persistence of Italianate

Notes to Chapter 1

fashions in seventeenth-century Crete (fully conquered by 1669), see Evliya, *Seyahatnamesi*, 8:174.

96. For contemporary descriptions of male outfits, see for example Chishull, *Travels*, 68; Dumont, *New Voyage*, 265–66; Hill, *Account*, 93–94. For a scholarly overview, see Hülya Tezcan, *The Topkapı Saray Museum* (Boston: Little, Brown, 1985), 25.

97. On women's eighteenth-century fad for shirts with a plunging neckline, see Onur İnal, "Ottoman Borderlands and the Anglo-Ottoman Exchange of Costumes," *Journal of World History* 22 (2011): 263.

98. In eighteenth-century Aleppo, men wore their furs at least half the year, "but the fashion continues the use of furs when the necessity ceases, and many of the people of rank retain them all the summer"; Russell, *Aleppo*, 1:100–101.

99. Ahmed Vasıf, *Mahasinü'l-Asar ve Haka'ikü'l-Ahbar* (Istanbul: Dar al-Taba`a al-`Amira, 1804), 1:76.

100. Tezcan, *Topkapı*, 43.

101. See for example the range of fur-lined garments in eighteenth-century Damascus; Grehan, *Everyday*, 215–16.

102. Mehmed Haşim, *İma*, 206.

103. See for example descriptions of Greek and Albanian dress: Chateaubriand, *Travels*, 2:200–201; Dodwell, *Tour*, 1:135–36; Hobhouse, *Journey*, 1:406–7. In his travels from the mid-seventeenth century, Evliya Çelebi refers to these styles as the "Algerian fashion"; Evliya, *Seyahatnamesi*, 8:106–7, 279; 9:37; 10:366.

104. Chateaubriand, *Travels*, 2:200–201.

105. Holland, *Travels*, 253. For other descriptions of Albanian attire, see Dodwell, *Tour*, 1:135–36; Hobhouse, *Journey*, 1:121.

106. Grehan, *Everyday Life*, 209–10.

107. D'Ohsson, *Tableau*, 4:158. See also van Egmont, *Travels*, 1:224; Febvre, *Théâtre*, 195; Lane, *Manners*, 31, 43–44.

108. Russell, *Aleppo*, 1:113.

109. On rural footwear in Bulgaria, Greece, and western Anatolia, see for example Chandler, *Travels*, 1:149; Dodwell, *Tour*, 1:136; Frankland, *Travels*, 1:53. On Romania, Wilkinson, *Account*, 159.

110. Kabudlu Mustafa Vasfı Efendi, *Tevarih: Analysis—Texts—Maps—Index—Facsimile*, ed. Ömer Koçyiğit (Cambridge, MA: Department of Near Eastern Languages and Civilizations, Harvard University, 2016), 289; Kabudlı Vasfi Efendi, "The Adventures of an Ottoman Horseman: The Autobiography of Kabudlı Vasfi Efendi, 1800–1825," in *The Joys of Philology: Studies in Ottoman Literature, History, and Orientalism (1500–1923)*, ed. Jan Schmidt (Istanbul: Isis Press, 2002), 1:215.

111. See for example Volney, *Travels*, 1:4.

112. Frankland, *Travels*, 1:53. On Romanian women going about barefoot, see Wilkinson, *Account*, 160.

113. Thomas Allom, *Constantinople and the Scenery of the Seven Churches of Asia Minor* (London: Fisher, Son, 1838), 1:42.

114. See for example Browne, *Travels*, 508; Ahmad al-Budayri, *Hawadith Dimashq al-yawmiyya*, ed. Ahmad `Izzat `Abd al-Karim (Cairo: Matbu`at al-Jam`iyya al-Misriyya li'l-Dirasat al-Tarikhiyya, 1959), 140; Mikha'il Burayk, *Tarikh al-Sham*, ed. Ahmad Ghassan

Sabbanu (Damascus: Dar Qutayba, 1982), 74–75; Griffiths, *Travels*, 88. On the practice of affluent women (in Aleppo) renting a garden for the day, see Russell, *Aleppo*, 1:255.

115. Griffiths, *Travels*, 337–38.

116. For depictions of such escorts, respectively in Izmir and Aleppo, see for example Chandler, *Travels*, 75; Russell, *Aleppo*, 1:259.

117. Pococke, *Description*, 3:10–11; Thévenot, *Travels*, 1:101–2; Wittman, *Travels*, 443; Chandler, *Travels*, 56. Mehmed Haşim Efendi, the Ottoman bureaucrat and traveler, attributed their boldness to the absence of their husbands, who had to seek employment off the island and send back remittances. Only about 10 percent of the women on the island were living, at any given time, with their husbands; Mehmed Haşim, *İma*, 52.

118. Selim Karahasanoğlu, *Kadı ve Günlüğü: Sadreddinzade Telhisi Mustafa Efendi Günlüğü (1711-1735) Üstüne Bir İnceleme* (Istanbul: Türkiye İş Bankası Kültür Yayınları, 2013), 110; Ahmet Refik, *Hicri On İkinci Asırda İstanbul Hayatı* (Istanbul: Devlet Matbaası, 1930), 86–88. For an overview of sartorial regulation in the eighteenth-century Ottoman Empire, see Donald Quataert, "Clothing Laws, State, and Society in the Ottoman Empire, 1720–1829," *International Journal of Middle East Studies* 29 (1997): 403–25; Madeline Zilfi, "Women, Minorities, and the Changing Politics of Dress in the Ottoman Empire, 1650–1830," in *The Right to Dress: Sumptuary Laws in a Global Perspective, c. 1200-1800*, ed. Giorgio Riello and Ulinka Rublack (Cambridge: Cambridge University Press, 2019), 393–415.

119. Shirine Hamadeh, *The City's Pleasures: Istanbul in the Eighteenth Century* (Seattle: University of Washington Press, 2008), esp. chap. 8.

120. Fındıklılı Süleyman Efendi Şemdanizade, *Mür'i't-Tevarih*, ed. Münir Aktepe (Istanbul: Edebiyat Fakültesi Matbaası, 1976), 1:26; Mustafa Sami, *Tarih-i Sami*, in *Tarih-i Sami ve Şakir ve Suphi* (Istanbul, 1784), 34. See also Joseph von Hammer, *Histoire de l'empire ottoman depuis son origine jusqu'à nos jours* (Istanbul: Isis Press, 2000), 14:138–39.

121. Mehmed Hakim, *Hakim Efendi Tarihi*, ed. Tahir Güngör and Ziya Yılmazer (Istanbul: Türkiye Yazma Eserler Kurumu Başkanlığı, 2019), 227–28; Refik, *On İkinci*, 174–75; von Hammer, *Histoire*, 16:13. On the peculiarities of Osman III's reign, see Zilfi, *Women*, 73–74.

122. Hakim, *Hakim Tarihi*, 274; Ahmed Vasıf, *Mahasinü'l-Asar*, 1:57. On the bright colors and floral themes incorporated into women's overcoats, see Sevin, *Kıyafet*, 120. For further discussion, see also Hamadeh, *Pleasures*, 129–32, 167–68; Quataert, "Clothing Laws"; Madeline Zilfi, "Goods in the Mahalle: Distributional Encounters in Eighteenth-Century Istanbul," in *Consumption Studies and the History of the Ottoman Empire, 1550-1922*, ed. Donald Quataert (Albany: State University of New York Press, 2000), chap. 9; Zilfi, "Women, Minorities."

123. Hakim, *Hakim Tarihi*, 548. See also von Hammer, *Histoire*, 16:22.

124. Hakim, *Hakim Tarihi*, 874.

125. Abdülkadir Özcan, ed., *Anonim Osmanlı Tarihi, 1099-1116 (1688-1704)* (Ankara: Türk Tarih Kurumu Basımevi, 2000), 176. For a short-lived wave of sartorial legislation directed against Christians and Jews in 1742, related to a riot that shook the markets of the capital in 1740, see Robert W. Olson, "Jews, Janissaries, Esnaf, and the Revolt of 1740 in Istanbul: Social Upheaval and Political Realignment in the Ottoman Empire," *Journal of the Economic and Social History of the Orient* 20 (1977): 199–207.

126. Hakim, *Hakim Tarihi*, 548; Refik, *On İkinci*, 182–83. These decrees could have teeth.

On the execution of two non-Muslims, an Armenian and a Jew, caught wearing "Muslim" articles of clothing (1758), see Hakim, *Hakim Tarihi*, 515–16. On the tight-fitting resemblance of "Frankish" and Indian fashions, see al-Jabarti, *'Aja'ib*, 4:75. On the general disapproval of European clothing, see Boué, *Turquie*, 2:399–400. Europeans would continue to wear local dress into the early decades of the nineteenth century; see for example Frankland, *Travels*, 2:59, 96.

127. Ahmed Vasıf, *Mahasinü'l-Asar*, 1:103–4; Teşrifatçı Mehmed Akif Bey, *Tarih-i Cülus-ı Sultan Mustafa Han-ı Salis* (Istanbul: Türkiye Yazma Eserler Kurumu Başkanları Yayınları, Istanbul, 2012), 21b; Refik, *On İkinci*, 182–83.

128. Hakim, *Hakim Tarihi*, 874. See also von Hammer, *Histoire*, 16:22.

129. Zilfi, *Women*, 76–78; Zilfi, "Goods," 301.

130. Dumont, *New Voyage*, 283; de Bruyn, *Voyages*, 1:140.

131. Febvre, *Théâtre*, 196. In eighteenth-century Aleppo, Christian women generally abstained from green in public, but were "eager to indulge their fancy within doors"; Russell, *Natural*, 2:45.

132. See for example Browne, *Travels*, 435–36; Volney, *Travels*, 2:21–22.

133. Van Egmont, *Travels*, 1:254. See also Mehmed Haşim, *İma*, 65.

134. Hüseyin Ayvansarayi, *The Garden of the Mosques: Hafız Hüseyin Ayvansarayi's Guide to the Muslim Monuments of Ottoman Istanbul*, trans. Howard Crane (Leiden: Brill, 2000), 2:343. See also Mustafa Naima, *Tarih-i Naima* (Istanbul: n.d.), 1:114.

135. Ahmad Shalabi, *Awdah al-isharat fi-man tawalla Misr al-Qahira min al-wuzara' wa al-bashat*, ed. 'Abd al-Rahim 'Abd al-Rahman 'Abd al-Rahim (Cairo: Tawzi' Maktabat al-Khanji, 1978), 120, 126.

136. On the color for Christians, see Niebuhr, *Travels*, 1:116; Russell, *Aleppo*, 2:42–43. On violet being assigned to Aleppan Jews, see Russell, *Aleppo*, 2:59. At the turn of the eighteenth century, violet seems to have been the main color of Jewish communities in Istanbul and Izmir as well; Dumont, *New Voyage*, 300; de Bruyn, *Voyages*, 1:130, 220. One chronicler insists that Jews were once told to wear blue (1726); Shalabi, *Awdah*, 469. By the 1820s, the "Copts and Jews" could choose from among "black, blue, gray, or light-brown" for their turbans; Lane, *Manners*, 34.

137. On the Greek elite wearing yellow shoes, see Hobhouse, *Journey*, 1:407. On eighteenth-century attempts to regulate footwear, Matthew Elliott, "Dress Codes in the Ottoman Empire: the Case of the Franks," in *Ottoman Costumes: From Textiles to Identity*, ed. Suraiya Faroqhi and Christoph Neumann (Istanbul: Eren, 2004), 111–14.

138. d'Ohsson, *Tableau*, 4:158; Russell, *Aleppo*, 2:46–47.

139. "Women of every class, when they walk abroad, wear thin, yellow boots, reaching half up the leg and over these yellow babooge or slippers"; Russell, *Aleppo*, 1:113. He continues, "it is only some of the common people . . . who wear red boots" (1:115).

140. Hakim, *Hakim Tarihi*, 919.

141. Vasıf, *Mahasinü'l-Asar*, 1:189. See also von Hammer, *Histoire*, 16:35.

142. Hakim, *Hakim Tarihi*, 1148, 1161–62.

143. See for example the trade in fine Indian textiles, which catered mainly to the markets of Istanbul; Katsumi Fukasawa, *Toilerie et commerce du Levant* (Paris: CNRS, 1987), 40–41.

144. Ahmet Cevdet, *Tarih-i Cevdet* (Istanbul: Matbaa-yi Osmaniye, 1893), 2:50–51. On

the wave of sartorial legislation in the late eighteenth and early nineteenth centuries, see Zilfi, *Women*, 86–95.

145. Ahmet Cevdet, *Tarih*, 2:359–60; Enver Ziya Karal, ed., *Selim III'ün Hatt-ı Hümayunları* (Ankara: Türk Tarih Kurumu Basımevi, 1942–46), 100–101. On earlier Ottoman reservations about Indian textile imports—which did not, however, lead to restrictions—see Halil İnalcık, "The Ottoman Economic Mind and Aspects of the Ottoman Economy," in *Studies in the Economic History of the Middle East*, ed. M.A. Cook (London: Oxford University Press, 1970), 207–18.

146. Karal, *Selim III*, 102. See too the complaint, issued at the same time, about state officials who were wearing turbans of unusual height; ibid., 102.

147. Ahmet Refik, *Hicri On Üçüncü Asırda İstanbul Hayatı* (İstanbul: Enderun Kitabevi, 1988), 4; Karal, *Selim III*, 102. On the order to snip overly long collars, see d'Ohsson, *Tableau*, 4:170. On the persistence of bright colors in women's overcoats, see Sevin, *Kıyafet*, 119–20.

148. Cabi Ömer Efendi, *Cabi Tarihi*, ed. Mehmet Ali Beyhan (Ankara: Türk Tarih Kurumu, 2003), 753. For other references to sartorial policing and official anxieties about social climbing from the same period, see Ahmed Cevdet, *Tarih*, 9:18–19; Cabi, *Tarih*, 766–67, 773; Refik, *On Üçüncü*, 11–12; Mehmed Ataullah Şanizade, *Şanizade Tarihi* (İstanbul: Trabzonlu Bakırcıbaşı Mehmed Efendizade Süleyman Efendi'nin Matbaası, 1867–74), 1:286–88.

149. al-Halabi, *Hawadith*, 88–90.

150. al-Halabi, *Hawadith*, 114–15. See also Marcus, *The Middle East*, 41–42, 98–99.

151. al-Halabi, *Hawadith*, 132.

152. Burayk, *Tarikh*, 73–74.

153. Rufa'il Karamah, *Hawadith Lubnan wa Suriya min sanat 1745 ila sanat 1800*, ed. Basiliyus Qattan (Beirut: Jarrus, 1983[?]), 74, 82–83, 86.

154. al-Jabarti, *'Aja'ib*, 3:341, 348.

155. al-Jabarti, *'Aja'ib*, 3:342.

156. al-Jabarti, *'Aja'ib*, 4:33.

157. For the text of the French pamphlets, see al-Jabarti, *'Aja'ib*, 4:288–91. On the French expedition in Egypt, see Juan Cole, *Napoleon's Egypt: Invading the Middle East* (New York: Palgrave Macmillan, 2007); André Raymond, *Égyptiens et français au Caire, 1798–1801* (Cairo: Institut Français d'Archéologie Orientale, 1998).

158. al-Jabarti, *'Aja'ib*, 4:312–13.

159. al-Jabarti, *'Aja'ib*, 4:310.

160. al-Jabarti, *'Aja'ib*, 5:20–21.

161. On the two revolts, see al-Jabarti, *'Aja'ib*, 4:330–32, 5:107–25. For a reconstruction of the first uprising, see Cole, *Napoleon*, 198–211.

162. al-Jabarti, *'Aja'ib*, 4:303; 5:12, 148–49, 239.

163. See for example al-Jabarti, *'Aja'ib*, 4:323, 5:76. On anti-Christian sentiment during the French occupation, see also Raymond, *Égyptiens*, 93, 124.

164. See for example al-Jabarti, *'Aja'ib*, 4:309; 5:18, 81–82, 136.

165. al-Jabarti, *'Aja'ib*, 5:292, 295. Less noticeable was the discreet persistence of Christians in bearing arms. Some of the local Orthodox Christians who had served in the French army now turned up in Ottoman units, openly carrying knives and guns; al-Jabarti, *'Aja'ib*, 5:292.

166. al-Jabarti, *'Aja'ib*, 7:428.

167. al-Jabarti, 'Aja'ib, 7:185.
168. al-Jabarti, 'Aja'ib, 7:478.
169. al-Jabarti, 'Aja'ib, 7:479–80.
170. al-Dimashqi, *Tarikh*, 23–24; al-Halabi, *Hawadith*, 297.
171. al-Dimashqi, *Tarikh*, 38, 41; Mishaqa, *Murder*, 63.
172. Mishaqa, *Murder*, 121.
173. Es'ad Efendi, *Es'ad Efendi Tarihi*, ed. Ziya Yılmazer (Istanbul: Osmanlı Araştırmaları Vakfı, 2000), 116–17.
174. James Grehan, "Imperial Crisis and Muslim-Christian Relations in Ottoman Syria and Palestine, c. 1770–1830," *Journal of the Economic and Social History of the Orient* 58 (2015): 490–531.
175. In eighteenth-century Aleppo, townspeople could keep their best clothes for many years "as fashions seldom change"; Russell, *Aleppo*, 1:290.
176. On the general stability of early modern Ottoman fashion, see Tezcan, *Topkapı*, 26–27; Suraiya Faroqhi, *A Cultural History of the Ottomans: The Imperial Elite and Its Artifacts* (London: IB Tauris, 2016), 166; Christoph Neumann, "How Did a Vizier Dress in the Eighteenth Century?," in *Ottoman Costumes: From Textiles to Identity*, ed. Suraiya Faroqhi and Christoph Neumann (Istanbul: Eren, 2004), 184; Sevin, *Kıyafet*, 101. Most shifts during this period were subtle and partook of the common Eurasian vogue for lighter and more comfortable fabrics; see Jennifer Scarce, "Principles of Ottoman Turkish Costume," *Costume* 22 (1988): 24–26. For contemporary impressions, see for example Russell, *Aleppo*, 1:108; Niebuhr, *Travels*, 1:111.
177. Sevin, *Kıyafet*, 101; Madeline Zilfi, "Whose Laws? Gendering the Ottoman Sumptuary Regime," in *Ottoman Costumes: From Textiles to Identity*, ed. Suraiya Faroqhi and Christoph Neumann (Istanbul: Eren, 2004), 129.
178. Volney, *Travels*, 2:17. See also his observation about Maronite bishops, whose dress was not very different from ordinary monks; ibid., 2:22.
179. Mehmed Haşim, *İma*, 119.
180. Hill, *Account*, 95.

Chapter 2

1. "Kahvehane köşelerinde kokma/ öyle süfli yerlere başını sokma"; Vehbi, *Lütfiyye*, 158–59.
2. See for example Muhammad al-Khadimi, *Bariqa mahmudiyya fi sharh tariqa muhammadiyya wa shari'a nabawiyya fi sira ahmadiyya* (Istanbul: Şirket-i Sihafiye, 1900), 3:18; Murtada al-Zabidi, *Ithaf al-sada al-muttaqin bi-sharh asrar ihya' 'ulum al-din* (Cairo, 1893), 7:431. On disapproval of "fun and games" in medieval Islamic treatises, see Franz Rosenthal, *Gambling in Islam* (Leiden: Brill, 1975), 9–26.
3. Mehmed Haşim, *İma*, 119. ("Ahalisinin tabi'atları zevk ü safaya mail olup leyl ü nehar hanende ve sazende ve rakkasan mel'abeleriyle imrar-ı vakit ederler.")
4. For an overview of these legal and moral debates, see for example Ralph Hattox, *Coffee and Coffeehouses: The Origins of a Social Beverage in the Medieval Near East* (Seattle: University of Washington Press, 1985); Eminegül Karababa and Güliz Ger, "Early Modern Ottoman Coffeehouse Culture and the Formation of the Consumer Subject," *Journal of Consumer Research* 37 (2011): 737–60; Hatim Mahamid and Chaim Nissim, "Sufis and

Coffee Consumption: Religio-Legal and Historical Aspects of a Controversy in the Late Mamluk and Early Ottoman Periods," *Journal of Sufi Studies* 7 (2018): 140–64; Massoud Vahedi, "Coffee Was Once *Haram*?: Dispelling Popular Myths Regarding a Nuanced Legal Issue," *Islamic Studies* 60 (2021): 125–56.

5. On debates about tobacco and smoking, see for example Ahmad al-Aqhisari, *Against Smoking*, ed. and trans. Yahya Michot (Leicestershire: Kube, 2010); James Grehan, "Smoking and Early Modern Sociability: The Great Tobacco Debate in the Ottoman Middle East (Seventeenth to Eighteenth Centuries)," *American Historical Review* 111 (2006): 1352–77; Evgenia Kermeli, "The Tobacco Controversy in Early Modern Ottoman Muslim and Christian Discourse," *Hacettepe University Journal of Turkish Studies* 11 (2014): 121–35.

6. The Kadızadeli movement has recently generated a vigorous scholarship. See for example Marc David Baer, *Honored by the Glory of Islam: Conversion and Conquest in Ottoman Europe* (New York: Oxford University Press, 2008), esp. chap. 3; Semiramis Çavuşoğlu, "The Kadızadeli Movement: An Attempt of Şeriat-Minded Reform in the Ottoman Empire," (unpublished PhD diss., Princeton University, 1990); Simeon Evstatiev, "The Qadizadeli Movement and the Revival of Takfir in the Ottoman Age," in *Accusations of Unbelief in Islam: A Diachronic Perspective on Takfir*, ed. Camilla Adang et al. (Leiden: Brill, 2016), 213–43; Dina Le Gall, "Kadızadelis, Nakşbendis, and Intra-Sufi Diatribe in Seventeenth-Century Istanbul," *Turkish Studies Association Journal* 28 (2004): 1–28; Marinos Sariyannis, "The Kadızadeli Movement as a Social and Political Phenomenon: The Rise of a 'Mercantile Ethic'?," in *Political Initiatives from the Bottom Up in the Ottoman Empire*, ed. Antonis Anastasopoulos (Rethymno: Crete University Press, 2012), 263–89; Nir Shafir, "Moral Revolutions: The Politics of Piety in the Ottoman Empire Reimagined," *Comparative Studies of Society and History* 61 (2019): 595–623; Mustapha Sheikh, *Ottoman Puritanism and Its Discontents: Ahmad al-Aqhisari and the Qadizadelis* (Oxford: Oxford University Press, 2016); Ahya Ulumiddin, "Socio-Political Turbulence of the Ottoman Empire: Reconsidering Sufi and Kadızadeli Hostility in 17th Century," *Ulumuna* 20 (2016): 319–52; Madeline Zilfi, "The Kadızadelis: Discordant Revivalism in Seventeenth-Century Istanbul," *Journal of Near Eastern Studies* 45 (1986): 251–69.

7. Mehmed Raşid, *Tarih-i Raşid* (Istanbul, n.d.), 2:52–53, 149.

8. D'Ohsson, *Tableau*, 4:144. On similar drinking habits in mid-seventeenth-century Istanbul, see Thévenot, *Travels*, 1:33.

9. Russell, *Aleppo*, 1:119–20.

10. Lane, *Manners*, 141.

11. See for instance the irritation of the diplomat Ahmed Resmi Efendi at mere tent-pitchers, eager to demand daily cups of coffee; Aksan, *Ottoman Statesman*, 190–91.

12. Mehmet Genç, "Contrôle et taxation du commerce du café dans l'Empire ottoman fin XVIIe–première moitié du XVIIIe siècle," in *La Commerce du café avant l'ère des plantations colonials*, ed. Michel Tuchscherer (Cairo: Institut Français d'Archéologie Orientale, 2001), 161–79.

13. On the Egyptian coffee trade, see Nelly Hanna, *Making Big Money in 1600: The Life and Times of Isma`il Abu Taqiyya, Egyptian Merchant* (Syracuse: Syracuse University Press, 1998); Jane Hathaway, "The Ottomans and the Yemeni Coffee Trade," *Oriente Moderno* 25 (2006): 161–71; André Raymond, "A Divided Sea: The Cairo Coffee Trade in the Red Sea Area during the Seventeenth and Eighteenth Centuries," in *Modernity and Culture*, ed.

Leila Tarazi Fawaz and C.A. Bayly (New York: Columbia University Press, 2002), chap. 2. On the intrusion of colonial coffee from the Atlantic, see McGowan, "Age of the Ayans," 726–27; André Raymond, "Les problèmes du café en Égypte au XVIIIe siècle," in *Le Café en Meditérranée* (Aix-Marseilles: CNRS, 1980), 31–71.

14. Burckhardt, *Syria*, 52. On the general scarcity of coffee in the Egyptian countryside, see Michel Tuchscherer, "Les cafés dans l'Égypte ottomane (XVIe–XVIIIe siècles)," in *Cafés d'Orient revisités*, ed. Hélène Desmet-Grégoire and François Georgeon (Paris: CNRS, 1997), 93.

15. See for example Chandler, *Travels*, 137; van Egmont, *Travels*, 1:133; Pococke, *Description*, 3:79.

16. See for example the Egyptian scholar, Khalil al-Misri (d. 1747), who had a positive passion for coffee and tobacco. In the tolerant estimation of his biographer, these habits neither clouded his character nor dimmed his intellect; al-Muradi, *Silk*, 2:103.

17. al-Jabarti, `Aja'ib, 2:26–27.

18. In Damascus, the eminent Sufi and scholar Murad al-Muradi bought a dilapidated caravansary, which he renovated and converted to a religious school (*madrasa*). No one could reside there who was a "bachelor, youth, or smoker of tobacco"; al-Muradi, *Silk*, 4:130.

19. al-Jabarti, `Aja'ib, 3:117. For references to Syrian scholars who went to extreme lengths in their objections to tobacco, see al-Muradi, *Silk*, 2:31. For a Tunisian enemy of tobacco, see Ahmad Ibn Abi'l-Diyaf, *Ithaf ahl al-zaman bi-akhbar muluk Tunis wa `ahd al-aman* (Tunis: Nashr Kitabat al-Dawla li'l-Shu'un al-Thaqafiyya wa al-Ikhbar, 1963–66), 7:104.

20. Vassaf, *Sefine*, 4:56.

21. `Abd al-Ghani al-Nabulsi, *al-Haqiqa wa al-majaz wa fi al-rihla ila Bilad al-Sham wa Misr wa al-Hijaz*, ed. Ahmad `Abd al-Majid al-Hariri (Cairo: al-Hay'a al-Misriyya al-`Amma li'l-Kitab, 1986), 58.

22. Enfi Hasan Hulus Halveti, *Tezkiretü'l-Müteahhirin: XVI. ve XVIIIe Asırda Yaşayan Veliler ve Deliler*, ed. Mustafa Tatçı ve Musa Yıldız (Istanbul: H Yayınları, 2014), 143–44.

23. Vassaf, *Sefine*, 2:189.

24. Vassaf, *Sefine*, 4:115.

25. See respectively Hakim, *Hakim Tarihi*, 516; Cabi, *Tarih*, 885.

26. al-Jabarti, `Aja'ib, 2:17–18.

27. Ibn Kannan, *Yawmiyat shamiyya*, ed. Akram al-`Ulabi (Damascus: Dar al-Tabba`, 1994), 21, 180, 203; al-Budayri, *Hawadith*, 130.

28. Munayyir, *al-Durr*, 18.

29. Cevdet, *Tarih*, 2:165, 337.

30. d'Ohsson, *Tableau*, 4:147. For seventeenth-century references to the enthusiasm for smoking, see Febvre, *Théatre*, 286; Thévenot, *Travels*, 2:45.

31. Russell, *Aleppo*, 1:120–21.

32. See for example Cevdet, *Tarih*, 2:165; al-Budayri, *Hawadith*, 140; Burayk, *Tarikh*, 74–75.

33. Allom, *Constantinople*, 1:24.

34. Hayati Develi, ed., *XVIII. Yüzyıl İstanbul Hayatına Dair Risale-i Garibe* (Istanbul: Kitabevi, 2001), 33.

35. al-Jabarti, 'Aja'ib, 3:233.
36. Ahmad al-Damurdashi, *al-Damurdashi's Chronicle of Egypt, 1688-1755: Al-Durra al-musana fi akhbar al-Kinana*, trans. Daniel Crecilius and Muhammad 'Abd al-Wahhab Bakr (Leiden: Brill, 1991), 164-65.
37. Cabi, *Tarih*, 106-7.
38. See for example Dihkanizade Ubeydullah Kuşmani and Ebubekir Efendi, *Asiler ve Gaziler: Kabakçı Mustafa Risalesi*, ed. Aysel Danacı Yıldız (Istanbul: Kitap Yayınevi, 2007), 110; Ibrahim al-'Awra, *Tarikh Wilayat Sulayman Basha al-'Adil*, ed. Antun Bishara Qiqanu (Beirut: Dar Lahad Khatir, 1989), 318-19.
39. Cabi, *Tarih*, 579.
40. For a description of pipes in early nineteenth-century Anatolia, see Allom, *Constantinople*, 1:42.
41. For an overview of Ottoman pipes and hookahs, see Boué, *Turquie*, 2:426-28; d'Ohsson, *Tableau*, 4:146-47; C.S. Sannini, *Travels in Upper and Lower Egypt* (London: J. Debrett, 1800), 158.
42. See for example al-Jabarti, 'Aja'ib, 2:283.
43. Craven, *Journey*, 206. For a description of long-stemmed pipes in Greece, see also Dodwell, *Tour*, 1:152-53.
44. Van Egmont, *Travels*, 1:161.
45. d'Ohsson, *Tableau*, 4:148; Russell, *Aleppo*, 1:126. By the early nineteenth century, some of it was being supplied by the Ottoman market. One soldier could affirm that Yanya, on Crete, "produced good snuff"; Kabudlu, *Tevarih*, 292; Kabudlı, "Adventures," 1:217. On the sale of snuff in Istanbul, see Cevdet Türkay, "XVIII. Yüzyıl Sonlarında İstanbul'da Enfiye Dükkanları," in *Ehlikeyfin Kitabı*, ed. Fatih Tığlı (Istanbul: Kitabevi, 2004), 353-60.
46. See for example Dodwell, *Tour*, 1:153; d'Ohsson, *Tableau*, 4:147.
47. al-Damurdashi, *Chronicle*, 357.
48. al-Jabarti, 'Aja'ib, 4:43-44.
49. Ibn Abi'l-Diyaf, *Ithaf*, 2:157.
50. Hakim, *Hakim Tarihi*, 822.
51. For an overview of these themes, see Marinos Sariyannis, "Sociability, Public Life, and Decorum," in *A Companion to Early Modern Istanbul*, ed. Shirine Hamadeh and Çiğdem Kafescioğlu (Leiden: Brill, 2022), 476-79.
52. Mehmed Haşim, *İma*, 127. (". . . bir sülüsü heman kahvehanelerde laf ve güzaf ederler.")
53. Cengiz Kırlı, "İstanbul: Bir Büyük Kahvehane," *İstanbul Dergisi* 47 (2003): 75-76. One British traveler put the total number for the capital at about 2,500; Charles White, *Three Years in Constantinople, or Domestic Manners of the Turks in 1844* (London: Henry Colburn, 1845), 1:282.
54. Doris Behrens-Abouseif, *Azbakiyya and Its Environs from Azbak to Isma'il, 1476-1879* (Cairo: Institut Français d'Archéologie Orientale, 1985), 44.
55. Ibn Kannan, *Yawmiyat*, 19.
56. Cabi, *Tarih*, 223-24.
57. Cabi, *Tarih*, 591.
58. Cemal Kafadar, "How Dark Is the History of the Night, How Black the Story of

Coffee, How Bitter the Tale of Love: The Changing Measure of Leisure and Pleasure in Early Modern Istanbul," in *Medieval and Early Modern Performance in the Eastern Mediterranean*, ed. Arzu Öztürkmen and Evelyn Birge Vitz (Turnhout: Brepols, 2014), 243-69.

59. Boué, *Turquie*, 2:401; Russell, *Aleppo*, 1:143-44.

60. al-Muradi, *Silk*, 4:98.

61. See in particular Avner Wishnitzer, *As Night Falls: Eighteenth-Century Ottoman Cities after Dark* (Cambridge: Cambridge University Press, 2021).

62. `Abd al-Rahman al-Kurdi, a Sufi from Damascus (d. 1781), won acclaim for converting a coffeehouse that he had purchased into a Sufi lodge. His biographer railed against the clientele as "the scum and riffraff of the people and those who practice deviance and vice and gambling" (*al-asafil wa al-ru`a` min al-nas wa ahl al-dilal wa al-fujur wa al-qumar*). Thanks to the Sufi's intervention, "God had expelled the building from the shadows into the light"; al-Muradi, *Silk*, 2:292-93. See the controversy (1626) kicked up by the enemies of one scholar in Mecca, accused of setting up a coffeehouse by the Ka`ba itself; Muhammad Amin al-Muhibbi, *Khulasat al-athar fi a`yan al-qarn al-hadi `ashar* (Beirut: Dar Sadr, n.d), 4:186.

63. Marcus, *The Middle East*, 224.

64. Herbert Bodman, *Political Factions in Aleppo, 1760-1826* (Chapel Hill: University of North Carolina Press, 1963), 64, f.65.

65. al-Jabarti, *`Aja'ib*, 3:104. For a Damascene Sufi who committed the same social infraction of mingling in coffeehouses, see al-Budayri, *Hawadith*, 192-93.

66. Russell, *Aleppo*, 1:146. For the same verdict, see d'Ohsson, *Tableau*, 4:144.

67. In his words, it contained "bir mecma`ü'l-irfan ve mesken-i dervişan-ı zarifandır"; Evliya, *Seyahatnamesi*, 9:190. For his observations on the Aegean town of Söke, where members of the elite had their own coffeehouses, see ibid., 9:83.

68. Thevenot, *Travels*, 1:33-34. On the social openness of early Ottoman coffeehouses, see Ayşe Saraçgil, "L'Introduction du café à Istanbul (XVIe-XVIIe siècles)," in *Cafés d'Orient revisités*, ed. Hélène Desmet-Grégoire and François Georgeon (Paris: CNRS Editions, 1997), 25-38.

69. Salah Birsel, *Kahveler Kitabı* (Ankara: Türkiye İş Bankası Kültür Yayınları, 1983), 51-52.

70. For an overview of several large coffeehouses in Aleppo, see Jean-Claude David, "Le Café â Alep au temps des Ottomans: entre le souk et le quartier," in *Cafés d'Orient revisités*, ed. Hélène Desmet-Grégoire and François Georgeon (Paris: CNRS, 1997), 113-26.

71. For depictions of coffeehouse interiors, see for example Febvre, *Théatre*, 286; Volney, *Travels*, 2:497.

72. Hill, *Account*, 123.

73. Browne, *Travels*, 92. On the prevalence of small, simple coffeehouses in Egypt, see Tuchscherer, "Les Cafés," 108-9.

74. On the neighborhood coffeehouse as a kind of home away from home for men, see Alan Mikhail, "The Heart's Desire: Gender, Urban Space, and the Ottoman Coffee House," in *Ottoman Tulips, Ottoman Coffee: Leisure and Lifestyle in the Eighteenth Century*, ed. Dana Sajdi (London: Tauris Academic Studies, 2007), 133-70. On the political implications of the new coffeehouse culture, in which patrons might debate the news of the day and the actions of officials, see Cengiz Kırlı, "Coffeehouses: Leisure and Sociability in

Ottoman Istanbul," in *Leisure Cultures in Urban Europe, c. 1700-1870*, ed. Peter Borsay and Jan Hein Furnée (Manchester: Manchester University Press, 2016), 161-82.

75. Murat Bardakçı, *Osmanlı'da Seks: Sarayda Gece Dersleri* (Istanbul: Gür Yayınları, 1992), 94.

76. See for example d'Ohsson, *Tableau*, 4:144; Febvre, *Théatre*, 286; Russell, *Aleppo*, 1:146-50; Griffiths, *Travels*, 336-37; Boué, *Turquie*, 2:406. On Ottoman coffeehouses as theatrical spaces, see Uğur Kömeçoğlu, "Homo Ludens ve Homo Sapiens Arasında Kamusallık ve Toplumsallık," in *Osmanlı Kahvehaneleri: Mekân, Sosyalleşme, İktidar*, ed. Ahmet Yaşar (Istanbul: Kitap Yayınevi, 2009), 64-69.

77. Mehmed Haşim, *İma*, 94.

78. For an overview of Ottoman music culture, see Cem Behar, "The Ottoman Musical Tradition," in *The Cambridge History of Turkey*, Vol. 3, *The Later Ottoman Empire, 1603-1839*, ed. Suraiya Faroqhi (New York: Cambridge University Press, 2006), 393-407; Cem Behar, *Zaman, Mekan, Müzik: Klasik Türk Musıkisinde Eğitim (Meşk), İcra ve Aktarım* (Istanbul: AFA Yayıncılık, 1992); Merih Erol, *Greek Orthodox Music in Ottoman Istanbul: Nation and Community in the Era of Reform* (Indianapolis: Indiana University Press, 2015); Walter Feldman, "The Emergence of Ottoman Music and Local Modernity," *Yıllık: Annual of Istanbul Studies* 1 (2019): 173-79; Ahmad Taymur, *al-Musiqa wa al-ghina' 'inda al-'arab* (Cairo: Lajnat Nashr al-Mu'allafat al-Taymuriyya, 1963); Habib Touma, *The Music of the Arabs*, trans. Laurie Schwartz (Portland, OR: Amadeus Press, 1996).

79. Even during the reign of Selim III (r. 1789-1807), a great music lover, only a dozen or so musicians were able to earn a stipend from the palace; İsmail Hakkı Uzunçarşılı, "Osmanlılar Zamanında Saraylarda Musiki Hayatı," *Belleten* 41 (1977): 103-7. On the recruitment and organization of musicians at the palace, see Walter Feldman, *Music of the Ottoman Court: Makam, Composition and the Early Modern Ottoman Instrumental Repertoire* (Berlin: VWB, 1996), 72-80.

80. Cemal Kafadar, "The City Opens Your Eyes Because It Wants to Be Seen," in *A Companion to Early Modern Istanbul*, ed. Shirine Hamadeh and Çiğdem Kafescioğlu (Leiden: Brill, 2022), 44-45. On the spread of musical composition in Istanbul far beyond the palace by 1700, see Owen Wright, *Words without Songs: A Musicological Study of an Early Ottoman Anthology and Its Precursors* (London: School of Oriental and African Studies, 1992), 204-5.

81. al-Jabarti, *'Aja'ib*, 2:141-42. See too descriptions of early nineteenth-century celebrations of the prophet's birthday (*mawlid*); Lane, *Manners*, 442-56. For scenes of coffeehouses and entertainments at seventeenth-century Egyptian festivals, see Evliya, *Seyahatnamesi*, 10:323-27, 340.

82. Pococke, *Description*, 2:125. Fleeing disturbances in Istanbul (1808), a former reformist official, now disguised as a dervish, arrived in Gemlik, a tiny port on the Sea of Marmara. He was looking for a room and went straight to the coffeehouse, which was full of nearby villagers who had "come to be entertained." See Cabi, *Tarih*, 350.

83. Pococke, *Description*, 2:65. For coffeehouses serving as inns on Mt. Lebanon, see Mishaqa, *Murder*, 13. On rural coffeehouses in the early nineteenth-century Balkans, which were located mostly along major commercial routes, see Boué, *Turquie*, 2:296. On the growth of coffeehouse culture in Ottoman Bulgaria from the turn of the nineteenth century onward, see Mary C. Neuburger, *Balkan Smoke: Tobacco and the Making of Modern Bulgaria* (Ithaca: Cornell University Press, 2013), 11-14.

84. Ioannes Makriyannis, *Makriyannis: The Memoirs of General Makriyannis, 1797–1864*, trans. H.A. Lidderdale (New York: Oxford University Press, 1966), 9.

85. Boué, *Turquie*, 2:401–2.

86. Kemal Beydilli, ed., *Osmanlı Döneminde İmamlar ve bir İmam'ın Günlüğü* (Istanbul: Tarih ve Tabiat Vakfı, 2001), 144–45.

87. Chandler, *Travels*, 1:231.

88. de la Mottraye, *Travels*, 193. See too the account of de Thévenot from the mid-seventeenth century: "Wine seems to be prohibited by the Alcoran, yet the good-fellows say that it is not more than an advice or council [sic] and not a precept: however, they drink it not publicly, unless it must be the Janizaries and other desperadoes that stand in awe of no man"; Thévenot, *Travels*, 1:33.

89. Hill, *Account*, 90–91.

90. Rudi Matthee, "Alcohol in the Islamic Middle East," *Past and Present* 222, Suppl. 9 (2014): 103.

91. Hill, *Account*, 90–91. The first successful breweries, opened in Izmir by German immigrants, began operations in the 1830s; Matthee, "Alcohol," 115.

92. Chishull, *Travels*, 10. For another scene of heavy drinking, see van Egmont, *Travels*, 2:36.

93. Mishaqa, *Murder*, 174.

94. Dodwell, *Tour*, 1:212.

95. Thevenot, *Travels*, 1:33.

96. An early practice was to flavor rakı with mastic (hence the name *mastika*) from the island of Chios; see François Georgeon, *Au Pays du rakı: Le vin et l'alcool de l'empire Ottoman à la Turquie d'Erdoğan* (Paris: CNRS, 2021), 58. On the variety of alcoholic beverages made in Egypt, see Browne, *Travels*, 27, 75. On drinking culture in Damascus, see Grehan, *Everyday*, 133–35.

97. François Georgeon, "Ottomans and Drinkers: The Consumption of Alcohol in Istanbul in the Nineteenth Century," in *Outside In: On the Margins of the Modern Middle East*, ed. Eugene Rogan (London: IB Tauris, 2002), 7–30.

98. Wishnitzer, *As Night Falls*, 101. On alcohol sold at caravansaries, see Chishull, *Travels*, 57.

99. Hobhouse, *Journey*, 2:884–85.

100. On the taverns of early modern Istanbul, see Georgeon, *Pays*, 65–68; on nineteenth-century Bulgarian taverns, Neuberger, *Smoke*, 11–12, 18–19, 22–23.

101. See for example the "Strange Essay," which imagines that pimps were the partners of many tavern keepers; Develi, ed., *Risale*, 23.

102. Van Egmont, *Travels*, 1:201. On the island of Tenedos (modern Bozcaada), the tavern was a "little hole in a stinking house," about "eight yards square," that doubled (1674) as a church. The priests managed the premises; Covel, "Diary," 156.

103. Fariba Zarinebaf, *Crime and Punishment in Istanbul, 1700–1800* (Berkeley: University of California Press, 2010), 101.

104. Mehmed Haşim, *İma*, 54–55.

105. Mehmed Haşim, *İma*, 193, 203.

106. Wishnitzer, *As Night Falls*, 81–86.

Notes to Chapter 2

107. Kırlı, "Struggle," 152.
108. Zarinebaf, *Crime*, 104.
109. Ahmed Cavid, *Hadika-i Vekayi*`, ed. Adnan Baycar (Ankara: Türk Tarih Kurumu Basımevi, 1998), 215–16.
110. Covel, *Diary*, 244–45, 269.
111. See for example the short-lived proscription of alcohol in Istanbul (1689) and the expulsion of tavern owners from Edirne (1703); Özcan, ed., *Anonim*, 10–11, 218. See too the bey of the Qasimi faction who took the deliberate step of shutting down a boza house at Girga, a small town in Upper Egypt; al-Jabarti, `Aja'ib, 1:339.
112. De Tott, *Memoirs*, 1:233. On the official decree (1687) that lifted the ban on alcohol, see Raşid, *Tarih*, 2:52–53. On the lucrative alcohol taxes collected in Istanbul, see Zarinebaf, *Crime*, 100; for Cairo, see Raymond, *Artisans*, 2:469.
113. al-Damurdashi, *Chronicle*, 117–24. For the proposal of a similar campaign (1731) to shut brothels and boza shops, see al-Damurdashi, *Chronicle*, 298. On the manufacture of boza in Egypt, see Lane, *Manners*, 94.
114. Ahmed Cavid, *Hadika*, 194–95, 203; Cabi, *Tarih*, 22; Karal, ed., *Selim III*, 99–100. European embassies were exempted from the restrictions; Refik, *Onüçüncü*, 7–9. See also Ahmet Yaşar, "'Külliyen Ref'ten 'İbreten li'l-Ğayr'e: Erken Modern Osmanlı'da Kahvehane Yasaklamaları," in *Osmanlı Kahvehaneleri: Mekân, Sosyalleşme, İktidar*, ed. Ahmet Yaşar (Istanbul: Kitap Yayınevi, 2009), 41.
115. Işıl Çokuğraş, *Bekar Odaları ve Meyhaneler: Osmanlı İstanbulu'nda Marjinalite ve Mekan (1789–1839)* (Istanbul: İstanbul Araştırmaları Enstitüsü, 2016), 155–61; Cengiz Kırlı, "The Struggle over Space: Coffeehouses of Ottoman Istanbul, 1780–1845" (unpublished PhD diss., SUNY-Binghamton, 2000), 58–62; Wishnitzer, *As Night Falls* 219–25.
116. Çokuğraş, *Bekar Odaları*, 157; Wishnitzer, *As Night Falls*, 103–4, 234–37.
117. al-Halabi, *Hawadith*, 317. See also Muhammad Raghib al-Tabbakh, *I`lam al-nubala' bi-tarikh Halab al-shahba* (Aleppo: Dar al-Qalam al-`Arabi), 3:302.
118. For the campaign of 1804, see al-Dimashqi, *Tarikh*, 29. For that of 1807, see al-Dimashqi, *Tarikh*, 36–37; Haydar Ahmad Shihab, *Tarikh Ahmad Basha al-Jazzar*, ed. Antuniyus Shibli and Ighnatiyus `Abdu Khalifa (Beirut: Maktabat Antoine, 1955), 185; Hasan Agha, *Tarikh*, 140, 143.
119. See for example d'Ohsson, *Tableau*, 4:137–38.
120. On this geographical distribution of taverns, see Çokuğraş, *Bekar Odaları*, 162–71. Around the turn of the nineteenth century, Istanbul held about six hundred taverns; Kırlı, "Struggle," 112. See also Wishnitzer, *As Night Falls*, 85–86.
121. Behrens-Abouseif, *Azbakiyya*, 38–40.
122. Daniel Goffman, "Izmir: From Village to Colonial Port City," in *The Ottoman City between East and West: Aleppo, Izmir, and Istanbul*, ed. Edhem Eldem et al. (Cambridge: Cambridge University Press, 1999), 94.
123. See for example Guillaume-Joseph Grelot, *A Late Voyage to Constantinople* (London: John Playford, 1683), 8.
124. Marie-Carmen Smyrnelis, "Coexistence et reseaux de sociabilité (fin du XVIIIe–milieu du XIXe siècle)," in *Une Ville Ottomane plurielle: Smyrne aux XVIIIe et XIXe siècles* (Istanbul: Isis, 2006), 47.

125. Paulina Lewicka, "Restaurants, Inns, and Taverns That Never Were: Some Reflections on Public Consumption in Medieval Cairo," *Journal of the Economic and Social History of the Orient* 48 (2005): 40–91.

126. Ahmad Ghassan Sabbanu, ed., *Mudhakkirat tarikhiyya 'an hamlat Ibrahim Basha 'ala Suriya* (Damascus: Dar Qutayba, 1980), 66.

127. For a similar verdict, see Georgeon, *Pays*, 70–83.

128. Jelena Mrgić, "Wine or 'Raki': The Interplay of Climate and Society in Early Modern Ottoman Bosnia," *Environment and History* 17 (2011): 633–35.

129. Pococke, *Description*, 3:70–71. On drinking among Greek Muslims (1805), see William Leake, *Travels in Northern Greece* (London: J. Rodwell, 1835), 1:63.

130. In Aleppo, townsmen showed "less abhorrence than formerly" for the drinking of alcohol; Russell, *Aleppo*, 1:183.

131. Claudius James Rich, *Narrative of a Residence in Koordistan* (London: James Duncan, 1836), 2:59.

132. Mishaqa, *Murder*, 26.

133. Kuşmani, *Asiler*, 106.

134. al-Jabarti, *'Aja'ib*, 7:92.

135. al-Tabbakh, *I'lam*, 3:308.

136. al-'Awra, *Tarikh*, 141–42.

137. On this military subculture of drinking, see d'Ohsson, *Tableau*, 4:137–38.

138. 'Abd al-Rahman al-Suwaydi, *Tarikh Hawadith Baghdad wa al-Basra*, ed. 'Imad 'Abd al-Salam Ru'uf (Baghdad: Wizarat al-Thaqafa wa al-Funun, 1978), 114–15. On drinking among the Janissaries of Aleppo, see Russell, *Aleppo*, 1:183.

139. Browne, *Travels*, 99. For portraits of hard-drinking officers in Egypt, see al-Damurdashi, *Chronicle*, 236, 269; al-Jabarti, *'Aja'ib*, 1:346. For an example from Baghdad, see al-Suwaydi, *Tarikh*, 111. For rumors about İbrahim Paşa, commander of Egyptian forces in Syria (1832–40), who allegedly became intoxicated at a drinking party in Jaffa, see Mishaqa, *Murder*, 201.

140. Cabi, *Tarih*, 198.

141. Van Egmont, *Travels*, 1:177.

142. On the complicated attitudes of medieval Muslim jurists toward hashish, see Franz Rosenthal, *The Herb: Hashish versus Medieval Muslim Society* (Leiden: Brill, 1971).

143. For a description, see d'Ohsson, *Tableau*, 4:140; von Hammer, *Histoire*, 16:36.

144. On the public smoking of tobacco-opium mixtures in Aleppo, see Marcus, *The Middle East*, 233.

145. Lane, *Manners*, 334. See also Sannini, *Travels*, 551–52.

146. Hobhouse, *Journey*, 2:945; Victor Fontanier, *Voyages en Orient* (Paris: Librarie Universelle, 1829), 1:282–83; de Tott, *Memoirs*, 1:160–61; von Hammer, *Histoire*, 16:36.

147. Charles Fellows, *A Journal Written during an Excursion in Asia Minor* (London: John Murray, 1839), 298.

148. Covel, *Diary*, 140.

149. Roger Owen, *The Middle East and the World Economy, 1800–1914* (London: Methuen, 1981), 28–30, 113; Şevket Pamuk, *The Ottoman Empire and European Capitalism, 1820–1913* (Cambridge: Cambridge University Press, 1987), 53, 85.

150. Özcan, ed., *Anonim*, 270.

151. Vasıf, *Tarih*, 1:195–96; Von Hammer, *Histoire*, 16:36.

152. Hill, *Account*, 123–24. Writing in the late eighteenth century, one French traveler thought that members of the Ottoman elite were more immoderate in their use of opium than their counterparts in the Iranian lands; Rudi Matthee, *The Pursuit of Pleasure: Drugs and Stimulants in Iranian History, 1500-1900* (Princeton: Princeton University Press, 2005), 208.

153. Şanizade, *Tarih*, 1:91.

154. Hakim, *Hakim Tarihi*, 964–65.

155. De Tott, *Memoirs*, 1:43.

156. Ahmed Asım, *Asım Tarihi* (Istanbul: Ceride-yi Havadis Matbaası, n.d.), 1:247.

157. Cevdet, *Tarih*, 10:110; Şanizade, *Tarih*, 2:170.

158. al-Muradi, *Silk*, 4:209–17. For another Syrian jurist who began to use opium after starting a career in Istanbul, see al-Muradi, *Silk*, 1:37–39.

159. Russell, *Aleppo*, 1:126–27. For a concurring opinion that opium use was not widespread, see Boué, *Turquie*, 2:144; Lane, *Manners*, 335.

160. al-Muradi, *Silk*, 1:42. For other references to opium use or addiction in Arab towns, see al-Muradi, *Silk*, 4:185; al-Muhibbi, *Khulasat*, 1:296–97; 3:17–19, 332–34; 4:2–9, 212–14, 290–94.

161. Van Egmont, *Travels*, 1:157.

162. Van Egmont, *Travels*, 2:82–83. Making his way through Ottoman Greece (1819), the British traveler Henry Dodwell rendered a somewhat envious verdict: "The life a Turkish gentleman consists almost entirely of smoking tobacco, drinking coffee, and counting his beads. The former is indispensably necessary for his happiness"; Dodwell, *Tour*, 1:152.

163. See for example Antonia Finnane, *Speaking of Yangzhou: A Chinese City, 1550-1850* (Cambridge, MA: Harvard University Asia Center, 2004), chaps. 8, 11; Howard Hibbett, *The Floating World in Japanese Fiction* (London: Oxford University Press, 1959); Matsunosuke Nishiyama, *Edo Culture: Daily Life and Diversions in Urban Japan, 1600-1868* (Honolulu: University of Hawaii Press, 1997); Conrad Totman, *Early Modern Japan* (Berkeley: University of California Press, 1993), chap. 10; Teruoka Yasutaka, "Pleasure Quarters and Tokugawa Culture," in *Eighteenth-Century Japan: Culture and Society*, ed. C. Andrew Girstle (Sydney: Allen&Unwin, 1989), 3–32.

164. From an extensive literature, see for example Thomas Brennan, *Public Drinking and Popular Culture in Eighteenth-Century Paris* (Princeton: Princeton University Press, 1988); Brian Cowan, *The Social Life of Coffee: The Emergence of the British Coffeehouse* (New Haven: Yale University Press, 2008); Beat A. Kümin, *Drinking Matters: Public Houses and Social Exchange in Early Modern Central Europe* (Basingstoke: Palgrave Macmillan, 2007); E. Wesley Reynolds, *Coffeehouse Culture in the Atlantic World, 1650-1789* (New York: Bloomsbury Academic, 2022); Ellen Rosand, *Opera in Seventeenth-Century Venice: The Creation of a Genre* (Berkeley: University of California Press, 2007); Downing A. Thomas, *Aesthetics of Opera in the Ancien Régime, 1647-1785* (Cambridge: Cambridge University Press, 2002).

Chapter 3

1. See Muhammad Khalil al-Muradi, ʿArf al-basham fī man waliya fatwa Dimashq al-Sham, ed. Muhammad Mutiʿ al-Hafiz and Riyad ʿAbd al-Hamid Murad (Damascus: Dar Ibn Kathir, 1988), 7–25.

2. On the medieval background to the practice of *adab*, see Samer M. Ali, *Arabic Literary Salons in the Islamic Middle Ages: Poetry, Public Performance, and the Presentation of the Past* (Notre Dame: University of Notre Dame Press, 2010).

3. See in particular Helen Pfeifer, *Empire of Salons: Conquest and Community in the Early Modern Ottoman Lands* (Princeton: Princeton University Press, 2022).

4. Volney, *Travels*, 2:460–61.

5. de la Mottraye, *Travels*, 233. In the coffeehouses of late seventeenth-century Istanbul, patrons sat "sometimes two or three hours in company without any discourse or saying anything one to another, but only some few broken half-words uttered between sip and sip"; Grelot, *Voyage*, 71–72.

6. Browne, *Travels*, 526. For an identical impression of conversation, see Boué, *Turquie*, 2:413–14; d'Ohsson, *Tableau*, 4:255.

7. See for example Chisull, *Travels*, 6.

8. D'Ohsson, *Tableau*, 4:242. Muslim scholars had the same aversion to interrupting the speech of others; see for example al-Khadimi, *Bariqa*, 3:369–71; ʿAbd al-Ghani al-Nabulsi, *al-Hadiqa al-nadiyya: sharh al-Tariqa al-Muhammadiyya* (Lyallpur: al-Maktaba al-nuriyya al-ridwiyya, 1977), 2:350–52.

9. Russell, *Aleppo*, 1:170.

10. Russell, *Aleppo*, 1:223.

11. Ulular yanında etme söylemek/ yeğdir anda söylemekden dinlemek/ ger soralar anda sana bir kelam/ anı söyle gayri deme ve's-selam; Zarifi, *Pendname*, 30. See too the expectations for students, who were to show an unwavering deference to their teachers. They should keep their words to a minimum, and in recognition of their elders' social and intellectual seniority, never open learned discussions, which might seem to place them on an equal footing; al-Nabulsi, *al-Hadiqa*, 2:303.

12. Oğulukyan, *Ruzname*, 15.

13. See for example al-Budayri, *Hawadith*, 152; Ibn Kannan, *Yawmiyat*, 485. For a more general sketch of these social expectations, see Leon Carl Brown, "The Religious Establishment in Husainid Tunisia," in *Scholars, Saints, and Sufis: Muslim Religious Institutions in the Middle East since 1500*, ed. Nikki Keddie (Berkeley: University of California Press, 1972), chap. 2.

14. al-Nabulsi, *al-Hadiqa*, 2:239–40. For ulama remembered for their "purity of tongue," see for example al-Muradi, *Silk*, 1:187; 2:327; 3:37, 166–67; 4:218.

15. The ulama considered speech mainly from a moral perspective and cautioned against such "calamities of the tongue" as lies, slanders, insults, invectives, obscenities, and quarrels; see the overview in al-Khadimi, *Bariqa*, 3:195–97, 4:1–12; al-Nabulsi, *al-Hadiqa*, 2:191–403.

16. Vehbi, *Lütfiyye*, 46.

17. al-Jabarti, ʿAjaʾib, 2:259. See also al-Muradi, ʿArf, 21; al-Nabulsi, *al-Hadiqa*, 2:292, 350–51.

18. Ibn Abi'l-Diyaf, *Ithaf*, 7:70.

19. The anonymous essay from eighteenth-century Istanbul rants against those who would join a gathering and sit "like iron shit" (*demir boki gibi*), neither uttering a word nor knowing how to enliven the company; Develi, ed., *Risale*, 37.

20. Pfeifer, *Empire of Salons*, chap. 3. Although Pfeifer deals mainly with the sixteenth century, the hierarchy and exclusivity embedded in salon culture were very much in evidence in the eighteenth and early nineteenth centuries as well. See for example the biography of Ahmad al-Budayr (Ibn Budayr), a barber from eighteenth-century Damascus. An author of a homespun chronicle, he nonetheless had no hope of entering the salons of the ulama and literati by virtue of literacy alone; see Dana Sajdi, *The Barber of Damascus: Nouveau Literacy in the Eighteenth-Century Levant* (Stanford: Stanford University Press, 2013), chap. 2.

21. On this rather unusual salon, see Ahmed Lütfi, *Tarih-i Lütfi* (Istanbul: Matbaa-yi Amire, 1873), 1:168–69; İsmail Hakkı Uzunçarşılı, "Nizam-i Cedid Ricalinden Valide Sultan Kethüdası Meşhur Yusuf Ağa ve Kethüdazade Arif Efendi," *Belleten* 20 (1956): 485–525.

22. al-Muradi, *Silk*, 2:231. See too the praise for a learned gathering in Damascus (1736) that was "free of singing, music, visiting, and playing *manqala* and chess, as is the custom among the people"; Ibn Kannan, *Yawmiyat*, 474–75. On the verbal jousting at sixteenth-century salons, see Pfeifer, *Empire*, chap. 4.

23. al-Jabarti, *'Aja'ib*, 4:258–59. For other scholars who had musical gifts, see for example Müstakimzade Süleyman Sadeddin Efendi, *Devhat ül-Meşayih ma Zeyl* (Istanbul: Çağrı Yayınları, 1978), 96–97; Aziz-zade Hüseyin Ramiz, *Adad-ı Zurafa: İnceleme, Tıpkıbasım, İndeks*, ed. Sadık Erdem (Ankara: Türk Tarih Kurumu, 2019), 30–31, 92–93, 195, 196.

24. al-Jabarti, *'Aja'ib*, 7:334–35, 337. From the same generation in Cairo was Musa al-Sirsi (d. 1804), a scholar who cut a figure as a charming bon vivant. He held a good deal of property and had many wives and concubines. He was social, quick-witted in conversation, and utterly disarming with his affectionate and unpretentious manner; al-Jabarti, *'Aja'ib*, 6:202.

25. On the variety of salons in Cairo, see Nelly Hanna, *In Praise of Books: A Cultural History of Cairo's Middle Class, Sixteenth to Eighteenth Century* (Syracuse: Syracuse University Press, 2003), 72–76.

26. al-Jabarti, *'Aja'ib*, 3:84.

27. Ramiz, *Zurafa*, 29.

28. See for example al-Muradi, *Silk*, 1:44–45, 116.

29. al-Muradi, *Silk*, 2:83. For another scholar gifted with eloquence and fluency, see the biography of Manevi Efendi, personal spiritual advisor of sultan Ahmed II (r. 1691–95); Enfi, *Tezkiret*, 176–77. On the celebration of scholars as models of verbal skill and expertise, see al-Nabulsi, *al-Hadiqa*, 2:292.

30. al-'Awra, *Tarikh*, 194–95.

31. Vehbi, *Lütfiyye*, 83.

32. al-Muradi, *Silk*, 1:162–63. See also al-Muradi, *Silk*, 1:11, 222; 3:9, 64–65, 89, 246, 257, 258; 4:40; Ibn Kannan, *Yawmiyat*, 181, 255, 314, 348–49.

33. See for example Saba al-Katib, a priest who had absolute command of literary Arabic, which he spoke with utter precision. He expected others to match his flawless model and could hardly bare an infelicity in conversation. "He loved only the compan-

ionship of the refined and elegant, those who had taste and understanding"; al-ʿAwra, *Tarikh*, 367.

34. Enfi, *Tezkiret*, 114–16.

35. al-Jabarti, *ʾAjaʾib*, 7:323.

36. al-Muradi, *Silk*, 2:183–89. See too the case of Saʿdi al-ʿUmari (d. 1734), a poet and scholar from Damascus (and no direct relation to Shakir al-ʿUmari). He traveled to Istanbul and used his poetry to launch his career. After celebratory verses for the new library at the imperial palace came to the attention of Ahmed III (r. 1703-30), he received a teaching position in Damascus; al-Muradi, *Silk*, 2:151–56.

37. al-Muradi, *Silk*, 2:293–94. For a snapshot of poetry at a learned Damascene salon, see Ibn Kannan, *Yawmiyat*, 295–96.

38. See for example Müstakimzade, *Meşayih*, 93–94, 101, 116–17, 129–31; Ramiz, *Zurafa*, 9, 30, 38, 46–47, 47–48, 55–57, 67–70, 81, 81–82, 83–84, 84–85, 85–87, 93–95, 95–96, 101–2, 146–50, 154–55, 159, 175, 176, 180–81, 207–8, 208–10, 240, 262–63.

39. al-Muradi, *Silk*, 2:216–17.

40. See for example the cutting assessment of one early seventeenth-century poet: "If he talked, one would suppose that he knew nothing"; al-Muhibbi, *Khulasat*, 2:81–84.

41. al-Muradi, *Silk*, 3:108–16. See also the scholar and poet, Yusuf al-Qabaqibi (d. 1706), who toiled in poverty as a scribe in the mills outside Damascene until a chance inheritance lifted him into affluence; al-Muradi, *Silk*, 4:240–41.

42. Hatice Aynur, "Ottoman Literature," in *The Cambridge History of Turkey*, Vol. 3, *The Later Ottoman Empire, 1603-1839*, ed. Suraiya Faroqhi (Cambridge: Cambridge University Press, 2006), 515; al-Muradi, *Silk*, 2:117–18. Zübeyde (Zubayda) was her first name.

43. Only four female poets appear in the biographical collections of the seventeenth and eighteenth centuries. See Aynur, "Ottoman Literature," 514–17. For an overview of female poets in Ottoman poetry collections, see Didem Havlioğlu, "On the Margins and Between the Lines: Ottoman Women Poets from the Fifteenth to the Twentieth Centuries," *Turkish Historical Review* 1 (2010): 25–54.

44. Elite women who gained an education might venture into scholarship as well. Faʾiza Molla Kadın (d. 1763/74) was the daughter of a chief judge of Istanbul. More than a poet, she excelled at the "Arabic sciences" (*ulum-ı arabiyye*), in which she was equal, her biographer agreed, to the best male scholars of her day; Ramiz, *Zurafa*, 237. For a Tunisian scholar who saw to the full education of all his daughters in such standard fields as Qurʾanic study, Islamic jurisprudence, and Sufism, see Ibn Abiʾl-Diyaf, *Ithaf*, 7:27.

45. Walter Andrews and Mehmet Kalpaklı, "Toward a Meclis-Centered Reading of Ottoman Poetry," *Journal of Turkish Studies* 33 (2009): 309–18.

46. On the cultural life of the eighteenth-century court and its environs, see for example Volkan Karagözlü, "Damad İbrahim Paşaʾnın Şiir Meclisleri Bağlamında Kültür, Oyun, Gazel," *1. Uluslararası Nevşehir Tarih ve Kültür Sempozyumu Bildirileri*, ed. Adem Öger (Ankara: Nevşehir Üniversitesi Yayınları, 2012), 119–31; Sevda Önal Kılıç, "Edebiyat Patronajı Açısından Damad İbrahim Paşa Dönemine Dair Genel Bir Değerlendirme," *Atatürk Üniversitesi Türkiyat Araştırmaları Enstitüsü Dergisi* 61 (2018): 1–14; Zehra Öksüz, "XVIII. Asır İstanbulʾnun Kültür Merkezleri Olarak Edebiyat Mahfilleri: Kültürel Mirasın Aktarımında ʿEdebiyat Mahfilleriʾnin Rölü," *International Journal of Sport Culture and Science* 3 (2015): 141–58; Namık Sinan Turan, "Osmanlı 18. Yüzyılında Müziğin Kamusal

Görünümü," in *Şehvar Beşiroğlu'ya Bir Armağan*, ed. Namık Sinan Turan and Şeyma Ersoy Çak (Istanbul: Pan Yayıncılık, 2019), 317–39.

47. al-Jabarti, *'Aja'ib*, 2:113. See too the biography of Hamuda al-Sadidi (d. 1750), a scholar who migrated to Cairo from Mahalla al-Kubra, a small town in the Delta. He later became a boon companion to the powerful Emir Kethüda and composed flattering odes and couplets that no doubt reinforced their friendship; al-Jabarti, *'Aja'ib*, 2:115.

48. Percy Kemp, "Power and Knowledge in Jalili Mosul," *Middle Eastern Studies* 19 (1983): 203.

49. For an overview of Ottoman defamatory poetry, see Hikmet Feridun Güven, "Klasik Türk Edebiyatında hiciv ve mizah," in *Türk Edebiyatı Tarihi*, ed. Talat Sait Halman (Istanbul: TC Kültür ve Turizm Bakanlığı Yayınları), 2:576–85.

50. For examples of satirical poems meant to be read out at gatherings, see al-Jabarti, *'Aja'ib*, 2:250–51; 4:9–11.

51. al-Jabarti, *'Aja'ib*, 2:115. Ahmad al-Sukuni (d. 1690/91), a poet from Damascus, made a name for himself trading jabs with his nemesis Yusuf al-Rahawi; al-Muradi, *Silk*, 1:128. On the feuding within the al-Bahnasi family of Damascus, which spilled into public view through defamatory poetry, see al-Muradi, *Silk*, 4:3–5. For examples of satirical poems meant to be read out loud at gatherings, see al-Jabarti, *'Aja'ib*, 2:250–51; 4:9–11. For other specialists in defamatory poetry, see also Ramiz, *Zurafa*, 77–79, 171–72.

52. al-Muradi, *Silk*, 2:47–49. Perfectly mainstream poets could dabble in this genre. See the defamatory poetry directed against "the people of Damascus" by 'Abd al-Ghani al-Nabulsi (d. 1731), the great scholar and Sufi, during a midlife period of depression and withdrawal; al-Muradi, *Silk*, 3:31–38.

53. al-Muradi, *Silk*, 2:285–91. For defamatory poetry aimed at other breaches of honor, see al-Muradi, *Silk*, 2:253; 3:275–79.

54. For an overview of Ottoman love poetry, see for example Walter G. Andrews and Mehmet Kalpaklı, *The Age of Beloveds: Love and the Beloved in Early-Modern Ottoman and European Culture and Society* (Durham: Duke University Press, 2005); Victoria Rowe Holbrook, *The Unreadable Shores of Love: Turkish Modernity and Mystic Romance* (Austin: University of Texas Press, 1994); Mehmet Karabella, "Lovers in the Age of the Beloveds: Classical Ottoman Divan Literature and the Dialectical Tradition (Adab al-Bahth)," in *The Beloved in Middle East Literatures: The Culture of Love and Languishing*, ed. Hanadi al-Samman, Alireza Korangy, and Michael Beard (London: IB Tauris, 2017), 285–300; Selim S. Kuru, "Generic Desires: Homoerotic Love in Ottoman Turkish Poetry," in *Mediterranean Crossings: Sexual Transgressions in Islam and Christianity (10th to 18th Centuries)* (Rome: Viella, 2020), 43–63; Khaled el-Rouayheb, "The Love of Boys in the Arabic Poetry of the Early Ottoman Period, 1500–1800," *Middle Eastern Literatures* 8 (2005): 3–22.

55. al-Jabarti, *'Aja'ib*, 3:8.

56. al-Muradi, *Silk*, 1:155–62. For examples of earlier storytellers from the sixteenth and seventeenth centuries who put their travels to good use in performance, see al-Muhibbi, *Khulasat*, 1:490–94; 2:172.

57. al-Muradi, *Silk*, 4:39–40. For others who partook of this style, see for example al-Jabarti, *'Aja'ib*, 6:140–41; al-Muradi, *Silk*, 1:173, 222; 2:231; 4:40.

58. al-Jabarti, *'Aja'ib*, 2:139.

59. See for example al-Muradi, *Silk*, 1:46–48; 2:5–6, 10–11, 141–49, 214–16; 3:144.

60. Ramiz, *Zurafa*, 117. See too the biography of Reşid Rüşdizade (d. 1739/40), a scholar and judge renowned for his puzzles and riddles; Ramiz, *Zurafa*, 128.

61. al-Muradi, *Silk*, 4:185–86.

62. van Egmont, *Travels*, 1:161.

63. Craven, *Journey*, 283.

64. de la Mottraye, *Travels*, 171; Le Bruyn, *Voyage*, 1:130; Hill, *Account*, 116; Thévenot, *Travels*, 1:30; van Egmont, *Travels*, 1:222. Muslims would knowingly extend this greeting only to other Muslims; Lane, *Manners*, 198.

65. d'Ohsson, *Tableau*, 4:239.

66. Russell, *Aleppo*, 2:62. See also Lane, *Manners*, 199.

67. Lane, *Manners*, 199.

68. Favorably impressed by Ottoman civility, one English traveler could fondly recall (1669): "When I came into any room where the Turks were sitting, they would salute me, and touching my hand, require me to sit down with them, then offer me to eat heartily"; Brown, *Brief Account*, 79.

69. Maillet, *Description*, 2:263–64.

70. See for example Hasırzade Mehmed Elif, *Tenşitu'l-muhibbin bi-menakıb-ı Hoca Hüsameddin* (Süleymaniye Library, Nafız Paşa 1217), 27.

71. de la Mottraye, *Travels*, 204. During Easter, Christians had their own expressive gestures that went beyond the normal greeting. In Istanbul, they would "salute one another with three kisses, one on the mouth, and on each cheek, at the same time, repeating the words . . . 'Christ is risen.'" See Dumont, *New Voyage*, 286.

72. On the taboo of talking about the women of the household, see for example Russell, *Aleppo*, 1:181. On the permissibility of oblique inquiries, see Lane, *Manners*, 201.

73. Mishaqa, *Murder*, 95.

74. d'Ohsson, *Tableau*, 4:240. See also Boué, *Turquie*, 2:433.

75. d'Ohsson, *Tableau*, 4:239–40. In one of the early memories of Ahmad Ibn Abi'l-Diyaf, a Tunisian scholar, his father took him to meet the mufti of Tunis, whose hand he kissed; Ibn Abi'l-Diyaf, *Ithaf*, 7:87.

76. Lane, *Manners*, 199–200.

77. al-Muradi, *Silk*, 1:227–29.

78. al-Jabarti, *'Aja'ib*, 3:307–8. For other references to the hand-kissing of religious leaders, see al-Muradi, *Silk*, 1:73; 2:208–9; 4:245–46.

79. al-Jabarti, *'Aja'ib*, 3:111.

80. Dodwell, *Tour*, 1:157–58. On the Romanian custom of kissing the hand of the priest, see Radu Florescu, "The Fanariot Regime in the Danubian Principalities," *Balkan Studies* 9 (1968): 312.

81. Burckhardt, *Travels*, 7.

82. al-Jabarti, *'Aja'ib*, 7:76–77. For another incident of refusing to kiss a hand, see al-Muradi, *Silk*, 4:245–46.

83. al-Jabarti, *'Aja'ib*, 2:36. See too the biography of Hasan al-Jabarti, father of the historian al-Jabarti, who insisted that people not kiss his hand and who had little patience with other forms of social deference as well; al-Jabarti, *'Aja'ib*, 3:82–83.

84. See for example Emir Bashir receiving guests who kissed his hand; Mishaqa, *Murder*, 42, 48. At the bey's court in Tunis, petitioners would automatically kiss the hand

of the bey; al-Hajj Hammuda ibn ʿAbd al-ʿAziz, *al-Kitab al-bashi*, ed. Muhammad al-Madur (Tunis: al-Dar al-Tunisiyya li'l-Nashr, 1970), 1:228. From 1740 onwards, European consuls had to conform to this custom as well; Ibn Abi'l-Diyaf, *Ithaf*, 2:124–25.

85. al-Jabarti, *ʿAja'ib*, 2:53.

86. al-Jabarti, *ʿAja'ib*, 5:149.

87. See for example Es'ad Efendi, *Teşrifat-ı Kadime* (Istanbul: Matbaa-yı Amire, 1870), 32–44, 93–97, 101, 114. On the enthronement ceremonies of the court, see Hakan T. Karateke, *Padişahım Çok Yaşa: Osmanlı Devletinin Son Yüz Yılında Merasimler* (Istanbul: Kitap Yayınevi, 2004), 33–40. For an image of the enthronement ceremony for Mahmud II (1808), in which leading officials kissed the hem of the new sultan's robe, see Kalost Arapyan, *Rusçuk Ayanı: Mustafa Paşa'nın Hayatı ve Kahramanlıkları*, trans. Esat Uras (Ankara: Türk Tarih Kurumu Basımevi, 1943), 13–14.

88. See for example the military commanders in Cairo who paraded before the governor and in a demonstration of loyalty kissed the hem of his robe; al-Jabarti, *ʿAja'ib*, 2:202. For a soldier who kissed the hem of the robe of a military commander, see al-Damurdashi, *Chronicle*, 136. At Acre, petitioners would routinely kiss the hem of Süleyman Paşa's robe, as well as that of his top advisor, Ali Paşa; al-ʿAwra, *Tarikh*, 232. On Romanian boyars kissing the hem of the robe of superiors, see Wilkinson, *Account*, 132.

89. Gazzizade Abdullatif Efendi, *Vekayi'-i Baba Paşa fi't-Tarih*, ed. Salih Erol (Ankara: Türk Tarih Kurumu, 2013), 303.

90. Leake, *Travels*, 1:40.

91. Ibn Abi'l-Diyaf, *Ithaf*, 7:109.

92. al-Jabarti, *ʿAja'ib*, 3:325.

93. al-Jabarti, *ʿAja'ib*, 7:56.

94. See for example Chishull, *Travels*, 69; al-Damurdashi, *Chronicle*, 24–25. In the Romanian lands, Greek princes (*hospodar*) would kiss a staff representing the sultan's authority during their investiture ceremony; Viorel Panaite, "Power Relationships in the Ottoman Empire: The Sultans and the Tribute-Paying Princes of Wallachia and Moldavia from the Sixteenth to the Eighteenth Century," *International Journal of Turkish Studies* 7 (2001): 38.

95. al-Jabarti, *ʿAja'ib*, 4:155. For other examples of religious figures receiving this public reverence, see Ibn Abi'l-Diyaf, *Ithaf*, 7:71–72, 121.

96. al-Jabarti, *ʿAja'ib*, 2:29.

97. Kabudlu, *Tevarih*, 349; Kabudlı, "Adventures," 243.

98. al-ʿAwra, *Tarikh*, 278.

99. al-ʿAwra, *Tarikh*, 246–50. The scene was as much political as social. Süleyman's future heir, Abdullah, accompanied him and performed exactly the same gestures, down to the relaxed interview in private.

100. al-Muradi, *Silk*, 4:210.

101. İbrahim Hilmi Bey, *Menakıbname-i Mustafa Safi-i Amedi*, ed. Serdar Uğurlu (Istanbul: Kriter Yayınevi, 2017), 101–2.

102. al-Jabarti, *ʿAja'ib*, 3:59. See too the biography of his lieutenant, Mehmed Bey Abu'l-Dhahab, who said little and kept his own grand, dignified manner; al-Jabarti, *ʿAja'ib*, 3:124.

103. al-ʿAwra, *Tarikh*, 246–47.

104. Mishaqa, *Murder*, 96.

105. al-ʿAwra, *Tarikh*, 313. This was a lesson that his successor as governor, Abdullah Paşa (r. 1819-31), failed to learn. He felt no inhibition about mingling with commoners—for instance, during the Sufi rituals that he became fond of attending. His chief scribe, much older and trying to act as a kind of mentor, reproved him and earned only the governor's enmity; Mishaqa, *Murder*, 106.

106. Tülay Artan, "Forms and Forums of Expression: Istanbul and Beyond, 1600-1800," in *The Ottoman World*, ed. Christine Woodhead (London: Routledge, 2012), 386-87; Ebru Boyar and Kate Fleet, *A Social History of Ottoman Istanbul* (Cambridge: Cambridge University Press, 2010), 250.

107. Marcus, *The Middle East*, 287. Marcus notes that the actual distribution of bathhouses was uneven, and that most were located in the central parts of Aleppo.

108. Astrid Meier, "Bathing as a Translocal Phenomenon? Bathhouses in the Arab Provinces of the Ottoman Empire," in *Bathing Culture of Anatolian Civilizations: Architecture, History, and Imagination*, ed. Nina Ergin (Leuven: Peeters, 2011), 189. The figure for eighteenth-century Cairo was slightly worse: about one bathhouse for every three thousand inhabitants; André Raymond, "Les bains publics du Caire à la fin du XVIIIe siècle," *Annales Islamologiques* 8 (1969): 129-50.

109. Ekrem Hakkı Ayverdi, *Avrupa'da Osmanlı Mimari Eserleri* (Istanbul: İstanbul Fetih Cemiyeti, 1978-82), vol. 4; Eleni Kanetaki, "Ottoman Baths in Greece: A Contribution to the Study of Their History and Architecture," in *Bathing Culture of Anatolian Civilizations: Architecture, History, and Imagination*, ed. Nina Ergin (Leuven: Peeters, 2011), 221-55; Machiel Kiel, "Ottoman Mineral Baths (Kaplıca) on the Balkans: A Study of Several Little-Known Examples," in Ergin, *Bathing Culture*, 198-219; Lyubomir Mikov, "Ottoman Bathhouses in Bulgaria (in the Context of Bathing Culture in the Balkans and Anatolia)," *Études Balkaniques* 4 (2012): 118-51.

110. See for example bathing practices in Ottoman Bulgaria; Svetla Ianeva, "Hygiene in Nineteenth-Century Ottoman Bulgaria," *Turkish Historical Review* 5 (2014): 16-31.

111. See for example Grelot, *Voyage*, 188.

112. See for example the case of eighteenth-century Aleppo; Marcus, *Middle East*, 231.

113. Montagu, *Letters*, 106.

114. Moralists counseled that the pious and proper should perform these bodily functions in silence. They should not, for instance, plead for help, "O Lord, O Lord!," as one Anatolian scholar sketched a scene; al-Khadimi, *Bariqa*, 3:328-29. See also al-Nabulsi, *al-Hadiqa*, 2:311-12.

115. Hill, *Account*, 122.

116. See for example Chandler, *Travels*, 60.

117. Boué, *Turquie*, 2:197; Russell, *Aleppo*, 1:113.

118. al-Muradi, *Silk*, 3:246. For an earlier case of a scholar who took his perfuming too far, see al-Muhibbi, *Khulasat*, 4:491-92.

119. On the use of censers in Damascus, see Grehan, *Everyday Life*, 168.

120. de la Mottraye, *Travels*, 194. See also Sannini, *Travels*, 160.

121. Volney, *Travels*, 2:460-61. For an almost identical impression of tranquility, see Browne, *Travels*, 526; d'Ohsson, *Tableau*, 4:242.

122. On the western European exception in using chairs, see Fernand Braudel, *The*

Structures of Everyday Life: Civilization and Capitalism, 1400–1800, Volume 1, trans. Sian Reynolds (New York: Harper and Row, 1981), 287–90.

123. d'Ohsson, *Tableau*, 4:147.

124. On the etiquette of sitting properly, see al-Nabulsi, *al-Hadiqa*, 2:506.

125. D'Ohsson, *Tableau*, 4:242; Lane, *Manners*, 201–2.

126. İbrahim Hilmi Bey, *Menakıbname*, 99.

127. Boué, *Turquie*, 2:432. For an overview of these manners for entering rooms and greeting guests, see Boué, *Turquie*, 2:438–41.

128. See for example al-Jabarti, *'Aja'ib*, 4:55. One further gesture of deference was to welcome an honored guest at the door or in the courtyard outside the room where the reception was being held; Lane, *Manners*, 201.

129. Wittman, *Travels*, 16.

130. deTott, *Memoirs*, 3:194. See also d'Ohsson, *Tableau*, 4:241. European officers were still taking offense decades later at Ottomans who would not seat them; see for example Adolphus Slade, *Records of Travels in Turkey, Greece, &c. and of a Cruise in the Black Sea* (London: Saunders and Otley, 1833), 1:142–43.

131. Aysel Yıldız, *Kenar Adamları ve Bendeleri: Tirsinikli İsmail Ağa ve Alemdar Mustafa Paşa'nın Adamları, Manuk Mirzayan ve Köse Ahmed Efendi* (Istanbul: Kitap Yayınevi, 2018), 137.

132. d'Ohsson, *Tableau*, 4:265. For a discussion of European goods that circulated mainly among the Ottoman elite in Istanbul, see Fatma Müge Göçek, *Rise of the Bourgeoisie, Demise of Empire: Ottoman Westernization and Social Change* (New York: Oxford University Press, 1996), 97–107. On cultural contact between Europeans and the Ottoman elite in eighteenth-century Istanbul, see Fatma Müge Göçek, *East Encounters West: France and the Ottoman Empire in the Eighteenth Century* (New York: Oxford University Press, 1987), chap. 8.

133. On the cultural formation of the Phanariot Greeks, see Christos G. Patrinelis, "The Phanariots before 1821," *Balkan Studies* 42 (2001): 177–98.

134. de Tott, *Memoirs*, 1:123.

135. Alan Duben and Cem Behar, *Ottoman Households: Marriage, Family, and Fertility, 1880–1940* (Cambridge: Cambridge University Press, 1991); Selçuk Esenbel, "The Anguish of Civilized Behavior: The Use of Western Cultural Forms in the Everyday Lives of the Meiji Japanese and the Ottoman Turks during the Nineteenth Century," *Nichibunken Japan Review* (1994): 145–85.

136. For an overview of dining manners, see Boué, *Turquie*, 2:449–52.

137. Denon, *Travels*, 1:156–57.

138. al-Jabarti, *'Aja'ib*, 7: 467. For accounts of imperial banquets from the late seventeenth century, see Covel, "Diary," 264; Galland, *Journal*, 1:186–87.

139. Russell, *Aleppo*, 1:175.

140. Galt, *Letters*, 86–87. Balkan dining manners, including the acceptability of controlled belching, were identical to those in other parts of the empire; see Boué, *Turquie*, 2:449–52.

141. For other dining scenes, see Chandler, *Travels*, 14; Dodwell, *Tour*, 1:156–57; Febvre, *Théatre*, 189–93; van Egmont, *Travels*, 2:35, 203–4; Griffiths, *Travels*, 111–12; Hill, *Account*, 116–19; Thevenot, *Travels*, 1:32–33.

142. For a sixteenth-century Arab manual, see Badr al-Din al-Ghazzi, *Risalat adab mu'akala*, ed. 'Umar Musa Basha (Rabat: Maktabat al-Ma'arif, 1984). For a study of this treatise, see Helen Pfeifer, "The Gulper and the Slurper: A Lexicon of Mistakes to Avoid While Eating with Ottoman Gentlemen," *Journal of Early Modern History* 24 (2020): 41–62.

143. Dumont, *New Voyage*, 279.

144. Panages Skouzes, *Apomnemoneumata: He tyrannia tou Chatze-Ale Chaseke sten tourkodratoumene Athena (1772-1796)* (Athens: Kedros, 1975), 80–81.

145. See for example van Egmont, *Travels*, 1:219; Maundrell, "Journey," 408.

146. Montagu, *Letters*, 158.

147. Browne, *Travels*, 525. By the early nineteenth century, the perfuming ceremony was apparently going out of fashion in Egypt; Lane, *Manners*, 203.

148. Browne, *Travels*, 442, 493.

149. For an overview of these attitudes in Aleppo, see Marcus, *Middle East*, 27–36.

Chapter 4

1. Browne, *Travels*, 51.

2. On the wealthy military officers of Cairo, see André Raymond, *Artisans*, chap. 14. On the rise in equality within *askeri* ranks in Damascus from the late seventeenth to the mid-eighteenth century, see respectively Colette Establet and Jean-Pascual, *La gent d'État dans la société ottomane damascène: Les 'askar à la fin du XVIIe siècle* (Damascus: Institut Français du Proche-Orient, 2011), chap. 3; Grehan, *Everyday Life*, 64–65, 230–31.

3. See for example Daniel Crecelius, *The Roots of Modern Egypt: A Study of the Regimes of Ali Bey al-Kabir and Muhammad Bey Abu al-Dhahab* (Minneapolis: Bibliotheca Islamica, 1981); Jane Hathaway, *The Politics of Households in Ottoman Egypt: The Rise of the Qazdağlıs* (Cambridge: Cambridge University Press, 1997), chap. 2; Jane Hathaway, "The Military Household in Ottoman Egypt," *International Journal of Middle East Studies* 27 (1995): 39–52.

4. Evliya, *Seyahatnamesi*, 1:120–21.

5. Naima, *Tarih*, 3:453–55.

6. Naima, *Tarih*, 3:408–9.

7. Evliya, *Seyahatnamesi*, 10:385. For other encounters in which he fought and displayed bravery against the bedouin or bandits, see Evliya, *Seyahatnamesi*, 5:312–13; 8:283–84; 9:57–58, 60–62, 71–73, 410.

8. al-Muradi, *Silk*, 2:31–33.

9. Rasul Karkukli, *Dawhat al-wuzara' fi tarikh waqa'i' Baghdad al-zawra'*, trans. 'Ala' Musa Kazim Nawras (Beirut: Dar al-Katib al-'Arabi, 1963), 28.

10. Shihab, *Tarikh*, 75. For other examples of a courageous warrior, see the tribute to Nasuh Paşa (d. 1714), governor of Damascus and scourge of the bedouin; and Süleyman Paşa the Little (r. 1807–10), governor of Baghdad. See respectively Ibn Kannan, *Yawmiyat*, 218; Karkukli, *Dawhat*, 250.

11. al-Jabarti, *'Aja'ib*, 1:94–95.

12. al-Jabarti, *'Aja'ib*, 4:176. See too the career of another Emir Ali, who rose to the position of head clerk at the imperial palace in Istanbul. A capable administrator, he was a good horseman and marksman as well; al-Jabarti, *'Aja'ib*, 2:215–16.

13. Evliya, *Seyahatnamesi*, 2:188–89. For another Circassian soldier, whom the sultan Osman II (r. 1618–22) hailed for his "horsemanship and courage," see the biography of

Derviş Mehmed Paşa (d. 1655); al-Muhibbi, *Khulasat*, 2:157–58. For the same model of courage and generosity, see the biography of al-Amir Farukh (d. 1620/21), a Circassian slave of the emir of Gaza. He became intendant (*hakim*) of Nablus after having served as commander of the pilgrimage caravan. His son, Amir Muhammad, ultimately succeeded him in Nablus and earned such a forbidding reputation among the bedouin that the mere mention of his name became a source of terror. See respectively al-Muhibbi, *Khulasat*, 3:271; 4:108–10. In Egypt, the emir Hüseyin Bey Kişkiş Kazdağlı (d. 1768) was another model of martial valor and daring. Bedouin were so terrified of his troops' raids that they used to mention his name to frighten their children; al-Jabarti, *'Aja'ib*, 2:305. The maternal great-grandfather of Muhammad Khalil al-Muradi, the mufti of Damascus, was a soldier of Circassian descent and twice became commander of the local Janissary garrison. His grandson memorialized him with the usual compliments about bravery and generosity; al-Muradi, *Silk*, 3:90.

14. Abdul-Rahim Abu-Husayn, *Provincial Leaderships in Syria, 1575-1650* (Beirut: American University of Beirut Press, 1985); Stefan Winter, *The Shiites of Lebanon under Ottoman Rule, 1516-1788* (Cambridge: Cambridge University Press, 2010).

15. al-Muhibbi, *Khulasat*, 3:427–28. On the horsemanship and bravery of the bedouin, which earned so much admiration, see the account of the chieftain 'Arar, who haunted the caravan routes around Aleppo toward the end of the sixteenth century; al-Muhibbi, *Khulasat*, 1:364.

16. al-Jabarti, *'Aja'ib*, 2:306. See also the biography of Amir Musa. Better known as Ibn Turkoman (d. 1670/71), he was a Damascene soldier who rose through the ranks, eventually gaining an appointment as intendant (*hakim*) of the Transjordanian frontier zone around 'Ajlun. An expert horseman and deft administrator, he got along so well with the local people that he willingly adopted bedouin dress and insisted on using only their dialect; al-Muhibbi, *Khulasat*, 4:434.

17. Sabbanu, ed., *Hamlat*, 102.
18. Ramiz, *Zurafa*, 268.
19. Ibn Kannan, *Yawmiyat*, 195.
20. Burayk, *Tarikh*, 47–48.
21. Vehbi, *Lütfiyye*, 68–69.
22. Vassaf, *Sefine*, 3:91.
23. Vassaf, *Sefine*, 3:101. For examples of other Sufis who participated in Ottoman campaigns, see Enfi, *Tezkiret*, 149–52, 188; Vassaf, *Sefine*, 1:433; 5:124.
24. See for example Mishaqa, *Murder*, 127, 129.
25. Mishaqa, *Murder*, 75.
26. Vassaf, *Sefine*, 4:167–68.
27. Vassaf, *Sefine*, 4:447–51.
28. Mishaqa, *Murder*, 85–86.
29. Mishaqa, *Murder*, 167–68.
30. Mishaqa, *Murder*, 169.
31. Mishaqa, *Murder*, 176. See also Ahmed Lutfi, *Tarih-i Lutfi* (Istanbul: Matbaa-yı Amire, 1875–1912), 4:23.
32. For accounts of this dramatic scene, see Arapyan, *Rusçuk Ayanı*, 17–19; Beydilli, ed., *İmamlar*, 111; Cevdet, *Tarih*, 9:28–30; Fahri Ç. Derin, ed., "Yayla İmamı Risalesi," *İs-*

tanbul Üniversitesi Tarih Enstitüsü Dergisi 3 (1973): 254–55. This self-annihilating bravado became something of a trope in political folklore. The warlord Tepedelenli Ali Paşa, who brought large parts of Greece and Albania under his control (1788–1822), ended his days facing a siege from an Ottoman army, sent to put down the incipient Greek war of independence and making a brief detour to depose him along the way. As Ottoman troops closed in, he sent word to a trusted subordinate, who guarded his stocks of gunpowder in the basement of the citadel of Yanina. If Ali should send his broken signet ring, the soldier was to blow up the fortress along with everyone inside. Ali would later opt for discretion over valor and try to retire to a nearby monastery. The Ottomans captured and executed him anyway. See Katherine E. Fleming, *The Muslim Bonaparte: Diplomacy and Orientalism in Ali Pasha's Greece* (Princeton: Princeton University Press, 1999), 28–29.

33. Cevdet, *Tarih*, 8:306–7.

34. Enderunlu Fazıl, *Der Vasf-ı Hubanname; Der Vasf-ı Zenanname-yi Fazıl; Rakkasname-yi Fazılın* (Istanbul, 1839), 88. On Georgian female slaves, see Zilfi, *Women*, 155–56.

35. Pertev Naili Boratav, *Köroğlu Destanı* (Istanbul: Kırmızı Yayınları, 2009), esp. part IV.

36. John W. Baggally, *Greek Historical Folksongs: The Klephtic Ballads in Relation to Greek History (1715–1821)* (Chicago: Argonaut, 1968; reprint of 1936 edition). See also John Campbell, "The Greek Hero," in *Honor and Grace in Anthropology*, ed. J.G. Peristiany and Julian Pitt-Rivers (Cambridge: Cambridge University Press, 1992), 129–49; Albert B. Lord, "The Heroic Tradition of Greek Epic and Ballad: Continuity and Change," in *Hellenism and the First Greek War of Liberation (1821–1830): Continuity and Change* (Thessaloniki: Institute for Balkan Studies, 1976), 79–94.

37. Gülay Yılmaz, "Janissaries in the Making: Coerced Labor and Chivalric Masculinity in the Early Modern Ottoman Empire," *Labor History* 64 (2023): 1–18.

38. On the enduring admiration for bedouin manhood in late Ottoman Syrian literature, see Fruma Zachs and Sharon Halevi, "Repaving the Path of *Muru'a*: Manly Virtue and the Emergence of a Modern Masculinity in Greater Syria," in *Gendering Culture in Greater Syria: Intellectuals and Ideology in the Late Ottoman Period* (New York: IB Tauris, 2015), 63–81.

39. See for example the biography of Muhammad bin ʿUmar (d. 1816/17), a Tunisian tribesman renowned for his warrior courage and for occasionally, as opportunity presented itself, resorting to brigandage. Having lost a son in battle, he claimed not to mourn him. Only if his son had fled the field of combat, he insisted, would he have felt any sorrow; Ibn Abi'l-Diyaf, *Ithaf*, 7:104–5.

40. Thomas Philipp, *Acre: The Rise and Fall of a Palestinian City, 1730–1831* (New York: Columbia University Press, 2001), chap. 3.

41. Mikha'il al-Sabbagh, *Tarikh al-Shaykh Zahir al-ʿUmar al-Zaydani, hakim ʿAkka wa Bilad Safad*, ed. Qastantin al-Basha al-Mukhlisi (Harisa, Lebanon: Matbaʿat al-Qiddis Bulus, n.d.), 16–17. Another grandson of Ibrahim al-Sabbagh, Zahir's Christian chief scribe, was ʿAbbud al-Sabbagh, whose account is relatively more scrupulous about dates and details and whose adulation is more measured. See ʿAbbud al-Sabbagh, *al-Rawd al-zahir fi tarikh Zahir*, ed. Muhammad ʿAbd al-Karim Muhafaza and ʿIsam Mustafa Hazayima (Irbid: Mu'assasat Hamadah li'l-Khidmat wa al-Dirasat al-Jamiʿiyya, 1999). For an overview of the career of Zahir (alternatively pronounced as Dahir in local Palestinian dialects), see

Ahmad Hasan Joudah, *Revolt in Palestine in the Eighteenth Century: The Era of Shaykh Zahir al-ʿUmar* (Princeton: Kingston Press, 1987).

42. al-Sabbagh, *Tarikh*, 21.
43. al-Sabbagh, *Tarikh*, 21–23.
44. al-Sabbagh, *Tarikh*, 31–33.
45. al-Sabbagh, *Tarikh*, 36–37.
46. al-Sabbagh, *Tarikh*, 121–22.
47. al-Sabbagh, *Tarikh*, 56–57.
48. al-Sabbagh, *Tarikh*, 67–68.
49. al-Sabbagh, *Tarikh*, 150–52.
50. al-Sabbagh, *Tarikh*, 81–83.
51. al-Sabbagh, *Tarikh*, 60, 62. See also al-Budayri, *Hawadith*, 45–46. For an alternative account of this campaign that makes no mention of any poisoning, see al-Sabbagh, *al-Rawd*, 36.
52. al-Sabbagh, *Tarikh*, 154–56. The "simplicity" of the bedouin was a cultural trope that endured far into the nineteenth century. To take a figure from a different region: it was said that Salih al-Zakrawi (d. 1855), a tribal leader from southern Tunisia, deliberately kept his bedouin manners and spurned all urban affectations; Ibn Abiʾl-Diyaf, *Ithaf*, 8:96.
53. al-Sabbagh, *Tarikh*, 110–11.
54. Philipp, *Acre*, 79.
55. al-ʿAwra, *Tarikh*, 389. See also the similar assessment in Mishaqa, *Murder*, 54.
56. al-ʿAwra, *Tarikh*, 226–27.
57. On these Ottoman images, see Cevdet, *Tarih*, 1:319–21.
58. Mishaqa, *Murder*, 92.
59. Mishaqa, *Murder*, 47. A similar character sketch was reserved for ʿAli Bey al-Asʿad, appointed as head of the district administration for Jabal ʿAkkar; al-ʿAwra, *Tarikh*, 135.
60. al-ʿAwra, *Tarikh*, 35–36.
61. For the participation of Mehmed IV (r. 1648–87) in Polish campaigns during the 1670s, see Baer, *Honored*, chap. 8.
62. The spending habits of the court during the so-called "Tulip Age" of the 1720s, condemned by so many commentators, were no more profligate than in other periods before or after; Selim Karahasanoğlu, "Challenging the Paradigm of the Tulip Age: The Consumer Behavior of Nevşehirli Damad İbrahim Paşa and His Household," in *Living the Good Life: Consumption in the Qing and Ottoman Empires of the Eighteenth Century*, ed. Elif Akçetin and Suraiya Faroqhi (Leiden: Brill, 2018), 134–60.
63. For a sketch of Selim III's personality, see Aysel Yıldız, "The 'Louis XVI of the Turks': The Character of an Ottoman Sultan," *Middle Eastern Studies* 50 (2014): 272–90.
64. See for example Ahmed Cavid, *Hadika*, 25–26; Cevdet, *Tarih*, 6:266; 7:101.
65. For an overview of these developments, see Aksan, *Ottoman Statesman*, 12–23; Itzkowitz, "Ottoman Realities"; Yeşil, *Aydınlanma*, 13–32.
66. Carter Findley, *Ottoman Civil Officialdom: A Social History* (Princeton: Princeton University Press, 1989), 22. By comparison, the Russian czar had thirty-eight thousand officials at his disposal by the end of the eighteenth century. Under Louis XVI, France had some ninety thousand, who swarmed through Europe's most bureaucratized state;

Simon Dixon, *The Modernization of Russia, 1676-1825* (Cambridge: Cambridge University Press, 1999), 132; Nancy Shields Kollmann, *The Russian Empire, 1450-1801* (Oxford: Oxford University Press, 2017), 313.

67. al-Jabarti, `Aja'ib, 2:210-11; Ramiz, *Zurafa*, 111-15; Ahmed Resmi, *Halifet ür-Rüesa* (Istanbul: Takvimhane-yi Amire, 1853), 70-73. On the career of Ahmed Resmi Efendi, a leading Ottoman bureaucrat who was recognized as a literary connoisseur, see al-Muradi, *Silk*, 1:73-80. On Ahmed Resmi's early formation, see Aksan, *Ottoman Statesman*, chap. 1. For examples of other bureaucrats recognized for their literary attainments, see Ahmed Resmi, *Halifet*, 48-51, 60-64, 104-5, 129-32, 157-60, 162-64; Abdülfettah Şefkat, *Zeyl-i Hadikat ül-Vüzera*, in Osmanzade Taib, *Hadikat ül-Vüzera* (Istanbul: Ceride-i Havadis Matbaası, 1854), 17.

68. Ahmed Resmi, *Halifet*, 66-70.

69. Ramiz, *Zurafa*, 156-57. For other bureaucrats recognized for their poetry, see for example ibid., 96-97, 99-100, 100-1, 102-2, 104-5, 118, 124-25, 129, 159, 161, 161-62, 170-71, 174-75, 176, 178, 180-81, 181-83, 186-87, 188, 190-91, 197, 197-98, 199, 201-2, 202, 208-10, 216-17, 218-19, 221-23, 223, 223-24, 224, 225-27, 229-30, 234-35, 238, 241-42, 244, 248, 266-67, 280.

70. Carter V. Findley, *Bureaucratic Reform in the Ottoman Empire* (Princeton: Princeton University Press, 1980), 79-91.

71. For scribes who became celebrated adepts of calligraphy, see for example Ramiz, *Zurafa*, 106, 125, 135-36, 137-39, 142, 158, 201-2, 281-83. For the fullest collection of Ottoman calligraphers, see Müstakimzade Süleyman Sadeddin Efendi, *Tuhfe-i Hattatin* (Istanbul: Devlet Matbaası, 1928).

72. Cevdet, *Tarih*, 3:147. For examples of other experts with penmanship, see Ahmed Cavid, *Zeyl-i Hadikat ül-Vüzera*, in Osmanzade Taib, *Hadikat*, 31; Ahmed Resmi, *Halifet*, 170, 182-83.

73. al-Damurdashi, *Chronicle*, 59.

74. Özcan ed., *Anonim*, 277-78.

75. Officials were not the only ones to feel the sting of such deficiencies. The father of Sa`id al-Sa`sa`ani (d. 1732), a renowned poet, was one of the notables of Damascus, but could not escape the cutting verdict that he was "an empty vessel with respect to learning"; al-Muradi, *Silk*, 2:128-33.

76. Ibn Abi'l-Diyaf, *Ithaf*, 7:84.

77. Yıldız, *Kenar Adamları*, 32.

78. Yıldız, *Kenar Adamları*, 73. On Alemdar's rise from provincial obscurity, see İsmail Hakkı Uzunçarşılı, *Meşhur Rumeli Ayanlarından Tirsinikli İsmail, Yılıkoğlu Süleyman Ağalar ve Alemdar Mustafa Paşa* (Ankara: Türk Tarih Kurumu Basımevi, 2010), 40-81.

79. Arapyan, *Rusçuk Ayanı*, 11.

80. al-Jabarti, `Aja'ib, 5:260-61.

81. Ramiz, *Zurafa*, 101-2. For another grand admiral who wrote poetry, ibid., 72-73.

82. During a second visit to Istanbul, Muhammad Khalil al-Muradi, future mufti of Damascus, met İbrahim in person. The Syrian scholar was so struck by his accomplishments that İbrahim received his own entry (as Ibrahim al-Rumi) in Muradi's biographical dictionary; al-Muradi, *Silk*, 1:14-15.

83. Mehmed Haşim, İma, 107.

84. al-Jabarti, ʿAjaʾib, 3:294. For references to two other bibliophiles among the Egyptian emirs, see al-Jabarti, ʿAjaʾib, 4:261; 6:342–43. As governor of Baghdad, Süleyman Abu Layla Paşa (r. 1749–62) did his part to perpetuate an eighteenth-century household of Georgian slave-soldiers by buying a large number of new mamluks. To prepare them for future service, he actively oversaw their education and training; Sulayman Faʾiq [Süleyman Faik], Tarikh Baghdad, trans. Musa Kazim Nawras (Beirut: al-Rafidin liʾl-Tibaʿa wa al-Nashr wa al-Tawziʿ, 2010), 18–19.

85. al-Jabarti, ʿAjaʾib, 6:142–43. See also the sketch of Murad Bey (d. 1803), which, though more mixed in its appraisal of his character, still applauded him for mingling with jurists and showing them favor; al-Jabarti, ʿAjaʾib, 5:255.

86. Faʾiq, Tarikh, 129–31. See also the impeccable education of Talib Aǧa, another mamluk purchased by Süleyman the Great; and Ahmed Paşa, Daud's brother; ibid., 132–34, 134–35.

87. Leon Carl Brown, *The Tunisia of Ahmad Bey, 1837–1855* (Princeton: Princeton University Press, 1974), 43–47. For several individual portraits of educated mamluks, see Ibn Abiʾl-Diyaf, Ithaf, 8:15, 129–30, 133, 144, 151. One of the Husayni governors of Tunisia, Muhammad Bey (r. 1756–59), was known for his love of books and learning, especially in the fields of history and literature; ibid., 2:156–57.

88. al-Muradi, Silk, 2:199.

89. Karl Barbir, "From Pasha to Efendi: The Assimilation of Ottoman into Damascene Society, 1516–1783," *International Journal of Turkish Studies* 1 (1979–80): 68–83.

90. al-Muradi, Silk, 4:166–78; see also al-Muradi, Silk, 1:97–107, 274–78.

91. al-Muardi, Silk, 4:16.

92. al-Muradi, Silk, 2:31–33; for Hasan's son, ibid., 3:209–12. For similar cases of outsiders settling into the provincial bureaucracy at Damascus, ibid., 3:39–41; 4:7–8, 38. See again Barbir, "From Pasha to Efendi," 68–83.

93. For an overview of Naima's life and career, see Lewis V. Thomas, *A Study of Naima*, ed. Norman Itzkowitz, (New York: New York University Press, 1972), 5–54.

94. al-Jabarti, ʿAjaʾib, 4:127. For examples of other scribes famed for their penmanship, see al-Jabarti, ʿAjaʾib, 3:294, 302–3; al-Muhibbi, Khulasat, 1:402–4; 3:227.

95. Mishaqa, Murder, 165–66. For a similar salute to the elegant script and fine character of Fadlullah Efendi (d. 1831), a scribe and notable of Kirkuk, see Faʾiq, Tarikh, 136–38.

96. al-Muradi, Silk, 3:119–23. For examples of other Syrian scribes who became expert poets, see al-Muradi, Silk, 1:163–67; 2:114; 3:104.

97. al-Muradi, Silk, 1:48–49. His Arabic biography refers to him as "Abu Bakr al-Murawi."

98. al-Muradi, Silk, 3:209–13.

99. See for example al-Muradi, Silk, 1:15–19; 2:42–46, 63–67, 118–19, 160–61; 4:23–24.

100. al-Muradi, Silk, 2:107–12.

101. On sixteenth-century literary salons, centered mainly at the courts of sultans and princes, see Haluk İpekten, *Divan Edebiyatında Edebi Muhitler* (Istanbul: Milli Eğitim Basımevi, 1996).

102. One celebrated soldier-poet from sixteenth-century Damascus was Mamaya al-Rumi (d. 1580), who quit soldiering as a young man and drifted into a literary career;

Clifford Edmund Bosworth, "A Janissary Poet of Sixteenth-Century Damascus: Mamayya al-Rumi," in *The Islamic World from Classical to Modern Times: Essays in Honor of Bernard Lewis*, ed. C.E. Bosworth et al. (Princeton: Darwin Press, 1989), 451–66.

103. al-Muhibbi, *Khulasat*, 4:229–30.
104. al-Muhibbi, *Khulasat*, 4:409–23.
105. al-Muradi, *Silk*, 4:40–41.
106. See for example al-Muradi, *Silk*, 4:166–78, 179–83.
107. al-Muradi, *Silk*, 1:97–107.
108. al-Muradi, *Silk*, 3:11–21.
109. al-Jabarti, *'Aja'ib*, 3:233.
110. al-Jabarti, *'Aja'ib*, 4:193. On eighteenth-century mamluks' sponsorship of salons, see Hanna, *In Praise*, 140–44.
111. al-Jabarti, *'Aja'ib*, 4:54–55.
112. al-Jabarti, *'Aja'ib*, 4:192.
113. al-Jabarti, *'Aja'ib*, 2:17.
114. al-Jabarti, *'Aja'ib*, 1:275.
115. al-Muradi, *Silk*, 3:135–36. See too the biography of Fathi al-Falaqansi (d. 1746), another treasurer of Damascus. Despite his violent downfall at the hands of the governor, 'Asad Paşa al-'Azm (r. 1743–57), he was celebrated as a connoisseur of poetry, music, and fine conversation, even if some grumbled about his taste for wine; al-Muradi, *Silk*, 3:279–87.
116. See for example the protocol in eighteenth-century Aleppo. The governor's military band had the privilege of playing twice a day in front of his palace; Bodman, *Factions*, 20.
117. Browne, *Travels*, 91–92.
118. See for example Kuşmani and Ebubekir, *Asiler*, 144. On complaints about him turning a blind eye to immorality among his troops, see Gazzizade, *Baba Paşa*, 214.
119. See for example Develi, ed., *Risale*, 32–33.
120. Cevdet, *Tarih*, 9:18–19.
121. al-Jabarti, *'Aja'ib*, 2:92–93.
122. al-Jabarti, *'Aja'ib*, 2:349–50.
123. al-Jabarti, *'Aja'ib*, 2:306. On the theory of "impression management," see Erving Goffman, *The Presentation of Self in Everyday Life* (New York: Anchor Books, 1959).
124. Shalabi, *Awdah*, 168.
125. On the case of Aleppo, see Russell, *Aleppo*, 1:324. On the absorption of Janissaries into the guild system at Istanbul, see Eunjeong Yi, *Guild Dynamics in Seventeenth-Century Istanbul* (Leiden: Brill, 2004), 132–43; for Cairo, see André Raymond, "Soldiers in Trade: The Case of Cairo," *British Journal of Middle East Studies* 18 (1991): 16–37.
126. Bodman, *Factions*, 138.
127. al-Jabarti, *'Aja'ib*, 5:250.
128. On the older tradition of equestrian preparation for battle, see Tülay Artan, "Ahmed I and 'Tuhfet'ül-mülük ve's-selatin," in *Animals and People in the Ottoman Empire*, ed. Suraiya Faroqhi (Istanbul: Eren, 2010), 235–69; David Ayalon, *Gunpowder and Firearms in the Mamluk Kingdom: A Challenge to Mediaeval Society*, 2nd ed. (London: F. Cass, 1978); Agnès Carayon, "City of the Cavalryman and House of the Rider: 'Landscaped-Hippodromes'

and Stable-Palaces in Mamluk Cairo," in *Echoing Hooves: Studies on Horses and Their Effects on Medieval Societies* (Leiden: Brill, 2022), 57–75; Hassanein Rabie, "The Training of the Mamluk Faris," in *War, Technology, and Society in the Middle East*, ed. V.J. Parry and Malcolm Yapp (London: Oxford University Press, 1978), chap. 9; Shihab al-Sarraf, "Furusiyya Literature of the Mamluk Period," in *Furusiyya: the Horse in the Art of the Near East*, ed. David Alexander (Riyadh: King Abdulaziz Public Library, 1996), 1:118–35.

129. Artan, "Forms and Forums," 394.

130. James Grehan, "Fun and Games in Ottoman Aleppo: The Life and Times of a Local Schoolteacher (1835–1865)," in *Entertainment among the Ottomans*, ed. Ebru Boyar and Kate Fleet (Leiden: Brill, 2019), 90–120.

131. See for example T.C.W. Blanning, *The Culture of Power and the Power of Culture: Old Regime Europe, 1660–178* (Oxford: Oxford University Press, 2002); Jeroen Duindam, *Vienna and Versailles: The Courts of Europe's Major Dynastic Rivals, 1550–1780* (Cambridge: Cambridge University Press, 2003); Mark Motley, *Becoming a French Aristocrat: The Education of the Court Nobility, 1580–1715* (Princeton: Princeton University Press, 1990); Louis de Rouvroy Saint-Simon, *Versailles, the Court, and Louis XIV* (New York: Harper & Row, 1966).

132. Mark C. Elliott, *The Manchu Way: The Eight Banners and Ethnic Identity in Late Imperial China* (Stanford: Stanford University Press, 2001), chaps. 7–8; Pei Huang, *Reorienting the Manchus: A Study of Sinicization, 1583–1795* (Ithaca: East Asia Program, Cornell University, 2011), chap. 6; Colin P. Mackerras, *The Rise of the Peking Opera, 1770–1870: Social Aspects of the Theatre in Manchu China* (Oxford: Clarendon Press, 1972).

133. Eiko Ikegami, *The Taming of the Samurai: Honorific Individualism and the Making of Modern Japan* (Cambridge, MA: Harvard University Press, 1995); Wai Lau, *On the Process of Civilisation in Japan: Sociogenetic and Psychogenetic Investigations* (Cham, Switz.: Palgrave Macmillan, 2022).

134. E.M. Collingham, *Imperial Bodies: The Physical Experience of the Raj, c. 1800–1947* (Cambridge: Polity Press, 2001), esp. chap. 1; William Dalrymple, *White Mughals: Love and Betrayal in Eighteenth-Century India* (London: Harper Collins, 2002); P.J. Marshall, *East India Fortunes: The British in Bengal in the Eighteenth Century* (London: Oxford University Press, 1976); James Raven, *Judging New Wealth: Popular Publishing and Responses to Commerce in England, 1750–1800* (New York: Oxford University Press, 1992); Percival Spear, *The Nabobs: A Study of the Social Life of the English in Eighteenth-Century India* (New York: Oxford University Press, 1998).

135. On the surge of urbanization in early modern Europe, see Jan de Vries, *European Urbanization, 1500–1800* (Cambridge, MA: Harvard University Press, 1984); Nico Voigtländer and Hans-Joachim Voth, "The Three Horsemen of Riches: Plague, War, and Urbanization in Early Modern Europe," *Review of Economic Studies* 80 (2013): 774–811.

Chapter 5

1. Vassaf, *Sefine*, 2:293.

2. See for example the place of honor in early modern European culture: Renato Barahona, *Sex Crimes, Honour, and Law in Early Modern Spain: Vizcaya, 1528–1735* (Toronto: University of Toronto Press, 2003); François Billacois, *The Duel: Its Rise and Fall in Early Modern France*, trans. Trista Sellou (New Haven: Yale University Press, 1990); Bryson, *Courtesy*, 232–42; Frederic Robertson Bryson, *The Point of Honor in Sixteenth-Century Italy: An Aspect*

of the Life of the Gentleman (New York: Columbia University Press, 1935); Stuart Carroll, *Blood and Violence in Early Modern France* (New York: Oxford University Press, 2006); V.G. Kiernan, *The Duel in European History: Honour and the Reign of Aristocracy* (Oxford: Oxford University Press, 1988); Edward Muir, *Mad Blood Stirring: Vendetta and Factions in Friuli during the Renaissance* (Baltimore: Johns Hopkins University Press, 1993); Markku Peltonen, *The Duel in Early Modern England: Civility, Politeness, and Honour* (Cambridge: Cambridge University Press, 2003); Kathy Stuart, *Defiled Trades and Social Outcasts: Honor and Ritual Pollution in Early Modern Germany* (Cambridge: Cambridge University Press, 1999); Scott K. Taylor, *Honor and Violence in Golden Age Spain* (New Haven: Yale University Press, 2008); Hillay Zmora, *The Feud in Early Modern Germany* (Cambridge: Cambridge University Press, 2011). On society and notions of honor in other parts of the early modern world, see for example: Nancy Shields Kollmann, *By Honor Bound: State and Society in Early Modern Russia* (Ithaca: Cornell University Press, 1999); Osvaldo F. Pardo, *Honor and Personhood in Early Modern Mexico* (Ann Arbor: University of Michigan Press, 2015).

3. Castellan, *Lettres*, 2:286–87.

4. Enfi, *Tezkiret*, 126–27. On the virtues of this taciturnity, see also ibid., 114–16, 127–30; al-Muradi, *Silk*, 4:24.

5. al-Muradi, *Silk*, 2:70–72. For a similar tribute, see ibid., 2:329–30.

6. Vehbi, *Lütfiyye*, 50. "Düşmanını sustursan bile yine hoş tutmaya gayret et."

7. Making explicit these limits of forbearance was ʿAbd al-Ghani al-Nabulsi, who conceded that barbs directed against a scholar's intelligence, learning, or faith were too outrageous to be overlooked; al-Nabulsi, *al-Hadiqa*, 2:237–38.

8. Cevdet, *Tarih*, 2:24–25; 6:271–72. For another scholar with a combustible temperament, see the biography of Ibrahim al-Atasi (d. 1782), a talented jurist from Homs who blighted his own career due to "his quarrelsome disposition and frequent heedlessness." Only a visit to Istanbul, where he successfully lobbied to become mufti of Tripoli, rescued him from self-inflicted setbacks; al-Muradi, *Silk*, 1:14. For references to other temperamental ulama, see al-Muradi, *Silk*, 2:324; 3:144; 4:30, 58, 210, 225.

9. al-Budayri, *Hawadith*, 50–51. For an earlier incident in which a soldier had physically struck a scholar (1717), see Ibn Kannan, *Yawmiyat*, 276. For a member of the governor's retinue insulting a religious student and causing an outcry (1711), see Ibn Kannan, *Yawmiyat*, 182.

10. al-ʿAwra, *Tarikh*, 371. The local Catholics so vexed the patriarch that he would sometimes succumb to his inner rage, clutching an icon and pleading with God to smite his religious rivals; see al-Dimashqi, *Tarikh*, 66–67. For correspondence between two church leaders who heaped abuse on one another (1783), see Karamah, *Hawadith*, 79.

11. Kuşmani and Ebubekir, *Asiler*, 111.

12. Shalabi, *Awdah*, 305.

13. Enfi, *Tezkiret*, 108. For a more veiled form of obscene banter, expressed through poetry, see al-Muradi, *Silk*, 3:275–76.

14. Mustafa Vazih Efendi, *Amasya Fetvaları ve İlk Amasya Şehir Tarihi (Belabilü'r-Rasiye fi Riyaz-ı Mesaili'l-Amasiyye)*, ed. Ali Rıza Ayar and Recep Orhan Özel (Amasya: Amasya Belediye Kültür Yayınları, 2011), 19.

15. al-Jabarti, *ʿAjaʾib*, 7:77.

16. al-Jabarti, 'Aja'ib, 2:199–200. For other incidents, see al-Muradi, Silk, 2:292; 4:10.

17. See for example al-Muradi, Silk, 1:41–42; Enfi, Tezkiret, 119–20.

18. al-Muradi, Silk, 2:291–92.

19. al-Jabarti, 'Aja'ib, 3:153–55. See too the case of Ahmed Efendi (d. 1748), a respectable preacher in Cairo, who was a member of the local Turcophone community. Leading military officers, also Turkish-speaking, would sometimes attend his sermons, only to be horrified by the tongue-lashing that they received in front of the entire congregation. Some muttered about sending their men to kill him, but none ever had the courage to follow through; al-Jabarti, 'Aja'ib, 2:39.

20. al-Jabarti, 'Aja'ib, 3:118.

21. On fifteenth- and sixteenth-century images of the sultan being stirred to righteous anger, see N. Zeynep Yelçe, "Royal Wrath: Curbing the Anger of the Sultan," in *Discourses of Anger in the Early Modern Period*, ed. Karl A.E. Enenkel and Anita Traninger (Leiden: Brill, 2015), 439–57.

22. Shalabi, Awdah, 202.

23. Shalabi, Awdah, 207. For a similar promise of dyeing an adversary's beard with blood, see al-Damurdashi, Chronicle, 100.

24. Shalabi, Awdah, 297. For a variation of this threat, see the reaction of the governor Sulayman Paşa al-`Azm during the siege of Tiberius (1743). Offered a bribe if he would only go back to Damascus, he swore to Zahir al-`Umar, his quarry hiding in the town, that the campaign would end "only with your head"; al-Budayri, Hawadith, 46. For other instances in which officials used threatening language, see for example Ibn Kannan, Yawmiyat, 41, 43, 158–59.

25. Shalabi, Awdah, 313.

26. See for example Ibn Kannan, Yawmiyat, 90; Raslan ibn Yahya al-Qari, *al-Wuzara' aladhina hakamu Dimashq*, in *Wulat Dimashq fi al-`ahd al-`uthmani*, ed. Salah al-Din al-Munajjid (Damascus, 1949), 81; al-Budayri, Hawadith, 214; al-Dimashqi, Tarikh, 12. One very interesting document is the brief chronicle of Ibn al-Siddiq, a soldier who served in the province of Damascus. For moments in which an official or soldier "lost his head" (tar `aqlu), see Ibn al-Siddiq, *Ghara'ib al-bada'i` fi `aja'ib al-waqa'i*`, ed. Yusuf al-Nu`aysa (Damascus: Matba`at al-`Ajluni, 1988), 20–21, 28–29, 33–34, 37, 39–40, 45, 50, 52, 54–56, 58, 60–62, 64, 66–67, 74, 79, 83, 88, 99.

27. Cevdet, Tarih, 7:266–67.

28. Fa'iq, Tarikh, 37.

29. al-Jabarti, 'Aja'ib, 2:70.

30. Russell, Aleppo, 1:223.

31. al-Jabarti, 'Aja'ib, 4:79.

32. Shihab, Tarikh, 73–74.

33. al-Jabarti, 'Aja'ib, 3:331; 4:44–45.

34. İsmail Hakkı Uzunçarşılı, "Cezayirli Gazi Hasan Paşa'ya Dair," *İstanbul Üniversitesi Edebiyat Fakültesi Türkiyat Mecmuası* 7/8 (1942): 17–40.

35. al-Halabi, Hawadith, 158–59. See too the short biography of an Afghan soldier who died in Damascus (1753). He always went about town fully armed, even in the bathhouse. He knew Turkish, Kurdish, and "Afghani," but hardly spoke a word at all, except to spit

out occasional curses. The chronicler supplies no linguistic details; al-Budayri, *Hawadith*, 174. For an imperial representative who "swore horribly" at the son of a Damascene scholar who owed a debt to the state, see al-Muradi, *Silk*, 1:170.

36. Shihab, *Tarikh*, 70.

37. al-ʿAwra, *Tarikh*, 385. Shown treasonous correspondence within his clan, Zahir al-ʿUmar threw down the document and swore that he could no longer trust anyone; al-Sabbagh, *Tarikh*, 70. See too the interview (1715) in which an Egyptian officer contemptuously threw down a receipt, which he regarded as inadequate, for supplies that he was to purchase; al-Jabarti, *ʿAjaʾib*, 1:142.

38. Sannini, *Travels*, 69.

39. Russell, *Aleppo*, 1:224.

40. Townspeople might even use litigation itself as a means for drawing attention to their disputes and winning public sympathy; see Leslie Peirce, *Morality Tales: Law and Gender in the Ottoman Court of Aintab* (Berkeley: University of California Press, 2003), esp. chap. 6.

41. Enfi, *Tezkiret*, 121–26.

42. al-Muradi, *Silk*, 3:188–90. See also the biography of Muhammad Emin-i Tevfiki (d. 1880), an ecstatic Sufi who settled in Istanbul. He once struck a student in the middle of a ceremony when the latter's mind started to wander; Vassaf, *Sefine*, 4:479.

43. Ibn Abi'l-Diyaf, *Ithaf*, 7:50.

44. See for example James E. Baldwin, *Islamic Law and Empire in Ottoman Cairo* (Edinburgh: Edinburgh University Press, 2017), 131–32.

45. al-Jabarti, *ʿAjaʾib*, 2:303–4.

46. al-Damurdashi, *Chronicle*, 138–39.

47. See for example altercations in Cairo between servants that drew masters or even entire military units into clashes; al-Damurdashi, *Chronicle*, 382–84; al-Jabarti, *ʿAjaʾib*, 1:95–96. So familiar was this theme of the head of the household taking vengeance for an offense committed against a servant that other officers could use it as a ruse to murder rivals; see for example al-Damurdashi, *Chronicle*, 237, 271.

48. Oğulukyan, *Ruzname*, 40.

49. Shalabi, *Awdah*, 207.

50. al-Jabarti, *ʿAjaʾib*, 7:192. For other examples of elite women as knowledgeable and self-confident politicians, see Browne, *Travels*, 98–99; al-Damurdashi, *Chronicle*, 309; al-Jabarti, *ʿAjaʾib*, 2:12–13, 20; 6:152. On the role of women in holding and transmitting the property of military factions in Cairo, see Mary Ann Fay, "Women and Waqf: Property, Power, and the Domain of Gender in Eighteenth-Century Egypt," in *Women in the Ottoman Empire*, ed. Madeline Zilfi (Leiden: Brill, 1997), 27–47; Hathaway, *Politics of Households*, chap. 6. On the women of political households in Tunisia, see Amy Aisen Kallander, *Women, Gender, and the Palace Households in Ottoman Tunisia* (Austin: University of Texas Press, 2013), 38–44, 96–99.

51. al-Budayri, *Hawadith*, 58–59. See too the rough interrogations meted out to the wives of the Egyptian emirs who fled the Ottoman expedition in 1786; al-Jabarti, *ʿAjaʾib*, 3:345. For a concubine willing to turn on her own household and act as a spy, ibid., 1:333.

52. al-Jabarti, *ʿAjaʾib*, 4:71–72.

53. Cevdet, *Tarih*, 2:17–18.
54. Hill, *Account*, 17.
55. de Tott, *Memoirs*, 3:192.
56. al-Jabarti, *'Aja'ib*, 6:318.
57. Cabi, *Tarih*, 888.
58. al-Damurdashi, *Chronicle*, 347.
59. al-Halabi, *Hawadith*, 125.
60. al-Jabarti, *'Aja'ib*, 3:307. For another physical altercation, see the chief judge of Cairo who personally dragged (1711) a "Rumi" preacher to the governor's council. Inspired by Kadızadeli rhetoric, the preacher had been railing against the cult of saints and other religious practices, and had further goaded his audience with taunts against the ulama of Cairo; Shalabi, *Awdah*, 251–53.
61. Hasan Agha, *Tarikh*, 164.
62. al-Jabarti, *'Aja'ib*, 4:130–31.
63. Kuşmani and Ebubekir, *Asiler*, 122.
64. Hasan Agha, *Tarikh*, 110. For references to other reprisals, see Sabbanu, ed., *Hamlat*, 28–29.
65. al-Jabarti, *'Aja'ib*, 3:297–98.
66. al-Jabarti, *'Aja'ib*, 1:82. See too the parading of a forger, with half his beard shaved, in the streets of Cairo (1814); al-Jabarti, *'Aja'ib*, 7:291.
67. van Egmont, *Travels*, 1:223.
68. Ahmed Resmi, *Halifet*, 124.
69. For a description of the proceedings, see de Tott, *Memoirs*, 1:137–45; von Hammer, *Histoire*, 16:6–7.
70. For a description of the imperial boats, see de Tott, *Memoirs*, 1:247–48.
71. For secret clucking about the Persian ambassador, who visited the court at Edirne (1695) without a military band that could match Ottoman ceremony, see Özcan, ed., *Anonim*, 133.
72. See for example Özcan, ed., *Anonim*, 33–34; Karkukli, *Dawhat*, 23. For a detailed description (minus the elephants) of one "Indian" embassy (1787), see Taylesanizade, *İstanbul*, 221–22. On the gifting of elephants to the Ottoman court, see Alan Mikhail, *The Animal in Ottoman Egypt* (New York: Oxford University Press, 2014), chap. 5; Hedda Reindl-Kiel, "Dogs, Elephants, Lions, a Ram, and a Rhino on Diplomatic Mission: Animals as Gifts to the Ottoman Court," in *Animals and People in the Ottoman Empire*, ed. Suraiya Faroqhi (Istanbul: Eren, 2010), 279–80.
73. Von Hammer, *Histoire*, 15:65. For an earlier procession by the Crimean khan, see Özcan, ed., *Anonim*, 99, 104.
74. Carter Vaughn Findley, "Political Culture and the Great Households," in *The Cambridge History of Turkey*, Vol. 3, *The Later Ottoman Empire, 1603–1839*, ed. Suraiya Faroqhi (Cambridge: Cambridge University Press, 2006), 65–80.
75. See for example al-Damurdashi, *Chronicle*, 28, 33, 59, 79, 104, 125, 130, 135, 143, 148, 176, 201, 215, 227, 253, 277, 303, 307, 317, 322, 338, 342, 355, 361, 370, 374, 376, 379, 388; Shalabi, *Awdah*, 134–35; van Egmont, *Travels*, 2:142. For official entries into Damascus, which had its own elaborate ceremonies, see Hasan Agha, *Tarikh*, 11, 37, 49, 55, 65, 68, 113,

122, 134, 154, 161, 163; Ibn Kannan, *Yawmiyyat*, 144. For a description of Ahmed Paşa al-Jazzar's entry into Damascus (1785)—one of four terms that he would serve as governor there—see Philipp, *Acre*, 140.

76. On the respective protocol for governors and chief judges, see Ibn Kannan, *al-Mawakib al-islamiyya fi al-mamalik al-shamiyya*, ed. Hikmet Isma`il (Damascus: Wizarat al-Thaqafa, 1992), 2:65–66, 339–44, 349–50. For an overview, see James Grehan, "The Legend of the Samarmar: Parades and Communal Identity in Syrian Towns, 1500–1800," *Past and Present* 204 (2009): 89–125. On the ceremonial entry for governors of Aleppo, see Kamil al-Ghazzi, *Nahr al-dhahab fi tarikh Halab*, ed. Shawqi Sha`ath and Mahmud Fakhuri, 2nd ed. (Aleppo: Dar al-Qalam al-`Arabi, 1991), 1:249–50.

77. See respectively Karahasanoğlu, *Kadı*, 69, 72; Hannes Grandits, "Social Stratification and Change in Herzegovinian Urban Life in the Tanzimat Era," in *Urban Governance under the Ottomans: Between Cosmopolitanism and Conflict*, ed. Ulrike Freitag and Nora Lafi (New York: Routledge, 2014), 79–81. On the reception of governors at Bulgarian towns, where local "elders" (*memleket ihtiyarlar ve vilayet hacıları*) came out for the greeting, see Mehmed Haşim, *İma*, 189.

78. al-Jabarti, *`Aja'ib*, 1:155.

79. al-Muradi, *Silk*, 1:170.

80. Sabbanu ed., *Hamlat*, 68–69. For a grand entry of the British consul into Aleppo (1803), see John Barker, *Syria and Egypt under the Last Five Sultans of Turkey* (London: Samuel Tinsley, 1876), 1:62–64.

81. Hourani, "Ottoman Reform," 67.

82. al-Jabarti, *`Aja'ib*, 4:86. He was technically the mufti of the Shafi`i legal tradition, which the Ottoman state did not sponsor, and so working as an arbitrator may have been a natural alternative. For another scholar whose social ascent brought him a mule and retinue, see al-Jabarti, *`Aja'ib*, 7:86. The head of one Sufi order in Tunis, `Uthman al-Bakri (d. 1762), carried himself with an air of magnificence and always rode through the streets on a horse whose decorated saddle "was fit only for kings"; Ibn Abi'l-Diyaf, *Ithaf*, 7:68.

83. See for example Ibn Kannan, *Yawmiyat*, 117–18, 462. It was not a proclivity of Ottoman Sufis. Damascenes did not hide (1719) their amazement at the entourage of Muhammad al-Naqshbandi, a Sufi from Central Asia who was making the pilgrimage in the company of his "two hundred" retainers, including his personal prayer-leader and muezzin; Ibn Kannan, *Yawmiyat*, 311–12.

84. al-Jabarti, *`Aja'ib*, 7:247.

85. Karamah, *Hawadith*, 128.

86. al-Dimashqi, *Tarikh*, 118. He led a second procession through Dayr al-Qamr later that year; al-Dimasqhi, *Tarikh*, 121.

87. Munayyir, *al-Durr*, 138.

88. See for example Karamah, *Hawadith*, 148; Munayyir, *al-Durr*, 102.

89. One of the rare soldiers who took a relaxed approached to processions was the emir Hüseyin Bey Kişkiş Kazdağlı (d. 1768), who displayed such bonhomie that he openly preferred to joke and banter. When he was riding and had no one with whom he could make quips, he would turn to the grooms and servants and jest with them; al-Jabarti, *`Aja'ib*, 2:305.

90. Taylesanizade, İstanbul, 118.

91. Beydilli ed., İmamlar, 145–46. On the extra ritual sensitivities of this procession of the Janissaries' meat supply, see Cemal Kafadar, "Janissaries and Other Riffraff in Ottoman Istanbul: Rebels without a Cause?," in *Identity and Identity Formation in the Ottoman World: A Volume of Essays in Honor of Norman Itzkowitz*, ed. Baki Tezcan and Karl Barbir (Madison: University of Wisconsin Press, 2008), 131–32.

92. Ibn Kannan, *Yawmiyat*, 144.

93. Shihab, *Tarikh*, 41.

94. al-Damurdashi, *Chronicle*, 146.

95. al-Jabarti, *'Aja'ib*, 4:6–7.

96. Vraçali Sofroni, *Osmanlı'da Bir Papaz: Günahkâr Sofroni'nin Çileli Hayat Hikâyesi, 1739-1813*, trans. Aziz Nazmi Şakir-Taş (Istanbul: Kitap Yayınevi, 2003), 38.

97. al-Muradi, *Silk*, 1:39–41.

98. al-Jabarti, *'Aja'ib*, 3:311. See also al-Jabarti, *'Aja'ib*, 4:236. Some members of the religious establishment might take the point farther. They would not ride under any circumstances, even for long voyages. See for example al-Muradi, *Silk*, 2:77, 4:16.

99. Vassaf, *Sefine*, 4:113. For another Sufi who was relaxed about the protocol of his order, see Vassaf, *Sefine*, 2:66–7.

100. al-Jabarti, *'Aja'ib*, 4:4. For another scholar who took his own dough to the baker, in plain sight on top of his head, see al-Jabarti, *'Aja'ib*, 4:263. See too the biography of Muhammad al-Khalwati (d. 1793), an ascetic Sufi who never married and lived by himself in Cairo. He cooked his own food and washed his own laundry despite being blind. Without servant or slave, he presided over a courtyard full of sheep, chicken, geese, and ducks and somehow managed the menagerie alone. Neighbors whispered that he must be getting household help from genies (*jinn*); al-Jabarti, *'Aja'ib*, 4:234–35.

101. See for example al-Budayri, *Hawadith*, 192–93; al-Jabarti, *'Aja'ib*, 4:257–58.

102. See for example the enormous celebration that Mehmed IV staged over more than two weeks in Edirne (1674) for the circumcision of his two sons; Ahmed Badi, *Riyaz-ı Belde-i Edirne: 20. Yüzyıla Kadar Osmanlı Edirne'si*, ed. Niyazi Adıgüzel and Raşit Gündoğdu (Edirne: Trakya Üniversitesi Yayınları, 2014), 1:485–511. Soon afterward came a slightly longer wedding celebration for an Ottoman princess; ibid., 1:517–28.

103. See for example the governor of Egypt who held a circumcision ceremony (1696/97) for his two sons. They were joined in requisite fashion by "two hundred boys" from the city, each of whom received a packet of underpants, a belt, skullcap, and shawl, together with a gold coin placed in his mouth to keep him from crying; al-Damurdashi, *Chronicle*, 64–65; al-Jabarti, *'Aja'ib*, 1:261–62. For examples of festivities in Baghdad, see Karkukli, *Dawhat*, 24, 49, 293.

104. al-Budayri, *Hawadith*, 38–39. See also the extravagant wedding feast that a leading Sufi, Ibrahim al-Jabawi, would throw for his grandson (1747); al-Budayri, *Hawadith*, 103.

105. al-Jabarti, *'Aja'ib*, 3:126–27. By the late eighteenth century, European coaches had become fashionable. For a second marriage procession (1792) in which the bride sat concealed in "an unusual carriage of European manufacture," see al-Jabarti, *'Aja'ib*, 4:200. For other Egyptian officers who tried to outdo each other in ceremonial display, see al-Jabarti, *'Aja'ib*, 2:196–97, 3:126–27, 4:194, 7:59. See too the celebration that Ibrahim Paşa threw (1820) for the circumcision of his nephew; al-Jabarti, *'Aja'ib*, 7:467.

106. al-Jabarti, ʿAjaʾib, 6:206–12. See too the extravagant circumcision ceremony organized (1809) by ʿUmar Makram, the naqib al-ashraf in Cairo, for his grandson; al-Jabarti, ʿAjaʾib, 7:59.

107. For a detailed description of this protocol, see Mehmed Haşim, İma, 196–201; Wilkinson, Account, 46–47.

108. Cevdet, Tarih, 1:306–7; al-Jabarti, ʿAjaʾib, 3:120.

109. al-Jabarti, ʿAjaʾib, 6:217. European diplomats might have recourse to the same gesture. In the opening years of the nineteenth century, the British residents in Baghdad moved through the streets with a large escort of Indian soldiers and scattered coins to the curious crowd; Dina Rizk Khoury, "Violence and Spatial Politics between the Local and Imperial: Baghdad, 1778–1810," in *The Spaces of the Modern City: Imaginaries, Politics, and Everyday Life*, ed. Gyan Prakash and Kevin M. Kruse (Princeton: Princeton University Press, 2008), 201.

110. al-Jabarti, ʿAjaʾib, 7:112–13.

111. Cabi, Tarih, 753–55.

Chapter 6

1. Toward the end of the eighteenth century, more than four out of every five coffeehouse owners in Istanbul were affiliated with the Janissary corps; see Başaran, *Selim III*, 215. See also Kırlı, "Struggle," 114–23. Soldiers made up a disproportionate share of coffeehouse owners in many Ottoman towns. For Cairo, see Raymond, "Soldiers in Trade," 18; for Damascus, see Grehan, *Everyday Life*, 143–44; for Tunis, see Dalenda Larguèche, "Le café à Tunis du XVIIIe au XIXe siècle: Produit de commerce et espace de sociabilité," in *Le Commerce du café avant l'ère des plantations coloniales*, ed. Michel Tuchscherer (Cairo: Institut Français d'Archéologie Orientale, 2001), 186.

2. Şemdanizade, *Tevarih*, 2B:87–88.

3. İsmail Hakkı Uzunçarşılı, *Osmanlı Devleti Teşkilatından Kapukulu Ocakları* (Ankara: Türk Tarih Kurumu Basımevi, 1988), 1:613–15. For an overview of this transformation, see Tezcan, *Second Ottoman Empire*, 198–212.

4. Gülay Yılmaz Diko, "Blurred Boundaries between Soldiers and Civilians: Artisan Janissaries in Seventeenth-Century Istanbul," in *Bread from the Lion's Mouth: Artisans Struggling for a Livelihood in Ottoman Cities*, ed. Suraiya Faroqhi (New York: Berghahn Books, 2015), 175–93; Cemal Kafadar, "On the Purity and Corruption of the Janissaries," *Turkish Studies Association Bulletin* 15 (1991): 273–80; Yi, *Guild Dynamics*.

5. This extreme cost-cutting was not entirely an Ottoman peculiarity. In the Habsburg Empire, state finances were not much sounder. In the aftermath of the Napoleonic wars (c. 1815–30), anywhere from one-third to one-half of the Austrian army would typically go "on leave" and forfeit their pay; Alan Sked, *The Decline and Fall of the Habsburg Empire, 1815–1918* (London: Longman, 1989), 14.

6. d'Ohsson, *Tableau*, 7:297. For a cautious analysis of eighteenth-century estimates, see also Uzunçarşılı, *Kapukulu*, 1:618–20.

7. See for example the case of Cairo; Raymond, "Soldiers in Trade"; for Aleppo, see Charles Wilkins, *Forging Urban Solidarities: Ottoman Aleppo, 1640–1700* (Leiden: Brill, 2010), esp. chap. 3. On the expansion of military recruitment in Tunis, most notably under Hamuda Bey (r. 1782–1814), see Brown, *Ahmad Bey*, 63.

8. al-Jabarti, `Aja'ib, 1:104.

9. Khoury, *State and Provincial Society*, 133.

10. Rossitsa Gradeva, "War and Peace along the Danube: Vidin at the End of the Seventeenth Century," *Oriente Moderno* NS 20 (2001): 149–75. So extensive did Janissary networks become in the hinterland of Vidin along the southern banks of the Danube that many peasants had converted to Islam and joined the Janissary corps by the early eighteenth century; see Evgeni Raduschev, "'Peasant' Janissaries?" *Journal of Social History* 42 (2008): 447–70.

11. On the greater dependence on locally raised militias by the eighteenth century, see Virginia Aksan, "Whatever Happened to the Janissaries?: Mobilization for the 1768–1774 Russo-Ottoman War," *War and History* 5 (1998): 23–36; Virginia Aksan, "Ottoman Military Recruitment Strategies in the Late Eighteenth Century," in *Arming the State: Military Conscription in the Middle East and Central Asia, 1775–1925*, ed. Erik Zürcher (London: IB Tauris, 1999), 21–39; Mustafa Cezar, *Osmanlı Tarihinde Levendler* (Istanbul: Çelikcilt Matbaası, 1965), 317–43; Khoury, *State and Provincial Society*, chap. 3; Fatih Yeşil, *İhtilaller Çağında Osmanlı Ordusu: Osmanlı İmparatorluğu'nda Sosyoekonomik ve Sosyopolitik Değişim Üzerine Bir İnceleme (1793–1826)* (Istanbul: Tarih Vakfı Yurt Yayınları, 2016), chap. 1.

12. For a snapshot of overlapping networks of military recruitment (which might easily slide into banditry) in the Balkans at the turn of the nineteenth century, see Tolga Esmer, "Economies of Violence, Bandits and Ottoman Governance in the Ottoman Empire around 1800," *Past and Present* 224 (2014): 163–99. On the recruitment of Albanians, see Frederick Anscombe, "Albanians and 'Mountain Bandits,'" in *The Ottoman Balkans, 1750–1830*, ed. Frederick Anscombe (Princeton: Markus Wiener, 2006), 87–113. At the other end of the empire, the search for soldiers tended to turn to pastoral populations. On the regularization of bedouin recruitment by the governors of Baghdad during the eighteenth century, see Khoury, "Violence," 190–91. On recruitment to the Ottoman navy, in which Christian sailors had practically disappeared by the early nineteenth century, see İdris Bostan, *Osmanlı Bahriye Teşkilatı: XVII. Yüzyılda Tersane-i Amire* (Ankara: Türk Tarih Kurumu Basımevi, 1992), 181–244; Daniel Panzac, "The Manning of the Ottoman Navy in the Heyday of Sail (1660–1850)," in *Arming the State: Military Conscription in the Middle East and Central Asia, 1775–1925*, ed. Erik Zürcher (London: IB Tauris, 1999), 41–57.

13. See Virginia Aksan, "Mobilization of Warrior Populations in the Ottoman Context, 1750–1850," in *Fighting for a Living*, ed. Erik Jan Zürcher (Amsterdam: International Institute for Social History, 2013), 323–43.

14. Dick Douwes, *The Ottomans in Syria: A History of Justice and Oppression* (New York: IB Tauris, 2000), chap. 5; `Abd al-Karim Rafeq, "The Local Forces in Syria in the Seventeenth and Eighteenth Centuries," in *War, Technology, and Society in the Middle East*, ed. V.J. Parry and M.E. Yapp (London: Oxford University Press, 1975), 277–307. On the multi-ethnic military recruitment conducted by al-Jazzar and his successors at Acre, see Philipp, *Acre*, 136–53.

15. al-Jabarti, `Aja'ib, 6:129. On the wider practice of blood brotherhood in the Balkans, see Mary Edith Durham, *Some Tribal Origins, Laws, and Customs of the Balkans* (New York: Macmillan, 1929), 153–59.

16. al-Jabarti, `Aja'ib, 1:310.

17. This use of nicknames was prevalent in Mediterranean cultures. See Anton Blok, "Nicknames as Symbolic Subversions," in *Honor and Violence* (Cambridge: Polity, 2001), chap. 9.

18. Faik Reşit Unat, ed., *1730 Patrona İhtilalı Hakkında Bir Eser: Abdi Tarihi* (Ankara: Türk Tarih Kurumu, 2020), 22, 29, 37, 50, 64, 73–74, 77.

19. See respectively Cabi, *Tarih*, 249, 594–95. One of the executed Janissaries in the "Auspicious Event" that abolished the corps (1826) was Drunk Mustafa; Esad Efendi, *Tarih*, 645. On nicknames among the soldiers of Cairo, see Denon, *Travels*, 2:254. In Istanbul, popular stories were full of colorful Janissaries (and their equally colorful nicknames); see Reşad Ekrem Koçu, *İstanbul Tulumbacıları* (Istanbul: Ana Yayınevi, 1981), 38–53.

20. This tactic did not always work; see for example Cabi, *Tarih*, 485. See also Kafadar, "Janissaries," 118.

21. Es'ad Efendi, *Üss-i Zafer (Yeniçeriliğin Kaldırılmasına Dair)*, ed. Mehmet Arslan (Istanbul: Kitabevi, 2005), 95. See also Hakan Erdem, "Recruitment for the 'Victorious Soldiers of Muhammad' in the Arab Provinces, 1826–1828," in *Histories of the Modern Middle East: New Directions*, ed. Israel Gershoni, Hakan Erdem, and Ursula Woköck (London: Lynne Rienner, 2002), 194.

22. The author who recounted this scene, Es'ad Efendi, was a partisan of the Tanzimat program and no doubt wished to discredit the Janissaries as "deviant" Muslims. On the ideological tensions between reformers and their opponents, see Butrus Abu-Manneh, "The Naqshbandi-Mujaddadi and the Bektashi Orders in 1826," in *Studies on Islam and the Ottoman Empire in the 19th Century (1826-1876)* (Istanbul: Isis Press, 2001), 59–72. On Christian elements in Bektashi Sufism, see for example John Kingsley Birge, *The Bektashi Order of Dervishes* (London: Luzac, 1937); Irène Mélikoff, *Hadji Bektach, un mythe et ses avatars: Genèse et évolution du soufisme populaire en Turquie* (Leiden: Brill, 1998); Emil B.H. Saggau, "Marginalised Islam: Christianity's Role in the Sufi Order of Bektashism," in *Exploring the Multitude of Muslims in Europe: Essays in Honor of Jorgen S. Nielsen*, ed. Niels Valdemar Vinding et al. (Leiden: Brill, 2018), chap. 12.

23. al-Jabarti, *'Aja'ib*, 1:91–92.

24. Cevdet, *Tarih*, 9:228. For another case of a Janissary switching units, see Cevdet, *Tarih*, 11:27.

25. Boué, *Turquie*, 2:147; d'Ohsson, *Tableau*, 4:245; de Tott, *Memoirs*, 1:229.

26. On soldiers' violence in the streets of Istanbul, see Zarinebaf, *Crime*, 119–21.

27. Makriyannis, *Memoirs*, 43.

28. Tolga Uğur Esmer, "The Precarious Intimacy of Honor in Late Ottoman Accounts of Para-militarism and Banditry," *European Journal of Turkish Studies* 18 (2014): 1–18.

29. al-Budayri, *Hawadith*, 181.

30. al-Budayri, *Hawadith*, 144.

31. On the imperial Janissaries and al-'Amara, see Linda Schatkowski Schilcher, *Families in Politics: Damascene Factions and Estates of the 18th and 19th Centuries* (Stuttgart: Steiner Verlag Wiesbaden, 1985), esp. chap. 1; on the Midan and the local Janissaries, see Brigitte Marino, *Le faubourg du Midan à Damas à l'époque Ottomane: Espace urbaine, société, et habitat (1742-1830)* (France: Presses de l'Ipfo, 1997).

32. Bodman, *Factions*, 97–98; Bruce Masters, "Aleppo's Janissaries: Crime Syndicate

or *Vox Populi?*" in *Popular Protest and Political Participation in the Ottoman Empire*, ed. Eleni Gara, M. Erdem Kabadayı, and Christoph Neumann (Istanbul: Bilgi University Press, 2011), 160–62. For an overview of this turbulent period, see Marcus, *The Middle East*, 86–101.

33. For a decree that tried to abolish these rackets along the wharves of the capital (1808), see Cabi, *Tarih*, 244–45.

34. Cabi, *Tarih*, 902–3.

35. al-`Awra, *Tarikh*, 39–42.

36. d'Ohsson, *Tableau*, 7:303. See also Uzunçarşılı, *Kapukulu*, 290–305.

37. Cabi, *Tarih*, 367.

38. At least this is the mocking image that lurked in urban culture; see for example Kuşmani and Ebubekir, *Asiler*, 131.

39. Bodman, *Factions*, 63. On the same practice in Mosul, see Kemp, "Power and Knowledge," 206. On the general phenomenon of the "Janissary coffeehouse," see Ali Çaksu, "Janissary Coffee Houses in Late Eighteenth-Century Istanbul," in *Ottoman Tulips, Ottoman Coffee: Leisure and Lifestyle in the Eighteenth Century*, ed. Dana Sajdi (London: Tauris Academic Studies, 2007), 117–32.

40. On the absorption of rural migrants into the Janissary corps around the turn of the nineteenth century, see Kırlı, "Struggle," 123–28. By profession, porters were among the best represented: of 2,919 officially registered in Istanbul (1822), about 84 percent were Muslim; of the latter, about two-thirds belonged to the Janissary corps; Nejdet Ertuğ, *Osmanlı Döneminde İstanbul Hammalları* (Istanbul: Timaş Yayınları, 2008), 64–67.

41. Cabi, *Tarih*, 703.

42. Beydilli, ed., *İmamlar*, 197.

43. Cabi, *Tarih*, 594. One Ottoman cavalryman could proudly recount how he vanquished a Greek rebel in the Morea with a sword thrust; Kabudlu, *Tevarih*, 415; Kabudlı, "Adventures," 270.

44. de Tott, *Memoirs*, 3:9–10.

45. See for example Kabudlu, *Tevarih*, 311; Kabudlı, "Adventures," 226.

46. Dennis N. Skiotis, "Bandit to Pasha: First Steps in the Rise to Power of Ali of Tepelen, 1750–1784," *International Journal of Middle East Studies* 2 (1971): 228. On the participation of Souliote (i.e., of Albanian ethnicity) and Maniote women in battles against Ottoman troops during the Greek war of independence, see Helen Angelomatis-Tsougarakis, "Women in the Greek War of Independence," in *Networks of Power in Modern Greece: Essays in Honor of John Campbell*, ed. Mark Mazower (New York: Columbia University Press, 2008), 60–62.

47. Karkukli, *Dawhat*, 41.

48. al-Jabarti, `Aja'ib, 2:290. Amid street clashes between military factions in Cairo (1711), soldiers were amazed by the appearance of a woman from Upper Egypt who urged them on in the thick of the fray; al-Damurdashi, *Chronicle*, 160.

49. al-`Awra, *Tarikh*, 41.

50. Şemdanizade, *Tevarih*, IIA:16. For a riot in 1808, in which stick-wielding women gathered around the chief judge of Istanbul, see Oğulukyan, *Ruzname*, 22.

51. Asım Bezirci, *Türk Halk Şiiri: Tarihçesi, Kaynakları, Şairleri, ve Seçme Şiirleri* (Ankara: Say Yayınları, 1993), 1:315.

52. al-Jabarti, `Aja'ib, 6:346. For an earlier demonstration, swelled by large numbers of women (1804), see al-Jabarti, `Aja'ib, 6:128–29. On women participating in bread riots in Aleppo, see Russell, Aleppo, 1:294–95, 328.

53. al-Jabarti, `Aja'ib, 7:269.

54. Ibn Kannan, Yawmiyat, 238.

55. Ibn Kannan, Yawmiyat, 411–12.

56. al-Halabi, Hawadith, 136.

57. On the rural origins of the Janissary rank-and-file in Aleppo, see Bodman, *Factions*, 23, 63–64. Most were Kurds, Turkomans, or central Anatolians (Karamanlı). By the early nineteenth century, recruitment seems to have drawn more heavily on Albanians; ibid., 15. In nearby Ayntab, too, the Janissary garrison had admitted large numbers of rural recruits by the late eighteenth century; see Canbakal, "Preliminary Observations," 43–44, 46. On the presence of rural recruits (mainly Albanians) in eighteenth-century Salonica, see Eyal Ginio, "Migrants and Workers in an Ottoman Port: Ottoman Salonica in the Eighteenth Century," in *Outside In: On the Margins of the Modern Middle East*, ed. Eugene Rogan (London: IB Tauris, 2002), 136–37.

58. Sabbanu, ed., *Hamlat*, 48–49.

59. Burckhardt, *Travels*, 204; Volney, *Travels*, 2:18–19. For numerous references to guns in the hands of sixteenth-century Druze on Mt. Lebanon, see Abdul-Rahim Abu-Husayn, *The View from Istanbul: Lebanon and the Druze Emirate in the Ottoman Chancery Documents, 1546-1711* (London: Center for Lebanese Studies in association with IB Tauris, 2004). A Druze emir, pleased with John Lewis Burckhardt's Arabic, invited him (1812) to stay longer so that the two of them could hunt together. He meant it as a great compliment; Burckhardt, *Travels*, 205.

60. Shalabi, *Awdah*, 161.

61. Grehan, *Everyday Life*, 204–5.

62. Shalabi, *Awdah*, 374–75.

63. Cabi, *Tarih*, 698–99.

64. Arapyan, *Rusçuk Ayanı*, 22; Beydilli, ed., *İmamlar*, 113; Derin, ed., "Yayla İmamı," 257.

65. al-Jabarti, `Aja'ib, 7:266.

66. al-Halabi, *Hawadith*, 135–36.

67. Cabi, *Tarih*, 600. For another war of words turning into a brawl, see the exchange between two officials quarreling over wood; Cabi, *Tarih*, 892.

68. For other cases of soldiers using coarse or questionable language, see for example al-Dimashqi, *Tarikh*, 52; al-Muradi, *Silk*, 1:184. On the meeting between Ahmed Paşa al-Jazzar and the mufti of Damascus, Muhammad Khalil al-Muradi, which degenerated into "inappropriate words" (*mukalamat ghayr layiqa*), see Hasan Agha, *Tarikh*, 9–10.

69. Cabi, *Tarih*, 844.

70. `Ali Ibrahim Abu Zayd, *Tamthiliyat khayal al-zill* (Cairo: Dar al-Ma`arif, 1982); Metin And, *Karagöz: Turkish Shadow Theater* (Ankara: Dost Yayınları, 1975); Nizar Aswad, *Karakuz Bilad al-Sham* (Damascus: al-Warda al-Shamiyya, 1994); Georg Jacob, *Türklerde Karagöz*, trans. Orhan Şaik Gökyay (Istanbul: Bürhaneddin Basımevi, 1938); Cevdet Kudret, *Karagöz* (Ankara: Bilgi Yayınevi, 1968–70), 3 vols.; Azza Maaoui, "Karakouz et le culte de la negativité," in *Mélanges Professeur Robert Mantran*, ed. Abdeljelil Temimi

(Zaghouan: Publiquations du Centre d'Etudes et de Recherches Ottomanes, Morisques, de Documentation et d'Information, 1988), 153–59; Linda S. Myrsiades and Kostas Myrsiades, *Karagiozis: Culture and Comedy in Greek Puppet Theater* (Lexington: University Press of Kentucky, 1992); Faruq Sa'd, *Khayal al-zill al-'arabi* (Beirut: Sharikat al-Matbu'at, 1993); Nureddin Sevin, *Türk Gölge Oyunu* (Istanbul: Devlet Kitapları, 1968); Sabri Esat Siyavuşgil, *Karagöz: Its History, Its Characters, Its Mystic and Satiric Spirit* (Ankara: Saim Toraman Basımevi, 1955); Andreas Tietze, *The Turkish Shadow Theater and the Puppet Collection of the L.A. Mayer Memorial Foundation* (Berlin: Gebr. Mann Verlag, 1977).

71. For the argument that meddah fully emerged as a distinct form of entertainment around the beginning of the eighteenth century, see Zeynep Altok, "The 18th-Century 'Istanbul Tale,'" in *A Companion to Early Modern Istanbul*, ed. Shirine Hamadeh and Çiğdem Kafescioğlu (Leiden: Brill, 2022), 581–603.

72. Officials mostly bore this barbed humor as a kind of safety valve for popular disaffection. Only at extreme moments did they dare to clamp down. In Istanbul, setbacks along the Danube frontier (1809) prompted temporary censorship of meddah performances. See Cabi, *Tarih*, 562. The edict was repeated in 1810 and 1812; ibid., 687, 892. The same political satire appeared in Karagöz. See for example the Janissaries of Aleppo, who were subject to ridicule after setbacks on the Russian front (1768); Marcus, *The Middle East*, 235.

73. For a collection of eighteenth-century meddah stories, see Özdemir Nutku, *Meddahlık ve Meddah Hikayeleri* (Istanbul: Atatürk Kültür Merkezi Başkanlığı Yayınları, 1997).

74. On the indecent gestures and language in shadow puppet performances in Istanbul, see d'Ohsson, *Tableau*, 4:255. For snapshots of puppet plays and meddah storytelling, see for example Allom, *Constantinople*, 1:60–61; 2:72–73; van Egmont, *Travels*, 2:142; Russell, *Aleppo*, 1:147–48; Robert Walsh, *A Residence at Constantinople* (London: Frederick Westley and A.H. Davis, 1836), 2:240. For an overview of the evidence, see Daryo Mizrahi, "Language and Sexuality in Ottoman Shadow-Puppet Performances," in *Celebration, Entertainment, and Theater in the Ottoman World*, ed. Suraiya Faroqhi and Arzu Öztürkmen (London: Seagull, 2014), 275–92; Dror Ze'evi, *Producing Desire: Changing Sexual Discourse in the Ottoman Middle East, 1500–1900* (Berkeley: University of California Press, 2006), 127–34.

75. Peter Burke, *Popular Culture in Early Modern Europe* (New York: Harper & Row, 1978), esp. chap. 9.

76. Van Egmont, *Travels*, 2:82. On dancing in Egypt, see also Denon, *Travels*, 1:232; Maillet, *Description*, 2:224–25. For scenes from Izmir, see Dumont, *New Voyage*, 284–85.

77. The search for dancers took place through informal channels. See for example the inquiries put out by a servant in Cairo (1799) who was trying to procure dancers for his neighborhood coffeehouse; al-Jabarti, *'Aja'ib*, 5:27. On the educated female dancers ('alma), whose status would progressively fall during the nineteenth century, see Karin van Nieuwkerk, *"A Trade Like Any Other": Female Singers and Dancers in Egypt* (Austin: University of Texas Press, 1995), chap. 2.

78. al-Jabarti, *'Aja'ib*, 7:78. For another depiction of male dancing, see Denon, *Travels*, 1:205. For a general discussion of these cross-dressing dancers, see Çiğdem Kılıç, "Men Acting as Women: The Zenne in Nineteenth-Century Popular Theater," in *Celebration, Entertainment, and Theater in the Ottoman World*, ed. Suraiya Faroqhi and Arzu Öztürkmen (London: Seagull, 2014), 303–18.

79. Kuşmani and Ebubekir, *Asiler*, 104. See too the tense exchange between Zahir al-ʿUmar and Osman Paşa after the Battle of Lake Hula (1771), in which the latter's forces were routed. Zahir taunted the defeated governor as a "traitor" and "dog"; al-Sabbagh, *Tarikh*, 107.

80. Mark Mazower, "Villagers, Notables, and Imperial Collapse: The Virgin Mary on Tinos in the 1820s," in *Networks of Power in Modern Greece: Essays in Honor of John Campbell* (New York: Columbia University Press, 2008), 78. "Dog" was a particular favorite of the Damascene soldier Ibn al-Siddiq; see Ibn al-Siddiq, *Ghara'ib*, 22, 26, 34, 40–41, 54, 63, 70, 76–77, 85, 87–88, 96.

81. Oğulukyan, *Ruzname*, 11–12. See also Ibn al-Siddiq, *Ghara'ib*, 30–31, 42, 99.

82. See for example Karal, *Selim III'ün*, 179, 182. See also Ibn al-Siddiq, *Ghara'ib*, 18, 73.

83. Dana Osborne, "Maledictive Language: Cursing and Swearing," in *International Encyclopedia of Linguistic Anthropology*, ed. James Stanlaw (Hoboken: Wiley-Blackwell, 2021), 1286–93; Karyn Stapleton, "Swearing," in *Interpersonal Pragmatics*, ed. Miriam A. Locher and Sage L. Graham (New York: de Gruyter Mouton, 2010), 289–305. For an analysis of this usage in European languages, see Jack Hoeksema, "Taboo Terms and Their Grammar," in *The Oxford Handbook of Taboo Words and Language*, ed. Keith Allan (New York: Oxford University Press, 2019), 161–64.

84. James Grehan, "The Mysterious Power of Words: Language, Law, and Culture in Ottoman Damascus (17th–18th Centuries)," *Journal of Social History* 37 (2004): 1003–6.

85. Judith Tucker, *In the House of the Law: Gender and Islamic Law in Ottoman Syria and Palestine* (Berkeley: University of California Press, 1998), 101–8, 181–82.

86. d'Ohsson, *Tableau*, 4:244–45. For lavish abuse of "infidels" and "heretics," see too Boué, *Turquie*, 2:146; Ibn al-Siddiq, *Ghara'ib*, 20, 22, 26, 30–31, 35–36, 39, 42, 57–59, 85, 87–89.

87. d'Ohsson, *Tableau*, 4:244; Boué, *Turquie*, 2:146. For this particular curse in actual use, see Karahasanoğlu, *Kadı*, 192.

88. ("Aman effendi, bok yeme, anafor vakti değil, akındıya girüb İstanbul yolunu tutmazsak ardımızdan berren ve bahren taʿkib eden tabyalar neferatı elbette şimdi çatarlar ve can-ı azizine sıçarlar..."); Kuşmani and Ebubekir, *Asiler*, 113–14. For soldiers insulting an enemy as "shit moustache" (*bok bıyık*), see Karahasanoğlu, *Kadı*, 192.

89. Khoury, *State and Provincial Society*, 136. For similar language in Konya (1736), during an altercation in which a *seyyid* struck and insulted a scholar, see Nil Tekgül, *Emotions in the Ottoman Empire: Politics, Society, and Family in the Early Modern Era* (New York: Bloomsbury Academic, 2023), 102.

90. Mishaqa, *Murder*, 104.

91. See for example the group of Janissaries who got into an argument (1815) with staff at the Yedikule slaughterhouse in Istanbul. They swore so profusely that the butcher's guild complained to the palace, which warned the head of the Janissaries (Yeniçeri Ağası) to arrest the offending members and punish them. Their lavish abuse had inadvertently set off a political crisis. Two suspects fled; two others were imprisoned. As the news spread, "several hundred" Janissaries gathered in the streets. Their protest would culminate in their capture and execution of the head of the corps. Beydilli, ed., *İmamlar*, 169–70.

92. al-Damurdashi, *Chronicle*, 362.

93. ("Behey boklar! Ne kaçıyorsunuz, meğer karga derneği imişsiniz!"); Kuşmani and Ebubekir, *Asiler*, 118.

94. Makariyannis, *Memoirs*, 86.
95. Kabudlu, *Tevarih*, 421; Kabudlı, "Adventures," 273.
96. al-Damurdashi, *Chronicle*, 284.
97. al-Damurdashi, *Chronicle*, 290.
98. See for example the biography of Islam Rais (d. 1822), leader of the Tunisian fleet. He was an imposing figure, brave and generous, pious and decent, courageous and daring. As contemporaries also noted, he was "severe" in upholding his honor; Ibn Abi'l-Diyaf, *Ithaf*, 7:128.
99. al-Budayri, *Hawadith*, 62, 66.
100. Ibn al-Siddiq, *Ghara'ib*, 89. For other references to this emasculating language of tears, see ibid., 20, 26, 34, 63, 100.
101. See for example al-'Awra, *Tarikh*, 388; al-Damurdashi, *Chronicle*, 158; Ibn Kannan, *Yawmiyat*, 127; al-Jabarti, *'Aja'ib*, 1:122.
102. ("Arsız namussuz bir zampara pezevengin oğlu olarak dünyaya gelmişti"); Kuşmani and Ebubekir, *Asiler*, 104. For an example of "catamite" (*puşt*) being used as an insult, see Derin ed., "Yayla İmamı," 224-25.
103. A brawl was ignited when the guards roughed up their prisoner, who, as it turned out, belonged to the same Janissary unit as the steward of the stable; Cabi, *Tarih*, 686-87.
104. For a discussion of this imagery, see Khaled el-Rouayheb, *Before Homosexuality in the Arab-Islamic World, 1500-1800* (Chicago: University of Chicago Press, 2005), chap. 1. It was almost certainly an extension of derogatory language that had been used since Roman antiquity; see Melissa Mohr, *Holy Shit: A Brief History of Swearing* (New York: Oxford University Press, 2013), chap. 1. For a different argument about an Ottoman "subculture" of homosexuality, in which the link between masculinity and domination was not so straightforward, see Delice, "Janissaries," 132-33.
105. "*Ninesini sikdiğim kafir*"; Cabi, *Tarih*, 665. For another instance of Janissary cursing, see Cabi, *Tarih*, 700-701.
106. "*Yeniçeriler avratlarını sikdi mi?*"; Cabi, *Tarih*, 486-87.
107. ("Aman gardaş, gavurun gulamparesine göt dayanamıyor!"); Kuşmani and Ebubekir, *Asiler*, 100.
108. Makriyannis, *Memoirs*, 21.
109. On verbal taunts against the honor of women in Europe, see for example Peter Burke, *The Historical Anthropology of Early Modern Italy: Essays on Perception and Communication* (Cambridge: Cambridge University Press, 1987), chap. 8; David Garrioch, "Verbal Insults in Eighteenth-Century Paris," in *The Social History of Language*, ed. Peter Burke and Roy Porter (Cambridge: Cambridge University Press, 1987), chap. 5.
110. Cabi, *Tarih*, 677.
111. Anton Blok, "The Meaning of 'Senseless' Violence," in *Honor and Violence*, chap. 6.
112. On the essentially "tribal" nature of feuding, see Jacob Black-Michaud, *Cohesive Force: Feud in the Mediterranean and the Middle East* (New York: St. Martin's Press, 1975), 38-54. For a definition embedded in notions of kinship, see J.K. Campbell, "The Kindred in a Greek Mountain Community," in *Mediterranean Countrymen*, ed. Julian Pitt-Rivers (Paris: Mouton, 1963), 73-96.
113. al-Halabi, *Hawadith*, 284-87, 292-94. See too the attack on the coffeehouse controlled by "Kurdish" mercenaries in Damascus (1750), who had become embroiled in a

blood feud with "Baghdadi" and "Mosuli" mercenaries backed up by imperial Janissaries; al-Budayri, *Hawadith*, 148.

114. Cabi, *Tarih*, 379. For an earlier raid (1786), in which one unit of Janissaries seized the coffeehouses of another, see Taylesanizade, *İstanbul*, 125.

115. Cabi, *Tarih*, 469-71. See also Beydilli, ed., *İmamlar*, 120; Oğulukyan, *Ruzname*, 53-54.

116. Cabi, *Tarih*, 728.

117. Cabi, *Tarih*, 729-30; Beydilli, ed., *İmamlar*, 141.

118. On the difference between feuding and raiding, see Christopher Boehm, *Blood Revenge: The Anthropology of Feuding in Montenegro and Other Tribal Societies* (Lawrence: University of Kansas Press, 1984), 194.

119. For anthropological perspectives on honor in Mediterranean society, see David D. Gilmore, ed., *Honor and Shame and the Unity of the Mediterranean* (Washington, DC: American Anthropological Association, 1987); J.G. Peristiany, ed., *Honor and Shame: The Values of Mediterranean Society* (Chicago: University of Chicago Press, 1966).

120. On the importance of having an "audience" for such bravura, see Michael Herzfeld, *The Poetics of Manhood: Contest and Identity in a Cretan Mountain Village* (Princeton: Princeton University Press, 1985), 80-81.

121. On the "rules" of feuding and raiding in the early nineteenth-century Balkans, see Boué, *Turquie*, 2:522-34; Durham, *Some Tribal Origins*, 162-71. For anthropological studies of feuding in the Balkans and Middle East, see for example Black-Michaud, *Cohesive Force*; Boehm, *Blood Revenge*; Eugene Hammel, *Alternative Social Structures and Ritual Relations in the Balkans* (Englewood Cliffs, NJ: Prentice-Hall, 1968); J.M.L. Hardy, *Blood Feuds and the Payment of Blood Money in the Middle East* (Leiden: Brill, 1963); Hasluck, *The Unwritten Law*; Zdenko Zlatar, *Njegoš's Montenegro: Epic Poetry, Blood Feud and Warfare in a Tribal Zone, 1830-1851* (Boulder, CO: East European Monographs, 2005).

122. On the placing of axes in Istanbul, see Esad Efendi, *Üss*, 114-15.

123. al-Jabarti, *'Aja'ib*, 1:138-39.

124. For a narrative of these events, see Şanizade, *Tarih*, 1:122-38. For a close analysis of this uprising, see Yaycıoğlu, *Partners*, chaps. 4-5; Yıldız, *Crisis and Rebellion*.

125. Kuşmani and Ebubekir, *Asiler*, 117; Beydilli, ed., *İmamlar*, 173, 177; Oğulukyan, *Ruzname*, 9.

126. The act evokes the threat, commonly uttered among feuding Greeks, that "I shall drink your blood!" They believed that in killing a foe in a blood feud, they appropriated their victim's strength, which flowed in the blood. See J.K. Campbell, *Honor, Family, and Patronage: A Study of Institutions and Moral Values in a Greek Mountain Community* (Oxford: Oxford University Press, 1964), 193-94. On literal blood-drinking in the Balkans, see Durham, *Some Tribal Origins*, 159-62.

127. Derin ed., "Yayla İmamı," 228. See also Aysel Yıldız, "The Anatomy of a Rebellious Social Group: The Yamaks of the Bosphorus at the Margins of Ottoman Society," in *Political Initiatives "From the Bottom Up" in the Ottoman Empire*, ed. Antonis Anastasopoulos (Rethymno: Crete University Press, 2012), 321. For other episodes in which soldiers took cannibalistic revenge on enemies, see for example Ibn Abi'l-Diyaf, *Ithaf*, 2:73-74, 123-24.

128. In early modern Europe, spectators at the execution of officials and even rulers often sought to daub the blood or carry away bits of the body as souvenirs or folk medical

cures. See for example Richard J. Evans, *Rituals of Retribution: Capital Punishment in Germany, 1600-1987* (Oxford: Oxford University Press, 1996), 90-98; V.A.C. Gatrell, *The Hanging Tree: Execution and the English People, 1770-1868* (Oxford: Oxford University Press, 1994), 81; Mabel Peacock, "Executed Criminals and Folk-Medicine," *Folklore* 7 (1896): 268-83.

129. For seventeenth-century examples of this abuse directed toward decapitated heads, see Günhan Börekçi, "Factions and Favorites at the Courts of Sultan Amhed I (r. 1603-17) and His Immediate Predecessors" (PhD diss., Ohio State University, 2010), 190-95. One of the most famous episodes was the butchering of the corpse of Hezarpare Ahmed Paşa, the grand vizier whose execution the Janissaries demanded during the fall of sultan Ibrahim (1648). They sliced it into "a thousand pieces" (*hezarpare*) at Atmeydanı (the Hippodrome) and sold the fat as a cure for "aches" (*sızı*); Ayvansarayı, *Garden*, 2:444; Evliya Çelebi, *Seyahatname*, 2:248; Naima, *Tarih*, 4:306-15. See too the fate of Esperanza Malchi, a Jewish confidante of the Queen Mother, whom Janissaries hacked to death (1600) before leaving pieces of her corpse in Atmeydanı for the dogs to devour; Naima, *Tarih*, 1:230-31.

130. Gülay Yılmaz, "Urban Protests, Rebellions, and Revolts," in *A Companion to Early Modern Istanbul*, ed. Shirine Hamadeh and Çiğdem Kafescioğlu (Leiden: Brill, 2022), 571.

131. Oğulukyan, *Ruzname*, 13; Yıldız, "Anatomy," 321.

132. Beydilli, ed., *İmamlar*, 173-74. See also Kuşmani and Ebubekir, *Asiler*, 121-22.

133. Beydilli, ed., *İmamlar*, 112-13; Derin, ed., "Yayla İmamı," 260. A second version of this grisly retribution varies only in a few details. Recalling earlier humiliations of fallen officials, the rebels compelled Christians to pull the body through the streets. Having hung the body upside down, they beat it with sticks, lit "filth" as mock incense before it, and took turns bowing before it; Arapyan, *Rusçuk Ayanı*, 19-20. A very similar spectacle had played out during a revolt by the town of Ayntab against their governor in 1788. The pasha's corpse was beheaded; his body was left overnight to the dogs before being buried. Townspeople reserved their greatest ferocity for the corpse of his lieutenant. Having cut off his head, they smeared the beard with excrement. They then took the body and impaled it with a long stick from the anus. See Mehmet Bayrak, *Eşkıyalık ve Eşkıya Türküleri: İnceleme, Antoloji* (Ankara: Yorum Yayınevi, 1985), 27-35; cit., Canbakal, "Preliminary Observations," 33.

134. Destari Salih, *Destari Salih Tarihi: Patrona Halil Ayaklanması Hakkında Bir Kaynak*, ed. Bekir Sıtkı Baykal (Ankara: Türk Tarih Kurumu Basımevi, 1962), 19-20; Unat, ed., *Abdi Tarihi*, 52-53. The inspiration for placing candles in the eye sockets may have come from earlier penal ceremonies in which condemned men had candles inserted into their backs and buttocks before they were paraded through the streets and executed; Wishnitzer, *As Night Falls*, 212-23. This ceremonial "sticking of candles" insinuated itself into the street slang of Istanbul: *"mum yapıştırmak"*; Mehmet Halit Bayri, *İstanbul Argosu ve Halk Tabirleri* (Istanbul: Burhaneddin Matbaası, 1934), 144.

135. al-Budayri, *Hawadith*, 74-75; al-Muradi, *Silk*, 3:287. For another scene of a pitiless execution of a rival, set during one of the frequent feuds among the military barracks of Egypt, see al-Damurdashi, *Chronicle*, 273. A bey listened (1727/28) to his prisoner, a fellow military commander, beg for his life and offer all his properties and tax-farms as surety. The bey had heard enough. "Smack him in the mouth!" he ordered. His men understood what he wanted. The prisoner was beaten, stripped, and led away to an ignominious public beheading.

136. Kuşmani and Ebubekir, *Asiler*, 120–21; Oğulukyan, *Ruzname*, 13. See too the posthumous humiliation of Feyzullah Efendi, the *şeyhülislam* who was murdered in the so-called Edirne Event (1703). Soldiers had "monks" drag his corpse in front of the army; Özcan, ed., *Anonim*, 253. One variation of this ritual humiliation was to have a condemned official paraded through the markets by Christians and/or Jews before execution. This was the fate of the lieutenant (*kethüda*) of Nevşehirli Damad İbrahim Paşa, grand vizier (1718–30) to Ahmed III, who was brought down in the Patrona Halil uprising; Destari, *Tarih*, 20.

137. Vazih, *Amasya*, 78–79.

138. Taylesanizade, *İstanbul*, 184–85. On the factional rivalry between religious students and Janissaries in Istanbul, see Nalan Turna, "The Everyday Life of Istanbul and Its Artisans, 1808–1839" (unpublished PhD diss., SUNY-Binghamton, 2006), 64–67.

139. See for example Beydilli, *İmamlar*, 118; al-Jabarti, *'Aja'ib*, 7:228. If not displayed from gates or ramparts, the heads of the executed might be placed either on an arm of the body, or as a mark of dishonor, on the buttocks; see de Tott, *Memoirs*, 1:231–32. Trying (unsuccessfully) to placate the Janissaries during the Kabakçı Mustafa uprising (1807), Selim III sent the head of an executed official to Etmeydanı, where the rebels put it on a pike; Oğulukyan, *Ruzname*, 9.

140. Halil Nuri Bey, *Nuri Tarihi*, ed. Seydi Vakkas Toprak (Ankara: Türk Tarih Kurumu, 2015), 733. For the heads of Albanian bandits being sent to Istanbul (1785), see Cevdet, *Tarih*, 3:123. The display of bandits' heads would continue into the early twentieth century. See for example Sabri Yetkin, *Ege'de Eşkiyalar* (Istanbul: Tarih Vakfı Yurt Yayınları, 1997). For the case of a posthumous beheading (1800), with an order to send the skull to Istanbul, see Hakan Kırımcı and Ali Yaycıoğlu, "Heirs of Chingis Khan in the Age of Revolutions: An Unruly Crimean Prince in the Ottoman Empire and Beyond," *Der Islam* 94 (2017): 513–54. Bandits, too, collected the same trophies as the Ottoman soldiers hunting them; see Esmer, "Economies of Violence," 191–93.

141. Simon Harrison, *Dark Trophies: Hunting and the Enemy Body in Modern War* (New York: Berghahn Books, 2012), chaps. 2–4; Andrew Lipman, "'A Meanes to Knitt Them Togeather': The Exchange of Body Parts in the Pequot War," *William and Mary Quarterly* 65 (2008): 3–28; Patricia Palmer, *The Severed Head and the Grafted Tongue: Literature, Translation, and Violence in Early Modern Ireland* (Cambridge: Cambridge University Press, 2014), chap. 1.

142. Gazzizade, *Baba Paşa*, 172. For other references to heads and ears being collected as trophies, see for example Beydilli, *İmamlar*, 118–19; Esad Efendi, *Tarih*, 86, 364–65; Kabudlu, *Tevarih*, 304, 391; Kabudlı, "Adventures," 223, 261; Taylesanizade, *İstanbul*, 258; Wittman, *Travels*, 302.

143. See for example Theodoros Kolokotrones, *Memoirs from the Greek War of Independence, 1821–1833*, trans. George J. Koutris (Chicago: Argonaut, 1969), 241; Makriyannis, *Memoirs*, 128; Mazower, "Villagers," 73. On the same practices in the Balkans, see Durham, *Some Tribal Origins*, 172–79.

144. al-Damurdashi, *Chronicle*, 217.

145. al-Jabarti, *'Aja'ib*, 2:285.

146. al-Jabarti, *'Aja'ib*, 6:356.

147. See for example al-Jabarti, ʾAjaʾib, 2:334; 3:168, 192–93. On sacks of heads being placed in public view, see for example al-Jabarti, ʾAjaʾib, 1:248–49, 2:196.

148. al-Jabarti, ʾAjaʾib, 5:81. By way of comparison, note the treatment that one governor meted out to a military commander (1788). After receiving the officer with hospitality, he had his retinue murder and decapitate him. They threw the head through a window to a crowd waiting below; al-Jabarti, ʾAjaʾib, 4:74. For another reference to a defenestrated head, see al-Jabarti, ʾAjaʾib, 1:257.

149. See for example al-Jabarti, ʾAjaʾib, 4:321, 5:3.

150. See for example William Beik, "The Violence of the French Crowd: From Charivari to Revolution," *Past and Present* 197 (2007): 75–110.

151. Durham, *Some Tribal Origins*, 173–74.

152. al-Halabi, *Hawadith*, 138.

153. Munayyir, *al-Durr*, 23.

154. Cabi, *Tarih*, 179–80; Cevdet, *Tarih*, 8: 283–84. See also Beydilli, ed., *İmamlar*, 179.

155. al-Damurdashi, *Chronicle*, 195.

156. Bodman, *Factions*, 118–19; Masters, "Aleppo's Janissaries," 162–65; al-Tabbakh, *Iʿlam*, 3:299–300.

157. Ibn Kannan, *Yawmiyat*, 509–10. For other episodes of soldiers firing from minarets in Damascus, see al-Dimashqi, *Tarikh*, 52; Sabbanu, ed., *Hamlat*, 30.

158. al-Halabi, *Hawadith*, 136–38. For soldiers firing from minarets during the disturbances of 1778 in Baghdad, see Khoury, "Violence," 196.

159. Karamah, *Hawadith*, 54.

160. On the cult of the Virgin Mary on Mt. Lebanon, see Joseph Goudard and Henri Jalabert, *La Sainte Vierge au Liban*, 2nd ed. (Beirut: Impr. Catholique, 1955). On the common sharing of religious sites in Syria, see James Grehan, *Twilight of the Saints: Everyday Religion in Ottoman Syria and Palestine* (New York: Oxford University Press, 2014); for Anatolia and the Balkans, see Frederick William Hasluck, *Christianity and Islam under the Sultans*, 2 vols. (Oxford: Clarendon Press, 1929).

161. Hasan Agha, *Tarikh*, 110. For references to other reprisals, see Sabbanu, ed., *Hamlat*, 28–29.

162. Kolokotrones, *Memoirs*, 293.

163. See for example the reaction of Istanbulites to the arrival of Alemdar Mustafa Paşa's Balkan militia; Yaycıoğlu, *Partners*, 190; Aysel Yıldız, "A City under Fire: Urban Violence in Istanbul during the Alemdar Incident (1808)," in *Urban Governance under the Ottomans: Between Cosmopolitanism and Conflict*, ed. Ulrike Freitag and Nora Lafi (New York: Routledge, 2014), 38. On the Anatolian origins of most Janissaries in Istanbul, see Mehmet Mert Sunar, "'When Grocers, Porters, and Riff-Raff Become Soldiers': Janissary Artisans and Laborers in Nineteenth-Century Istanbul and Edirne," *Kocaeli Üniversitesi Sosyal Bilimler Enstitüsü* 17 (2009): 189–90.

Conclusion

1. al-Jabarti, ʾAjaʾib, 4:113. See too the disparaging depiction of Mehmed Ali's troops (1815); al-Jabarti, ʾAjaʾib, 7:313.

2. Taylesanizade, *İstanbul*, 282–83. For a similar reaction to Janissary brawling in

1812, see Şanizade, *Tarih*, 2:76–78. For the same language about "respectable people" reacting with unease to political disorder in late eighteenth-century Aleppo, see al-Halabi, *Hawadith*, 105–6, 130–31.

3. On European soldiers' low opinion of Ottoman military discipline and organization, see for example de Tott, *Memoirs*, 3:20–24; Wittman, *Travels*, 303. In Aleppo, European consuls watched (1811) as a mobilization of Janissaries failed before their eyes. Having received an order to muster three to four thousand men, Janissaries could only manage to assemble some nine hundred, most of whom soon slipped back home; Bodman, *Factions*, 67.

4. Dihkanizade Ubeydullah Kuşmani, *Nizam-ı Cedide Bir Risale: Zebire-i Kuşmani fi Ta'rif-i Nizam-ı Ilhami*, ed. Ömer İşbilir (Ankara: Türk Tarih Kurumu, 2006), 34; Kuşmani and Ebubekir, *Asiler*, 135–45; Kemal Beydilli and İlhan Şahin, eds., *Mahmud Raif Efendi ve Nizam-ı Cedid'e Dair Eseri* (Ankara: Türk Tarih Kurumu, 2001), 63. For the quote from the memorandum (*layiha*) proposing the New Order, see Nuri, *Tarih*, 197. For other praise of the "organization" (*tertib*) imposed by the New Order, see also Gazzizade, *Baba Paşa*, 122. On the general impression of disorder, see too the cutting judgment of al-Jabarti as he watched the departure of the pilgrimage caravan (1814) with its armed escort. It seemed to his eyes more ragged and disorganized than in the past; al-Jabarti, `Aja'ib, 7:289–90.

5. See for example al-Halabi, *Hawadith*, 74–75, 99–100, 116–17, 192.

6. Osman Paşa ordered (1781) troops to be quartered in the homes around the governor's mansion; al-Halabi, *Hawadith*, 118–19. In an earlier expedition against Kilis, the governor sacked the town and quartered troops in local homes; al-Halabi, *Hawadith*, 110–12. Fears about quartering predated these incidents. Notables in Aleppo had arranged a payment (1772) to a detachment of Janissaries so that they would not be quartered inside the city; Bodman, *Factions*, 38.

7. Robert W. Zens, "In the Name of the Sultan: Haci Mustafa Pasha of Belgrade and Ottoman Provincial Rule in the Late 18th Century," *International Journal of Middle East Studies* 44 (2012): 129–46; Robert W. Zens, "Pasvanoglu Osman Pasha and the Pashalik of Belgrade, 1791–1807," *International Journal of Turkish Studies* 8 (2002): 88–114.

8. Virginia Aksan, "The Ottoman Military and State Transformation in a Globalizing World," *Comparative Studies of South Asia, Africa, and the Middle East* 27 (2007): 266; Khaled Fahmy, *All the Pasha's Men: Mehmed Ali, His Army, and the Making of Modern Egypt* (Cairo: American University in Cairo Press, 1997), 85–86.

9. See for example Beydilli, ed., *İmamlar*, 123; Cevdet, *Tarih*, 9:228; Derin, ed., "Yayla İmamı," 270.

10. Cabi, *Tarih*, 570.

11. Cabi, *Tarih*, 628. On a blaze set in 1831 by "discontented adherents of the Janissaries," who by that point had been outlawed, see Allom, *Constantinople*, 2:61. On persistent rumors of Janissary involvement in arson, see Wishnitzer, *As Night Falls*, 213–14.

12. Cabi, *Tarih*, 836–37.

13. Cevdet, *Tarih*, 11:27; Şanizade, *Tarih*, 3:50–52.

14. al-Jabarti, `Aja'ib, 4:77–78.

15. al-Jabarti, `Aja'ib, 7: 314–15. For complaints about the same violations the next year, see al-Jabarti, `Aja'ib, 7:288.

16. Hasan Agha, *Tarikh*, 62.

17. See for example a decree (1796) calling for the expulsion of any resident who lacked a guarantor (*kefil*); Nuri, *Tarih*, 351–52. See also Başaran, *Selim III*, 36–38, 107–10, 161–67; Nalan Turna, "Pandemonium and Order: Suretyship, Surveillance, and Taxation in Early Nineteenth-Century Istanbul," *New Perspectives on Turkey* 39 (2008): 167–89. On chain migration into Istanbul, see Başaran, *Selim III*, 141, 143–46; Behar, *Neighborhood*, 98–103, 114–20; Nina Ergin, "The Albanian *Tellak* Connection: Labor Migration to the Hamams of Eighteenth-Century Istanbul Based on the 1752 *İstanbul Hamamları Defteri*," *Turcica* 43 (2012): 231–56; Suraiya Faroqhi, "Migration into Eighteenth-Century 'Greater Istanbul' as Reflected in the Kadı Registers of Eyüp," in *Stories of Ottoman Men and Women* (Istanbul: Eren, 2002), 289–305.

18. On the population estimate, see Çokuğraş, *Bekar Odaları*, 106.

19. On "bachelor rooms" and other accommodations for workers, see Başaran, *Selim III*, 35–37, 106–7, 113–16, 133–35; Çokuğraş, *Bekar Odaları*, 69–90; Zarinebaf, *Crime*, 40–41. One official from the late seventeenth century put the total number of bachelor rooms at around twelve thousand; Shirine Hamadeh, "Invisible City: Istanbul's Migrants and the Politics of Space," *Eighteenth-Century Studies* 50 (2017): 176.

20. Cabi, *Tarih*, 196, 761–62; Beydilli, ed., *İmamlar*, 144; Şanizade, *Tarih*, 2:51–52. See also Shirine Hamadeh, "Mean Streets: Space and Moral Order in Early Modern Istanbul," *Turcica* 44 (2013): 259–64.

21. Şanizade, *Tarih*, 2:151.

22. The quarrels were not entirely new or confined to Istanbul. See for example the deadly brawl among troops attached to the governor of Aleppo (1766). The scuffle concerned the affections of a "woman of ill-repute"; Bodman, *Factions*, 24. On the social ties between soldiers and prostitutes in Aleppo, see Elyse Semerdjian, *"Off the Straight Path": Illicit Sex, Law, and Community in Ottoman Aleppo* (Syracuse: Syracuse University Press, 2008), 105–9; for Damascus, see Abd al-Karim Rafeq, "Public Morality in Eighteenth-Century Ottoman Damascus," *Revue du monde musulman et de la Méditerranée* 55/56 (1990): 180–96.

23. Cabi, *Tarih*, 422–23. See a similar scuffle between Janissaries and palace guards over a "prostitute" from Üsküdar; Cabi, *Tarih*, 374–75.

24. Cabi, *Tarih*, 380.

25. Cabi, *Tarih*, 439–40.

26. Cabi, *Tarih*, 732. Tradesmen may have felt free to take matters into their own hands after previously clashing with porters in the markets (1810). The authorities afterwards gave permission to merchants and shopkeepers to discipline unruly porters; Mehmet Mert Sunar, "Cauldron of Dissent: a Study of the Janissary Corps, 1807–1826" (unpublished PhD diss., SUNY-Binghamton, 2006), 166–67. For the incident, also in 1810, in which porters had fought over a women at Balkapanı, see Cabi, *Tarih*, 624; Derin, ed., "Yayla İmamı," 270.

27. Karahasanoğlu, *Kadı*, 191; Şanizade, *Tarih*, 3:88.

28. On the different categories of prostitutes in Istanbul, see Zarinebaf, *Crime*, 90–97. On attempts by neighbors and officials in Istanbul to police prostitutes and other women whose morals were suspect, see Başaran, *Selim III*, 190–200; Hamadeh, "Mean Streets," 264–71.

29. Cabi, *Tarih*, 466. See also Cabi, *Tarih*, 469–70.

30. See for example Cabi, *Tarih*, 490, 527–28; Taylesanizade, *İstanbul*, 145. For other rumors of women and children being kidnapped from the streets (1822), see Oğulukyan, *Ruzname*, 54.

31. Cabi, *Tarih*, 476–77. Fears about rape could extend to young men who might have to endure the amorous advances of soldiers. See for example a gruesome account (1816) from Cairo; al-Jabarti, *'Aja'ib*, 7:358.

32. Yıldız, "Anatomy," 313. In earlier episodes, soldiers had molested European women; ibid., 313. In a similar report from Aleppo (1812), women faced so much harassment from Janissaries that they could only leave for the bathhouse in groups. One woman who had ventured out alone, it was said, had been raped; al-Tabbakh, *I'lam*, 3:303. For complaints of soldiers' unruliness in early nineteenth-century Tunis, see Ibn Abi'l-Diyaf, *Ithaf*, 3:56–57, 115.

33. Cabi, *Tarih*, 787–88.

34. Cabi, *Tarih*, 913. See too the Christian youth who suffered the same fate after he tried (1813) to kidnap a Muslim girl from the streets near Küçükçekmece; see Cabi, 997. For the incident in which a Janissary "accosted" a respectable woman, only to be hauled away by a passing Janissary patrol, see Cabi, *Tarih*, 915–16.

35. Cabi, *Tarih*, 756. See too the account of a group of "wicked" soldiers who were harassing women in the market of Küçükpazar (1809); Cabi, *Tarih*, 504.

36. See for example Hasanoğlu, *Kadı*, 192.

37. On the sensitivities of the Ottoman Old Regime to the threats of sexual violence against honor, see Başak Tuğ, *Politics of Honor: Sexual Violence and Socio-Legal Surveillance in the Eighteenth Century* (Leiden: Brill, 2017), chap. 3. For the same questions in earlier Ottoman society, see Leslie Peirce, "Abduction with (Dis)honor: Sovereigns, Brigands, and Heroes in the Ottoman World," *Journal of Early Modern History* 15 (2011): 311–29.

38. Sabbanu, ed., *Hamlat*, 52.

39. For an overview of these sartorial reforms, see Quataert, "Clothing Laws."

40. Yıldız, *Crisis and Rebellion*, 22–25.

41. Ahmet Cevat Eren, *Mahmud II. Zamanında Bosna-Hersek* (Istanbul: Nurgök Matbaası, 1965), 82. The same strident criticism met the adoption of modern Ottoman-style (*nizami*) uniforms in Tunisia after 1831. For one suspicious scholar who viewed them as an emblem of "infidelity," see Ibn Abi'l-Diyaf, *Ithaf*, 8:173.

42. Eren, *Bosna-Hersek*, 115; Fatma Sel Turhan, "The Rebellious Kapudan of Bosnia: Hüseyin Kapudan (1802–1834)," *Osmanlı Araştırmaları* 44 (2014): 460. On the reluctance of soldiers along the eastern frontier in Erzurum to wear the new uniforms (1829), see Sunar, "Cauldron," 229.

43. Donald Quataert, "Janissaries, Artisans, and the Question of Ottoman Decline, 1730–1826," in *Workers, Peasants, and Economic Change in the Ottoman Empire, 1730–1914*, ed. Donald Quataert (Istanbul: Isis Press, 1993), 197–203.

44. ("Bunların meramları yoldaş gavgası değil, ancak İstanbul'a ateş verüp, yağma edüp, vilayetlerine gitmekdir"); Cabi, *Tarih*, 731–32.

45. Quataert, "Clothing Laws," 413–15.

46. Reşat Ekrem Koçu, *Türk Giyim, Kuşam ve Süslenme Sözlüğü* (Ankara: Başnur Matbaası, 1967), 114.

47. John S. Koliopoulos, *Brigands with a Cause: Brigandage and Irredentism in Modern*

Greece, 1821-1912 (Oxford: Clarendon Press, 1987), chap. 4; Nicholas Pappas, "Brigands and Brigadiers: The Problem of Banditry and the Military in Nineteenth-Century Greece," *Athens Journal of History* 4 (2018): 183-85.

48. In Egypt (1815), Mehmed Ali required his troops to dress in European-style uniforms. Al-Jabarti, a Muslim scholar, could not hide his revulsion for this "tight and disfiguring" dress; al-Jabarti, *'Aja'ib*, 7:305.

49. "The turban was everywhere resumed, and the obnoxious fez discarded. 'How do you expect them to fight,' said an old Osmanley to me, whom I was rallying on the pusillanimity displayed by the troops at Aidos, 'with this thing on their heads?' pointing to his own fez with unmixed contempt." Slade, *Travels*, 1:370.

50. In the Anatolian town of Sivas, the affluent were the first to adopt the fez; among other segments of the population, it was much slower to catch on; Ömer Demirel, *II. Mahmud Döneminde Sivas'ta Esnaf Teşkilatı ve Üretim-Tüketim İlişkileri* (Ankara: Kültür Bakanlığı, 1989), 57.

51. Cemal Kutay, *İki Rıfat Paşa'nın Ahlak Dünyası* (Istanbul: Sile Matbaası, 1970). For more background on Mehmed Sadık Rifat Paşa, see Şerif Mardin, *The Genesis of Young Ottoman Thought: A Study in the Modernization of Turkish Political Ideas* (Princeton: Princeton University Press, 1962), chap. 6.

52. See for example the lifestyle of the reforming bureaucrat Ahmed Vefik Paşa (1823-1891); Hanifi Vural, *Ahmet Vefik Paşa: Hayatı—Şahsiyeti—Eserleri* (Istanbul: Kesit, 2016), 21-22.

53. For an overview of this reformulation of nineteenth-century court protocol, see Karateke, *Padişahım*, chap. 5. The same ceremonial evolution took place in the now autonomous provinces of Egypt and Tunisia; see for example Brown, *Ahmad Bey*, 242; A.A. Paton, *History of the Egyptian Revolution* (London: Trübner, 1870), 2:238-39; James Augustus St. John, *Egypt and Mohammed Ali* (London: Longman, Rees, Orme, Brown, Green & Longman, 1834), 1:49-51.

54. Karateke, *Padişahım*, 178-79.

55. On the fashions of the late-Ottoman modern middle class, see for example Toufoul Abou-Hodeib, *A Taste for Home: The Modern Middle Class in Ottoman Beirut* (Stanford: Stanford University Press, 2017); Pelin Başcı, "Advertising Modernity in *Woman's World*: Women's Lifestyle and Leisure in Late-Ottoman Istanbul," *Hawwa* 2 (2004): 34-63; Duben and Behar, *Istanbul Households*; Paul Dumont, "Said Bey: The Everyday Life of an Istanbul Townsman at the Beginning of the Twentieth Century," in *The Modern Middle East: A Reader* (Berkeley: University of California Press, 1993), 271-87; Haris Exertzoglou, "The Cultural Uses of Consmption: Negotiating Class, Gender, and Nation in the Ottoman Urban Centers during the 19th Century," *International Journal of Middle East Studies* 35 (2003): 77-101; Elizabeth Frierson, "Cheap and Easy: The Creation of Consumer Culture in Late Ottoman Society," in *Consumption Studies and the History of the Ottoman Empire, 1550-1922*, ed. Donald Quataert (Albany: State University of New York Press, 2000), 243-60; Akram Fuad Khater, *Inventing Home: Emigration, Gender, and the Middle Class in Lebanon, 1870-1920* (Berkeley: University of California Press, 2001); Şerif Mardin, "Super-Westernization in Urban Life in the Ottoman Empire in the Last Quarter of the Nineteenth Century," in *Turkey: Geographic and Social Perspectives* (Leiden: Brill, 1974), 403-49; Lisa Pollard, *Nurturing the Nation: The Family Politics of Modernizing, Colonizing, and Liber-*

ating Egypt, 1805-1923 (Berkeley: University of California Press, 2005); Mona L. Russell, *Creating the New Egyptian Woman: Consumerism, Education, and National Identity, 1863-1922* (New York: Palgrave Macmillan, 2004); Salim Tamari, "Jerusalem's Ottoman Modernity: The Times and Lives of Wasif Jawhariyyeh," *Jerusalem Quarterly* 9 (2000): 5-27; Keith Watenpaugh, *Being Modern in the Middle East: Revolution, Nationalism, and Colonialism and the Arab Middle Class* (Princeton: Princeton University Press, 2006); Stefan Weber, *Damascus: Ottoman Modernity and Urban Transformation, 1808-1918* (Aarhus: Aarhus University Press, 2009); Einar Wigen, "The Education of Ottoman Man and the Practice of Orderliness," in *Civilizing Emotions: Concepts in Nineteenth-Century Asia and Europe*, ed. Margrit Pernau and Helge Jordheim (Oxford: Oxford University Press, 2015), 107-25.

56. Es'ad Efendi, *Üss-i Zafer*, 146. Eighteenth-century Ottoman reformers had been citing the success of Russian reform as far back as the writings of İbrahim Müteferrika (d. 1745), the Hungarian convert to Islam who had set up the first printing press in Turkish during the 1720s. Also making a big impression on Ottoman observers were the reforms of Joseph II (r. 1780-90) in Austria. See Aksan, "Ottoman Political Writing."

57. On the general hostility of early Ottoman reformers to the ideals of the French revolution, see Marinos Sariyannis, "Ottoman Ideas on Monarchy before the Tanzimat Reforms: Toward a Conceptual History of Ottoman Political Notions," *Turcica* 47 (2016): 33-72. See too the intellectual debt that Reşid Paşa, an early Tanzimat reformer, and Mehmed Sadık Rifat Paşa both owed to Prince Metternich, Europe's most notorious conservative; Mardin, *Genesis*, 178-82.

58. For partial agreement with this argument about the conservative nature of early Ottoman reform, see Ali Yaycıoğlu, "Guarding Traditions and Laws—Disciplining Bodies and Souls: Tradition, Religion, and Science in the Age of Ottoman Reform," *Modern Asian Studies* 52 (2018): 1542-603. Yaycıoğlu also places early Ottoman reform within a "Euro-Ottoman military enlightenment" and thereby draws on a recent trend in Ottoman historiography which has made the case for an "Ottoman Enlightenment" in the eighteenth and early nineteenth centuries. See for example Edhem Eldem, "Début des lumières ou simple plagiat? La très voltairienne préface de l'histoire de Şanizade Mehmed Ataullah Efendi?" *Turcica* 45 (2014): 269-318; Vefa Erginbaş, "Enlightenment in the Ottoman Context: İbrahim Müteferrika and His Intellectual Landscape," *Historical Aspects of Printing and Publishing in Languages of the Middle East*, ed. Geoffrey Roper (Leiden: Brill, 2014), 53-100; Bekir Harun Küçük, *Science without Leisure: Practical Naturalism in Istanbul, 1660-1732* (Pittsburgh: University of Pittsburgh Press, 2020). These arguments have an antecedent in an earlier debate for a proposed eighteenth-century "Islamic Enlightenment." For the full argument from its original exponent, see Reinhard Schulze, "Was ist die islamische Aufklärung?," *Die Welt des Islams* 36 (1996): 276-325. For critiques of this idea, which has not fared well, see R.S. O'Fahey and Bernd Radtke, "Neo-Sufism Reconsidered," *Der Islam* 70 (1993): 52-87; Rudolph Peters, "Reinhard Schulze's Quest for an Islamic Enlightenment," *Die Welt des Islams* 30 (1990): 160-62; Bernd Radtke, "Sufism in the 18th Century: An Attempt at a Provisional Appraisal," *Die Welt des Islams* 36 (1996): 326-64; Khaled el-Rouayheb, "Was There a Revival of Logical Studies in Eighteenth-Century Egypt?," *Die Welt des Islams* 45 (2005): 1-19. The debate about an 'Ottoman Enlightenment' is ongoing. Proponents tend to link it to what they characterize as a wider 'global' Enlightenment. On this latter concept, see especially Sebastian Conrad, "Enlightenment

in Global History: A Historiographical Critique," *American Historical Review* 117 (2012): 999–1027. In the Ottoman setting, though, one will search in vain for figures like the French philosophes, an intelligentsia who exalted reason and wielded it as an oppositional weapon against both the political and cultural establishment. For a general complaint about 'Enlightenment inflation'—i.e., use of the term which is entirely too loose and unmoored from its original context—see Robert Darnton, *George Washington's False Teeth: an Unconventional Guide to the Eighteenth Century* (New York: W.W. Norton, 2003).

59. Frederick W. Kagan, *The Military Reforms of Nicolas I: The Origins of the Modern Russian Army* (New York: St. Martin's Press, 1999); Marc Raeff, *Michael Speransky, Statesman of Imperial Russia, 172-1839* (The Hague: M. Nijhoff, 1957); David Saunders, *Russia in the Age of Reaction and Reform, 1801-1881* (New York: Longman, 1992); Paul W. Werth, *1837: Russia's Quiet Revolution* (Oxford: Oxford University Press, 2021); William Benton Whisenhunt, *In Search of Legality: Mikhail M. Speranskii and the Codification of Russian Law* (Boulder, CO: East European Monographs, 2001).

60. See for example Hermann Beck, *The Origins of the Authoritarian Welfare State in Prussia: Conservatives, Bureaucracy, and the Social Question, 1815-1870* (Ann Arbor: University of Michigan Press, 1995); David Good, *The Rise of the Austrian Empire, 1750-1914* (Berkeley: University of California Press, 1984); Matthew Bernard Levinger, *Enlightened Nationalism: The Transformation of Prussian Political Culture, 1806-1848* (Oxford: Oxford University Press, 2000); Gabor Vermes, *Hungarian Culture and Politics in the Habsburg Monarchy, 1711-1848* (Budapest: Central European University Press, 2014); Gerhard Wegner, "Defensive Modernization in Germany and the Habsburg Empire: A Historical Study of Capitalist Transformation," *Journal of Institutional Economics* 12 (2016): 443–69.

61. Cevdet, *Tarih*, 6:72. On similar opposition to state reform in Egypt, see Daniel Crecelius, "Nonideological Responses of the Egyptian Ulama to Modernization," in *Scholars, Saints, and Sufis: Muslim Religious Institutions since 1500*, ed. Nikki Keddie (Los Angeles: University of California Press, 1972), 167–209.

62. "Westernization" has become a loaded word in Ottoman historiography. Some twentieth-century historians attached it to the so-called "Tulip Age," set at the court of Ahmet III (r. 1703-30) during the 1720s. The decade gained fame as a time of lavish courtly consumption, in which the Ottoman elite allegedly took a new interest in all things European. Unfortunately for this argument, contemporary observers made no mention of any "Tulip Age," which as an expression did not come into use until the early twentieth century. See Can Erimtan, *Ottomans Looking West?: The Origins of the Tulip Age and Its Development in Modern Turkey* (London: IB Tauris, 2008). Recent research has also expressed doubt about any special "Westernizing" tendencies in Ottoman art and architecture during this period. The Ottoman court was cosmopolitan in outlook. It amused itself with an aesthetic eclecticism that had as much curiosity about Persian and Indian styles as any of those from Europe. See Hamadeh, *The City's Pleasures*, esp. chap. 8; Ünver Rüstem, *Ottoman Baroque: The Architectural Refashioning of Eighteenth-Century Istanbul* (Princeton: Princeton University Press, 2019).

BIBLIOGRAPHY

Abdel-Nour, Antoine. *Introduction à l'histoire urbaine de la Syrie ottomane (XVIe–XVIIIe siècle)*. Beirut: Université Libanaise, 1982.
Abou-El-Haj, Rif`aat `Ali. *Formation of the Modern State: The Ottoman Empire, Sixteenth to Eighteenth Centuries*, 2nd ed. Syracuse: Syracuse University Press, 2005.
———. *The 1703 Rebellion and the Structure of Ottoman Politics*. Leiden: Nederlands Historisch-Archaeologisch Instituut te Istanbul, 1984.
———. "The Ottoman Vezir and Paşa Households, 1683–1703: A Preliminary Report." *Journal of the American Oriental Society* 94 (1974): 438–47.
Abou-Hodeib, Toufoul. *A Taste for Home: The Modern Middle Class in Ottoman Beirut*. Stanford: Stanford University Press, 2017.
Abu-Husayn, Abdul-Rahim. *The View from Istanbul: Lebanon and the Druze Emirate in the Ottoman Chancery Documents, 1546–1711*. London: Center for Lebanese Studies in association with I.B. Tauris, 2004.
———. *Provincial Leaderships in Syria, 1575–1650*. Beirut: American University of Beirut Press, 1985.
Abu-Manneh, Butrus. *Studies on Islam and the Ottoman Empire in the 19th Century (1826–1876)*. Istanbul: Isis Press, 2001.
Abu Zayd, `Ali Ibrahim. *Tamthiliyat khayal al-zill*. Cairo: Dar al-Ma`arif, 1982.
Ágoston, Gabor. "Military Transformation in the Ottoman Empire and Russia, 1500–1800." *Kritika: Explorations in Russian and Eurasian History* 12 (2011): 281–319.
Ahmed Cavid. *Hadika-i Vekayi`*. Edited by Adnan Baycar. Ankara: Türk Tarih Kurumu Basımevi, 1998.
Ahmed Efendi. *III. Selim'in Sırkatibi Ahmed Efendi Tarafından Tutulan Ruzname*. Edited by Sema Arıkan. Ankara: Türk Tarih Kurumu, 1993.
Ahmed Lütfi. *Tarih-i Lütfi*. 8 vols. Istanbul: Matbaa-yi Amire, 1873.
Ahmed Resmi. *Halifet ür-Rüesa*. Istanbul: Takvimhane-yi Amire, 1853.

Akarlı, Engin. "Provincial Power Magnates in Ottoman Bilad al-Sham and Egypt, 1740-1840." In *La Vie sociale dans les provinces Arabes à l'époque Ottomane*, edited by Abdeljelil Temimi, 3:41–56. Zaghouan: Centre d'Études et de Recherches sur les Provinces Arabes à l'Époque Ottomane, 1988.

Aksan, Virginia. "Mobilization of Warrior Populations in the Ottoman Context, 1750-1850." In *Fighting for a Living*, edited by Erik Jan Zürcher, 323–43. Amsterdam: International Institute for Social History, 2013.

———. *Ottoman Wars, 1700-1870: An Empire Besieged*. London: Pearson-Longman, 2007.

———. "The Ottoman Military and State Transformation in a Globalizing World." *Comparative Studies of South Asia, Africa, and the Middle East* 27 (2007): 257–70.

———. "Breaking the Spell of the Baron de Tott: Reframing the Question of Military Reform in the Ottoman Empire, 1760-1830." *International History Review* 24 (2002): 253–77.

———. "Ottoman Military Recruitment Strategies in the Late Eighteenth Century." In *Arming the State: Military Conscription in the Middle East and Central Asia, 1775-1925*, edited by Erik Zürcher, 21–39. London: IB Tauris, 1999.

———. "Whatever Happened to the Janissaries? Mobilization for the 1768-1774 Russo-Ottoman War." *War in History* 5 (1998): 23–36.

———. *An Ottoman Statesman in War and Peace: Ahmed Resmi Efendi, 1700-1783*. Leiden: Brill, 1995.

———. "Ottoman Political Writing, 1768-1808." *International Journal of Middle East Studies* 25 (1993): 53–69.

Alexander, William, and Octavian Dalvimart. *Picturesque Representations of the Dress and Manners of the Turks*. London: T. M'Lean, 1816.

Ali, Samer M. *Arabic Literary Salons in the Islamic Middle Ages: Poetry, Public Performance, and the Presentation of the Past*. Notre Dame: University of Notre Dame Press, 2010.

Allom, Thomas. *Constantinople and the Scenery of the Seven Churches of Asia Minor*. 2 vols. London: Fisher, Son, 1838.

Altok, Zeynep. "The 18th-Century 'Istanbul Tale.'" In *A Companion to Early Modern Istanbul*, edited by Shirine Hamadeh and Çiğdem Kafescioğlu, 581–603. Leiden: Brill, 2022.

And, Metin. *Karagöz: Turkish Shadow Theater*. Ankara: Dost Yayınları, 1975.

Anastasopoulos, Antonis. "Crisis and State Intervention in Late Eighteenth-Century Karaferye (mod. Veroia)." In *The Ottoman Balkans, 1750-1830*, ed. Frederick Anscombe, 11–33. Princeton: Marcus Wiener, 2006.

Andrews, Walter G., and Mehmet Kalpaklı. "Toward a Meclis-Centered Reading of Ottoman Poetry." *Journal of Turkish Studies* 33 (2009): 309–18.

———. *The Age of Beloveds: Love and the Beloved in Early-Modern Ottoman and European Culture and Society*. Durham: Duke University Press, 2005.

Angelomatis-Tsougarakis, Helen. "Women in the Greek War of Independence." In *Networks of Power in Modern Greece: Essays in Honor of John Campbell*, edited by Mark Mazower, 45–68. New York: Columbia University Press, 2008.

Anscombe, Frederick F. "Albanians and 'Mountain Bandits.'" In *The Ottoman Balkans, 1750-1830*, edited by Frederick Anscombe, 87–113. Princeton: Markus Wiener, 2006.

App, Urs. *The Birth of Orientalism*. Philadelphia: University of Pennsylvania Press, 2010.

al-Aqhisari, Ahmad. *Against Smoking*. Edited and translated by Yahya Michot. Leicestershire: Kube, 2010.

Arapyan, Kalost. *Rusçuk Ayanı: Mustafa Paşa'nın Hayatı ve Kahramanlıkları*. Translated by Esat Uras. Ankara: Türk Tarih Kurumu Basımevi, 1943.
Armitage, David, and Sanjay Subrahmanyam, eds. *The Age of Revolutions in a Global Context, 1760–1840*. New York: Palgrave Macmillan, 2010.
Artan, Tülay. "Forms and Forums of Expression: Istanbul and Beyond, 1600–1800." In *The Ottoman World*, edited by Christine Woodhead, 378–406. London: Routledge, 2012.
———. "Ahmed I and 'Tuhfet'ül-mülük ve's-selatin." In *Animals and People in the Ottoman Empire*, edited by Suraiya Faroqhi, 235–69. Istanbul: Eren, 2010.
Asım, Ahmed. *Asım Tarihi*. 2 vols. Istanbul: Ceride-yi Havadis Matbaası, n.d.
Aswad, Nizar. *Karakuz Bilad al-Sham*. Damascus: al-Warda al-Shamiyya, 1994.
al-`Awra, Ibrahim. *Tarikh Wilayat Sulayman Basha al-`Adil*. Edited by Antun Bishara Qiqanu. Beirut: Dar Lahad Khatir, 1989.
Ayalon, David. *Gunpowder and Firearms in the Mamluk Kingdom: A Challenge to Mediaeval Society*, 2nd ed. London: F. Cass, 1978.
Aynur, Hatice. "Ottoman Literature." In *The Cambridge History of Turkey*, Vol. 3, *The Later Ottoman Empire, 1603–1839*, edited by Suraiya Faroqhi, 481–520. Cambridge: Cambridge University Press, 2006.
Ayvansarayi, Hüseyin. *The Garden of the Mosques: Hafız Hüseyin Ayvansarayi's Guide to the Muslim Monuments of Ottoman Istanbul*. 2 vols. Translated by Howard Crane. Leiden: Brill, 2000.
Ayverdi, Ekrem Hakkı. *Avrupa'da Osmanlı Mimari Eserleri*. 4 vols. Istanbul: İstanbul Fetih Cemiyeti, 1978–82.
Badi, Ahmed. *Riyaz-ı Belde-i Edirne: 20. Yüzyıla Kadar Osmanlı Edirne'si*. Edited by Niyazi Adıgüzel and Raşit Gündoğdu. 5 vols. Edirne: Trakya Üniversitesi Yayınları, 2014.
Baer, Marc David. *Honored by the Glory of Islam: Conversion and Conquest in Ottoman Europe*. New York: Oxford University Press, 2008.
Baggally, John W. *Greek Historical Folksongs: The Klephtic Ballads in Relation to Greek History (1715–1821)*. Chicago: Argonaut, 1968 (reprint of 1936 edition).
Baldwin, James E. *Islamic Law and Empire in Ottoman Cairo*. Edinburgh: Edinburgh University Press, 2017.
Barahona, Renato. *Sex Crimes, Honour, and Law in Early Modern Spain: Vizcaya, 1528–1735*. Toronto: University of Toronto Press, 2003.
Barbir, Karl. "From Pasha to Efendi: The Assimilation of Ottoman into Damascene Society, 1516–1783." *International Journal of Turkish Studies* 1 (1979–80): 68–83.
Bardakçı, Murat. *Osmanlı'da Seks: Sarayda Gece Dersleri*. Istanbul: Gür Yayınları, 1992.
Barker, John. *Syria and Egypt under the Last Five Sultans of Turkey*. 2 vols. London: Samuel Tinsley, 1876.
Barkey, Karen. *Empire of Difference: The Ottomans in Comparative Perspective*. Cambridge: Cambridge University Press, 2008.
Başaran, Betül. *Selim III, Social Control, and Policing in Istanbul at the End of the Eighteenth Century*. Leiden: Brill, 2014.
Başcı, Pelin. "Advertising Modernity in *Woman's World*: Women's Lifestyle and Leisure in Late-Ottoman Istanbul." *Hawwa* 2 (2004): 34–63.
Bayly, C.A. *The Birth of the Modern World, 1780–1914*. Malden, MA: Blackwell, 2004.

Bayrak, Mehmet. *Eşkıyalık ve Eşkıya Türküleri: İnceleme, Antoloji.* Ankara: Yorum Yayınevi, 1985.
Bayrı, Mehmet Halit. *İstanbul Argosu ve Halk Tabirleri.* Istanbul: Burhaneddin Matbaası, 1934.
Beck, Hermann. *The Origins of the Authoritarian Welfare State in Prussia: Conservatives, Bureaucracy, and the Social Question, 1815-1870.* Ann Arbor: University of Michigan Press, 1995.
Behar, Cem. "The Ottoman Musical Tradition" In *The Cambridge History of Turkey*, Vol. 3, *The Later Ottoman Empire, 1603-1839*, edited by Suraiya Faroqhi, 393-407. New York: Cambridge University Press, 2006.
———. *A Neighborhood in Istanbul: Fruit Vendors and Civil Servants in the Kasap İlyas Mahalle.* Albany: State University of New York Press, 2003.
———. *Osmanlı İmparatorluğunun ve İstanbul'un Nüfusu (1500-1927).* Ankara: Türkiye Cumhuriyeti Başbakanlık Devlet İstatistik Enstitüsü, 1996.
———. *Zaman, Mekan, Müzik: Klasik Türk Musıkisinde Eğitim (Meşk), İcra ve Aktarım.* Istanbul: AFA Yayıncılık, 1992.
Behrens-Abouseif, Doris. *Azbakiyya and Its Environs from Azbak to Isma`il, 1476-1879.* Cairo: Institut Français d'Archéologie Orientale, 1985.
Beik, William. "The Violence of the French Crowd: From Charivari to Revolution." *Past and Present* 197 (2007): 75-110.
Beydilli, Kemal, ed. *Osmanlı Döneminde İmamlar ve bir İmam'ın Günlüğü.* Istanbul: Tarih ve Tabiat Vakfı, 2001.
Beydilli, Kemal, and İlhan Şahin, eds. *Mahmud Raif Efendi ve Nizam-ı Cedid'e Dair Eseri.* Ankara: Türk Tarih Kurumu, 2001.
Bezirci, Asım. *Türk Halk Şiiri: Tarihçesi, Kaynakları, Şairleri, ve Seçme Şiirleri.* 2 vols. Ankara: Say Yayınları, 1993.
Billacois, François. *The Duel: Its Rise and Fall in Early Modern France.* Translated by Trista Sellou. New Haven: Yale University Press, 1990.
Birge, John Kingsley. *The Bektashi Order of Dervishes.* London: Luzac, 1937.
Birsel, Salah. *Kahveler Kitabı.* Ankara: Türkiye İş Bankası Kültür Yayınları, 1983.
Black-Michaud, Jacob. *Cohesive Force: Feud in the Mediterranean and the Middle East.* New York: St. Martin's Press, 1975.
Blanning, T.C.W. *The Culture of Power and the Power of Culture: Old Regime Europe, 1660-1789.* Oxford: Oxford University Press, 2002.
Blok, Anton. *Honor and Violence.* Cambridge: Polity, 2001.
Bodman, Herbert. *Political Factions in Aleppo, 1760-1826.* Chapel Hill: University of North Carolina Press, 1963.
Boehm, Christopher. *Blood Revenge: The Anthropology of Feuding in Montenegro and Other Tribal Societies.* Lawrence: University of Kansas Press, 1984.
Bonney, Richard. *The Rise of the Fiscal State in Europe, c. 1200-1815.* New York: Oxford University Press, 1999.
Boratav, Pertev Naili. *Köroğlu Destanı.* Istanbul: Kırmızı Yayınları, 2009.
Börekçi, Günhan. "Factions and Favorites at the Courts of Sultan Amhed I (r. 1603-17) and His Immediate Predecessors." Unpublished PhD diss., Ohio State University, 2010.
Bostan, İdris. *Osmanlı Bahriye Teşkilatı: XVII. Yüzyılda Tersane-i Amire.* Ankara: Türk Tarih Kurumu Basımevi, 1992.

Bosworth, Clifford Edmund. "A Janissary Poet of Sixteenth-Century Damascus: Mamayya al-Rumi." In *The Islamic World from Classical to Modern Times: Essays in Honor of Bernard Lewis*, edited by C.E. Bosworth et al., 451–66. Princeton: Darwin Press, 1989.

Boué, Ami. *Turquie d'Europe*. 6 vols. Paris: Arthus Bertrand, 1840.

Boyar, Ebru, and Kate Fleet. *A Social History of Ottoman Istanbul*. Cambridge: Cambridge University Press, 2010.

Braudel, Fernand. *The Structures of Everyday Life: Civilization and Capitalism, 1400–1800 (Volume One)*. Translated by Sian Reynolds. New York: Harper and Row, 1981.

Brennan, Thomas. *Public Drinking and Popular Culture in Eighteenth-Century Paris*. Princeton: Princeton University Press, 1988.

Brockedon, William. *The Holy Land, Syria, Idumea, Arabia, Egypt & Nubia*. Illustrated by David Roberts. London: Day and Son, 1855–56.

Brown, Edward. *A Brief Account of Some Travels*. London: Benjamin Tooke, 1673.

Brown, Leon Carl. *The Tunisia of Ahmad Bey, 1837–1855*. Princeton: Princeton University Press, 1974.

——. "The Religious Establishment in Husainid Tunisia." In *Scholars, Saints, and Sufis: Muslim Religious Institutions in the Middle East since 1500*, edited by Nikki Keddie, chap. 2. Berkeley: University of California Press, 1972.

Browne, W.G. *Travels in Africa, Egypt, and Syria*. London: Cengage Gale, 1799.

de Bruyn, Cornelis. *Voyages de Corneille le Bruyn au Levant*. 5 vols. The Hague: P. Gosse and J. Neaulme, 1732.

Bryson, Anna. *From Courtesy to Civility: Changing Codes of Conduct in Early Modern England*. Oxford: Clarendon Press, 1998.

Bryson, Frederic Robertson. *The Point of Honor in Sixteenth-Century Italy: An Aspect of the Life of the Gentleman*. New York: Columbia University Press, 1935.

al-Budayri, Ahmad. *Hawadith Dimashq al-yawmiyya*. Edited by Ahmad ʿIzzat ʿAbd al-Karim. Cairo: Matbuʿat al-Jamʿiyya al-Misriyya liʾl-Dirasat al-Tarikhiyya, 1959.

Burayk, Mikha'il. *Tarikh al-Sham*. Edited by Ahmad Ghassan Sabbanu. Damascus: Dar Qutayba, 1982.

Burckhardt, John Lewis. *Travels in Syria and the Holy Land*. London: John Murray, 1822.

Burke, Peter. *The Historical Anthropology of Early Modern Italy: Essays on Perception and Communication*. Cambridge: Cambridge University Press, 1987.

——. *Popular Culture in Early Modern Europe*. New York: Harper & Row, 1978.

Burke, Peter, Brian Harrison, and Paul Slack, eds. *Civil Histories: Essays Presented to Sir Keith Thomas*. Oxford: Oxford University Press, 2000.

Bursalı Mehmet Tahir. *Ahlak Kitaplarımız*. Istanbul: Necm-i İstikbal Matbaası, 1909.

Cabi Ömer Efendi. *Cabi Tarihi*. Edited by Mehmet Ali Beyhan. 2 vols. Ankara: Türk Tarih Kurumu, 2003.

Çaksu, Ali. "Janissary Coffee Houses in Late Eighteenth-Century Istanbul." In *Ottoman Tulips, Ottoman Coffee: Leisure and Lifestyle in the Eighteenth Century*, edited by Dana Sajdi, 117–32. London: Tauris Academic Studies, 2007.

Campbell, John. "The Greek Hero." In *Honor and Grace in Anthropology*, edited by J.G. Peristiany and Julian Pitt-Rivers, 129–49. Cambridge: Cambridge University Press, 1992.

——. *Honor, Family, and Patronage: A Study of Institutions and Moral Values in a Greek Mountain Community*. Oxford: Oxford University Press, 1964.

———. "The Kindred in a Greek Mountain Community." In *Mediterranean Countrymen*, edited by Julian Pitt-Rivers, 73–96. Paris: Mouton, 1963.

Canbakal, Hülya. "Preliminary Observations on Political Unrest in Eighteenth-Century Ayntab: Popular Protest and Faction." In *Political Initiatives "From the Bottom Up" in the Ottoman Empire*, edited by Antonis Anastasopoulos, 33–58. Rethymno: Crete University Press, 2012.

Carayon, Agnès. "City of the Cavalryman and House of the Rider: 'Landscaped-Hippodromes' and Stable-Palaces in Mamluk Cairo." In *Echoing Hooves: Studies on Horses and Their Effects on Medieval Societies*, 57–75. Leiden: Brill, 2022.

Carroll, Stuart. *Blood and Violence in Early Modern France*. New York: Oxford University Press, 2006.

Casalilla, Bartolomé Yun, and Patrick O'Brien, eds. *The Rise of Fiscal States: A Global History, 1500–1914*. Cambridge: Cambridge University Press, 2012.

Castellan, Antoine-Laurent. *Lettres sur la Morée, l'Hellespont et Constantinople*. 2 vols. Paris: A. Nepveu, 1811.

Çavuşoğlu, Semiramis. "The Kadızadeli Movement: An Attempt of Şeriat-Minded Reform in the Ottoman Empire." Unpublished PhD diss., Princeton University, 1990.

Cevdet, Ahmet. *Tarih-i Cevdet*. 12 vols. Istanbul: Matbaa-yi Osmaniye, 1893.

Cezar, Mustafa. *Osmanlı Tarihinde Levendler*. Istanbul: Çelikcilt Matbaası. 1965.

Cezar, Yavuz. "18. Ve 19. Yüzyıllarda Osmanlı Taşrasında Oluşan Yeni Mali Sektörün Mahiyet ve Büyüklüğü Üzerine." *Toplum ve Ekonomi* 9 (1996): 89–145.

———. *Osmanlı Maliyesinde Bunalım ve Değişim Dönemi: XVIII. Yüzyıldan Tanzimat'a Mali Tarihi*. Istanbul: Alan Yayıncılık, 1986.

Chandler, Richard. *Travels in Asia Minor and Greece*. 2 vols., 3rd ed. London: Joseph Booker, 1817.

Chartier, Roger. "Introduction." In *A History of Private Life*, Vol. 3, *The Passions of the Renaissance*, edited by Philippe Ariès and Georges Duby, translated by Arthur Goldhammer. Cambridge, MA: Belknap Press, 1989.

———. *Cultural History: Between Practices and Representations*. Translated by Lydia Cochrane. Ithaca: Cornell University Press, 1988.

Chateaubriand, François-Réné. *Travels in Greece, Palestine, Egypt, and Barbary*. Translated by Frederic Shoberl. 2 vols. London: Henry Colburn, 1812.

Chishull, Edmund. *Travels in Turkey and Back to England*. London: W. Bowyer, 1747.

Choiseul-Gouffier, Marie-Gabriel-August-Florent. *Voyage pittoresque de la Grèce*. Paris, 1782.

Çizakça, Murat. *A Comparative Evolution of Business Partnerships: The Islamic World and Europe, with Specific Reference to the Ottoman Archives*. Leiden: Brill, 1996.

Çokuğraş, Işıl. *Bekar Odaları ve Meyhaneler: Osmanlı İstanbulu'nda Marjinalite ve Mekan (1789–1839)*. Istanbul: İstanbul Araştırmaları Enstitüsü, 2016.

Cole, Juan. *Napoleon's Egypt: Invading the Middle East*. New York: Palgrave Macmillan, 2007.

Collingham, E.M. *Imperial Bodies: The Physical Experience of the Raj, c. 1800–1947*. Cambridge: Polity Press, 2001.

Conrad, Sebastian. "Enlightenment in Global History: A Historiographical Critique." *American Historical Review* 117 (2012): 999–1027.

Conway, Stephen, and Rafael Torres Sánchez, eds. *The Spending of States: Military Expen-*

diture during the Long Eighteenth Century: Patterns, Organization, and Consequences, 1650-1815. Saarbrücken: VDM Verlag Dr. Müller, 2011.

Covell, John. "Extracts from the Diaries of John Covell." In *Early Travels and Voyages in the Levant*, edited by Theodore Bent, 99–287. London: Hakluyt Society, 1893.

Cowan, Brian. *The Social Life of Coffee: The Emergence of the British Coffeehouse*. New Haven: Yale University Press, 2008.

Cracraft, James. *The Petrine Revolution in Russian Culture*. Cambridge, MA: Harvard University Press, 2004.

Craven, Elizabeth. *A Journey through the Crimea to Constantinople*. Dublin: H. Chamberlaine et al, 1789.

Crecelius, Daniel. *The Roots of Modern Egypt: A Study of the Regimes of Ali Bey al-Kabir and Muhammad Bey Abu al-Dhahab*. Minneapolis: Bibliotheca Islamica, 1981.

———. "Nonideological Responses of the Egyptian Ulama to Modernization." In *Scholars, Saints, and Sufis: Muslim Religious Institutions since 1500*, edited by Nikki Keddie, 167–209. Los Angeles: University of California Press, 1972.

Dalrymple, William. *White Mughals: Love and Betrayal in Eighteenth-Century India*. London: HarperCollins, 2002.

al-Damurdashi, Ahmad. *al-Damurdashi's Chronicle of Egypt, 1688-1755: Al-Durra al-musana fi akhbar al-Kinana*. Translated by Daniel Crecilius and Muhammad ʿAbd al-Wahhab Bakr. Leiden: Brill, 1991.

Dandini, Girolamo. *A Voyage to Mount Libanus*. London: A. Roper and R. Basset, 1698.

Darling, Linda T. *Revenue-Raising and Legitimacy: Tax Collection and Financial Administration in the Ottoman Empire, 1560-1660*. Leiden: Brill, 1996.

Darnton, Robert. *George Washington's False Teeth: An Unconventional Guide to the Eighteenth Century*. New York: W.W. Norton, 2003.

David, Jean-Claude. "Le Café à Alep au temps des Ottomans: Entre le souk et le quartier." In *Cafés d'Orient revisités*, edited by Hélène Desmet-Grégoire and François Georgeon, 113–26. Paris: CNRS, 1997.

Delice, Serkan. "The Janissaries and Their Bedfellows: Masculinity and Male Friendship in Eighteenth-Century Ottoman Istanbul." In *Gender and Sexuality in Muslim Cultures*, edited by Gül Özyeğin, 115–36. Burlington, VT: Ashgate, 2015.

Demeerseman, André. *Aspects de la société Tunisienne d'après Ibn Abi'l-Dhiyaf*. Tunis: Institut des Belles Lettres Arabes, 1996.

Demirel, Ömer. *II. Mahmud Döneminde Sivas'ta Esnaf Teşkilatı ve Üretim-Tüketim İlişkileri*. Ankara: Kültür Bakanlığı, 1989.

Denon, Vivant. *Travels in Upper and Lower Egypt*. Translated by Arthur Aikin. London: T.N. Longman and O. Rees, 1803; reprinted in New York: Arno Press, 1973.

Derin, Fahri Ç., ed. "Yayla İmamı Risalesi." *İstanbul Üniversitesi Tarih Enstitüsü Dergisi* 3 (1973): 213–72.

Destari Salih. *Destari Salih Tarihi: Patrona Halil Ayaklanması Hakkında Bir Kaynak*. Edited by Bekir Sıtkı Baykal. Ankara: Türk Tarih Kurumu Basımevi, 1962.

De Vries, Jan. *European Urbanization, 1500-1800*. Cambridge, MA: Harvard University Press, 1984.

Develi, Hayati, ed. *XVIII. Yüzyıl İstanbul Hayatına Dair Risale-i Garibe*. Istanbul: Kitabevi, 2001.

Diko, Gülay Yılmaz. "Blurred Boundaries between Soldiers and Civilians: Artisan Janissaries in Seventeenth-Century Istanbul." In *Bread from the Lion's Mouth: Artisans Struggling for a Livelihood in Ottoman Cities*, edited by Suraiya Faroqhi, 175–93. New York: Berghahn Books, 2015.

al-Dimashqi, Mikha'il. *Tarikh Hawadith al-Sham wa Lubnan, 1782-1841*. Edited by Ahmad Ghassan Sabbanu. Damascus: Dar Qutayba, 1982.

Dixon, Simon. *The Modernization of Russia, 1676-1825*. Cambridge: Cambridge University Press, 1999.

Dodwell, Edward. *A Classical and Topographical Tour through Greece*. 2 vols. London: Rodwell and Martin, 1819.

Douwes, Dick. *The Ottomans in Syria: A History of Justice and Oppression*. New York: IB Tauris, 2000.

Duben, Alan, and Cem Behar. *Ottoman Households: Marriage, Family, and Fertility, 1880-1940*. Cambridge: Cambridge University Press, 1991.

Duerr, Hans Peter. *Intimität*. Frankfurt am Main: Suhrkamp, 1990.

———. *Nacktheit und Sham*. Frankfurt am Main: Suhrkamp, 1988.

Duindam, Jeroen. *Vienna and Versailles: The Courts of Europe's Major Dynastic Rivals, 1550-1780*. Cambridge: Cambridge University Press, 2003.

———. *Myths of Power: Norbert Elias and the Early Modern European Court*. Translated by Lorri S. Granger and Gerard T. Moran. Amsterdam: Amsterdam University Press, 1994.

Dumont, Jean. *A New Voyage to the Levant*. London: M. Gillyflower et al., 1696.

Dumont, Paul. "Said Bey: The Everyday Life of an Istanbul Townsman at the Beginning of the Twentieth Century." In *The Modern Middle East: A Reader*, 271–87. Berkeley: University of California Press, 1993.

Dupré, Louis. *Voyage à Athènes et à Constantinople*. Paris: Imprimerie de Dondey-Dupré, 1825.

Durham, Mary Edith. *Some Tribal Origins, Laws, and Customs of the Balkans*. New York: Macmillan, 1929.

van Egmont, J. Aegidius. *Travels through Part of Europe, Asia Minor, the Islands of the Archipelago; Syria, Palestine, Egypt, Mt. Sinai*. Translated by John Heyman. 2 vols. London: Cengage Gale, 1759.

Eldem, Edhem. "Début des lumières ou simple plagiat? La très voltairienne préface de l'histoire de Şanizade Mehmed Ataullah Efendi?" *Turcica* 45 (2014): 269–318.

Elias, Norbert. *The Civilizing Process*. Translated by Edmund Jephcott. Oxford: Blackwell, 1994.

———. *The Court Society*. Translated by Edmund Jephcott. New York: Pantheon Books, 1983.

Elliott, Mark C. *The Manchu Way: The Eight Banners and Ethnic Identity in Late Imperial China*. Stanford: Stanford University Press, 2001.

Elliott, Matthew. "Dress Codes in the Ottoman Empire: The Case of the Franks." In *Ottoman Costumes: From Textiles to Identity*, edited by Suraiya Faroqhi and Christoph Neumann, 111–14. Istanbul: Eren, 2004.

Enderunlu Fazıl. *Der Vasf-ı Hubanname; Der Vasf-ı Zenanname-yi Fazıl; Rakkasname-yi Fazılın*. Istanbul, 1839.

Enfi Hasan Hulus Halveti. *Tezkiretü'l-Müteahhirin: XVI. ve XVIIIe Asırda Yaşayan Veliler ve Deliler*. Edited by Mustafa Tatçı ve Musa Yıldız. Istanbul: H Yayınları, 2014.

Erdem, Hakan. "Recruitment for the 'Victorious Soldiers of Muhammad' in the Arab Provinces, 1826–1828." In *Histories of the Modern Middle East: New Directions*, edited by Israel Gershoni, Hakan Erdem, and Ursula Woköck, 189–206. London: Lynne Rienner, 2002.

Eren, Ahmet Cevat. *Mahmud II. Zamanında Bosna-Hersek*. Istanbul: Nurgök Matbaası, 1965.

Ergin, Nina. "The Albanian *Tellak* Connection: Labor Migration to the Hamams of Eighteenth-Century Istanbul Based on the 1752 *İstanbul Hamamları Defteri*." *Turcica* 43 (2012): 231–56.

Erginbaş, Vefa. "Enlightenment in the Ottoman Context: İbrahim Müteferrika and His Intellectual Landscape." In *Historical Aspects of Printing and Publishing in Languages of the Middle East*, edited by Geoffrey Roper, 53–100. Leiden: Brill, 2014.

Erimtan, Can. *Ottomans Looking West?: The Origins of the Tulip Age and Its Development in Modern Turkey*. London: IB Tauris, 2008.

Erol, Merih. *Greek Orthodox Music in Ottoman Istanbul: Nation and Community in the Era of Reform*. Indianapolis: Indiana University Press, 2015.

Ertuğ, Nejdet. *Osmanlı Döneminde İstanbul Hammalları*. Istanbul: Timaş Yayınları, 2008.

Es'ad Efendi. *Üss-i Zafer (Yeniçeriliğin Kaldırılmasına Dair)*. Edited by Mehmet Arslan. Istanbul: Kitabevi, 2005.

———. *Es'ad Efendi Tarihi*. Edited by Ziya Yılmazer. Istanbul: Osmanlı Araştırmaları Vakfı, 2000.

———. *Teşrifat-i Kadime*. Istanbul: Matbaa-yı Amire, 1870.

Esenbel, Selçuk. "The Anguish of Civilized Behavior: The Use of Western Cultural Forms in the Everyday Lives of the Meiji Japanese and the Ottoman Turks during the Nineteenth Century." *Nichibunken Japan Review* (1994): 145–85.

Esmer, Tolga. "Economies of Violence, Bandits and Ottoman Governance in the Ottoman Empire around 1800." *Past and Present* 224 (2014): 163–99.

———. "The Precarious Intimacy of Honor in Late Ottoman Accounts of Para-militarism and Banditry." *European Journal of Turkish Studies* 18 (2014): 1–18.

Establet, Colette, and Jean-Paul Pascual. *La gent d'État dans la société ottomane damascène: Les 'askar à la fin du XVIIe siècle*. Damascus: Institut Français du Proche-Orient, 2011.

Evans, Richard J. *Rituals of Retribution: Capital Punishment in Germany, 1600-1987*. Oxford: Oxford University Press, 1996.

Evliya Çelebi. *Evliya Çelebi Seyahatnamesi*. Edited by Yücel Dağlı et al. 10 vols. Istanbul: Yapı Kredi Yayınları, 1999–2006.

Evstatiev, Simeon. "The Qadizadeli Movement and the Revival of Takfir in the Ottoman Age." In *Accusations of Unbelief in Islam: A Diachronic Perspective on Takfir*, edited by Camilla Adang, 213–43. Leiden: Brill, 2016.

Exertzoglou, Haris. "The Cultural Uses of Consmption: Negotiating Class, Gender, and Nation in the Ottoman Urban Centers during the 19th Century." *International Journal of Middle East Studies* 35 (2003): 77–101.

Fahmy, Khaled. *All the Pasha's Men: Mehmed Ali, His Army, and the Making of Modern Egypt*. Cairo: American University in Cairo Press, 1997.

Fa'iq, Sulayman [Süleyman Faik]. *Tarikh Baghdad*. Translated by Musa Kazim Nawras. Beirut: al-Rafidin li'l-Tiba'a wa al-Nashr wa al-Tawzi', 2010.

Faroqhi, Suraiya. *A Cultural History of the Ottomans: The Imperial Elite and Its Artifacts*. London: IB Tauris, 2016.

———. "The Adventures of Tunisian Fez-Sellers in Eighteenth-Century Istanbul." In *Travel and Artisans in the Ottoman Empire*, 143–55. London: IB Tauris, 2014.

———. "Migration into Eighteenth-Century 'Greater Istanbul' as Reflected in the Kadı Registers of Eyüp." In *Stories of Ottoman Men and Women*, 289–305. Istanbul: Eren, 2002.

Fay, Mary Ann. "Women and Waqf: Property, Power, and the Domain of Gender in Eighteenth-Century Egypt." In *Women in the Ottoman Empire: Middle Eastern Women in the Early Modern Era*, edited by Madeline Zilfi, 27–47. Leiden: Brill, 1997.

Febvre, Michel. *Théâtre de la Turquie*. Paris: E. Couterot, 1682.

Feldman, Walter. "The Emergence of Ottoman Music and Local Modernity." *Yıllık: Annual of Istanbul Studies* 1 (2019): 173–79.

———. *Music of the Ottoman Court: Makam, Composition and the Early Modern Ottoman Instrumental Repertoire*. Berlin: VWB, 1996.

Fellows, Charles. *A Journal Written during an Excursion in Asia Minor*. London: John Murray, 1839.

Findley, Carter Vaughn. *Enlightening Europe on Islam and the Ottomans: Mouradgea d'Ohsson and His Masterpiece*. Leiden: Brill, 2019.

———. "Political Culture and the Great Households." In *The Cambridge History of Turkey*, Vol. 3, *The Later Ottoman Empire, 1603-1839*, edited by Suraiya Faroqhi, 65–80. Cambridge: Cambridge University Press, 2006.

———. *Ottoman Civil Officialdom: A Social History*. Princeton: Princeton University Press, 1989.

———. *Bureaucratic Reform in the Ottoman Empire*. Princeton: Princeton University Press, 1980.

Finnane, Antonia. *Speaking of Yangzhou: A Chinese City, 1550-1850*. Cambridge, MA: Harvard University Asia Center, 2004.

Fleischer, Cornell H. *Bureaucrat and Intellectual in the Ottoman Empire: The Historian Mustafa Ali (1541-1600)*. Princeton: Princeton University Press, 1986.

Fleming, Katherine E. *The Muslim Bonaparte: Diplomacy and Orientalism in Ali Pasha's Greece*. Princeton: Princeton University Press, 1999.

Florescu, Radu. *Essays on Romanian History*. Portland: Center for Romanian Studies, 1999.

———. "The Fanariot Regime in the Danubian Principalities." *Balkan Studies* 9 (1968): 301–18.

Fontanier, Victor. *Voyages en Orient*. 2 vols. Paris: Librarie Universelle, 1829.

Frangakis-Syrett, Elena. *The Commerce of Smyrna in the Eighteenth Century (1700-1820)*. Athens: Center for Asia Minor Studies, 1992.

Frankland, Charles Colville. *Travels to and from Constantinople in the Years 1827 and 1828*. 2 vols. London: Henry Colburn and Richard Bentley, 1830.

Frierson, Elizabeth. "Cheap and Easy: The Creation of Consumer Culture in Late Ottoman Society." In *Consumption Studies and the History of the Ottoman Empire, 1550-1922*, edited by Donald Quataert, 243–60. Albany: State University of New York Press, 2000.

Fukasawa, Katsumi. *Toilerie et commerce du Levant*. Paris: CNRS, 1987.

Galland, Antoine. *Journal d'Antoine Galland*. Edited by Charles Schefer. 2 vols. Paris: Ernest Leroux, 1881.

Galt, John. *Letters from the Levant*. London: T. Cadell and W. Davies, 1812.

Garrioch, David. "Verbal Insults in Eighteenth-Century Paris." In *The Social History of*

Language, edited by Peter Burke and Roy Porter, 104–19. Cambridge: Cambridge University Press, 1987.

Gatrell, V.A.C. *The Hanging Tree: Execution and the English People, 1770–1868*. Oxford: Oxford University Press, 1994.

Gazzizade Abdullatif Efendi. *Vekayi'-i Baba Paşa fî't-Tarih*. Edited by Salih Erol. Ankara: Türk Tarih Kurumu, 2013.

Genç, Mehmet. "Contrôle et taxation du commerce du café dans l'Empire ottoman fin XVIIe–première moitié du XVIIIe siècle." In *La Commerce du café avant l'ère des plantations colonials*, edited by Michel Tuchscherer, 161–79. Cairo: Institut Français d'Archéologie Orientale, 2001.

———. "Osmanlı Maliyesinde Malikane Sistemi." In *Osmanlı İmparatorluğunda Devlet ve Ekonomi*, 99–152. Ankara: Ötüken, 2000.

———. "18. Yüzyıla Ait Osmanlı Mali Verilerinin İktisadi Faaliyetin Göstergisi Olarak Kullanılabilirliği Üzerinde Bir Çalışma." In *Osmanlı İmparatorluğunda Devlet ve Ekonomi*, 153–85. Ankara: Ötüken, 2000.

———. "18. Yüzyılda Osmanlı Ekonomisi ve Savaş." In *Osmanlı İmparatorluğunda Devlet ve Ekonomi*, 211–25. Istanbul: Ötüken, 2000.

Georgeon, François. *Au Pays du rakı: Le vin et l'alcool de l'empire Ottoman à la Turquie d'Erdoğan*. Paris: CNRS, 2021.

———. "Ottomans and Drinkers: The Consumption of Alcohol in Istanbul in the Nineteenth Century." In *Outside In: On the Margins of the Modern Middle East*, edited by Eugene Rogan, 7–30. London: IB Tauris, 2002.

al-Ghazzi, Badr al-Din. *Risalat adab mu'akala*. Edited by ʿUmar Musa Basha. Rabat: Maktabat al-Maʿarif, 1984.

al-Ghazzi, Kamil. *Nahr al-dhahab fi tarikh Halab*. Edited by Shawqi Shaʿath and Mahmud Fakhuri, 2nd ed. 3 vols. Aleppo: Dar al-Qalam al-ʿArabi, 1991.

Gilmore, David D. *Honor and Shame and the Unity of the Mediterranean*. Washington, DC: American Anthropological Association, 1987.

Ginio, Eyal. "Migrants and Workers in an Ottoman Port: Ottoman Salonica in the Eighteenth Century." In *Outside In: On the Margins of the Modern Middle East*, edited by Eugene Rogan, 126–48. London: IB Tauris, 2002.

Glete, Jan. *War and the State in Early Modern Europe: Spain, the Dutch Republic, and Sweden as Fiscal-Military States, 1500–1660*. New York: Routledge, 2002.

Göçek, Fatma Müge. *Rise of the Bourgeoisie, Demise of Empire: Ottoman Westernization and Social Change*. New York: Oxford University Press, 1996.

———. *East Encounters West: France and the Ottoman Empire in the Eighteenth Century*. New York: Oxford University Press, 1987.

Godsey, William D., and Petr Mata, eds. *The Habsburg Monarchy as a Fiscal-Military State: Contours and Perspectives, 1648–1815*. Oxford: Oxford University Press, 2022.

Goffman, Daniel. "Izmir: From Village to Colonial Port City." In *The Ottoman City between East and West: Aleppo, Izmir, and Istanbul*, edited by Edhem Eldem, Daniel Goffman, and Bruce Masters. Cambridge: Cambridge University Press, 1999.

———. *Izmir and the Levantine World, 1550–1650*. Seattle: University of Washington Press, 1990.

Goffman, Erving. *The Presentation of Self in Everyday Life*. New York: Anchor Books, 1959.

Good, David. *The Rise of the Austrian Empire, 1750-1914*. Berkeley: University of California Press, 1984.
Goody, Jack. *The Theft of History*. Cambridge: Cambridge University Press, 2006.
———. "The 'Civilizing Process' in Ghana." *European Journal of Sociology* 44 (2003): 61–73.
———. "Elias and the Anthropological Tradition." *Anthropological Theory* 2 (2002): 401–12.
Gordon, Daniel. *Citizens without Sovereignty: Equality and Sociability in French Thought, 1670-1789*. Princeton: Princeton University Press, 1994.
Goudard, Joseph, and and Henri Jalabert. *La Sainte Vierge au Liban*, 2nd ed. Beirut: Impr. Catholique, 1955.
Gradeva, Rossitsa. "War and Peace along the Danube: Vidin at the End of the Seventeenth Century." *Oriente Moderno* NS 20 (2001): 149–75.
Graham, Aaron, and Patrick Walsh. *The British Fiscal-Military States, 1660-c. 1783*. London: Routledge/Taylor and Francis Group, 2016.
Grandits, Hannes. "Social Stratification and Change in Herzegovinian Urban Life in the Tanzimat Era." In *Urban Governance under the Ottomans: Between Cosmopolitanism and Conflict*, edited by Ulrike Freitag and Nora Lafi, 79–96. New York: Routledge, 2014.
Grehan, James. "Fun and Games in Ottoman Aleppo: The Life and Times of a Local Schoolteacher (1835-1865)." In *Entertainment among the Ottomans*, edited by Ebru Boyar and Kate Fleet, 90–120. Leiden: Brill, 2019.
———. "Imperial Crisis and Muslim-Christian Relations in Ottoman Syria and Palestine, c. 1770-1830." *Journal of the Economic and Social History of the Orient* 58 (2015): 490–531.
———. *Twilight of the Saints: Everyday Religion in Ottoman Syria and Palestine*. New York: Oxford University Press, 2014.
———. "The Legend of the Samarmar: Parades and Communal Identity in Syrian Towns, 1500-1800." *Past and Present* 204 (2009): 89–125.
———. *Everyday Life and Consumer Culture in Eighteenth-Century Damascus*. Seattle: University of Washington Press, 2007.
———. "Smoking and Early Modern Sociability: The Great Tobacco Debate in the Ottoman Middle East (Seventeenth to Eighteenth Centuries)." *American Historical Review* 111 (2006): 1352–77.
———. "The Mysterious Power of Words: Language, Law, and Culture in Ottoman Damascus (17th-18th Centuries)." *Journal of Social History* 37 (2004): 991–1015.
Grelot, Guillaume-Joseph. *A Late Voyage to Constantinople*. London: John Playford, 1683.
Griffiths, J. *Travels in Europe, Asia Minor, and Arabia*. London: T. Cadell and W. Davies, 1805.
Guido, Alfani, and Matteo di Tullio. *The Lion's Share: Inequality and the Rise of the Fiscal State in Preindustrial Europe*. Cambridge: Cambridge University Press, 2019.
Güven, Hikmet Feridun. "Klasik Türk Edebiyatında hiciv ve mizah." In *Türk Edebiyatı Tarihi*. Edited by Talat Sait Halman. 4 vols. Istanbul: TC Kültür ve Turizm Bakanlığı Yayınları.
Hakim, Mehmed. *Hakim Efendi Tarihi*. Edited by Tahir Güngör and Ziya Yılmazer. 2 vols. Istanbul: Türkiye Yazma Eserler Kurumu Başkanlığı, 2019.
al-Halabi, Yusuf. *Hawadith Halab al-yawmiyya, 1771-1805*. Aleppo, 2006.
Hamadeh, Shirine. "Invisible City: Istanbul's Migrants and the Politics of Space." *Eighteenth-Century Studies* 50 (2017): 173–93.
———. "Mean Streets: Space and Moral Order in Early Modern Istanbul." *Turcica* 44 (2013): 249–77.

———. *The City's Pleasures: Istanbul in the Eighteenth Century.* Seattle: University of Washington Press, 2008.
Hammel, Eugene A. *Alternative Social Structures and Ritual Relations in the Balkans.* Englewood Cliffs, NJ: Prentice-Hall, 1968.
von Hammer, Joseph. *Histoire de l'empire ottoman depuis son origine jusqu'à nos jours.* 17 vols. Istanbul: Isis Press, 2000.
Hammuda ibn ʿAbd al-ʿAziz. *al-Kitab al-bashi.* Edited by Muhammad al-Madur. Tunis: al-Dar al-Tunisiyya li'l-Nashr, 1970.
Hanna, Nelly. *In Praise of Books: A Cultural History of Cairo's Middle Class, Sixteenth to Eighteenth Century.* Syracuse: Syracuse University Press, 2003.
———. *Making Big Money in 1600: The Life and Times of Ismaʿil Abu Taqiyya, Egyptian Merchant.* Syracuse: Syracuse University Press, 1998.
Hardy, M.J.L. *Blood Feuds and the Payment of Blood Money in the Middle East.* Leiden: Brill, 1963.
Harrison, Simon. *Dark Trophies: Hunting and the Enemy Body in Modern War.* New York: Berghahn Books, 2012.
Hasan Agha al-ʿAbd. *Tarikh Hasan Agha.* Edited by Yusuf Nuʿaysa. Damascus: Wizarat al-Thaqafa wa al-Irshad al-Qawmi, 1979.
Haşırzade Mehmed Elif. *Tenşitu'l-muhibbin bi-menakıb-ı Hoca Hüsameddin.* Süleymaniye Library, Nafız Paşa 1217.
Hasluck, Frederick William. *Christianity and Islam under the Sultans.* 2 vols. Oxford: Clarendon Press, 1929.
Hasluck, Margaret. *The Unwritten Law of Albania.* Edited by J.H. Hutton. Cambridge: Cambridge University Press, 1954.
Hathaway, Jane. *The Arab Lands under Ottoman Rule, 1516-1800.* New York: Pearson Longman, 2008.
———. "The Ottomans and the Yemeni Coffee Trade." *Oriente Moderno* 25 (2006): 161–71.
———. "Rewriting Eighteenth-Century Ottoman History." *Mediterranean Historical Review* 19 (2004): 29–53.
———. *The Politics of Households in Ottoman Egypt: The Rise of the Qazdağlıs.* Cambridge: Cambridge University Press, 1997.
———. "The Military Household in Ottoman Egypt." *International Journal of Middle East Studies* 27 (1995): 39–52.
Hattox, Ralph. *Coffee and Coffeehouses: The Origins of a Social Beverage in the Medieval Near East.* Seattle: University of Washington Press, 1985.
Havlioğlu, Didem. "On the Margins and between the Lines: Ottoman Women Poets from the Fifteenth to the Twentieth Centuries." *Turkish Historical Review* 1 (2010): 25–54.
des Hayes, Louis. *Voiage du Levant par le commandement du roy en l'année 1621.* Paris: Adrian Taupinart, 1632.
He, Wenkai. *Paths toward the Modern Fiscal State: England, Japan, and China.* Cambridge, MA: Harvard University Press, 2013.
Herzfeld, Michael. *The Poetics of Manhood: Contest and Identity in a Cretan Mountain Village.* Princeton: Princeton University Press, 1985.
Hibbett, Howard. *The Floating World in Japanese Fiction.* London: Oxford University Press, 1959.

Hill, Aaron. *A Full and Just Account of the Present State of the Ottoman Empire in All Its Branches.* London: Cengage Gale, 1709.

Hobhouse, J.C. *A Journey through Albania.* 2 vols. New York, 1817.

Hoeksema, Jack. "Taboo Terms and Their Grammar." In *The Oxford Handbook of Taboo Words and Language,* edited by Keith Allan, 160–79. New York: Oxford University Press, 2019.

Holbrook, Victoria Rowe. *The Unreadable Shores of Love: Turkish Modernity and Mystic Romance.* Austin: University of Texas Press, 1994.

Holland, Henry. *Travels in the Ionian Isles, Albania, Thessaly, Macedonia.* London: Longman, Hurst, Rees, Orme, and Brown, 1815.

Horta, Paulo Lemos. "Heterotopia as a Site of Cross-Cultural Collaboration: Ibrahim al-Dusuqi and Edward Lane." *Middle Eastern Literatures* 15 (2012): 273–85.

Hourani, Albert. *Arabic Thought in the Liberal Age, 1798-1939.* Cambridge: Cambridge University Press, 1983.

———. "Ottoman Reform and the Politics of Notables." In *The Beginnings of Modernization in the Middle East: The Nineteenth Century,* edited by William Polk and Richard L. Chambers, 41–68. Chicago: University of Chicago Press, 1968.

———. "The Changing Face of the Fertile Crescent in the XVIIIth Century." *Studia Islamica* 8 (1957): 89–122.

Huang, Pei. *Reorienting the Manchus: A Study of Sinicization, 1583-1795.* Ithaca: East Asia Program, Cornell University, 2011.

Hughes, Lindsey. "'The Crown of Maidenly Honor and Virtue': Redefining Femininity in Peter I's Russia." In *Women and Gender in 18th-Century Russia,* edited by Wendy Rosslyn, 35–49. Burlington, VT: Ashgate, 2003.

Hughes, Thomas Smart. *Travels in Sicily, Greece, and Albania.* 2 vols. London: J. Mawman, 1820.

Ianeva, Svetla. "Hygiene in Nineteenth-Century Ottoman Bulgaria." *Turkish Historical Review* 5 (2014): 16–31.

Ibn Abi'l-Diyaf, Ahmad. *Ithaf ahl al-zaman bi-akhbar muluk Tunis wa ʿahd al-aman.* 8 vols. Tunis: Nashr Kitabat al-Dawla li'l-Shu'un al-Thaqafiyya wa al-Ikhbar, 1963–67.

Ibn Kannan. *Yawmiyat shamiyya.* Edited by Akram al-ʿUlabi. Damascus: Dar al-Tabbaʿ, 1994.

———. *al-Mawakib al-islamiyya fi al-mamalik al-shamiyya.* Edited by Hikmet Ismaʿil. 2 vols. Damascus: Wizarat al-Thaqafa, 1992.

Ibn al-Siddiq. *Gharaʾib al-badaʾiʿ fi ʿajaʾib al-waqaʾiʿ.* Edited by Yusuf al-Nuʿaysa. Damascus: Matbaʿat al-ʿAjluni, 1988.

İbrahim Hilmi Bey. *Menakıbname-i Mustafa Safi-i Amedi.* Edited by Serdar Uğurlu. Istanbul: Kriter Yayınevi, 2017.

Ikegami, Eiko. *The Taming of the Samurai: Honorific Individualism and the Making of Modern Japan.* Cambridge, MA: Harvard University Press, 1995.

İnal, Onur. "Ottoman Borderlands and the Anglo-Ottoman Exchange of Costumes." *Journal of World History* 22 (2011): 243–72.

İnalcık, Halil. "Military and Fiscal Transformation in the Ottoman Empire, 1600-1700." *Archivum Ottomanicum* 6 (1980): 283–337.

———. "Centralization and Decentralization in Ottoman Administration." In *Studies in*

Eighteenth-Century Islamic History, ed. Thomas Naff and Roger Owen, 27-52. Carbondale: Southern Illinois University Press, 1977.

———. The Ottoman Empire: The Classical Age, 1300-1600. New York: Praeger, 1973.

———. "The Ottoman Economic Mind and Aspects of the Ottoman Economy." In Studies in the Economic History of the Middle East, edited by M.A. Cook, 207-18. London: Oxford University Press, 1970.

İnalcık, Halil, and Donald Quataert, eds. An Economic and Social History of the Ottoman Empire, Vol. 1, 1300-1600. New York: Cambridge University Press, 1997.

İpekten, Haluk. Divan Edebiyatında Edebi Muhitler. Istanbul: Milli Eğitim Basımevi, 1996.

Itzkowitz, Norman. "Eighteenth-Century Ottoman Realities." Studia Islamica 16 (1962): 73-94.

Ivanyi, Katherina. "Adab, Akhlaq, and Early Modern Ottoman Parenesis: Birgivi Mehmed Efendi's (d. 981/1573) al-Tariqa al-Muhammadiyya." In Adab and Modernity: A "Civilizing Process"? (Sixteenth-Twenty-First Century), edited by Catherine Mayeur Jaouen, 49-62. Leiden: Brill, 2020.

al-Jabarti, ʿAbd al-Rahman. ʿAjaʾib al-athar fi al-tarajim al-akhbar. Edited by Hasan Muhammad Jawhar, ʿAbd al-Fattah Sirinjawi, Ibrahim Salim, and ʿUmar Dusuqi. 7 vols. Cairo: Lajnat al-Bayan al-ʿArabi, 1958-67.

Jacob, Georg. Türklerde Karagöz. Translated by Orhan Şaik Gökyay. Istanbul: Bürhaneddin Basımevi, 1938.

Jianu, Angela. "Women, Fashion, and Europeanization: The Romanian Principalities, 1750-1830." In Women in the Ottoman Balkans, edited by Amila Buturovic and İrvin Cemil Schick, 201-30. New York: IB Tauris, 2007.

Jirousek, Charlotte. "Ottoman Influence in Balkan Dress." In Resplendent Dress from Southeastern Europe: A History in Layers, edited by Elizabeth Wayland Barber and Barbara Belle Sloan, 143-76. Los Angeles: Fowler Museum at UCLA, 2013.

Jory, Patrick. A History of Manners and Civility in Modern Thailand. Cambridge: Cambridge University Press, 2022.

Joudah, Ahmad Hasan. Revolt in Palestine in the Eighteenth Century: The Era of Shaykh Zahir al-ʿUmar. Princeton: Kingston Press, 1987.

Kabudlı Vasfi Efendi. "The Adventures of an Ottoman Horseman: The Autobiography of Kabudlı Vasfi Efendi, 1800-1825." In The Joys of Philology: Studies in Ottoman Literature, History, and Orientalism (1500-1923), edited by Jan Schmidt, vol. 1. Istanbul: Isis Press, 2002.

Kabudlu Mustafa Vasfı Efendi. Tevarih: Analysis—Texts—Maps—Index—Facsimile. Edited by Ömer Koçyiğit. Cambridge, MA: Department of Near Eastern Languages and Civilizations, Harvard University, 2016.

Kafadar, Cemal. "The City Opens Your Eyes Because It Wants to Be Seen." In A Companion to Early Modern Istanbul, edited by Shirine Hamadeh and Çiğdem Kafescioğlu, 25-60. Leiden: Brill, 2022.

———. "How Dark Is the History of the Night, How Black the Story of Coffee, How Bitter the Tale of Love: The Changing Measure of Leisure and Pleasure in Early Modern Istanbul." In Medieval and Early Modern Performance in the Eastern Mediterranean, edited by Arzu Öztürkmen and Evelyn Birge Vitz, 243-69. Turnhout: Brepols, 2014.

———. "Janissaries and Other Riffraff of Ottoman Istanbul: Rebels without a Cause?" In

Identity and Identity Formation in the Ottoman World: A Volume of Essays in Honor of Norman Itzkowitz, edited by Baki Tezcan and Karl Barbir, 113–34. Madison: University of Wisconsin Press, 2008.

———. "The Question of Ottoman Decline." *Harvard Middle Eastern and Islamic Review* 4 (1997–98): 30–75.

———. "On the Purity and Corruption of the Janissaries." *Turkish Studies Association Bulletin* 15 (1991): 273–80.

Kagan, Frederick W. *The Military Reforms of Nicolas I: The Origins of the Modern Russian Army*. New York: St. Martin's Press, 1999.

Kallander, Amy Aisen. *Women, Gender, and the Palace Households in Ottoman Tunisia*. Austin: University of Texas Press, 2013.

Kanetaki, Eleni. "Ottoman Baths in Greece: A Contribution to the Study of Their History and Architecture." In *Bathing Culture of Anatolian Civilizations: Architecture, History, and Imagination*, edited by Nina Ergin, 221–55. Leuven: Peeters, 2011.

Karababa, Emineğül, and Güliz Ger. "Early Modern Ottoman Coffeehouse Culture and the Formation of the Consumer Subject." *Journal of Consumer Research* 37 (2011): 737–60.

Karabella, Mehmet. "Lovers in the Age of the Beloveds: Classical Ottoman Divan Literature and the Dialectical Tradition (Adab al-Bahth)." In *The Beloved in Middle East Literatures: The Culture of Love and Languishing*, edited by Hanadi al-Samman, Alireza Korangy, and Michael Beard, 285–300. London: IB Tauris, 2017.

Karagözlü, Volkan. "Damad İbrahim Paşa'nın Şiir Meclisleri Bağlamında Kültür, Oyun, Gazel." In *1. Uluslararası Nevşehir Tarih ve Kültür Sempozyumu Bildirileri*, edited by Adem Öger, 119–31. Ankara: Nevşehir Üniversitesi Yayınları, 2012.

Karahasanoğlu, Selim. "Challenging the Paradigm of the Tulip Age: The Consumer Behavior of Nevşehirli Damad İbrahim Paşa and His Household." In *Living the Good Life: Consumption in the Qing and Ottoman Empires of the Eighteenth Century*, edited by Elif Akçetin and Suraiya Faroqhi, 134–60. Leiden: Brill, 2018.

———. *Kadı ve Günlüğü: Sadreddinzade Telhisi Mustafa Efendi Günlüğü (1711-1735) Üstüne Bir İnceleme*. Istanbul: Türkiye İş Bankası Kültür Yayınları, 2013.

Karal, Enver Ziya, ed. *Selim III'ün Hatt-ı Hümayunları*. Ankara: Türk Tarih Kurumu Basımevi, 1942–46.

Karamah, Rufa'il. *Hawadith Lubnan wa Suriya min sanat 1745 ila sanat 1800*. Edited by Basiliyus Qattan. Beirut: Jarrus, 1983(?).

Karaman, K. Kivanç, and Şevket Pamuk. "Different Paths to the Modern State in Europe: the Interaction between Warfare, Economic Structure, and Political Regime." *American Political Science Review* 107 (2013): 603–26.

———. "Ottoman State Finances in European Perspective, 1500–1914." *Journal of Economic History* 70 (2010): 593–629.

Karateke, Hakan T. *Padişahım Çok Yaşa: Osmanlı Devletinin Son Yüz Yılında Merasimler*. Istanbul: Kitap Yayınevi, 2004.

Karkukli, Rasul. *Dawhat al-wuzara' fi tarikh waqa'i' Baghdad al-zawra'*. Translated by `Ala' Musa Kazim Nawras. Beirut: Dar al-Katib al-`Arabi, 1963.

Katsaites, Markos Antonios. *Dio Taxidia ste Smyrne, 1740 and 1742*. Athens: Ekdoseis "Henoseos Smyrnnaion," 1972.

Kemp, Percy. "Power and Knowledge in Jalili Mosul." *Middle Eastern Studies* 19 (1983): 201–12.
Kermeli, Evgenia. "The Tobacco Controversy in Early Modern Ottoman Muslim and Christian Discourse." *Hacettepe University Journal of Turkish Studies* 11 (2014): 121–35.
al-Khadimi, Muhammad. *Bariqa mahmudiyya fi sharh tariqa muhammadiyya wa shari`a nabawiyya fi sira ahmadiyya*. 4 vols. Istanbul: Şirket-i Sihafiye, 1900.
Khater, Akram Fouad. *Inventing Home: Emigration, Gender, and the Middle Class in Lebanon, 1870-1920*. Berkeley: University of California Press, 2001.
Khoury, Dina Rizk. "Political Community in the Age of Reform: Rebellion and Empire, 1780–1820." In *Arabic Thought beyond the Liberal Age: Towards an Intellectual History of the Nahda*, edited by Jens Hanssen and Max Weiss, 101–20. Cambridge: Cambridge University Press, 2016.
———. "Violence and Spatial Politics between the Local and Imperial: Baghdad, 1778–1810." In *The Spaces of the Modern City: Imaginaries, Politics, and Everyday Life*, edited by Gyan Prakash and Kevin M. Kruse, 181–213. Princeton: Princeton University Press, 2008.
———. *State and Provincial Society in the Ottoman Empire: Mosul, 1540-1834*. Cambridge: Cambridge University Press, 1997.
Kiel, Machiel. "Ottoman Mineral Baths (Kaplıca) on the Balkans: A Study of Several Little-Known Examples." In *Bathing Culture of Anatolian Civilizations: Architecture, History, and Imagination*, edited by Nina Ergin, 198–219. Leuven: Peeters, 2011.
Kiernan, V.G. *The Duel in European History: Honour and the Reign of Aristocracy*. Oxford: Oxford University Press, 1988.
Kılıç, Çiğdem. "Men Acting as Women: The *Zenne* in Nineteenth-Century Popular Theater." In *Celebration, Entertainment, and Theater in the Ottoman World*, edited by Suraiya Faroqhi and Arzu Öztürkmen, 303–18. London: Seagull, 2014.
Kılıç, Sevda Önal. "Edebiyat Patronajı Açısından Damad İbrahim Paşa Dönemine Dair Genel Bir Değerlendirme." *Atatürk Üniversitesi Türkiyat Araştırmaları Enstitüsü Dergisi* 61 (2018): 1–14.
Kınlı, İrem Özgören. "Principal Elements of the Ottoman State-Formation Process through an Eliasian Perspective." In *Norbert Elias and Empirical Research*, edited by Tatiana Savoia Landini and François Dépelteau, 161–78. New York: Palgrave Macmillan, 1974.
Kırımcı, Hakan, and Ali Yaycıoğlu. "Heirs of Chingis Khan in the Age of Revolutions: An Unruly Crimean Prince in the Ottoman Empire and Beyond." *Der Islam* 94 (2017): 496–526.
Kırlı, Cengiz. "Coffeehouses: Leisure and Sociability in Ottoman Istanbul." In *Leisure Cultures in Urban Europe, c. 1700-1870*, edited by Peter Borsay and Jan Hein Furnée, 161–82. Manchester: Manchester University Press, 2016.
———. "İstanbul: Bir Büyük Kahvehane." *İstanbul Dergisi* 47(2003): 75–78.
———. "The Struggle over Space: Coffeehouses of Ottoman Istanbul, 1780–1845." Unpublished PhD diss., SUNY-Binghamton, 2000.
Koçu, Reşad Ekrem. *İstanbul Tulumbacıları*. Istanbul: Ana Yayınevi, 1981.
———. *Türk Giyim Kuşam ve Süslenme Sözlüğü*. Ankara: Başnur Matbaası, 1967.
Koliopoulos, John S. *Brigands with a Cause: Brigandage and Irredentism in Modern Greece, 1821-1912*. Oxford: Clarendon Press, 1987.

Kolokotrones, Theodoros. *Memoirs from the Greek War of Independence, 1821-1833*. Translated by George J. Koutris. Chicago: Argonaut, 1969.

Kollmann, Nancy Shields. *The Russian Empire, 1450-1801*. Oxford: Oxford University Press, 2017.

———. "Etiquette for Peter's Time: The Honorable Mirror for Youth." *Russian History* 35 (2008): 63-83.

———. *By Honor Bound: State and Society in Early Modern Russia*. Ithaca: Cornell University Press, 1999.

Kömeçoğlu, Uğur. "*Homo Ludens* ve *Homo Sapiens* Arasında Kamusallık ve Toplumsallık." In *Osmanlı Kahvehaneleri: Mekân, Sosyalleşme, İktidar*, edited by Ahmet Yaşar, 49-84. Istanbul: Kitap Yayınevi, 2009.

Krieken, Robert van. *Norbert Elias*. London: Routledge, 1998.

Küçük, Bekir Harun. *Science without Leisure: Practical Naturalism in Istanbul, 1660-1732*. Pittsburgh: University of Pittsburgh Press, 2020.

Kudret, Cevdet. *Karagöz*. 3 vols. Ankara: Bilgi Yayınevi, 1968-70.

Kudsieh, Suha. "Beyond Colonial Binaries: Amicable Ties among Egyptian and European Scholars, 1820-1850." *Journal of Comparative Poetics* 36 (2016): 44-68.

Kümin, Beat A. *Drinking Matters: Public Houses and Social Exchange in Early Modern Central Europe*. Basingstoke: Palgrave Macmillan, 2007.

Kuru, Selim S. "Generic Desires: Homoerotic Love in Ottoman Turkish Poetry." In *Mediterranean Crossings: Sexual Transgressions in Islam and Christianity (10th to 18th Centuries)*, 43-63. Rome: Viella, 2020.

Kuşmani, Dihkanizade Ubeydullah. *Nizam-ı Cedide Bir Risale: Zebire-i Kuşmani fi Ta'rif-i Nizam-ı Ilhami*. Edited by Ömer İşbilir. Ankara: Türk Tarih Kurumu, 2006.

Kuşmani, Dihkanizade Ubeydullah, and Ebubekir Efendi. *Asiler ve Gaziler: Kabakçı Mustafa Risalesi*. Edited by Aysel Danacı Yıldız. Istanbul: Kitap Yayınevi, 2007.

Kutay, Cemal. *İki Rifat Paşa'nın Ahlak Dünyası*. Istanbul: Sile Matbaası, 1970.

Kuzmics, Helmut. "The Civilizing Process." In *Civil Society and the State*, edited by John Keane, 147-76. New York: Verso, 1988.

Ladurie, Emmanuel Le Roy, with Jean-François Fitou. *Saint-Simon and the Court of Louis XIV*. Translated by Arthur Goldhammer. Chicago: University of Chicago Press, 2001.

Lafi, Nora. *Esprit civique et organization citadine dans l'Empire ottoman (Xve-XXe siècles)*. Leiden: Brill, 2018.

Lane, Edward Lane. *An Account of the Manners and Customs of the Modern Egyptians*. London: John Murray, 1860; reprint: New York, Dover, 1973.

Larguèche, Dalenda. "Le café à Tunis du XVIIIe au XIXe siècle: Produit de commerce et espace de sociabilité." In *Le Commerce du café avant l'ère des plantations coloniales*, edited by Michel Tuchscherer, 181-210. Cairo: Institut Français d'Archéologie Orientale, 2001.

Lau, Wai. *On the Process of Civilisation in Japan: Sociogenetic and Psychogenetic Investigations*. Cham, Switz.: Palgrave Macmillan, 2022.

Leake, William. *Travels in Northern Greece*. 4 vols. London: J. Rodwell, 1835.

Le Gall, Dina. "Kadızadelis, Nakşbendis, and Intra-Sufi Diatribe in Seventeenth-Century Istanbul." *Turkish Studies Association Journal* 28 (2004): 1-28.

Levinger, Matthew Bernard. *Enlightened Nationalism: The Transformation of Prussian Political Culture, 1806-1848*. Oxford: Oxford University Press, 2000.

Lewicka, Paulina. "Restaurants, Inns, and Taverns That Never Were: Some Reflections on Public Consumption in Medieval Cairo." *Journal of the Economic and Social History of the Orient* 48 (2005): 40-91.

Lipman, Andrew. "'A Meanes to Knitt Them Togeather': The Exchange of Body Parts in the Pequot War." *William and Mary Quarterly* 65 (2008): 3-28.

Liston, Katie, and Stephen Mennell. "Ill Met in Ghana: Jack Goody and Norbert Elias on Process and Progress in Africa." *Theory, Culture, and Society* 26 (2009): 52-70.

Lord, Albert B. "The Heroic Tradition of Greek Epic and Ballad: Continuity and Change." In *Hellenism and the First Greek War of Liberation (1821-1830): Continuity and Change*, 79-94. Thessaloniki: Institute for Balkan Studies, 1976.

Lotman, Yuri M. "The Poetics of Everyday Behavior in Eighteenth-Century Russian Culture." In *The Semiotics of Russian Culture*, edited by Yuri M. Lotman and Boris Uspenskii, 231-56. Ann Arbor: University of Michigan Press, 1984.

Lucas, Paul. *Voyage au Levant*. 2 vols. Paris: Nicolas Simart, 1714.

Lutfî, Ahmed. *Tarih-i Lutfî*. 8 vols. Istanbul: Matbaa-yi Amire, 1875-1912.

Maaoui, Azza. "Karakouz et le culte de la negativité." In *Mélanges Professeur Robert Mantran*, edited by Abdeljelil Temimi, 153-59. Zaghouan: Publiquations du Centre d'Etudes et de Recherches Ottomanes, Morisques, de Documentation et d'Information, 1988.

Mackerras, Colin P. *The Rise of the Peking Opera, 1770-1870: Social Aspects of the Theatre in Manchu China*. Oxford: Clarendon Press, 1972.

Mahamid, Hatim, and Chaim Nissim. "Sufis and Coffee Consumption: Religio-Legal and Historical Aspects of a Controversy in the Late Mamluk and Early Ottoman Periods." *Journal of Sufi Studies* 7 (2018): 140-64.

de Maillet, Benoit. *Description de l'Egypte*. 2 vols. Paris: Louis Genneau and Jacques Rollin, 1735.

Makriyannis, Ioannes. *Makriyannis: The Memoirs of General Makriyannis, 1797-1864*. Translated by H.A. Lidderdale. New York: Oxford University Press, 1966.

Mantran, Robert. *Istanbul dans la seconde moitié du XVIIe siècle*. Paris: Librairie Adrien Maisonneuve, 1962.

Marcus, Abraham. *The Middle East on the Eve of Modernity: Aleppo in the Eighteenth Century*. New York: Columbia University Press, 1989.

Mardin, Şerif. "Super-Westernization in Urban Life in the Ottoman Empire in the Last Quarter of the Nineteenth Century." In *Turkey: Geographic and Social Perspectives*, 403-49. Leiden: Brill, 1974.

———. *The Genesis of Young Ottoman Thought: A Study in the Modernization of Turkish Political Ideas*. Princeton: Princeton University Press, 1962.

Marino, Brigitte. *Le faubourg du Midan à Damas à l'époque Ottomane: Espace urbaine, société, et habitat (1742-1830)*. France: Presses de l'Ipfo, 1997.

Marshall, P.J. *East India Fortunes: The British in Bengal in the Eighteenth Century*. London: Oxford University Press, 1976.

Masters, Bruce. "Aleppo's Janissaries: Crime Syndicate or *Vox Populi*?" In *Popular Protest and Political Participation in the Ottoman Empire: Studies in Honor of Suraiya Faroqhi*, edited by Eleni Gara, M. Erdem Kabadayı, and Christoph Neumann. Istanbul: Bilgi University Press, 2011.

Matthee, Rudi. "Alcohol in the Islamic Middle East." *Past and Present* 222, Suppl. 9 (2014): 100–25.

———. *The Pursuit of Pleasure: Drugs and Stimulants in Iranian History, 1500-1900*. Princeton: Princeton University Press, 2005.

Mazower, Mark. "Villagers, Notables, and Imperial Collapse: The Virgin Mary on Tinos in the 1820s." In *Networks of Power in Modern Greece: Essays in Honor of John Campbell*, edited by Mark Mazower 69–87. New York: Columbia University Press, 2008.

McGowan, Bruce. "The Age of the Ayans, 1699–1812." In *A Social and Economic History of the Ottoman Empire*, Vol. 2, *1600–1914*, edited by Halil İnalcık and Donald Quataert, New York: Cambridge University Press, 1999.

Mehmed Haşim Efendi. *İma-yi Törehat-ı Büldanan*. Edited by Feridun Emecen and İlhan Şahin. Ankara: Neyir Matbaacılık, 2022.

Meier, Astrid. "Bathing as a Translocal Phenomenon? Bathhouses in the Arab Provinces of the Ottoman Empire." In *Bathing Culture of Anatolian Civilizations: Architecture, History, and Imagination*, edited by Nina Ergin, 167–97. Leuven: Peeters, 2011.

Mélikoff, Irène. *Hadji Bektach, un mythe et ses avatars: Genèse et évolution du soufisme populaire en Turquie*. Leiden: Brill, 1998.

Mennell, Stephen. *Norbert Elias: An Introduction*. Oxford: Blackwell, 1989.

Mikhail, Alan. *The Animal in Ottoman Egypt*. New York: Oxford University Press, 2014.

———. "The Heart's Desire: Gender, Urban Space, and the Ottoman Coffee House." In *Ottoman Tulips, Ottoman Coffee: Leisure and Lifestyle in the Eighteenth Century*, edited by Dana Sajdi, 133–70. London: Tauris Academic Studies, 2007.

Mikov, Lyubomir. "Ottoman Bathhouses in Bulgaria (in the Context of Bathing Culture in the Balkans and Anatolia)." *Études Balkaniques* 4 (2012): 118–51.

Mishaqa, Mikha'il. *Murder, Mayhem, Pillage, and Plunder: The History of the Lebanon in the 18th and 19th Centuries*. Translated by Wheeler M. Thackston. Albany: State University of New York Press, 1988.

Mizrahi, Daryo. "Language and Sexuality in Ottoman Shadow-Puppet Performances." In *Celebration, Entertainment, and Theater in the Ottoman World*, edited by Suraiya Faroqhi and Arzu Öztürkmen, 275–92. London: Seagull, 2014.

Mohr, Melissa. *Holy Shit: A Brief History of Swearing*. New York: Oxford University Press, 2013.

Montagu, Lady Mary Wortley. *Letters from the Levant during the Embassy to Constantinople, 1716-1718*. New York: Arno Press, 1971.

Motley, Mark. *Becoming a French Aristocrat: The Education of the Court Nobility, 1580-1715*. Princeton: Princeton University Press, 1990.

de la Mottraye, Aubry. *Travels through Europe, Asia, and into Part of Africa*. 3 vols. London: T. Woodward, 1732.

Mrgić, Jelena. "Wine or 'Raki': The Interplay of Climate and Society in Early Modern Ottoman Bosnia." *Environment and History* 17 (2011): 613–37.

al-Muhibbi, Muhammad Amin. *Khulasat al-athar fi a'yan al-qarn al-hadi 'ashar*. 4 vols. Beirut: Dar Sadr, n.d.

Muir, Edward. *Mad Blood Stirring: Vendetta and Factions in Friuli during the Renaissance*. Baltimore: Johns Hopkins University Press, 1993.

Munayyir, Hananiya. *al-Durr al-marsuf fi al-tarikh al-Shuf*. Beirut, 1984.
al-Muradi, Muhammad Khalil. *Silk al-durar fi a'yan al-qarn al-thani 'ashar*. 4 vols. Beirut: Dar Ibn Hazm, 1988.
———. *'Arf al-basham fi man waliya fatwa Dimashq al-Sham*. Edited by Muhammad Muti' al-Hafiz and Riyad 'Abd al-Hamid Murad. Damascus: Dar Ibn Kathir, 1988.
Mustafa Ali. *XVI. Yüzyıl Osmanlı Efendisi Mustafa Ali: Meva'idü'n-Nefais fi Kava'idi'l-Mecalis*. Translated by Douglas Scott Brookes. Cambridge, MA: Dept. of Near Eastern Languages and Civilizations, Harvard University, 2003.
Müstakimzade Süleyman Sadeddin Efendi. *Devhat ül-Meşayih ma Zeyl*. Istanbul: Çağrı Yayınları, 1978.
———. *Tuhfe-i Hattatin*. Istanbul: Devlet Matbaası, 1928.
Myrsiades, Linda S., and Kostas Myrsiades. *Karagiozis: Culture and Comedy in Greek Puppet Theater*. Lexington: University Press of Kentucky, 1992.
Nabi. *Hayriyye*. Edited by İskender Pala. Istanbul: Bedir Yayınevi, 1989.
al-Nabulsi, 'Abd al-Ghani. *al-Haqiqa wa al-majaz wa fi al-rihla ila Bilad al-Sham wa Misr wa al-Hijaz*. Edited by Ahmad 'Abd al-Majid al-Hariri. Cairo: al-Hay'a al-Misriyya al-'Amma li'l-Kitab, 1986.
———. *al-Hadiqa al-nadiyya: Sharh al-Tariqa al-Muhammadiyya*. 2 vols. Lyallpur: al-Maktaba al-Nuriyya al-Ridwiyya, 1977.
Naima, Mustafa. *Tarih-i Naima*. Istanbul, n.d.
Neuburger, Mary C. *Balkan Smoke: Tobacco and the Making of Modern Bulgaria*. Ithaca: Cornell University Press, 2013.
Neumann, Christoph. "How Did a Vezir Dress in the Eighteenth Century?" In *Ottoman Costumes: From Textiles to Identity*, edited by Suraiya Faroqhi and Christoph Neumann, 181–217. Istanbul: Eren, 2004.
———. "Ottoman Provincial Towns from the Eighteenth to the Nineteenth Century." In *The Empire in the City: Arab Provincial Capitals in the Late Ottoman Empire*, edited by Jens Hanssen, Thomas Philipp, and Stefan Weber, 131–44. Beirut: Ergon Verlag Würzburg, 2002.
Niebuhr, Carsten. *Travels through Arabia and Other Countries of the East*. Translated by Robert Heron. 2 vols. Edinburgh: R. Morison and Son, 1792.
Nishiyama, Matsunosuke. *Edo Culture: Daily Life and Diversions in Urban Japan, 1600–1800*. Honolulu: University of Hawai'i Press, 1997.
Nuri Bey, Halil. *Nuri Tarihi*. Edited by Seydi Vakkas Toprak. Ankara: Türk Tarih Kurumu, 2015.
Nutku, Özdemir. *Meddahlık ve Meddah Hikayeleri*. Istanbul: Atatürk Kültür Merkezi Başkanlığı Yayınları, 1997.
O'Fahey, R.S., and Bernd Radtke. "Neo-Sufism Reconsidered." *Der Islam* 70 (1993): 52–87.
Oğulukyan, Georg. *Georg Oğulukyan'ın Ruznamesi 1806–1810 İsyanları: III. Selim, IV. Mustafa, II. Mahmud ve Alemdar Mustafa Paşa*. Translated by Hrand D. Andreasyan. Istanbul: Edebiyat Fakültesi Basımevi, 1972.
d'Ohsson, Ignatius Mouradgea. *Tableau général de l'empire ottoman*. 7 vols. Istanbul: Isis, 2001.
Öksüz, Zehra. "XVIII. Asır İstanbulu'nun Kültür Merkezleri Olarak Edebiyat Mahfilleri: Kültürel Mirasın Aktarımında 'Edebiyat Mahfilleri'nin Rölü." *International Journal of Sport Culture and Science* 3 (2015): 141–58.

Olson, Robert W. "Jews, Janissaries, Esnaf, and the Revolt of 1740 in Istanbul: Social Upheaval and Political Realignment in the Ottoman Empire." *Journal of the Economic and Social History of the Orient* 20 (1977): 185–207.

Osborne, Dana. "Maledictive Language: Cursing and Swearing." In *International Encyclopedia of Linguistic Anthropology*, edited by James Stanlaw, 1286–93. Hoboken: Wiley-Blackwell, 2021.

Osmanzade Taib. *Hadikat ül-Vüzera*. Istanbul: Ceride-i Havadis Matbaası, 1854.

Osterhammel, Jürgen. *Unfabling the East: The Englightenment's Encounter with Asia*. Translated by Robert Savage. Princeton: Princeton University Press, 2018.

Özvar, Erol. *Osmanlı Maliyesinde Malikane Uygulaması*. Istanbul: Kitabevi, 2003.

Owen, Roger. *The Middle East and the World Economy, 1800–1914*. London: Methuen, 1981.

Özcan, Abdülkadir, ed. *Anonim Osmanlı Tarihi, 1099–1116 (1688–1704)*. Ankara: Türk Tarih Kurumu Basımevi, 2000.

Özkaya, Yücel. *18. Yüzyılda Osmanlı Toplumu*. Istanbul: Yapı Kredi Yayınları, 2007.

———. *Osmanlı İmparatorluğunda Ayanlık*. Ankara: Türk Tarih Kurumu Basımevi, 1994.

Özvar, Erol. "Transformation of the Ottoman Empire into a Military-Fiscal State: Reconsidering the Financing of War from a Global Perspective." In *The Battle for Central Europe: The Siege of Szigetvár and the Death of Süleyman the Magnificent and Nicolas Zrínyi (1566)*, edited by Pál Fodor, 21–63. Leiden: Brill, 2019.

Palmer, Patricia. *The Severed Head and the Grafted Tongue: Literature, Translation, and Violence in Early Modern Ireland*. Cambridge: Cambridge University Press, 2014.

Pamuk, Şevket. "Fiscal Centralisation and the Rise of the Modern State in the Ottoman Empire." *Medieval History Journal* 17 (2014): 1–26.

———. "Institutional Change and the Longevity of the Ottoman Empire, 1500–1800." *Journal of Interdisciplinary History* 35 (2004): 225–47.

———. "The Evolution of Financial Institutions in the Ottoman Empire, 1600–1914." *Financial History Review* 11 (2004): 7–32.

———. *A Monetary History of the Ottoman Empire*. New York: Cambridge University Press, 2000.

———. "The Ottoman Empire in the Eighteenth Century." *Itinerario* 24 (2000): 104–16.

———. *The Ottoman Empire and European Capitalism, 1820–1913*. Cambridge: Cambridge University Press, 1987.

Panaite, Viorel. "Power Relationships in the Ottoman Empire: The Sultans and the Tribute-Paying Princes of Wallachia and Moldavia from the Sixteenth to the Eighteenth Century." *International Journal of Turkish Studies* 7 (2001): 26–53.

Panzac, Daniel. "The Manning of the Ottoman Navy in the Heyday of Sail (1660–1850)." In *Arming the State: Military Conscription in the Middle East and Central Asia, 1775–1925*, edited by Erik Zürcher, 41–57. London: IB Tauris, 1999.

Pappas, Nicholas. "Brigands and Brigadiers: The Problem of Banditry and the Military in Nineteenth-Century Greece." *Athens Journal of History* 4 (2018): 175–96.

Pardo, Osvaldo F. *Honor and Personhood in Early Modern Mexico*. Ann Arbor: University of Michigan Press, 2015.

Paton, A.A. *History of the Egyptian Revolution*. 2 vols. London: Trübner, 1870.

Patrinelis, Christos G. "The Phanariots before 1821." *Balkan Studies* 42 (2001): 177–98.

Peacock, Mabel. "Executed Criminals and Folk-Medicine." *Folklore* 7 (1896): 268–83.

Peirce, Leslie. "Abduction with (Dis)honor: Sovereigns, Brigands, and Heroes in the Ottoman World." *Journal of Early Modern History* 15 (2011): 311–29.

——. *Morality Tales: Law and Gender in the Ottoman Court of Aintab*. Berkeley: University of California Press, 2003.

Peltonen, Markku. *The Duel in Early Modern England: Civility, Politeness, and Honour*. Cambridge: Cambridge University Press, 2003.

Pepperell, Nicole. "The Unease with Civilization: Norbert Elias and the Violence of the Civilizing Process." *Thesis Eleven* 137 (2016): 3–21.

Peristiany, J.G., ed. *Honor and Shame: The Values of Mediterranean Society*. Chicago: University of Chicago Press, 1966.

Peters, Rudolph. "Reinhard Schulze's Quest for an Islamic Enlightenment." *Die Welt des Islams* 30 (1990): 160–62.

Pfeifer, Helen. *Empire of Salons: Conquest and Community in the Early Modern Ottoman Lands*. Princeton: Princeton University Press, 2022.

——. "The Gulper and the Slurper: A Lexicon of Mistakes to Avoid While Eating with Ottoman Gentlemen." *Journal of Early Modern History* 24 (2020): 41–62.

Philipp, Thomas. *Acre: The Rise and Fall of a Palestinian City, 1730-1831*. New York: Columbia University Press, 2001.

Philliou, Christine M. *Biography of an Empire: Governing Ottomans in an Age of Revolution*. Berkeley: University of California Press, 2011.

Pitt-Rivers, Julian. "Postscript: The Place of Grace in Anthropology." In *Honor and Grace in Anthropology*, edited by J.G. Peristiany and Julian Pitt-Rivers. Cambridge: Cambridge University Press, 1992.

Pococke, Richard. *A Description of the East*. 3 vols. London: Cengage Gale, 1745.

Pollard, Lisa. *Nurturing the Nation: The Family Politics of Modernizing, Colonizing, and Liberating Egypt, 1805-1923*. Berkeley: University of California Press, 2005.

al-Qari, Raslan ibn Yahya. *al-Wuzara' fi aladhina hakamu Dimashq*, in *Wulat Dimashq fi al-'ahd al-'uthmani*. Edited by Salah al-Din al-Munajjid. Damascus, 1949.

Quataert, Donald. *The Ottoman Empire, 1700-1922*, 2nd ed. Cambridge: Cambridge University Press, 2005.

——. "Clothing Laws, State, and Society in the Ottoman Empire, 1720–1829." *International Journal of Middle East Studies* 29 (1997): 403–25.

——. "Janissaries, Artisans, and the Question of Ottoman Decline, 1730–1826." In *Workers, Peasants, and Economic Change in the Ottoman Empire, 1730-1914*, edited by Donald Quataert, 197–203. Istanbul: Isis Press, 1993.

Quilley, Stephen, and Steven Loyal. "Towards a 'Central Theory': The Scope and Relevance of the Sociology of Norbert Elias." In *The Sociology of Norbert Elias*, edited by Steven Loyal and Stephen Quilley, 1–22. Cambridge: Cambridge University Press, 2004.

Quinlan, Maurice J. *Victorian Prelude: A History of English Manners, 1700-1830*, 2nd ed. Hamdon, CT: Archon Books, 1964.

Rabie, Hassanein. "The Training of the Mamluk Faris." In *War, Technology, and Society in the Middle East*, edited by V.J. Parry and Malcolm Yapp, chap. 9. London: Oxford University Press, 1978.

Radtke, Bernd. "Sufism in the 18th Century: An Attempt at a Provisional Appraisal." *Die Welt des Islams* 36 (1996): 326–64.

Raduschev, Evgeni. "'Peasant' Janissaries?" *Journal of Social History* 42 (2008): 447-70.
Raeff, Marc. *Michael Speransky, Statesman of Imperial Russia, 1772-1839*. The Hague: M. Nijhoff, 1957.
Rafeq, Abd al-Karim. "Public Morality in Eighteenth-Century Ottoman Damascus." *Revue du monde musulman et de la Méditerranée* 55/56 (1990): 180-96.
———. "The Local Forces in Syria in the Seventeenth and Eighteenth Centuries." In *War, Technology, and Society in the Middle East*, edited by V.J. Parry and M.E. Yapp, 277-307. London: Oxford University Press, 1975.
Ramiz, Aziz-zade Hüseyin. *Adab-ı Zurafa: İnceleme, Tıpkıbasım, İndeks*. Edited by Sadık Erdem. Ankara: Türk Tarih Kurumu, 2019.
Ranum, Orest. "Courtesy, Absolutism, and the Rise of the French State, 1630-1660." *Journal of Modern History* 52 (1980): 426-51.
Raşid, Mehmed. *Tarih-i Raşid*. Istanbul, n.d.
Raven, James. *Judging New Wealth: Popular Publishing and Responses to Commerce in England, 1750-1800*. New York: Oxford University Press, 1992.
Raymond, André. "A Divided Sea: The Cairo Coffee Trade in the Red Sea Area during the Seventeenth and Eighteenth Centuries." In *Modernity and Culture*, edited by Leila Tarazi Fawaz and C.A. Bayly, chap. 2. New York: Columbia University Press, 2002.
———. *Égyptiens et français au Caire, 1798-1801*. Cairo: Institut Français d'Archéologie Orientale, 1998.
———. "Soldiers in Trade: The Case of Ottoman Cairo." *British Journal of Middle Eastern Studies* 1 (1991): 16-37.
———. *Grandes villes arabes à l'époque ottomane*. Paris: Sindbad, 1985.
———. "The Economic Crisis of Egypt in the Eighteenth Century." In *The Islamic Middle East, 700-1900*, edited by Abraham Udovitch, 687-707. Princeton: Princeton University Press, 1981.
———. "Les problèmes du café en Égypte au XVIIIe siècle." In *Le Café en Meditérranée*, 31-71. Aix-Marseilles: CNRS, 1980.
———. *Artisans et commerçants au Caire au XVIIIe siècle*. 2 vols. Damascus: Insitut Français de Damas, 1974.
———. "Les bains publics du Caire à la fin du XVIIIe siècle." *Annales Islamologiques* 8 (1969): 129-50.
Refik, Ahmet. *Hicri On Üçüncü Asırda İstanbul Hayatı*, Istanbul: Enderun Kitabevi, 1988.
———. *Hicri On İkinci Asırda İstanbul Hayatı*. Istanbul: Devlet Matbaası, 1930.
Reindl-Kiel, Hedda. "Dogs, Elephants, Lions, a Ram, and a Rhino on Diplomatic Mission: Animals as Gifts to the Ottoman Court." In *Animals and People in the Ottoman Empire*, edited by Suraiya Faroqhi, 271-85. Istanbul: Eren, 2010.
Revel, Jacques. "The Uses of Civility." In *A History of Private Life*, Vol. 3, *The Passions of the Renaissance*, edited by Philippe Ariès and Georges Duby, translated by Arthur Goldhammer, 167-205. Cambridge, MA: Belknap Press, 1989.
Reynolds, E. Wesley. *Coffeehouse Culture in the Atlantic World, 1650-1789*. New York: Bloomsbury Academic, 2022.
Rich, Claudius James. *Narrative of a Residence in Koordistan*. 2 vols. London: James Duncan, 1836.
Rizopoulou-Egoumenidou, Euphrosyne. "From Oriental (Ottoman) to European (Frank-

ish) Dress: Dress as Key Indicator of the Lifestyle and Role of the Elites of Cyprus during the Eighteenth and Nineteenth Centuries." In *From Traditional Attire to Modern Dress: Modes of Identification, Modes of Recognition in the Balkans (XVIth–XXth Centuries)*, edited by Constant Vintila-Ghitulescu, 129–43. Newcastle upon Tyne: Cambridge Scholars, 2011.

Rosand, Ellen. *Opera in Seventeenth-Century Venice: The Creation of a Genre.* Berkeley: University of California Press, 2007.

Rosenthal, Franz. *Gambling in Islam.* Leiden: Brill, 1975.

———. *The Herb: Hashish versus Medieval Muslim Society.* Leiden: Brill, 1971.

Rosenwein, Barbara H. *Emotional Communities in the Early Middle Ages.* Ithaca: Cornell University Press, 2006.

el-Rouayheb, Khaled. *Before Homosexuality in the Arab-Islamic World, 1500–1800.* Chicago: University of Chicago Press, 2005.

———. "The Love of Boys in the Arabic Poetry of the Early Ottoman Period, 1500–1800." *Middle Eastern Literatures* 8 (2005): 3–22.

———. "Was There a Revival of Logical Studies in Eighteenth-Century Egypt?" *Die Welt des Islams* 45 (2005): 1–19.

Ruff, Julius R. *Violence in Early Modern Europe, 1500–1800.* Cambridge: Cambridge University Press, 2001.

Russell, Alexander and Patrick. *The Natural History of Aleppo.* 2 vols., 2nd ed. London, 1794.

Russell, Mona L. *Creating the New Egyptian Woman: Consumerism, Education, and National Identity, 1863–1922.* New York: Palgrave Macmillan, 2004.

Rüstem, Ünver. *Ottoman Baroque: The Architectural Refashioning of Eighteenth-Century Istanbul.* Princeton: Princeton University Press, 2019.

al-Sabbagh, ʿAbbud. *al-Rawd al-Zahir fi tarikh Zahir.* Edited by Muhammad ʿAbd al-Karim Muhafaza and ʿIsam Mustafa Hazayima. Irbid: Muʾassasat Hamadah liʾl-Khidmat wa al-Dirasat al-Jamiʿiyya, 1999.

al-Sabbagh, Mikhaʾil. *Tarikh al-Shaykh Zahir al-ʿUmar al-Zaydani, hakim ʿAkka wa Bilad Safad*, edited by Qastantin al-Basha al-Mukhlisi. Harisa, Lebanon: Matbaʿat al-Qiddis Bulus, n.d.

Sabbanu, Ahmad Ghassan, ed. *Mudhakkirat tarikhiyya ʿan hamlat Ibrahim Basha ʿala Suriya.* Damascus: Dar Qutayba, 1980.

Saʿd, Faruq. *Khayal al-zill al-ʿarabi.* Beirut: Sharikat al-Matbuʿat, 1993.

Sadat, Deena R. "Rumeli Ayanları: The Eighteenth Century." *Journal of Modern History* 44 (1972): 346–63.

Saggau, Emil B.H. "Marginalised Islam: Christianity's Role in the Sufi Order of Bektashism." In *Exploring the Multitude of Muslims in Europe: Essays in Honor of Jorgen S. Nielsen*, edited by Niels Valdemar Vinding et al., chap. 12. Leiden: Brill, 2018.

Saint-Simon, Louis de Rouvroy. *Versailles, the Court, and Louis XIV.* New York: Harper & Row, 1966.

Sajdi, Dana. *The Barber of Damascus: Nouveau Literacy in the Eighteenth-Century Levant.* Stanford: Stanford University Press, 2013.

———. "Decline, Its Discontents, and Ottoman Cultural History." In *Ottoman Tulips, Ottoman Coffee: Lifestyle and Leisure in the Eighteenth Century*, edited by Dana Sajdi, 1–40. London: Tauris Academic Studies, 2007.

Salzmann, Ariel. "The Old Regime and the Ottoman Middle East." In *The Ottoman World*, edited by Christine Woodhead, 409–22. London: Routledge, 2012.

———. *Tocqueville in the Ottoman Empire: Rival Paths to the Modern State*. Leiden: Brill, 2004.

———. "An Ancien Régime Revisited: 'Privatization' and Political Economy in the Eighteenth-Century Ottoman Empire." *Politics and Society* 21 (1993): 393–423.

Sami, Mustafa. *Tarih-i Sami*. In *Tarih-i Sami ve Şakir ve Suphi*. Istanbul, 1784.

Sander, Elizabeth Clara. *Social Dancing in Peter the Great's Russia: Observations by Holstein Nobleman Friedrich Wilhelm Von Bergholz, 1721 to 1725*. Hildesheim: G. Olms, 2007.

Şanizade, Mehmed Ataullah. *Şanizade Tarihi*. 4 vols. Istanbul: Trabzonlu Bakırcıbaşı Mehmed Efendizade Süleyman Efendi'nin Matbaası, 1867–74.

Sannini, C.S. *Travels in Upper and Lower Egypt*. London: J. Debrett, 1800.

Saraçgil, Ayşe. "L'Introduction du café à Istanbul (XVIe–XVIIe siècles)." In *Cafés d'Orient revisités*, edited by Hélène Desmet-Grégoire and François Georgeon, 25–38. Paris: CNRS Editions, 1997.

Sarı Mehmed Paşa. *Zübde-i Vekayiat: Tahlil ve Metin (1066-1116 / 1656-1704)*. Edited by Abdülkadir Özcan. Ankara: Türk Tarihi Kurumu Basımevi, 1995.

Sariyannis, Marinos. "Sociability, Public Life, and Decorum." In *A Companion to Early Modern Istanbul*, edited by Shirine Hamadeh and Çiğdem Kafesçioğlu, 473–502. Leiden: Brill, 2022.

———. "Ottoman Ideas on Monarcy before the Tanzimat Reforms: Toward a Conceptual History of Ottoman Political Notions." *Turcica* 47 (2016): 33–72.

———. "The Kadızadeli Movement as a Social and Political Phenomenon: The Rise of a 'Mercantile Ethic'?" In *Political Initiatives from the Bottom Up in the Ottoman Empire*, edited by Antonis Anastasopoulos, 263–89. Rethymno: Crete University Press, 2012.

al-Sarraf, Shihab. "Furusiyya Literature of the Mamluk Period." In *Furusiyya: The Horse in the Art of the Near East*, edited by David Alexander, vol. 1, 118–35. Riyadh: King Abdulaziz Public Library, 1996.

Saunders, David. *Russia in the Age of Reaction and Reform, 1801-1881*. New York: Longman, 1992.

Sauvaget, Jean. *Alep: Essai sur le développement d'une grande ville syrienne, des origins au milieu du XIXe siècle*. Paris: Libraire Orientaliste Paul Geuthner, 1941.

Scarce, Jennifer. "Principles of Ottoman Turkish Costume." *Costume* 22 (1988): 13–31.

———. *Women's Costume of the Near and Middle East*. London: Unwin Hyman, 1987.

Schatkowski Schilcher, Linda. *Families in Politics: Damascenes Factions and Estates of the 18th and 19th Centuries*. Stuttgart: Steiner Verlag Wiesbaden, 1985.

Schulze, Reinhard. "Was ist die islamische Aufklärung?" *Die Welt des Islams* 36 (1996): 276–325.

Sevin, Nureddin. *Onüç Asırlık Türk Kıyafet Tarihine Bir Bakış*. Ankara: Kültür Bakanlığı, 1990.

———. *Türk Gölge Oyunu*. Istanbul: Devlet Kitapları, 1968.

Şemdanizade, Fındıklılı Süleyman Efendi. *Mür'i't-Tevarih*. Edited by Münir Aktepe. 3 vols. Istanbul: Edebiyat Fakültesi Matbaası, 1976.

Semerdjian, Elyse. *"Off the Straight Path": Illicit Sex, Law, and Community in Ottoman Aleppo*. Syracuse: Syracuse University Press, 2008.

Shafir, Nir. "Moral Revolutions: The Politics of Piety in the Ottoman Empire Reimagined." *Comparative Studies of Society and History* 61 (2019): 595–623.

Shalabi, Ahmad. *Awdah al-isharat fi-man tawalla Misr al-Qahira min al-wuzara' wa al-bashat*.

Edited by ʿAbd al-Rahim ʿAbd al-Rahman ʿAbd al-Rahim. Cairo: Tawziʿ Maktabat al-Khanji, 1978.

Sheikh, Mustapha. *Ottoman Puritanism and Its Discontents: Ahmad al-Aqhisari and the Qadizadelis.* Oxford: Oxford University Press, 2016.

Shihab, Haydar Ahmad. *Tarikh Ahmad Basha al-Jazzar.* Edited by Antuniyus Shibli and Ighnatiyus ʿAbdu Khalifa. Beirut: Maktabat Antoine, 1955.

Siyavuşgil, Sabri Esat. *Karagöz: Its History, Its Characters, Its Mystic and Satiric Spirit.* Ankara: Saim Toraman Basımevi, 1955.

Sked, Alan. *The Decline and Fall of the Habsburg Empire, 1815–1918.* London: Longman, 1989.

Skiotis, Dennis N. "Bandit to Pasha: First Steps in the Rise to Power of Ali of Tepelen, 1750–1784." *International Journal of Middle East Studies* 2 (1971): 219–44.

Skouzes, Panages. *Apomnemoneumata: He tyrannia tou Chatze-Ale Chaseke sten tourkodratoumene Athena (1772-1796).* Athens: Kedros, 1975.

Slade, Adolphus. *Records of Travels in Turkey, Greece, &c. and of a Cruise in the Black Sea.* 2 vols. London: Saunders and Otley, 1833.

Smith, Dennis. *Norbert Elias and Modern Social Theory.* London: Sage, 2001.

Smyrnelis, Marie-Carmen. *Une Ville ottomane plurielle: Smyrne aux XVIIIe et XIXe siècles.* Istanbul: Isis, 2006.

Sofroni, Vraçalı. *Osmanlı'da Bir Papaz: Günahkâr Sofroni'nin Çileli Hayat Hikâyesi, 1739–1813.* Translated by Aziz Nazmi Şakir-Taş. Istanbul: Kitap Yayınevi, 2003.

Sonnini, C.S. *Travels in Upper and Lower Egypt.* London: J. Debrett, 1800.

Spear, Percival. *The Nabobs: A Study of the Social Life of the English in Eighteenth-Century India.* New York: Oxford University Press, 1998.

St. John, James Augustus. *Egypt and Mohammed Ali.* 2 vols. London: Longman, Rees, Orme, Brown, Green & Longman, 1834.

Stapleton, Karyn. "Swearing." In *Interpersonal Pragmatics*, edited by Miriam A. Locher and Sage L. Graham, 289–305. New York: de Gruyter Mouton, 2010.

Stillman, Yedida. *Arab Dress: A Short History.* Leiden: Brill, 2000.

Stuart, Kathy. *Defiled Trades and Social Outcasts: Honor and Ritual Pollution in Early Modern Germany.* Cambridge: Cambridge University Press, 1999.

Sunar, Mehmet Mert. " 'When Grocers, Porters, and Riff-Raff Become Soldiers': Janissary Artisans and Laborers in Nineteenth-Century Istanbul and Edirne." *Kocaeli Üniversitesi Sosyal Bilimler Enstitüsü* 17 (2009): 175–94.

———. "Cauldron of Dissent: A Study of the Janissary Corps, 1807–1826." Unpublished PhD diss., SUNY-Binghamton, 2006.

al-Suwaydi, ʿAbd al-Rahman. *Tarikh Hawadith Baghdad wa al-Basra.* Edited by ʿImad ʿAbd al-Salam Ru'uf. Baghdad: Wizarat al-Thaqafa wa al-Funun, 1978.

al-Tabbakh, Muhammad Raghib. *Iʿlam al-nubala' bi-tarikh Halab al-shahba'.* 7 vols. Aleppo: Dar al-Qalam al-ʿArabi.

Tamari, Salim. "Jerusalem's Ottoman Modernity: The Times and Lives of Wasif Jawhariyyeh." *Jerusalem Quarterly* 9 (2000): 5–27.

Taylesanizade Hafız Abdullah Efendi. *İstanbul'un Uzun Dört Yılı (1785-1789): Taylesanizade Hafız Abdullah Efendi Tarihi.* Edited by Feridun Emecen. Istanbul: Tatav, 2003.

Taylor, Scott K. *Honor and Violence in Golden Age Spain.* New Haven: Yale University Press, 2008.

Taymur, Ahmad. *al-Musiqa wa al-ghina' `inda al-`arab*. Cairo: Lajnat Nashr al-Mu'allafat al-Taymuriyya, 1963.
Tekgül, Nil. *Emotions in the Ottoman Empire: Politics, Society, and Family in the Early Modern Era*. New York: Bloomsbury Academic, 2023.
Teşrifatçı Mehmed Akif Bey. *Tarih-i Cülus-ı Sultan Mustafa Han-ı Salis*. Istanbul: Türkiye Yazma Eserler Kurumu Başkanları Yayınları, Istanbul, 2012.
Tezcan, Baki. *The Second Ottoman Empire: Political and Social Transformation in the Early Modern World*. Cambridge: Cambridge University Press, 2010.
Tezcan, Hülya. *The Topkapı Saray Museum*. Boston: Little, Brown, 1986.
de Thévenot, Jean. *The Travels of Monsieur de Thévenot into the Levant*. Translated by Archibald Lovell. 3 vols. London: Gregg Farnborough, 1971.
Thieck, Jean-Pierre. "Décentralisation Ottomane et affirmation urbaine à Alep à la fin du XVIIIe siècle." In *Mouvements communautaires et espaces urbains au Machreq*, edited by Mona Zakariya, 117–68. Beirut: Centre d'études et de recherches sur le Moyen-Orient contemporain, 1985.
Thomas, Downing A. *Aesthetics of Opera in the Ancien Régime, 1647–1785*. Cambridge: Cambridge University Press, 2002.
Thomas, Keith. *In Pursuit of Civility: Manners and Civilization in Early Modern England*. Waltham, MA: Brandeis University Press, 2018.
Thomas, Lewis V. *A Study of Naima*. New York: New York University Press, 1972.
Thompson, Jason. "Edward Lane in Egypt." *Journal of the American Research Center in Egypt* 34 (1997): 243–61.
Tietze, Andreas. *The Turkish Shadow Theater and the Puppet Collection of the L.A. Mayer Memorial Foundation*. Berlin: Gebr. Mann Verlag, 1977.
Tilly, Charles. 'War-Making and State-Making as Organized Crime." In *Bringing the State Back In*, edited by Peter Evans, Dietrich Rueschemeyer, and Theda Skocpal, 169–87. Cambridge: Cambridge University Press, 1985.
Todorov, Nikolai. *The Balkan City, 1400–1900*. Seattle: University of Washington Press, 1983.
Toledano, Ehud. "The Emergence of Ottoman-Local Elites: A Framework for Research." In *Middle East Politics and Ideas*, edited by Ilan Pappé and Moshe Moaz, 145–62. London: IB Tauris, 1997.
Totman, Conrad. *Early Modern Japan*. Berkeley: University of California Press, 1993.
de Tott, François. *Memoirs of Baron de Tott*. 2 vols. London: G.G.J. and J. Robinson, 1785; reprint: New York: Arno Press, 1973.
Touma, Habib. *The Music of the Arabs*. Translated by Laurie Schwartz. Portland, OR: Amadeus Press, 1996.
de Tournefort, Joseph Pitton. *Voyage into the Levant*. 3 vols. London: D. Midwinter et al., 1741.
Tuchscherer, Michel. "Les cafés dans l'Égypte ottomane (XVIe–XVIIIe siècles)." In *Cafés d'Orient revisités*, edited by Hélène Desmet-Grégoire and François Georgeon, 91–112. Paris: CNRS, 1997.
Tucker, Judith. *In the House of the Law: Gender and Islamic Law in Ottoman Syria and Palestine*. Berkeley: University of California Press, 1998.
Tuğ, Başak. *Politics of Honor in Ottoman Anatolia: Sexual Violence and Socio-Legal Surveillance in the Eighteenth Century*. Leiden: Brill, 2017.

Turan, Namık Sinan. "Osmanlı 18. Yüzyılında Müziğin Kamusal Görünümü." In *Şehvar Beşiroğlu'ya Bir Armağan*, edited by Namık Sinan Turan and Şeyma Ersoy Çak, 317–39. Istanbul: Pan Yayıncılık, 2019.

Turhan, Fatma Sel. "The Rebellious Kapudan of Bosnia: Hüseyin Kapudan (1802–1834)." *Osmanlı Araştırmaları* 44 (2014): 457–74.

Türkay, Cevdet. "XVIII. Yüzyıl Sonlarında İstanbul'da Enfiye Dükkanları." In *Ehlikeyfin Kitabı*, edited by Fatih Tığlı, 353–60. Istanbul: Kitabevi, 2004.

Turna, Nalan. "Pandemonium and Order: Suretyship, Surveillance, and Taxation in Early Nineteenth-Century Istanbul." *New Perspectives on Turkey* 39 (2008): 167–89.

———. "The Everyday Life of Istanbul and Its Artisans, 1808–1839." Unpublished PhD diss., SUNY-Binghamton, 2006.

Ulumiddin, Ahya. "Socio-Political Turbulence of the Ottoman Empire: Reconsidering Sufi and Kadızadeli Hostility in 17th Century." *Ulumuna* 20 (2016): 319–52.

Unat, Faik Reşit, ed. *1730 Patrona İhtilalı Hakkında Bir Eser: Abdi Tarihi*. Ankara: Türk Tarih Kurumu, 2020.

Uzunçarşılı, İsmail Hakkı. *Meşhur Rumeli Ayanlarından Tirsinikli İsmail, Yılıkoğlu Süleyman Ağalar ve Alemdar Mustafa Paşa*. Ankara: Türk Tarih Kurumu Basımevi, 2010.

———. *Osmanlı Devleti Teşkilatından Kapukulu Ocakları*. 2 vols. Ankara: Türk Tarih Kurumu Basımevi, 1988.

———. "Osmanlılar Zamanında Saraylarda Musiki Hayatı." *Belleten* 41 (1977): 79–114.

———. "Nizam-i Cedid Ricalinden Valide Sultan Kethüdası Meşhur Yusuf Ağa ve Kethüdazade Arif Efendi." *Belleten* 20 (1956): 485–525.

———. "Cezayirli Gazi Hasan Paşa'ya Dair." *İstanbul Üniversitesi Edebiyat Fakültesi Türkiyat Mecmuası* 7/8 (1942): 17–40.

Vahedi, Massoud. "Coffee Was Once *Haram*?: Dispelling Popular Myths Regarding a Nuanced Legal Issue." *Islamic Studies* 60 (2021): 125–56.

Valensi, Lucette. "Islam et capitalism: Production et commerce des chéchias en Tunisie et en France au XVIIIe et XIXe siècles." *Revue d'Histoire Moderne et Contemporaine* 17 (1969): 376–400.

van Nieuwkerk, Karin. *"A Trade Like Any Other": Female Singers and Dancers in Egypt*. Austin: University of Texas Press, 1995.

van Velsen, H.U.E. "The Djuka Civilization." *Netherlands Journal of Sociology* 20 (1984): 85–97.

Vasıf, Ahmed. *Mahasinü'l-Asar ve Haka'ikü'l-Ahbar*. 2 vols. Istanbul: Dar al-Taba`a al-`Amira, 1804.

Vassaf, Hüseyin. *Sefine-i Evliya*. 5 vols. Istanbul: Kitabevi, 2006.

Vazih, Mustafa. *Amasya Fetvaları ve İlk Amasya Şehir Tarihi (Belabilü'r-Rasiye fi Riyaz-ı Mesaili'l-Amasiyye)*. Edited by Ali Rıza Ayar and Recep Orhan Özel. Amasya: Amasya Belediye Kültür Yayınları, 2011.

Vehbi, Sünbülzade. *Lütfiyye: Metin Tespiti, Özet, Yorum, ve Açıklamalar*. Edited by Süreyya Ali Beyzadeoğlu. Istanbul: Milli Eğitim Bakanlığı Yayınları, 2004.

Veinstein, Gilles. "Ayan de la region d'Izmire et la commerce du Levant dans la deuxième moitié du XVIIIe siècle." *Études Balkaniques* 1 (1976): 71–83.

Vermes, Gabor. *Hungarian Culture and Politics in the Habsburg Monarchy, 1711–1848*. Budapest: Central European University Press, 2014.

Vintila-Ghitulescu, Constanta. "Constructing a New Identity: Romanian Aristocrats between Oriental Heritage and Western Prestige (1780–1866)." In *From Traditional Attire to Modern Dress: Modes of Identification, Modes of Recognition in the Balkans (XVIth–XXth Centuries)*, edited by Constanta Vintila-Ghitulescu, 104–28. Newcastle upon Tyne: Cambridge Scholars, 2011.

Voigtländer, Nico, and Hans-Joachim Voth. "The Three Horsemen of Riches: Plague, War, and Urbanization in Early Modern Europe." *Review of Economic Studies* 80 (2013): 774–811.

Volney, C.-F. *Travels through Egypt and Syria in the Years 1783, 1784, and 1785*. 2 vols. Dublin: Cengage Gale, 1793.

Vural, Hanifi. *Ahmet Vefik Paşa: Hayatı—Şahsiyeti—Eserleri*. Istanbul: Kesit, 2016.

Walsh, Robert. *A Residence at Constantinople*. 2 vols. London: Frederick Westley and A.H. Davis, 1836.

Watenpaugh, Keith. *Being Modern in the Middle East: Revolution, Nationalism, and Colonialism and the Arab Middle Class*. Princeton: Princeton University Press, 2006.

Weber, Stefan. *Damascus: Ottoman Modernity and Urban Transformation, 1808–1918*. Aarhus: Aarhus University Press, 2009.

Wegner, Gerhard. "Defensive Modernization in Germany and the Habsburg Empire: A Historical Study of Capitalist Transformation." *Journal of Institutional Economics* 12 (2016): 443–69.

Werth, Paul W. *1837: Russia's Quiet Revolution*. Oxford: Oxford University Press, 2021.

Whisenhunt, William Benton. *In Search of Legality: Mikhail M. Speranskii and the Codification of Russian Law*. Boulder, CO: East European Monographs, 2001.

White, Charles. *Three Years in Constantinople, or Domestic Manners of the Turks in 1844*. 3 vols. London: Henry Colburn, 1845.

Wigen, Einar. "The Education of Ottoman Man and the Practice of Orderliness." In *Civilizing Emotions: Concepts in Nineteenth-Century Asia and Europe*, edited by Margrit Pernau and Helge Jordheim, 107–25. Oxford: Oxford University Press, 2015.

Wilkins, Charles. *Forging Urban Solidarities: Ottoman Aleppo, 1640–1700*. Leiden: Brill, 2010.

Wilkinson, William. *An Account of the Principalities of Wallachia and Moldavia*. London: Longman, Hurst, Rees, Orme, and Brown, 1820; reprint: New York: Arno Press, 1971.

Winter, Stefan. *The Shiites of Lebanon under Ottoman Rule, 1516–1788*. Cambridge: Cambridge University Press, 2010.

Wishnitzer, Avner. *As Night Falls: Eighteenth-Century Ottoman Cities after Dark*. Cambridge: Cambridge University Press, 2021.

Wittman, William. *Travels in Turkey, Asia Minor, Syria, and Egypt*. London: Richard Phillips, 1803; reprint: New York: Arno Press, 1971.

Wright, Owen. *Words without Songs: A Musicological Study of an Early Ottoman Anthology and Its Precursors*. London: School of Oriental and African Studies, 1992.

Yaşar, Ahmet. "'Külliyen Ref'ten 'İbreten li'l-Ġayr'e: Erken Modern Osmanlı'da Kahvehane Yasaklamaları." In *Osmanlı Kahvehaneleri: Mekân, Sosyalleşme, İktidar*, edited by Ahmet Yaşar, 37–47. Istanbul: Kitap Yayınevi, 2009.

Yasutaka, Teruoka. "Pleasure Quarters and Tokugawa Culture." In *Eighteenth-Century Japan: Culture and Society*, edited by C. Andrew Girstle, 3–32. Sydney: Allen & Unwin, 1989.

Yaycıoğlu, Ali. "Guarding Traditions and Laws—Disciplining Bodies and Souls: Tradition, Religion, and Science in the Age of Ottoman Reform." *Modern Asian Studies* 52 (2018): 1542–603.

———. *Partners of the Empire: The Crisis of the Ottoman Order in the Age of Revolutions*. Stanford: Stanford University Press, 2016.

Yelçe, N. Zeynep. "Royal Wrath: Curbing the Anger of the Sultan." In *Discourses of Anger in the Early Modern Period*, edited by Karl A.E. Enenkel and Anita Traninger, 439–57. Leiden: Brill, 2015.

Yeşil, Fatih. *İhtilaller Çağında Osmanlı Ordusu: Osmanlı İmparatorluğu'nda Sosyoekonomik ve Sosyopolitik Değişim Üzerine Bir İnceleme (1793-1826)*. Istanbul: Tarih Vakfı Yurt Yayınları, 2016.

———. *Aydınlanma Çağında Bir Osmanlı Katibi: Ebubekir Ratib Efendi (1750-1799)*. Istanbul: Tarih Vakfı Yurt Yayınları, 2010.

Yetkin, Sabri. *Ege'de Eşkiyalar*. Istanbul: Tarih Vakfı Yurt Yayınları, 1997.

Yi, Eunjeong. *Guild Dynamics in Seventeenth-Century Istanbul: Fluidity and Leverage*. Leiden: Brill, 2004.

Yıldız, Aysel. *Kenar Adamları ve Bendeleri: Tirsinikli İsmail Ağa ve Alemdar Mustafa Paşa'nın Adamları, Manuk Mirzayan ve Köse Ahmed Efendi*. Istanbul: Kitap Yayınevi, 2018.

———. *Crisis and Rebellion in the Ottoman Empire: The Downfall of a Sultan in the Age of Revolution*. London: IB Tauris, 2017.

———. "The 'Louis XVI of the Turks': The Character of an Ottoman Sultan." *Middle Eastern Studies* 50 (2014): 272–90.

———. "A City under Fire: Urban Violence in Istanbul during the Alemdar Incident (1808)." In *Urban Governance under the Ottomans: Between Cosmopolitanism and Conflict*, edited by Ulrike Freitag and Nora Lafi, 37–57. New York: Routledge, 2014.

———. "The Anatomy of a Rebellious Social Group: The Yamaks of the Bosphorus at the Margins of Ottoman Society." In *Political Initiatives "From the Bottom Up" in the Ottoman Empire*, edited by Antonis Anastasopoulos, 291–324. Rethymno: Crete University Press, 2012.

Yılmaz, Gülay. "Janissaries in the Making: Coerced Labor and Chivalric Masculinity in the Early Modern Ottoman Empire." *Labor History* 64 (2023): 1–18.

———. "Urban Protests, Rebellions, and Revolts." In *A Companion to Early Modern Istanbul*, edited by Shirine Hamadeh and Çiğdem Kafescioğlu, 555–80. Leiden: Brill, 2022.

al-Zabidi, Murtada. *Ithaf al-sada al-muttaqin bi-sharh asrar ihya' 'ulum al-din*. 10 vols. Cairo: 1893.

Zachs, Fruma, and Sharon Halevi. "Repaving the Path of Muru'a: Manly Virtue and the Emergence of a Modern Masculinity in Greater Syria." In *Gendering Culture in Greater Syria: Intellectuals and Ideology in the Late Ottoman Period*, 63–81. New York: IB Tauris, 2015.

Zarifi, Ömer. *Pendname-i Zarifi*. Edited by Mehmet Arslan. Sivas: Dilek Matbaacılık, 1994.

Zarinebaf, Fariba. *Crime and Punishment in Istanbul, 1700-1800*. Berkeley: University of California Press, 2010.

Ze'evi, Dror. *Producing Desire: Changing Sexual Discourse in the Ottoman Middle East, 1500-1900*. Berkeley: University of California Press, 2006.

Zens, Robert W. "In the Name of the Sultan: Haci Mustafa Pasha of Belgrade and Ottoman Provincial Rule in the Late 18th Century." *International Journal of Middle East Studies* 44 (2012): 129–46.

———. "Pasvanoglu Osman Pasha and the Pashalik of Belgrade, 1791–1807." *International Journal of Turkish Studies* 8 (2002): 88–114.

Zilfi, Madeline. "Women, Minorities, and the Changing Politics of Dress in the Ottoman Empire, 1650–1830." In *The Right to Dress: Sumptuary Laws in a Global Perspective, c. 1200–1800*, edited by Giorgio Riello and Ulinka Rublack, 393–415. Cambridge: Cambridge University Press, 2019.

———. *Women and Slavery in the Late Ottoman Empire*. Cambridge: Cambridge University Press, 2010.

———. "Goods in the Mahalle: Distributional Encounters in Eighteenth-Century Istanbul." In *Consumption Studies and the History of the Ottoman Empire, 1550–1922*, edited by Donald Quataert, chap. 9. Albany: State University of New York Press, 2000.

———. "The Kadızadelis: Discordant Revivalism in Seventeenth-Century Istanbul." *Journal of Near Eastern Studies* 45 (1986): 251–69.

Zlatar, Zedenko. *Njegoš's Montenegro: Epic Poetry, Blood Feud and Warfare in a Tribal Zone, 1830–1851*. Boulder, CO: East European Monographs, 2005.

Zmora, Hillay. *The Feud in Early Modern Germany*. Cambridge: Cambridge University Press, 2011.

INDEX

Page numbers in italics refers to illustrations.

Abdülaziz, Ottoman sultan, 229
Abdülhamid I, 175
Abdülhamid II, 229
Abdülkerim Efendi, 49
Abdullah Paşa (governor of Acre), 84, 128, 266n105
Acre, 56, 84, 108–10, 132, 135, 163; Egyptian siege of, 128
Adana, 35
al-`Afifi, `Abd al-Wahhab, 76–77
Afranj Ahmad Bey, 179
Africa, 6–7, 187
Ahmed III, 46–47, 127, 137, *149*, 262n36, 292n136, 299n62
Ahmed Paşa (governor of Baghdad), 125
Ahmed Paşa al-Jazzar, 52, 84, 110, 132, 135–36, 162, 173, 191, 193–94, 214
Ahmed Resmi Efendi, 251n11
Aksan, Virginia, 187
Albania, 58, 217, 219, 241n21, 269–70nn32; *fustanella*, *27*, 42
alcohol, 78–81, 83–84, 86, 90; campaigns against, 82. *See also* taverns
Alemdar Mustafa Paşa, 115, 129, 140, 148, 207; death of, 196, 209

Aleppo, 14, 22, 24, 29, 34, 45, 48–49, 52, 56, 66, 94, 99–100, 104, 120, 131, 141, 144, 151–52, 165, 171, 191, 195, 218, 248n131, 250n175, 294n3, 294n6; bathhouses, 111, 266n107; coffeehouses in, 72–74, 76, 192, 206; drinking in, 84; factional clashes, 213; furs, wearing of, 246n98; opium in, 88; uprisings in 213–14; women, harassment of, 296n32
Alexandria, 41, 53, 108, 164
al-Alfi, Mehmed Bey, 170
Algeria, 38
Algiers, 171
Ali Fenai Efendi, 127
Ali Paşa (governor of Baghdad), 161
Ali Paşa, Tepedelenli, 107, 193, 269–70nn32
Amir Manjik, 145–46
Amir Qanbaq, 143
Anatolia, 30, 36–37, 43, 58, 61, 67, 77, 79, 86–87, 120, 187, 221
ancien régime, 8
Anglo-Ottoman War, 67, 203, 204
Ankara, 71
al-Arna'ut, Mustafa, 140

333

Arpaeminizade, Mustafa Sami, 139
Aşık Halil, 194
Athens, 30, 38
Atıf Efendi (*reisülküttab*), 84
Austrian Empire, 11, 82, 228-29, 231, 298n56
Ayvansarayi, Hüseyin, 49
al-ʿAzizi, Muhammad, 180
al-ʿAzizi, Mustafa, 106-7
al-ʿAzm, Asʿad Paşa (governor of Damascus), 109, 169, 202-3, 210, 274n115, 277n24
al-ʿAzm, Sulayman Paşa (governor of Damascus), 133-34, 181, 190

Baghdad, 14, 85, 102, 282n109
Bakhkhash, Naʿum, 152
al-Bakri, Ahmad, 108
Balkans, 22-23, 25-28, 37-38, 43, 62, 67, 92, 111, 120, 130, 185, 187, 198, 213, 217, 221, 240n7, 241n21, 245n92; dining manners, 267n140
al-Barkawi, İbrahim Kethüda, 142
al-Barudi, Ahmed Ağa, 106
al-Barudi, Mehmed Ağa, 146-47
bathhouses, 44, 110, 113, 266n107, 266n108; female sociability, 111-12; fun and
recreation, 111; hygiene, 111; urbanity, as emblems of, 111
battle of Lake Hula, 288n79
battle of Lerna, 202
battle of Konya, 129
Baz, Jirjis, 177-78
beards: depriving of, as folk punishment, 174-75; respect, 28; as rite of passage, 172-73; shaving of, 29, 54, 241n31; as symbolic passage to male adulthood, 28
bedouin, 268-69nn13; Banu Asad tribe, 131; Hawwara tribe, 126; "simplicity" of, 271n52
Beirut, 35, 52, 98, 111
Belgrade, 218
"Beşiktas incident", 224

Beşiktaş Scientific Society (Beşiktaş Cemiyet-i İlmiyesi), 96
Bijut, Rufaʾil, 29
biographical dictionaries, 17
blood brothers, 188, 208
Blok, Anton, 205
bodily decoration, 30-35
bodily deportment, 118-19, 228-29, 232; European-style cutlery and furniture, 115; good hygiene, 110
Bosnia, 172, 226
breweries, 256n91
brigandage, 6
British Empire, 12
Browne, William, 122
Bucharest, 14, 182
Bulgaria, 43, 240n7
Bulutkapan Ali Bey (al-Kabir), 109, 160, 167, 181
Burayk, Mikhaʾil, 52
Burckhardt, John Lewis, 24, 63, 106, 286n59

Cairo, 13, 24, 30, 36-37, 53, 55, 64, 66-67, 70, 73, 76, 82, 85, 90, 95, 100, 106, 108-9, 113, 116, 122, 139, 142, 146-51, 157-58, 167, 169, 172-73, 176-77, 179, 180-82, 186, 195, 201-2, 212, 219-20, 225, 261n24, 278n47; bathhouses, 266n108; bawdy street entertainment, 199; camel incident, 197; coffeehouses in, 71, 287n77; Faqari faction, 207; revolts in, 54; salons, 96-97, 101-2; skirmishes between soldiers, 213; smoking of hashish, among poor, 86; storytelling, 103; street violence, 196, 285n48; taverns in, 83
caravansary, 77
Catholics, 20, 157, 200, 241n31, 276n10
ceremony: ceremonial entry, 178-79; ceremonial forms, 171; ceremonial jewelry, 178; ceremonial kissing, 108; ceremonial occasions, 63; ceremonial pageantry, 175-76; ceremonial processions, 175; ceremonial salutes, 175; ceremo-

nial self-defense, 155; ceremonial tools, 173; disorder, 70; evolution, 297n53; headpieces, 244n80; intimidation and social distance, 110; language of power and status, 38; of older warrior ethic, 151; robes of office, 182; self-defense, 155; splendor, 7; "sticking of candles," 291n34; turbans, 244n81; weapons of choice, 196. *See also* public processions

Çerkes Mehmed Bey al-Kabir, 202

Cevri Kalfa, 129

Chartier, Roger, 5

Chateaubriand, François-René, 41

China, 90, 152

Chios, 45, 46, 49, 112

Christians, 78, 163, 169, 185, 192, 291n133, 292n136; alcohol, 79, 81–83; color codes, 48–49, 52, 54–55, 58; dress codes, 54; greetings of, 264n71; gun ownership, 195; headgear 37, *37*; and Jews, 37, *37*, 47–49, 53, 55–58, 79, 80, 82–83, 161, 195, 210, 227, 247n125; militia, forming of, 218–19; Muslims, hostility against, 54, 214; Orthodox, 165, 200, 249n165; slaves, selling of, 53; subordinate status of, 227; suspicion toward, 57; turbans, 38, 48–49, 54–55

civility, 136, 161–62, 264n68; appeal of, 5; code of, 4; courtly model, 6; as kind of seduction, 153; manners, 18–19; poetry, association with, 144–45; self-restraint, 4–7; urban gentleman, 140; "urbanitas," 7; veneer of, 156

Civilizing Process, The (Norbert), 4

clothing, 14, 21, *23*, 31, 33–34, 44, 53, 59, 84, 119, 232; Christian, 52, 55; of countryside, 43; outer cloaks, 41; regulating of, 57, 225; sartorial legislation, 47, 49, 51–52, 56–58; shielding body from view, 40; shoes, 43; status, 48; symbolic hierarchies, reinforcing of, 57; women's 46–49, 51, 199, 225. *See also* fashion

coffee, 45, 70, 89–90, 119; as unaffordable, 63; vendors, 71; popularity of, 60–63, 71

coffee-drinking, 62–63, *64*, 71; campaign against, 64

coffeehouses, 70, 80–81, 82, 90, 92, 99–100, 154, 193–95, 220, 255n82, 260n5; attacks on, 289–90nn113; campaigns against, 18, 59–60, 71–72; doubling as inns, 77; closing of, 60, 71–72; conspicuous lounging, 191–92; dancers, 287n77; entertainment in, 76, 198; escapism, 60, 77, 86; guns in, 196; as home away from home, for men, 254–55nn74; hookah, 68; as immoral, 61; as innovation, 71; Janissary corps, affiliation with, 184, 192, 206, 282n1; leisure culture, 71; as male spaces, 73; open atmosphere of, and chance encounters, 76 opium in, 86–87, 89; paramilitary presence in, 191–92; plundering of, 206; popularity of, 76–77; public sociality, acceleration of, 75; in rural areas, 77–78; shadow puppet theater, 198; social consequences of, 75; as social hubs, 77; social segregation, 74; storytelling, 198; as Sufi lodge, 254n62; turf war over, 206; unsavory images, 73; urban clientele, 72–74; as urban demimonde, 192; as urban equivalents of military stations, 192; women in, 73.

colonialism, 7

color codes, 56, 58, 248n136

Congress of Vienna, 231

corpse defilement, 184, 208–11, 291n129, 291n133, 291n134, 291n135, 292n136, 292n139, 292n140

courtiers, 4, 7, 36, 87, 101, 123, 152, 161, 200

Court Society, The (Norbert), 4

Covell, John, 81, 87

Craven, Elizabeth, 33, 68, 103

Crete, 253n45

Crimea, 11

Croatia, 11

Cyprus, 38, 40, 243n63, 245n89

al-Daftari, ʿAli, 144
al-Daftari, Fathi, 181, 210
al-Daftari, Hasan, 124–25, 143
al-Dalaji, Yusuf, 103
dalatiyya (Anatolian mercenaries), 39
Damad İbrahim Paşa, Nevşehirli, 209–10, 292n136
Damascus, 14, 28–30, 56, 66, 82, 88–89, 91, 96, 98–99, 101–2, 109, 131–32, 143, 157, 159, 169, 172, 176, 178, 180–81, 188, 190–91, 193, 195, 203, 210, 220, 252n18, 261n22, 262n36; coffeehouses in, 71–72, 289–90nn113; Egyptian occupation of, 225; gun ownership, 196; street battles, 213; taverns in, 83
Daud Paşa (governor of Baghdad), 142
"decentralization" (Ottoman), 10, 18
Derendeli Ali, 161
de Tott, Baron, 1, 88, 115–16, 170, 193, 233n1
Dodwell, Edward, 33–34, 259n162
d'Ohsson, Mouradgea, 20, 63, 66, 93, 186. See also Tosunyan, Ignatius Muradcan
domestic space, 113–15
Druze, 39, 128, 177
Duçe Mehmed Paşa, 124
Duerr, Hans Peter, 5
al-Dusuqi, Muhammad, 98

East Asia: "floating towns," 90
East India Company (EIC), 12, 152–53
Edirne, 14, 78, 81, 103, 137, 170, 181, 228, 281n102; Edirne incident, 144
Egypt, 11, 22, 24, 29–30, 43, 49, 52–55, 63–64, 66, 70, 82, 108, 122, 140, 142, 147, 150, 160–62, 170, 176, 179, 188, 195, 202, 217, 297n48, 297n53; coffeehouses in, 74, 75, 75, 93; French occupation, 56, 181–82, 212, 245n92; perfuming ceremony, 268n147; popular dress in, 25
Elias, Norbert, 4–6, 92, 153; civilizing process, 239n44; sociogenic process, 7
Enderunlu Fazıl, 101, 129
English Event, 204. *See also* Anglo-Ottoman war
Erasmus, Desiderius, 5, 7

Erib (poet), 97
escapism, 18, 60, 77, 81, 86, 89
Esmihan Hamko, 193
Ethiopia, 61
etiquette, 91–92, 229, 232; conversational, as simple and honest, 103; dining etiquette, 115–19; greetings of, 103–6; manuals, 5, 15–16, 59, 228–29; public, 155; wide application of, 118–19. *See also* greetings, manners
Eurasia, 12, 90, 153, 231
Europe, 6–7, 12–13, 90, 93, 113, 115, 130, 153, 204, 228, 231, 247–48nn126, 271–72nn66, 290–91nn128, 299n62; code of civility, 4; courtesy of medieval courts, as turning point, 4–5
Eurocentrism: courtly model of manners, 6–7
Evliya Çelebi, 74, 123–24, 126, 245n85
Eyüp Sultan, 174–75

factional violence, 222, 224; houses of worship, 213–14; rituals of vengeance, 207
Faʾiza Molla Kadın, 262n44
Fakhr al-Din (ibn Maʿn), 125, 143
al-Falaqansi, ʿAbd al-Muʿti, 148
fashion, 16–17, 33, 35–36, 47–48, 56, 59, 88, 232; Algerian, 246n103; Croatian, 26; decency, 20–21, 57–58; footwear, 43; geography, 21; headgear, 21; male, 41; manners, 21; modesty, 58; nose rings, 30; Ottoman, 7–8, 31, 228, 243n54; pipes, as accessories, 66; social order, 51. *See also* clothing
al-Falaqansi, Fathi, 274n115
el-Fenayi, Muhammad Laʿli, 166
feuds, 135, 213, 219, 289–90nn113, 290n126, 291n135; poetic, 101
fez, 297n50; as emblem of modernity, 230; as emblem of reform, 227; as foreign "cap fashion", 228; as official headgear, 228; as too egalitarian, 227
Fitnat Hanım, 100
fly whisk, 171

folk justice, 173
folk poetry, 130
footwear, 43
France, 171, 200, 213, 271–72nn66; sociability in, 235n15
Frankland, Charles Colville, 22–23
French occupation of Egypt, 54–56, 181–82; legacies of, 55
French Revolution, 53
fustanella (loose kilt), 27, 42, *42*

Galata Event (Galata Vakası), 184–85
Genç Yusuf Paşa (governor of Damascus), 29, 56
al-Ghazzi, `Abd al-Rahman, 99
al-Ghazzi, Muhammad, 102–3
Goffman, Erving: impression management, 150
good life, 192; taste for, 150
Great Britain, 226–27; nabob, figure of, 153
Great Crisis, 11–12, 15, 21, 72, 82, 121, 182, 184, 215–16, 218; as destabilizing, 217
Greater Syria, 111
Great Powers, 226, 227
Greece, 12, 38, 77–79, 107, 119, 269–70nn32; feuding, 290n126; *fustanella*, 27; Greek war of independence, 56, 204, 214, 227
greetings, 232; ceremonial kissing, as sign of respect, 108–9, 265n87, 265n88, 265n94; deference, gestures of, 107–10; informality, 109; kissing of hand, 106–7, 264n75, 264n83, 264–65nn84; prostrating, 229; rural society, social structures of, 110; social distance, 110; social station, 106–7. *See also* etiquette, manners

Habsburg Empire, 282n5
Haci Ali (*voyvoda* of Athens), 119
hair: beard, as symbolic passage of male adulthood, 28; facial hair, pride in, 29; head, baring of, 22, 25; men's hair, 25–28; women's hair, anxiety about, 22–24.

al-Hakawati, Ahmad Shakir, 102
al-Halabi, Salih, 99
al-Hamaqi, Ahmad, 73–4
Hamevi Ali Efendi, 87
al-Hanafi, `Ali, 64
al-Hariri, Rajab, 101
Hasan Paşa (governor of Egypt), 139–40
hashish, 86
Haşim Efendi (see Mehmed Haşim Efendi)
al-Hawwari, Humam, 150
headgear, 21, 36–39, 48, 58, 228; caps, 35; fez, as official headgear, 228; male, 35; Ottoman, 226; regional styles, 35; and social status, 35–36. *See also* individual types, turbans
hedonism, 60–61, 86, 89, 149–50; of paramilitary culture, 220. *See also* escapism, leisure culture
Hezarpare Ahmed Paşa (grand vizier), 291n129
hierarchy, 8, 74, 109–10, 120, 161; clothing decrees, 57; of furs, 41; of household, 169; and order, 51; salon culture, 261n20; social, 47, 106, 134, 155, 171, 178–79; symbolic, 55; use of violence, 165–66
al-Hifnawi, Muhammad, 95
Hijaz, 220
Hill, Aaron, 58, 74, 79
Holy Cities, 142; pilgrimage to, 56
hookah, 68
hospitality, 2, 63, 126, 150; rites of, 119
Hourani, Albert, 176
humiliation, 114, 173, 213; public, 209; ritual, 292n136; sexual, 204
Hungary, 11
hunting: as genteel status symbol, 152; royal hunting parties, 151
Husaynid dynasty (of Ottoman Tunisia), 142
Hüseyin Bey Kişkiş Kazdağlı, 268–69nn13, 280n89
hygiene, 110; Ottoman women, 111–12; noxious odors, battles against, 112–13; propriety, 112

Ibn Abi'l Diyaf, Ahmad, 107–8, 264n75
Ibn Kannan, 194
Ibn al-Siddiq, 203
İbrahim Bey Abu'l-Shanab, 148
İbrahim Bey Katamiş, 201
İbrahim Kethüda (İbrahim Nesim Efendi), 201–2, 208–9
İbrahim Paşa (of Egypt), 116
Ibrahim bin Sa'ad al-Din (al-Jabawi), 89
al-Idkawi, 'Abdullah, 101–2
imperial court, 174–75
India, 12, 36, 102, 152
inflation, 11, 12, 57, 186, 217; "Enlightenment" inflation, 298–99n58
Ipsos, 22
Iran, 102
Iraq, 120, 142
Islam, 122, 127, 134; new uniforms, as insult to, 226
"Islamic Enlightenment", 298–99n58
Islamic law, 18, 45, 54–55, 59, 61, 70, 78, 81, 91, 101, 124, 159, 168, 200
Ismail: attack on, 212
İsmail Hakkı, Bursevi, 127
İsmail Paşa (governor of Bosnia), 139
İsmail Paşa (governor of Egypt), 146
Istanbul, 13–15, *23*, 28, 31, 33, 38, 40, 46, 48–49, *50*, 56, 58, 63, 65–68, 78–79, 98, 99, 101, 112, 128, 140, 145, 162, 170–71, 174–75, 181, 183, 189, 197, 200, 203–4, 208–9, 211, 213, 219, 225, 228, 262n36, 264n71, 284n19, 294n6; bathhouses, 111; coffeehouses in, 71–72, 74, 76, 86, 192, 255n82, 260n5, 282n1, 288n91; Egyptian Market, 45; Janissaries, expulsion from, 218; kidnapping of "prostitutes," 222; meddah, 198, 287n72; opium in, 86–88; porters in, 285n40; revolt in, 201–2; rice riots, 194; salons, 96; social order, anxiety over, 221; soldiers in, 84–85, 221; street skirmishes, 227; street slang, 291n134; taverns in, 80–83, 85; women in, as poor and unattached, 223–24
Izmir, 33

al-Jabarti, 'Abd al-Rahman, 97, 217
al-Jabarti, Hasan, 97, 106, 264n83
Janissary corps, 1, 4, 11–12, 29, 36, 67, 82, 86, 122, 129–30, *138*, 143, 145–46, 151, 167–68, 175–76, 178, 197, 201–4, 213–14, 222, 283n10, 284n22, 292n139, 294n3; abducting of women, 224; as boors and ruffians, 215; brawls of, 185, 189, 191, 218, 288n91, 289n103; coffeehouses, affiliation with, 184, 206; coffeehouses, as "under their sword," 192; corpse, defiling of, 210–11, 291n129; crimes and offenses, concerns over, 218; elimination of, 225–26; ethnic organizations, 190; expulsion, from Istanbul, 218; extortion, 219; guilds, links to, 195, 226; lawlessness, flaunting of, 219–20; membership in units, 189; military discipline, 185–86, 219; nicknames, 284n19; profanity of, 288n91; rebellions, 208–9; recruitment, 215, 286n57; recruitment, as piecemeal and opportunistic, 187; revenge, acts of, 207–10; rough manners of, 185; as rural migrants, 185; as shock troops, 185; as slave-soldiers, 185–86; as sultan's personal guards, 185–86, 190, 215; symbolic gestures, 208; talking parrot incident, 2–3; tattoos, use of, 189; as thugs, 227; as unruly rabble, 218; in urban markets, 186; women, dispute over, 223; women, harassment of, 296n32, 296n34
al-Jalfi, Ali Kethüda, 107
al-Jalfi, Osman Ağa, 147
al-Jalfi, Ridvan Kethüda, 149
Japan: kabuki theater, 90; samurai, 152
al-Jawish, Muhammad, 143
al-Jaziri, 'Ali, 166
Jerusalem, 111
al-Jinaji, Muhammad, 180
Joseph II, 298n56
Jumblat, Bashir, 127
al-Jundi, 'Abd al-Razzaq, 146

Kabakçı Mustafa rebellion, 51, 173, 200, 201, 207-8, 210-11, 226, 292n139
Kadızadeli movement, 60-62, 71, 81
al-Kafrawi, Hasan, 177
kalpak (hat), 36-37, *37*, 38-39, 48, 52, 245n84, 245n85
Kapıdağlı, Konstantin, *138*
Kapodistrias, Yannis, 214
Kapudan Hasan Paşa, 53, 108, 162-63
Kapudan Hüseyin Paşa, 161
Karaiskakis, Georgios, 204
al-Karimi, ʿAli, 113
Kashf al-Zunun, 141
Katsaites, Antonio, 28
Kazancızade Ahmed Ağa, 154
Ketağaç Paşa, 125-26
al-Khalifa, Mustafa, 103
al-Khashshab, Ismaʿil, 96
al-Khuri, Yusuf, 135-36
Kiblelizade Ali Bey, 140
al-Kilani, ʿAbd al-Qadir, 114
kinship, 24, 190
al-Kiwani, Ahmad, 146
Kiyamizade Efendi, 157
Kléber, Jean-Baptiste, 107
klepht (mountain bandit), 130
Köprülü, Mehmet, 9
Köroglu, 130
kovrdjak (headpiece), 37
Küçük Laz Ali, 192
al-Kurani, ʿAbd al-Latif, 144
Kurds, 36, 187, 188, 245n84, 286n57, 289-90nn113
Kuşadalı İbrahim Efendi, 66, 180

Lane, Edward, 17, 24
Latin America, 12
Leake, William, 107
leisure culture, 60-61, *85*, 86, 90; in coffeehouses, 71, 198; military embrace of, 147; urban, 123, 147
Lesbos, 33
Levni, Abdülcelil, *32*, *149*
Liotard, Jean-Etienne, *44*

London, 13
Louis XIV, 137, 152, 271-72nn66

Macedonia, 35, 67
Madrid, 13-14
Mahmud II, 12, 51, 109, 129; military reform, 220
al-Mahruqi, Ahmad, 181-2
Mahtumi (folk poet), *see* Vahid.
Makriyannis, Yannis, 77, 190, 202
al-Maktabi, ʿAbd al-Latif, 26-7
mamluks (slave-soldiers), 29, 52, 108, 122, 146-47, 182, 187, 212-13
manners, 3, 5-8, 59, 91-92, 232, 234-35nn13; acts of effrontery, 170; breach of, 154-55; civility, 18-19; code of honor, 19; fashion, 21; formality of speech, of religious establishment, 95; headgear, 21; notions of honor, 155; throughout Ottoman Empire, 120; pacification, 6; politesse, 155; and violence, 19; war-making, 4. *See also* etiquette, greetings
Maronite Church, 66
Mecca, 28, 36, 56, 98-99, 182, 220
meddah, 198-99; censorship of, 287n72
Medina, 56, 182, 220
Mehmed IV, 281n102
Mehmed Ağa ibn al-Qattan, 151
Mehmed Ali (governor of Egypt), 55, 84, 108, 116, 128-9, 170, 182, 194-95, 212, 219, 297n48
Mehmed Bey Abu'l-Dhahab ("Gold-Bearer"), 134, 147, 179, 182
Mehmed Haşim Efendi, 61, 76, 247n117
Mehmed Hayri Efendi (*reisülküttab*), 173-74
Mehmed Kadızade, 62
Mehmed Sadık Rifat Paşa, 228-30, 298n57
Metternich, Prince, 298n57
Middle East, 7, 62, 92, 120, 198
Midhat Paşa (grand vizier), 229
Milan, 13-14
military factions: rivalries and grudges between, 190

military notables, 160; sumptuous lifestyle, 148
military reform, 220; European style of jackets and pants, 225, 227-28; fez, as "Muslim" touch, 225-28; new uniforms, 225-28
Mirzayan, Manuk, 115, 140
Mishaqa, Mikha'il, 79, 105, 143
al-Misri, 'Umar, 166
modernity, 7, 19; fez, as emblem of, 230
modernization, 225, 228, 231; dandy, 230; European models of comportment, look toward, 229-30; material culture, innovations in, 230; middle class, 229-30; modern state and missionary schools, 230; of state reform, 229
modesty, 24, 41, 58
Moldovia, 28, 38, 39, 182
Montagu, Lady Mary Worley, 31, 33, 112, 119
morality, 64-65, 73, 130-31, 135, 221-22; guardians of, 72, 158; policing of, 56; public, 15, 132; regulation of, 90; threat to, 232
Morea, 11-12, 28, 117, 220
Mosul, 14, 100, 102, 187, 201
Mt. Lebanon, 35, 39, 66, 109, 127, 135-36, 195, 214; egalitarian lifestyle, 58
Mughal, 175
al-Mughassil, Muhammad, 194-5
al-Mughayzal, 'Abd al-Baqi, 96
Muhammad (prophet), 29, 53-54, 106, 158, 176, 201, 232
Muhammad Bey, 70
Muhammad Nasuhi, 65
al-Muhibbi, Muhammad Amin, 145
Murad III, 49
Murad IV, 71, 123-24, 137
Murad Bey, 108, 151-52
al-Muradi, Husayn, 156
al-Muradi, Muhammad Khalil, 91-92, 100, 105-6, 144, 268-69nn13
al-Muradi, Murad, 106, 252n18
Mustafa II, 137
Mustafa III, 49-50, 87, 161
Mustafa IV, 94, 129, 140; overthrow of, 207

Mustafa Ali, Gelibolulu, 234-5nn13
Mustafa Efendi (*reisülküttab*), 139
Mustafa Refik Efendi, 168
Mustafa Safi-i Amedi, 109, 169
Müteferrika, İbrahim, 298n56
mystics, 127

al-Nabulsi, 'Abd al-Ghani, 26, 65, 276n7
al-Nabulsi, 'Umar, 127
Naima (historian), 124, 143
Naples, 13-14
Napoleon, 11-12, 53, 107, 116, 122; defeat of, 54
Napoleonic wars, 231, 282n5
Nasuh Paşa (governor of Damascus), 179
Naxos, 33
New Army, 196
New Order, 11, 138, 175, 197, 219, 226, 231; revenge on, 207
Nicholas I, 231
Niebuhr, Carsten, 22
North Africa, 38, 41, 120
North America, 12

offensive speech, 197, 199; derogatory language, 289n104; "Islamic swearing," 200; scatological references, 201; street slang, 198, 291n134; 'ulama' (Muslim scholars), crude language, use of, 158. *See also* profanity
Old Regime, 8, 12-14, 18-21, 23, 45, 57-58, 62, 63, 80-82, 90, 105, 125, 134, 182, 194-95, 198-99, 229; civility, 136; crisis of confidence, 225; cultural matters, debates over, 232; culture of, 130; customs of, and popular thinking, 228; etiquette, 116; fall of, 216; gender roles, 203; hierarchy, belief in, 165; loyalty to, 226-27; military elite, 141; physical strength, admiration of, 128; polite manners of, 92, 94; reinvention of, 232; salons of, 96, 101; street violence, 220, 225. *See also* Ottoman Empire
opium, 86, 90, 259n152; among Ottoman elite, 87-89

Osman II, 268–69nn13
Osman III, 47
Osman Bey Zülfakar (Dhu'l-Faqar), 147, 161
Osman Kazdağlı, 202
Osman Paşa (al-Sadiq), Gürcü (governor of Damascus), 179, 203
Ottoman Empire, 1–2, 10–13, 20, 22, 60, 101, 145, 181, 215, 239–40nn47; acquisition of firearms, 195; alcohol, 79–80; biographical dictionaries, 17; bodily deportment, 115, 118–19; carnivalesque language, 201; ceremonial self-defense, 155; chronicles, 16–17; churches, as places of pilgrimage, 214; "classical age", 10; clothing fashion, 40–44; clothing regulations, 57; coffee-drinking, as entrenched, 61; coffeehouses in, 60–61, 71, 75, 77; coffee and tobacco, 60–61, 70; coffee trade, 64; conservative cultural outlook, 232; conservative reform, embracing of, 231; court, 100; dancing street girls, 199; defense of religion, 231; dining, 116, 117, 118; etiquette manuals, 15–16; European travelers to, 17; elite, stability of, 183; face-veil (burqu'), 24–25, 34; female modesty, 45–47, 58; fez, as official headgear, 228; folk heroism, 130; Galata Event, as microcosm of difficulties in, 185; good life, taste for, 150; grandees, 9, 31, 38, 90, 100, 109, 123, 142, 182–83; grand vizier, 9, 138, 156, 174, 229; Great Crisis, 184; headgear, 37, 37, 38–39, 46, 58; hierarchy, 164, 165; Islamic culture, misconception of, 17–18, 21; leisure culture, 18, 85, 86, 198; manners, 7–8, 18, 155; military defeats, 217; military discipline, lack of, 219; military expansion, 186; military recruitment, ethnic warrior bands, 187–88; military recruitment, and social mobility, 185; military reform, 220, 225–26; military weakness, 11, 184–85; modernization, 230–31; New Order, 138; opium trade, 87–88; Ottoman Algeria: fly whisk, as pretext for French invasion, 171; Ottoman army, drinking of, 84–85; Ottoman Bulgaria, 22–23; Ottoman conquest, 40; Ottoman court, as cosmopolitan, 299n62; Ottoman Enlightenment, 298–99n58; Ottoman Greece, 38; outer cloak, 41; Ottoman studies, 8; Ottoman Syria, 56, 126; Ottoman Tunisia, 96; outlaws, punishment of, 208, 211–12; paramilitary complex, 18–19, 185, 188, 193, 215–18; paramilitary complex, backlash against, 225; paramilitary subculture, defiance of, 185; pashas, 9; polite manners, 92, 120–21; pomp and ceremony, diffusion of, 182–83; poverty, and communal restrictions, 24, 58; protocol, 175; public ceremonies, downward infusion, 181; reform, 298–99n58; sartorial legislation, 57–58; sectarian tensions, 57; self-presentation, ideals of, 18; sociability, 95; social anxieties, 15; social distinction, inflation of, 183; social finesse, as asset, 140–41; social networks, necessity of, 223; social practice, 16 soft power of, 18; soldiers, 126–27; state-led modernization, 19, 57; street violence, and sense of disorder, 220; tobacco, 61–62; tulips, as symbol of imperial extravagance, 210; urban culture, as deeply rooted, 153; urbane warrior, 122–23; urbanism, 13–14; veiling, 24, 31; violent feuds, 219; war-making, 21. *See also* Great Crisis
Ottoman-Romanov war, 1, 184, 193

Palestine, 27, 130, 135
paramilitary culture, 185, 191, 195, 214, 218, 223; backlash against, 225; coarseness and indiscipline of, 220; hesitation in battle, sensitivity to, 202–3; honor of women, as target for slander, 204–5; local power struggles, 212; outlaws, as special target for

paramilitary culture (cont.)
  wrath, 211–12; profanity, use of, 201, 203–4; public display and mutilation of rivals, 211; sexual innuendo, 203–4; social networks, 223; unbridled hedonism of, 220; underclass, 215–16; violent rituals, 212–13; women, affiliation with, 223
Paris, 13, 230
patriarchy: crisis of, 225
Patrona Halil uprising, 47, 137, 188, 209, 292n136
Peter the Great, 14, 230
Phanariot families, 38, 46, 115
pilgrimages, 220, 280n83, 294n4
pipes, 67-9
Pitt-Rivers, Julian, 239–40nn47
Pococke, Richard, 22, 77
poetry, 99; civility, association with, 144–45; defamatory, 100–101, 263n51, 263n52; erotic, 102; love, 101
profane violence, 214
profanity, 158, 201, 288n79, 288n80, 288n88, 288n91. See also offensive speech
Prussia, 231
public processions, 173, 280n89, 281n105; in countryside, 177; deference, 178; status symbols, 178, 179; symbolic charge, 178; violence, risk of, 178; pageantry, expansion of, 181

al-Qal`i, Abu'l-Hasan, 106, 172
al-Qasafi, Husayn, 101
al-Qasimi, Salih Bey, 126, 150
Qing conquest, 152

Ragıb Mehmed Paşa (grand vizier), 98–99, 139
al-Rahawi, Yusuf, 263n51
Ramiz, 103
Ratib Ahmed Paşa (grand admiral), 141
religious establishment, 157, 171, 172, 176–77, 232, 281n98; breaches of decorum, 158, 160; fondness for public ostentation, 180; as models of urbanity, 155–56; respectability, 180
Reşid Mehmed Paşa (grand vizier), 129
Rhodes, 243n63
al-Rishmani, Ibrahim Agha, 128–29
Roberts, David, 75
Romanov Empire, 2, 231
Rome, 13–14
royal hunting parties, 151–52
Rüşdü Paşa (grand vizier), 229
Russell, Alexander, 22, 63, 66–67, 74, 88, 94, 104, 161
Russia, 1, 3, 11, 14, 36, 52–53, 82, 231; Pruth campaign against, 127; reforms, 298n56
Russian Empire, 41, 230

al-Sabbagh, Mikha'il, 131
al-Sadidi, Hamuda, 101, 263n47
al-Safaqisi, `Abd al-Rahman, 96
al-Safarjalani, Mustafa, 88, 109
Safavids, 123, 126
Said Ağa (of Acre), 84
al-Sa`idi, `Ali, 65, 159
Salonika, 14
salons, 110–11, 261n20; conviviality of, 95–96; etiquette, 234–35nn13; military manners, taming of, 147; poetry competitions, 100; poets at, 100–102; serious and playful, combination of, 97; storytelling in, 102; types of, 96
Saravejo, 83, 226
segbanbaşı, 206
Selim III, 11, 51, 72, 82, 137, 140, 194, 200, 204, 255n79, 292n139; New Order, 138; overthrow of, 201–2, 207, 219, 222, 226
Selim Ağa (of Acre), 136
Selim Giray, 175
Sepastyan, Bogos, 140
Serbia, 12, 68, 211, 241n21; Christian militia, forming of, 218, 219
şeyhülislam (head of religious establishment), 100, 140, 157, 170
shadow puppet theater, 198–99
Shafi`i legal tradition, 280n82

al-Shamma', 'Ali, 191, 193–94
Shams al-Din ibn al-'Arifin, 177
al-Sharayibi, Ahmad, 100
al-Sharif, Hasan, 95
al-Shihabi, Bashir, 109–10, 136, 177–78, 264–65nn84
al-Shihabi, Yusuf, 132, 214
al-Siddiqi, Khalil, 98
Simi, 243n63
al-Sinti, Muhammad Efendi, 146
Sırkatibi Ahmed Efendi, 210–11
smoking, 18, 60, 62, 65–66, 68, *68*, 70, 86, 124; crackdown on, 71; social hierarchies, 69–70; by soldiers, 67. *See also* tobacco
snuff, 69, 253n45
sociability, 61, 95, 232, 235n15; bathhouses, and Ottoman women, 111–12; of coffeehouses, acceleration of, 75; coffee and tobacco, as part of, 62; female, 111; patterns of, 3; pipes, *68, 69*; public, 95; of taverns, 81; urban, 123; violence, patterns of, 3–4
social elite, 36, *50*, 74–75, 77, 92, 105, 145, 147, 155, 157, 171, 173, 199; old ways, as durable, 228; wives and concubines, 168–69
socialization, 3
social mobility, 14–15, 215; military recruitment, 185
social order, 15, 22, 54, 94–95, 99, 116, 155, 165, 171, 200, 220, 227; anxiety over, 221; endangering of, 51; idealized, 45; preserving of, 232; social control, 6; upholding, 45, 53
social privilege, 167; shield against interpersonal violence, 169
social rank, 71, 94; beards, emblem of, 28
Sofia, 112
soft power, 18
soldiers, 122, 168; bachelor rooms, 221–22; as blood brothers, 188; brawling of, 220; crimes and offenses, concerns over, 218; distrust of, 217; domestication of, 150–51; factional violence of, 205, 207; female companionship, 221–23; fondness for hunting, 151–52; honor, as paramount, 207; lawlessness, flaunting of, 219–20; military discipline, 219; Ottoman, 107; as outsiders, 217–18; poetry, 144–46; religious insolence, 220–21; resolving disputes, through assassinations and ambushes, 189–90; rough manners, 217; rural honor system, 205; secret "insider" codes, 188, 189; self-conscious, 150; social bonds, 223; social idioms of villages and clans, 205; training and discipline, as lax, 151; turf, control of, 205–6; urban respectability, scoffing at, 220; urban society, revulsion toward, 217–18. *See also* Janissary corps
Soutzos, Michail, *39*
Spain, 12
state reform: inherited lifestyles, preservation of, 228; Islamic tradition, appeals to, 231; modernization of, 229; piety and morality, emphasis on, 229; struggle for legitimacy, 231–32; Westernization, as dirty word, 231–32
storytelling, 102, 198; humor in, 103
Sufis, 102, 128, 180, 280n82, 280n83; Bakriyya order, 53–54, 108; Celveti order, 127; Khalwati order, 142; mystics, 51; Wafa'i order, 177
Süleyman I, 7, 142, 243n63
Süleyman Feyzi Paşa (governor of Aleppo), 141
Suleyman the Magnificent. *See* Süleyman I
Süleyman Paşa (governor of Acre), 84, 108–10, 135
Şumnu, 67
Sünbülzade Vehbi, 15, 59, 60, 95, 98, 127, 156
symbolic messages, 172
Syria, 24, 54, 63, 67, *75*, 93, 100, 120, 125–26, 131, 134, 143, 245n92; Egyptian invasion of, 225

Tahazadeh, Muhammad Efendi, 163
al-Tahtawi, Ahmad, 158
al-Taji, 'Abd al-Rahman, 101
talking birds, 2, 233n1
Tamburi, Osman Bey, 85
al-Tamurtashi, Najm al-Din, 179
Tanzimat project, 220, 226, 228–31, 284n22
al-Tarzi, Mustafa, 143
taverns, 83, 85, 89; as brothels, 80–81; closing of, 82; as countercultural bastion of masculine sociability, 81; underworld denizens, 80
Tevfik (poet), 99
Thévenot, Jean, 74
Tiberius: siege of, 277n24
tobacco, 61–62, 69, 78, 81, 86, 89–90, 119; campaigns against, 65–66; convenience of, 67, 70–71; low cost of, 67. *See also* smoking
Tosunyan, Ignatius Muradcan, 20. *See also* D'Ohsson, Mouradgea
Transylvania, 11
Tripoli, 111
Tulip Age, 210, 271n62; Westernization, 299n62
Tunis, 14, 140, 166, 225, 244n81, 264–65nn84, 280n82
Tunisia, 142, 228, 296n41, 297n53
turbans, 35–36, 38, 54–55, 228, 243n63, 244n80, 244n81, 245n89, 297n49
Turkey, 33, 93

'ulama' (Muslim scholars), 56, 88–89, 96, 260n15, 261n20; crude language, use of, 158
al-'Umar, Zahir, 27, 101, 130–31, 134, 163, 213, 277n24, 278n37; martial virility, appeal of, 135; sense of honor, 132; as ruthless, 133
al-'Umari, Shakir, 98-9
al-'Urban, Shibli, 126
urbane warrior: aptitude for repartee and banter, 146; fortunes, amassing of, 123; rise of, 122; sociality, ideals of, 123. *See also* warrior society

urban gentleman, 41, 92, 96–97, 123, 140, 144, 215, 224; command of poetry, 99; elevated speech, 98; public face of, 95
urbanization, 13–14, 90, 153
urban society, 18, 31, 62–63, 91–92, 141, 214, 217–18, 221; bathhouses, 111; paramilitary culture, 195, 225; soldier-poet, as familiar figure, 146; urban elite, 74, 177; urban politesse, 160–61; women's safety, concern about, 225

Vahid, 127. *See also* Mahtumi
van Egmont, Aegidius, 27
Vani Mehmed Efendi, 61
Vanmour, Jean-Baptiste, *23, 50, 64, 85, 117*
veiling, 24, 31, *32*
Venice, 11, 13–14
Vienna, 230
Volney, Constantin-François, 26, 58, 93, 113–14
Vrachanski, Sofroniy, 180

Wahhabi forces, 56, 82, 182
Wallachia, 28, 38, *39*, 182
warfare, 6, 9, 11–12, 19, 62, 90, 185; costs of, 10; cultural consequences of, 4; manners, relationship between, 4; prolonged, 11, 62; urban, 206
War of the Holy League, 11, 47–48, 71
war-making, 18, 21; and manners, 4
warrior society, 125, 192; bureaucrat, figure of, 147; courageous deeds, 129; dandy, 150; guilds, 195; horsemanship and stamina, 126–27; martial virility, 136, 160–61, 195, 202; military bands (*mehter*), 148, *149*; military swagger, 193; mystics, 127; physical valor, ideals of, 194; religious establishment, 127; swashbuckling gallantry, ideal of, 193; violent rituals, 212–13; women, bravery of, 193–94
Westernization: as dirty word, 231–32; Tulip Age, 299n62; Western civilization, 249–40nn47
World War I, 225–26

Yemen, 36, 61, 63
Yusuf Bey al-Kabir, 159–60
al-Yusufi, ʿAbdullah, 99-100

al-Zabidi, Murtada, 36, 108
Zarifi, Ömer, 94
Zenanname (*Book of Women*) (Enderunlu Fazıl), 101, 129

STANFORD **OTTOMAN WORLD** SERIES
Critical Studies in Empire, Nature, and Knowledge

Nükhet Varlık and Ali Yaycioğlu, editors

EDITORIAL BOARD
Julia Phillips Cohen, Nahyan Fancy, John-Paul Ghobrial, Mayte Green-Mercado, Tijana Krstić, Harun Küçük, Dana Sajdi, Fatih Yeşil

The Stanford Ottoman World Series showcases cutting-edge interdisciplinary scholarship in Ottoman history from the thirteenth to the twentieth centuries. Books in the series are concerned with three major themes—empire, nature, and knowledge—and the connections among them. The books in this series foster ambitious and innovative scholarship and open new paths in Ottoman studies and beyond.

A. TUNÇ ŞEN, *Forgotten Experts: Astrologers, Science, and Authority in the Ottoman Empire 1450–1600* **2025**

ROBERT G. MORRISON, *Merchants of Knowledge: Intellectual Exchange in the Ottoman Empire and Renaissance Europe* **2025**

NIR SHAFIR, *The Order and Disorder of Communication: Pamphlets and Polemics in the Seventeenth-Century Ottoman Empire* **2024**

UĞUR ZEKERIYA PEÇE, *Island and Empire: How Civil War in Crete Mobilized the Ottoman World* **2024**

ELIZABETH R. WILLIAMS, *States of Cultivation: Imperial Transition and Scientific Agriculture in the Eastern Mediterranean* **2023**